The papers presented in this book take as their subject the military, political and economic changes forced upon inhabitants of Gaul during the fifth century AD. They seek to describe and explain how Gallo-Romans of all orders of society reacted to barbarian invasion and the growing debilitation of the western imperial government. The unusually wide range of topics dealt with by contributors allows the Gallic experience to be viewed and interpreted from many different directions. Much is made of the problematic, because highly subjective, nature of the literary sources; but close attention is also given to modern advances in our understanding of the archaeological and numismatic data. The whole presents a picture of a society under immense stress, as the people of the Gallic provinces abandoned, perforce, their allegiance to Roman emperors and yielded to the rule of Germanic kings, while yet preserving a significant element of their late antique culture.

Historians and archaeologists of the late Roman and early Medieval periods in western Europe will welcome the publication of this stimulating collection of essays.

Fifth-century Gaul: a crisis of identity?

Fifth-century Gaul:
a crisis of identity?

Edited by

John Drinkwater and Hugh Elton

CAMBRIDGE
UNIVERSITY PRESS

Published by the Press Syndicate of the University of Cambridge
The Pitt Building, Trumpington Street, Cambridge CB2 1RP
40 West 20th Street, New York, NY 10011-4211, USA
10 Stamford Road, Oakleigh, Victoria 3166, Australia

First published 1992

Printed in Great Britain at the University Press, Cambridge

A cataloguing in publication record for this book is available from the British Library

Library of Congress cataloguing in publication data

Fifth-century Gaul: a crisis of identity? / edited by John Drinkwater and Hugh Elton.
p. cm.
'The title and the main contents derive from a conference organized by the editors at
the University of Sheffield in April of 1989' – Acknowledgements.
Includes bibliographical references and index.
ISBN 0 521 41485 7 (hardcover)
1. Gaul – History – 58 BC – 511 AD – Congresses. 2. Rome – History – Germanic
Invasions, 3rd – 6th centuries – Congresses. 3. Romans – Gaul – History –
Congresses.
I. Drinkwater, J.F. II. Elton, Hugh.
DC62.F54 1992
936.4–dc20 91-18375 CIP

ISBN 0 521 41485 7 hardback

Contents

Contents

Figures

Contributors

Dr S. Barnish

The Queen's College,
Oxford OX1 4AW

Dr R. W. Burgess

Department of Classical
Studies,
University of Ottawa,
30 Stewart Street,
Ottawa, Ontario K1N 6N5

Professor T. S. Burns

Department of History,
Emory University,
Atlanta, GA 30322

Dr J. F. Drinkwater

Department of Classical and
Archaeological Studies,
The University,
Nottingham NG7 2RD

Dr H. Elton

The Queen's College,
Oxford OX1 4AW

Professor S. Fanning

Department of History,
University of Illinois at
Chicago,
Box 4348, Chicago, IL 60680

Dr G. Halsall

Birkbeck College,
Malet St.,
London WC1E 7HX

Dr J. D. Harries

Department of Ancient History,
St Salvator's College,
St Andrews, Fife KY16 9AL

Dr P. Heather

Worcester College,
Oxford OX1 2HB

Dr M. Heinzelmann

Institut historique allemand,
9 rue Maspéro,
F-75116 Paris

Contributors

Professor R. B. Hitchner

Department of History,
University of Dayton,
300 College Park,
Dayton, OH 45469

Dr E. D. Hunt

Department of Classics,
University of Durham,
38 North Bailey,
Durham DH1 4PS

Professor D. H. Kelley

2432 Sovereign Cr. S.W.,
Calgary, Alberta T3C 2M2

Dr C. E. King

Heberden Coin Room,
Ashmolean Museum,
Beaumont Street,
Oxford OX1 2PH

Professor J. H. W. G. Liebeschuetz

Department of Classical and
Archaeological Studies,
The University,
Nottingham NG7 2RD

S. T. Loseby, Esq.

St Anne's College,
Oxford OX2 6HS

Dr M. Maas

Department of History,
Rice University,
Houston, TX 77251

Professor R. W. Mathisen

Department of History,
University of South Carolina,
Columbia, SC 29208

T. S. Mommaerts, Esq.

Lincoln Meadows,
2415 Winding Way,
Lincoln, NE 68506

Dr S. Muhlberger

Nipissing University College,
100 College Drive,
Box 5002, North Bay,
Ontario P1B 8L7

Dr C. E. V. Nixon

School of History,
Macquarie University,
Sydney, NSW 2109

Professor J. Percival

School of History and
Archaeology,
University of Wales College of
Cardiff,
PO Box 909,
Cardiff CF1 3XU

Professor M. Roberts

Department of Classics,
Wesleyan University,
Middletown, CT 06457

R. Samson, Esq.

University of Glasgow,
Department of Archaeology,
10 The Square,
Glasgow G12 8QQ

Dr H. Sivan

Department of Classics,
University of the
Witwatersrand,
1 Jan Smuts Avenue,
Johannesburg, WITS 2050

Dr H. C. Teitler

Department of History,
University of Utrecht,
Lucas Bolwerk 5,
N-3512 EG Utrecht

Dr R. Van Dam

Department of History,
University of Michigan,
Ann Arbor, MI 48109-1045

Dr M. A. Wes

Department of History,
University of Groningen,
Oude Kijk in't Jatstraat 26,
PO Box 716,
N-9700 Groningen

Dr I. N. Wood

School of History,
University of Leeds,
Leeds LS2 9JT

Acknowledgements

The title and the main content of this book derive from a conference organized by the editors at the University of Sheffield in April 1989. We would like to express our thanks to all who attended – and especially to the many who travelled very long distances – for helping to make the gathering so stimulating and enjoyable an occasion. The conference lasted for just under four working days, and consisted of twenty-nine papers and seven Round Table sessions. The successful implementation of so full a programme was owed to punctilious time-keeping. We gratefully acknowledge the debt we owe to the sessional chairmen – Jill Harries, Wolf Liebeschuetz, Robert Markus, Ralph Mathisen, Hagith Sivan, Brian Warmington and Ian Wood – for gently, but firmly, keeping to the tight schedule we set them. Ralph Mathisen further deserves our thanks for his enthusiastic support for the idea of a conference when it was first broached, and for his subsequent advice and encouragement. We would also like to make particular mention of the six student helpers from the Department of History, University of Sheffield – Jo Bellamy, Alison MacDonald, Josie Porter, Monica Rorison, Jim Wadman and Alex Woolf – who gave us indispensable support in receiving and entertaining conference delegates. We would also record our appreciation of the invaluable financial assistance given to us in the running of the conference and the publication of its Proceedings by the Department of History, University of Sheffield, the Department of Classical and Archaeological Studies, University of Nottingham, and the British Academy.

Revised versions of all but one of the twenty-nine papers delivered are presented here. We are grateful to our contributors for the patience with which they endured the lengthy, and on occasions very strict, editing of their texts. Ralph Mathisen and Ray Van Dam very kindly read the finished book in its penultimate draft, and offered much useful criticism, as did the two anonymous readers of Cambridge University Press. The figures were prepared by Richard Sheppard; and Russell Adams played an indispensable role in transforming our computer disks into camera-ready copy. The mistakes and omissions that remain are our own, and for these we take full responsibility.

JFD, HE

Abbreviations

AA	*Auctores Antiquissimi*
AE	*L'Année Epigraphique*
ASHAL	*Annuaire de la Société d'Histoire et d'Archéologie Lorraine* (before 1919, *Jahrbuch der Gesellschaft für Lotharingisches Geschicht- und Altertümskunde*)
BAR(B)	British Archaeological Reports (British Series)
BAR(S)	British Archaeological Reports (Supplementary Series)
BLAFAM	*Bulletin de Liaison de l'Association Française de l'Archéologie Merovingienne*
BSFN	*Bulletin de la Société Française de Numismatique*
CIL	*Corpus Inscriptionum Latinarum*
CJ	*Codex Justinianus*
CSEL	*Corpus Scriptorum Ecclesiasticorum Latinorum*
CTh	*Codex Theodosianus*
Ep.	*Epistula*
FC	*Fathers of the Church*, Catholic University of America, Washington, DC
GM	*Liber in Gloria Martyrum Beatorum*
GT	Gregory of Tours
HF	*Historiae Francorum*
ILCV	*Inscriptiones Latinae Christianae Veteres*
ILS	*Inscriptiones Latinae Selectae*, ed. H. Dessau, Berlin
PL	*Patrologia Latina*, ed. J.-P. Migne, Paris
PLRE	*The Prosopography of the Later Roman Empire*, vols. I, II (Jones, Martindale and Morris, 1971; Martindale, 1980)
MGH	*Monumenta Germaniae Historica*
RE	*Real-Encyclopädie der classischen Altertumswissenschaft*, ed. F. Pauly, G. Wissowa and W. Kroll, Stuttgart
SRL	*Scriptores Rerum Langobardorum*
SRM	*Scriptores Rerum Merovingicarum*

Chronological table of main historical events

(based on Bury, 1923)

376	The Goths enter the Roman empire
378	Battle of Adrianople
379	Accession of Theodosius I
383–8	Magnus Maximus emperor in the west
392	Revolt of Arbogast and Eugenius
394	Theodosius I suppresses Arbogast and Eugenius
395	Death of Theodosius I; accession of Honorius and Arcadius; Stilicho regent in the west; approximate date of transfer of seat of Gallic prefecture from Trier to Arles; defection of Alaric
401	Alaric's first invasion of Italy
405–6	Radagaisus invades Italy
406–7	Vandals, Sueves and Alans invade Gaul
407	Usurpation of Constantine III in Britain and Gaul
408	Death of Stilicho; Alaric's second invasion of Italy; Constantine III takes Spain
409	Vandals, Alans and Sueves cross from Gaul into Spain; revolt of Gerontius in Spain against Constantine III
410	Fall of Rome to Goths; death of Alaric; succession of Athaulf
411	Fall of Constantine III; death of Gerontius; usurpation of Jovinus in Mainz
412	The Goths, under Athaulf, enter Gaul
413	The Goths crush Jovinus for Honorius; Cl. Postumus Dardanus persecutes his sympathisers; the Goths

	break with Honorius, fail to take Marseille, but seize Narbonne, Toulouse and Bordeaux; the Burgundians settled on the Rhine
414	Athaulf marries Galla Placidia in Narbonne; sets up Attalus as puppet-emperor
414–15	Fl. Constantius drives the Goths into Spain; Aquitania ravaged; flight of Paulinus of Pella
415	Death of Athaulf; rise and fall of Singeric; accession of Wallia
416	Wallia in difficulty in Spain; agrees to treaty with western empire
416–18	The Goths fight for western empire against other barbarians in Spain
418	Death of Wallia; accession of Theoderic I; the Goths settled in Aquitania; establishment of the Gallic Council, at Arles
421	Elevation and death of Fl. Constantius; dynastic disharmony in the western court
422	The Goths (now 'Visigoths') used against Vandals in Spain
423	Death of Honorius; usurpation of John
425	Death of John; accession of Valentinian III; beginning of troubled regency of Galla Placidia; Visigoths troublesome in southern Gaul; Aëtius given responsibility for defence of Gaul
427	Aëtius lifts Visigothic siege of Arles
428	Aëtius victorious over Franks
429	Vandals, under Gaiseric, cross from Spain to Africa
429/30	Hilary made bishop of Arles
430–2	Aëtius victorious over Visigoths, near Arles, over Franks in northern Gaul, and over Bacaudae
432–4	Aëtius victorious in civil war in Italy

c. 435	Revolt in Aremorica
436	Aëtius destroys first Burgundian kingdom
436–9	War with Visigoths; Arles and Narbonne attacked
438–9	Aremorica subdued
439	Capture of Litorius at Toulouse; peace with Visigoths arranged through Avitus; fall of Carthage to Vandals
440	Aëtius moves from Gaul to Italy to face Vandal threat; Alans settled in Gaul; Franks sack Trier
442	Further trouble in Aremorica; Germanus travels to Ravenna
443	Burgundians settled in Sapaudia
444	Western government in severe fiscal difficulties
444–5	Hilary of Arles involved in the 'Chelidonius affair'
451	Attila invades Gaul; is defeated at Catalaunian Plains; death of Theoderic I; accession of Thorismund
453	Death of Thorismund; accession of Theoderic II
454	Death of Aëtius
455	Death of Valentinian III; accession of Petronius Maximus; Vandal expedition against Rome; death of Petronius Maximus; proclamation of Avitus by Theoderic II at Toulouse
456	First Visigothic invasion of Spain; deposition of Avitus; dominance of Ricimer in west; expansion of Burgundian kingdom beyond Sapaudia
457	Accession of Majorian
458–9	Majorian in Gaul, dealing with Burgundians, Visigoths and Gallic supporters of Avitus
460	Failure of Majorian's African expedition
461	Majorian at Arles; death of Majorian in Italy; accession of Libius Severus; defection of Aegidius; Burgundians receive imperial favour

462–3	Visigoths' expansion to Mediterranean
463	Aegidius defeats Frederick, brother of Theoderic II, at Orleans
464	Aegidius treats with Vandals;　death of Aegidius; succeeded by Syagrius
465	Death of Libius Severus
466	Death of Theoderic II;　accession of Euric; acceleration of Visigothic expansion
467	Accession of Anthemius
468	Sidonius Apollinaris *Praefectus Urbi*;　beginning of the 'Arvandus affair';　failure of imperial African expedition
469	Arvandus condemned;　failure of Roman expedition against Euric, under Anthemiolus
469/70	Sidonius Apollinaris made bishop of Clermont; Visigoths begin to pressure Auvergne
471	Beginning of Visigothic summer blockade of Clermont
472	Death of Anthemius;　accession of Olybrius;　death of Olybrius
473	Accession of Glycerius;　death of Glycerius; accession of Julius Nepos
474–5	The 'Seronatus affair' (? or 470–1)
475	Auvergne ceded to Visigoths;　accession of Romulus
476	Deposition of Romulus;　Provence ceded to Euric
486	Clovis defeats Syagrius at Soissons
498	Franks raid Bordeaux
507	Clovis defeats Visigoths, under Alaric II, at Vouillé

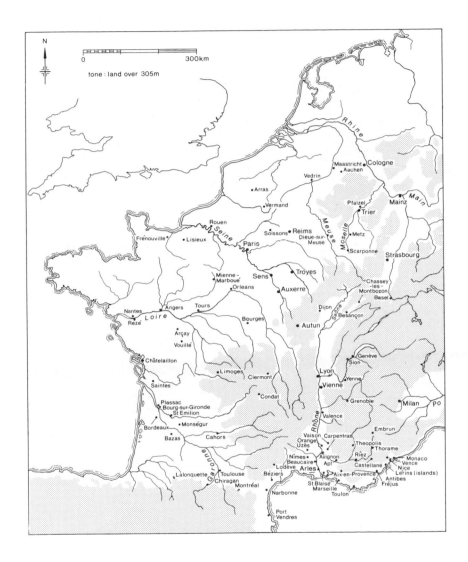

N

0   300km

tone : land over 305m

Rhine

Maastricht • Cologne
• Aachen

Vedrin •

Pfalzel
• Trier   Main

• Arras   Mainz

• Vermand

Meuse   Metz

Rouen   Scarponne •   Strasbourg

Frénouville •   • Lisieux   Seine   Soissons • Reims   Moselle
            Paris   Dieue-sur-
                 Meuse

Mienne -   • Troyes   Chassey
Marboué   Sens   -les-
      • Orleans   • Auxerre   Montbozon
                   Dijon   Basel
Nantes   Angers   Tours   Besançon
Rezé   Loire   • Bourges   Saône

            • Autun

Arçay
Vouillé

                     Genève
   • Châtelaillon   Sion
           • Limoges   Lyon
Saintes   • Clermont   Yenne
                Vienne

Plassac   • Condat   Grenoble   Milan   Po
Bourg-sur-Gironde
St Emilion   Rhône   Valence
• Monségur
Bordeaux   Embrun
       Bazas   Cahors   Vaison Carpentras   Theopolis
                   Orange   • Thorame
      Garonne   Uzès   Riez
              Nîmes •   Avignon   Monaco
Lalonquette   Beaucaire   Apt   Castellane   Vence
      Toulouse   Lodève   Arles   Nice
   Chiragan   Béziers   Aix-en-Provence   Lérins (islands)
    Montréal   St Blaise   Antibes
        Narbonne   Marseille   Fréjus
                 Toulon

Port
Vendres

Gaul in the fifth century

Introduction

In 375, no one could have doubted that Gaul was an integral and important part of the Roman empire. By then, Rome had been the dominant power in the country for five centuries; and in that year, the seventeen-year-old Gratian, having succeeded Valentinian I as effective ruler of the west, showed himself eager to continue his father's policy of locating the imperial court in Trier, on the Mosel. What is more, during the early years of Gratian's reign many native Gauls rose to great prominence in the imperial administration, thanks to the patronage of the emperor's former tutor, now senior counsellor, Ausonius of Bordeaux. One hundred years later, however, the situation was wholly changed, as a western imperial government now firmly based in Italy abandoned its Gallic subjects and ceded the last of its possessions in Gaul to king Euric of the Visigoths. The beginning of the establishment of the barbarians as sovereign powers in the land is conventionally dated to the invasions of 406–7 and their aftermath.

The disappearance of Roman power from Gaul and all that this implies for the decline and fall of the Roman empire and the transformation from Late Antiquity to the Middle Ages have long exercised the minds of scholars. The papers presented in this volume seek to identify and discuss the factors that so radically altered the position of Gaul in the Empire. Their authors were invited to consider the ways in which the inhabitants of Gaul reacted to the military, political and social changes consequent upon the invasions of 406–7 and, in particular, the manner and extent to which these people altered their perceptions of themselves as citizens of a world Empire: in brief, whether they suffered 'a crisis of identity'.

Such questions are usefully – indeed, given the fragmentary condition of the evidence, are perhaps best – approached from a number of different directions, employing the expertise of a wide range of disciplines. Contributions were therefore sought from archaeologists, genealogists, church historians, secular historians, literary scholars and numismatists. In order to give so varied a volume structure and coherency, and to make its contents as accessible as possible to the reader, the editors have taken the liberty of ordering its papers in roughly chronological sequence, and of allotting them to discrete Parts, for each of which they have provided introductory commentary. They would, however, emphasize that throughout their aim has been to allow the form and direction of the work to emerge without strain from the essays of which it is made up. They trust that their editorial contributions will be seen as pointing up those ideas which were at the forefront of their authors' minds, and not as attempting to trim these ideas to fit their own conceptions of the evolution of fifth-century Gallic history. They leave it to the reader to form his or her own general picture of the age, and of the problems involved in its study.

Given the theme of 'a crisis of identity?', it is not surprising that authors pay relatively little attention to straightforward reconstruction of political and military history; in fact, a number of them express serious doubts as to whether the writing of a narrative history of fifth-century Gaul is possible, or even proper. The emphasis is instead on the complex of social, economic, cultural and even, one might say, ideological processes by which Gaul slipped from Roman to barbarian rule. Much is made of the inherent brittleness of Roman control over Gaul following the settlement of barbarians west of the Rhine, and of the ways in which local ambitions, concerns and imperatives inexorably brought the leaders of Gallo-Roman society, lay and clerical, 'official' and 'unofficial', into contact and co-operation with Germanic kings and aristocrats not averse to adopting a Gallo-Roman lifestyle. Conversely, some Gallo-Roman leaders are characterized as acting themselves like barbarian kings. The distinction between 'Roman' and 'barbarian' is seen to blur. On the other hand, clear recognition of the emergence of a new order was remarkably slow to develop and, as a number of contributors stress, as far as the individuals involved were concerned, the change was often disruptive, costly and confusing: a matter of necessity, not choice. Gaul was destined to leave the womb of Rome but, like any other birth, her departure was laboured and painful.

Throughout, for the reasons already stated, the editors have avoided any direct attempt to set these papers in a general historical or historiographical context, or to offer direct comment on the validity or priority of particular issues raised. However, they would here draw attention to two points which seem likely to attract further comment and encourage more work. First, the 'maximalist' interpretation of the effect of the fifth-century disturbances on Gallo-Roman society stands in marked contrast to the 'minimalist' view – the emphasis on continuity – which has held sway in recent years. This may, in part at least, be attributed to the circumstance that many of the contributors to this volume can be categorized as scholars of the 'Ancient' as opposed to the 'Medieval' world; and it gives promise of a lively debate to follow. Second, a recurrent sub-theme throughout the book is the importance of Africa, and the disastrous consequences for the western empire of civil war and barbarian invasion in the African provinces. It appears that 'fifth-century Africa' would be an ideal subject for a similar multi-disciplinary investigation in the near future.

I

The literary sources

The modern historian of fifth-century Gaul has available no reliable contemporary account of the period, and must therefore depend for information upon the works of chroniclers, Christian apologists, littérateurs and hagiographers. A natural impulse is simply to draw on these writings to produce as consistent and plausible a narrative as possible. However, the grave problems involved in such an approach are underlined by *Wood*.

Wood points out that the establishment of even a basic chronology of the main political and military events of fifth-century Gallic history is hampered by the lack of entirely trustworthy texts of many of the authors concerned (in particular, the chroniclers); and, in respect of attempts at more detailed narratives, he warns against the practice of simply quarrying all available sources to obtain a supply of usable 'facts'. Fifth-century writers were not disinterested recorders of contemporary or near-contemporary happenings. Their observations were shaped by personal experience. The nature of this experience and the way they expressed it in their writings were themselves very much shaped by their class, education, family and social relationships, and their motives in setting pen to paper. With regard to all of these, authors in fifth-century Gaul were remarkably similar. Wood argues that such writers may be really understood only when they are read in their specific literary and political contexts, with a keen appreciation of their 'strategies' of the moment and with recognition and consideration of those matters which they omit, or distort, as much as of those which they include. We should resist the temptation to employ what they have to say as the basis for generalizations on the condition of Gaul as a whole.

Confirmation of this view is provided by *Burgess*, in a paper based on work for a new edition of Hydatius' *Chronicle*. Burgess demonstrates that Hydatius' interpretation of developments in Gaul was entirely determined by his sources and his Spanish viewpoint. The climax of Hydatius' doom-laden account is the Visigothic invasion of Spain in 456–7, and what followed. Hence he regards in a very favourable light those who administered a Gaul in which the Visigoths were still confined; but he reviles those who allowed Gaul to be used as a spring-board for Visigothic expansion over the Pyrenees. Particularly interesting in this respect is Hydatius' positive view of Aëtius, his purely negative estimation of Avitus – in his view a Gothic dupe or traitor – and his very favourable verdict on Aegidius, whose death marked the end of Roman Gaul.

A very similar plea for the precise identification of the contemporary preoccupations of our sources is made by *Muhlberger*, who contrasts the historical perspectives of Prosper of Aquitaine and the anonymous Chronicler of 452. Prosper's picture of secular developments in early fifth-century Gaul has to be teased out of his mainly ecclesiastical concerns, but it shows clearly that he thought little had changed as a result of the turmoil of 406–18: Constantius III had successfully restored the position of the Theodosian dynasty after what had amounted to no more than a struggle over the imperial throne; the barbarians were of only marginal importance. In 433, however, Prosper was worried lest Constantius III's unworthy successors, the quarrelling generals of his own day – in particular Aëtius – endanger the established order by allowing the barbarians an opportunity to make trouble. The Chronicler of 452, on the other hand, writing at a time when the African question had taken Aëtius' main attention from Gaul, and a year after Attila's invasion of the country, is much more pessimistic, seeing the invasion of 406 and its aftermath as a complete disaster, brought about by Theodosian incompetence and even treachery, that had exposed the whole of the western empire to barbarian invasion and settlement. He virtually ignores the achievements of Constantius III, and dismisses Aëtius' main Gallic campaigns as having brought only temporary respite – merely postponing the barbarian dismemberment of Gaul, and leaving the country prey to renegade Huns. His idealizing of Magnus Maximus, as the champion of the west, may be seen as a harbinger of Gallic support for Avitus. Muhlberger observes that the stark contrast between Prosper and the Chronicler of 452 may ultimately be explained by the undeniable decline in Roman power during the two decades that separate these writers, but that such an explanation in no way makes the Chronicler the more observant witness of the two, since much of what he says is derived more from ignorance, fear and religious prejudice than informed objectivity.

Burgess and Muhlberger concern themselves exclusively with writers who set down the events of their own day. Another approach is taken by *Barnish*, who examines successive treatments of a single significant historical event – Attila's defeat on the Catalaunian Plains in 451. Beginning with a contemporary, Sidonius Apollinaris, he shows how the battle fired the imagination of writers and resounded through the following half millennium, being reported in different ways according to whether an author's general perspective was secular or religious, and according to which particular lines of interest he was intent on pursuing. Though the battle was primarily reported as a good story, Barnish again demonstrates how important an acute sensitivity to a writer's likely personal, political and moral preoccupations is in grasping the shifting nuances in the accounts of the conflict that have come down to us in the works of Jordanes, Gregory of Tours, Fredegar, Paul the Deacon and anonymous hagiographers. He also shows how we cannot afford to neglect the concerns of the authors who were the sources for these writers, and lays particular emphasis on Cassiodorus, here the main source for Jordanes. Barnish sees Cassiodorus as having depicted the Ostrogothic Theoderic the Great as a second Aëtius-cum-Theoderic I, the defender of civilization against the Frankish Clovis, a second Attila. Ironically, as the legend of the battle of the Catalaunian Plains developed, it was used to buttress the prestige, power and legitimacy of Merovingian and Carolingian monarchs, and to tie them into the history of Christian Roman Gaul.

Overall, therefore, the reconstruction of the history of fifth-century Gaul is an activity that has to be undertaken with much care. Wood, indeed, advises against the writing of narrative history, and prefers the examination of the period through investigation of 'authorial concerns', in the manner of Burgess, Muhlberger, Barnish and, later in the volume, Harries. However, exploration of the often confusing and contradictory reactions of Gauls to changing circumstances – their 'shifting perceptions of identity' – from within their own thinking cannot be pursued in isolation. To understand the Gallic response to events we must also determine what those events were: as Maas suggests below (at the same time proposing comparative studies as a way of approaching authorial concerns 'without the frustration of seeking linear developments of ideas between writers divorced from historical context'), we need both narrative history and 'a history of changing perceptions and evaluations of cultural differences'. In brief, the creation of narrative history and the re-creation of authorial concerns should, if executed with prudence, be complementary rather than opposing aspects of the work of the modern scholar, as is demonstrated in the remaining papers in this volume.

CHAPTER 1

Continuity or calamity?: the constraints of literary models

I. N. Wood

The late fourth and fifth centuries were a significant period for literary production in Gaul, as in other provinces of the western empire. It is indeed possible that this period was one of greater literary production and achievement in the provinces than any that had come before, although such a contention could not be proved; it may be that the dominant role of the Church in the transmission of texts ensured the survival of Christian writings, and the loss of provincial texts of the pagan period. Nevertheless, it is clear that the fall of the western empire did not mark a caesura in written culture. Nor did the decline of schools of rhetoric during the later fifth and sixth centuries lead to any absolute break (Riché, 1962; for Merovingian Gaul, see also Wood, 1990).

At the same time, the message of the writers of the first half of the fifth century was one of discontinuity with the past. The moralists associated with Lérins, and other centres of Provençal monasticism, as well as those associated with St Martin, were concerned with new cultural and spiritual values. Moreover, some of them, including the poet Orientius, his predecessors and, above all, Salvian, set these values against a background of internal corruption, and of disasters inflicted by invading barbarians. Not surprisingly, those modern historians who have studied the period through these particular sources have presented a very bleak vision (Courcelle, 1964).

By contrast, the writers of the late fifth century looked back deliberately to the literature of the fourth century, to the epistolary traditions of Symmachus, and their development under Paulinus of Nola (Fabre, 1949), and to the panegyrics of Claudian. Gaul as seen through the letter-collections of Sidonius Apollinaris and of his acolytes of the following generation is dominated by the exercise of *amicitia*, much like that of the fourth century (Matthews, 1974). This assertion of cultural continuity after a period of disruption might reasonably be seen as part of the *ordo renascendi* vaunted by Rutilius Namatianus, the social and political manifestations of which have been exposed by John Matthews (Matthews, 1975: 329ff.).

That there was continuity of a sort, despite the visions of Orientius and Salvian, can be seen prosopographically, since many of the moralists and literati of fifth-century Gaul were connected in one way or another (see Mommaerts and Kelley, below). Thus, to begin firmly in the Merovingian period, the letter-writers Avitus, bishop of Vienne, and Ruricius, bishop of Limoges, were relatives of Sidonius (Stroheker, 1948: nos. 60, 327), and they were admirers of his literary achievements (Avitus, *Ep.* 51; Ruricius, *Ep.* 1.8–9, 16, 2.26). Ruricius was also an admirer of Faustus, bishop of Riez (Ruricius, *Ep.* 1.1–2; see also Faustus, *Ep.* 1–5), as was Sidonius, whose brother was influenced by the bishop (Sidonius, *Carm.* 16; *Ep.* 9.3.9). Faustus, however, was one of the leading members of the Lérinian community, which also included Salvian, as well as numerous other ascetics, among them Honoratus, Hilary, Eucherius and later Caesarius of Arles.

In fact, almost every major writer from fifth-century Gaul can be placed within a single, well-defined nexus of family, social and religious relationships. In certain respects the group was almost too tightly knit, given the religious debates and disagreements then current. This can be most neatly illustrated by the problems caused by the *De Statu Animae* of Claudianus Mamertus (Fortin, 1959; Wood, 1980: 56ff.). Claudianus was a priest of Vienne, where his brother, Mamertus, was bishop. He may well have taught the young Avitus, while Mamertus must have witnessed Avitus' early ecclesiastical career. He will also have been aware of the early career of his own successor as bishop of Vienne, Avitus' father, Isicius, who was perhaps the *tribunus legatus* sent by the emperor Avitus to the Goths in 456 (Stroheker, 1948: no. 190; Hydatius, 177). At all events, there were close links between Claudianus, the Aviti of Vienne and Sidonius. Thus, when Claudianus came across an anonymous tract on the corporeality of the soul, Sidonius commissioned a reply to it (Claudianus Mamertus, *De Statu Animae*, praef., 1.1–2; Sidonius, *Ep.* 4.2). This Claudianus did, with devastating effect. Unfortunately, the unnamed author of the original tract was none other than Faustus, himself a friend and spiritual mentor of Sidonius. The appearance of the *De Statu Animae* may have been partly responsible for a temporary break in relations between Sidonius and the bishop of Riez (Sidonius, *Ep.* 9.9.1).

These connections between the literati of the later fifth century and their ascetic predecessors provide a useful reminder that, for all the difference in tone between the moralizing of Salvian and his contemporaries and the letters of Sidonius, Avitus and Ruricius, they shared a common ecclesiastical culture. Indeed, Sidonius himself needs to be placed firmly in the ascetic traditions of fifth-century Gaul (Rousseau, 1976), as do the writers of the next generation. Avitus, in particular, in his poem *De Consolatoria Castitatis Laude*, shows a strong affinity for the ascetic life (Wood, 1980: 85ff.). And the same association between asceticism and rhetoric can be detected in the career of Pomerius, master and pupil of Caesarius of Arles (Delage, 1971: 48f., 52ff.), as well as religious guide to Ruricius (Ruricius, *Ep.* 1.17, 2.10–11).

The fact that the literature of the fifth century is the creation of a single social and cultural group gives pause for thought. For the modern historian there are both advantages and disadvantages in a recognition of this. On the one hand, it implies that our evidence comes from a limited circle which is restricted in social, religious and geographical terms. Because of these limitations it is necessary to be especially cautious about the voids in the evidence for all those areas which are not within the purview of this one section of the population; it is particularly dangerous here to argue from the known to the unknown. On the other hand, this one group can be discussed in relative detail, with an awareness of the complexity of its social, religious and literary relations.

Thus, it is instructive to recognize the fact that the doom-laden apologists were not the representatives of a class or society that was destroyed by the barbarian invasions, although they will have sustained some losses. In fact they were members of an aristocracy that, in southern and central Gaul at least, survived relatively unharmed into the period of the successor states (Stroheker, 1948; cf. Mommaerts and Kelley, below). Their sense of disaster, therefore, which may have represented only too accurately the realities of the first half of the fifth century, needs to be set against the letter-collections of the end of the century. Equally, the letter-collections need to be read against the background of the works of Salvian and his fellow moralists.

The responses of Orientius and Salvian, like those of Sidonius, Ruricius and Avitus, are, however, not mere reflections of reality, they are literary constructs. Seen in this perspective, the divergent tones to be found within the literature of the period provide a clear indication of the range of form and style open to the senatorial aristocracy of late and sub-Roman Gaul. Further, this exploitation of the full range of rhetorical devices available to the writers makes it abundantly clear that there was nothing ingenuous about their products; rather the style and form of each work, however short, is determined by the author's current literary strategy.

Nowhere is this more apparent than in Sidonius' letter to bishop Basilius of Marseilles, of the year 475 (*Ep*. 7.6; see Harries, below p. 299). The date of the letter, in the months preceding the cession of Clermont to Euric, and the recipient, Basilius, one of those involved in negotiations with the Visigothic king (*Ep*. 7.6.10), provide a very specific context for Sidonius' tirade against the policies both of Nepos and of Euric, the last of whom is depicted, through a manipulation of Biblical language, as an archetypal persecutor (*Ep*. 7.6.6). The rhetorical nature of this letter is all the more clear when set against that to Lampridius, with its laudatory verses on Euric's court (*Ep*. 7.9), written a year later, when the bishop of Clermont was trying to curry favour with one of the courtiers.

The dangers of reading Sidonius' letters without regard to their literary and political context are particularly apparent from Gregory of Tours's interpretation of Euric's religious policy (GT *HF* 2.25), which was accepted as an accurate record until K. F. Stroheker's devastating dissection of the evidence in 1937 (Stroheker, 1937: 40ff.). And even Stroheker's words have not always been fully heeded. Gregory's account of Euric's reign depends largely on the letter of Sidonius to Basilius, which provides the only 'hard' evidence for his account of Euric's persecution. As we have seen, however, the letter to Lampridius throws the validity of that to Basilius into question; are both letters to be taken at face value? In which case, the situation described by Sidonius lasted for only a year, and Gregory was quite wrong historically to take the letter to Basilius out of context, although to do so suited the bishop of Tours very well. Or are either or both of the letters to be regarded as little more than rhetorical exercises? Whatever the answer, Gregory's interpretation of events needs to be rejected (Stroheker, 1937: 40ff.; Wood, 1985: 255).

Sidonius' two letters provide an alarming insight into just how much we do not know; without the letter to Basilius we would know nothing about Euric's ecclesiastical policy in the year 475, but without the letter to Lampridius we would have no check on the applicability of that information. For much of the time we have no such control. As a result, although we can be certain that most of our sources for the fifth century are conditioned by literary strategies, we do not always have the evidence to evaluate the validity of the strategy in question.

It might be argued that so negative an approach to the evidence is unhelpful and extreme, not least because the letters of Sidonius are more likely to be suspect than other less rhetorical works. This may be so, but writings uncontaminated by literary devices are not easy to find. The only full narrative history of fifth-century Gaul is that contained in Book Two of Gregory's *Histories*. Although the bishop of Tours's skill as a writer used not to be recognized, there can no longer be any doubt about his sophistication (Goffart, 1988), and about his ability to manipulate his information (Wood, 1985). Essentially the account of fifth-century Gaul offered by Gregory in his *Histories* is intended, on the one hand, to denigrate the Arian Goths and Burgundians, and, on the other, to elevate the Franks and their king, the Catholic convert, Clovis. The interpretation set out by Gregory depended, in part, on the religious and political climate of the period in which he himself was writing. Significantly his hagiography makes different and sometimes contradictory points to those in his *Histories* (Wood, 1985: 256f.; 1988: 122). Even if this were not the case, his misuse of Sidonius should stand as a warning to any reader in search of 'hard' fact. And since his reading of Sidonius can be shown to be misleading, there must be a suspicion that the same is true of his use of Renatus Profuturus Frigeridus and Sulpicius Alexander (GT *HF* 2.8–9). Moreover, since their works survive only in the passages quoted by Gregory, it is impossible to ascertain the aims and reliability of these authors. The same difficulties hold true when it comes to assessing the other main source cited by Gregory for the period, the *Angers Chronicle*, which provides the chief evidence for the reign of Childeric I, although here there is the additional difficulty that the chronicle's entries are so concise as to be ambiguous, if not inscrutable (GT *HF* 2.18–19).

It might, however, be thought that other fifth-century Gallic chronicles provide a more reliable foundation for writing a narrative of the period. This, however, assumes that chronicles are less prone to manipulation than are other texts, and unfortunately the assumption is unwarranted. By the inclusion and omission of material, by grouping events and by placing them in particular years, a chronicler could embark on an interpretation of his period every bit as contrived as that of Gregory, and all the more misleading, because the literary form may be thought of as not being open to rhetorical abuse.

All the fifth-century chroniclers can be said to have their own voices. Each one is interested in different issues, whether political or ecclesiastical. Prosper's papal viewpoint is clear enough from what he says, as also is his recognition of the significance of civil war (Muhlberger, 1984: 57). So too is the Gallaecian perspective of Hydatius (see Burgess, below). Equally well known is the anti-Augustinian stance of the Chronicler of 452, as well as his concerns with the region round Valence and with the provinces of Britain (Wood, 1987: 255). Here the identifiable concerns of the Chronicler, who also included a number of entries relevant to the monastic culture of Lérins (e.g. 86, 104, 134), may suggest that he was in some way associated with Faustus of Riez. Were such a suggestion to be correct, it could add considerably to an understanding of the context in which one of the few contemporary sources for Britain and northern Gaul in the fifth century was composed, and it might, therefore, be possible to be more specific about the implications of the entries relevant to those areas.

What chroniclers included in their works is one key to their intentions; what they excluded is another. Of course, it is not always possible to say whether an omission or an error is deliberate. One error that can scarcely be anything other than deliberate is the placing by Prosper of the conclusion of the Council of Chalcedon in 453. Since he was a member of the papal household he must have known better. His annal for 451, however, already had enough to keep the reader's interest, with Attila's invasion of Gaul. Moreover, Attila's invasion is the beginning of a narrative stretching over two annals, which culminates in pope Leo's involvement in the withdrawal of the Huns from Italy. Part, but perhaps only part, of the explanation for the error over Chalcedon must lie in the demands of narrative. Similarly, the Chronicler of 452's peculiar date of 444 for the fall of Carthage is best explained by reference to the cluster of other disasters placed in the previous years. Indeed, the chronicler seems to have been particularly keen on grouping evidence, regardless of chronological accuracy; thus the sack of Rome, which is misplaced in

411, is preceded by disasters in Britain, Gaul and Spain, while the fall of Carthage comes after barbarian success or settlement in Valence, Britain, Gallia Ulterior and Sapaudia (Wood, 1987: 255; for an alternative reading, Jones and Casey, 1988: 376ff., 397).

But there are other instances where it is less easy to be certain whether an event is deliberately misplaced, or indeed whether it is misplaced at all. This obviously holds true for those events for which we have only one witness; thus, granted the amount of chronological re-arrangement in the *Chronicle of 452*, is it reasonable to assume that the entry for the settlement of the Burgundians in Sapaudia (128) is accurate, simply because we have no alternative source to discredit it? Or should the entry be treated in the same way as that for the fall of Carthage, and be seen as part of an interpretative scheme?

Equally problematic, despite the inclusion of the event in various chronicles and histories, is the date for the settlement of the Visigoths in Aquitaine. That in the *Chronicle of 452*, at 415, is wildly out of line, but of the other two dates, which is more accurate; Hydatius' 418 or Prosper's 419 (Wood, 1987: 254)? The difference is important, since it affects the relationship between the institution of the Council of the Gauls in Arles (in 418) (Matthews, 1975: 325, 334f.) and the Visigothic settlement. The assumption that 418 is correct seems largely to derive from Mommsen's edition of the *Chronica Gallica*, in which he inserted his own marginal dates, giving the texts a spurious similarity. Indeed, it is probably true to say that Mommsen's edition of the *Chronicles* has hindered scholarship considerably more than it has helped, and that the confusions generated can be disentangled only by separate editions of and commentaries on the various chronicles and their major recensions.

In one way or another it is clear that the Chronicles do not provide the unquestionable chronology that is required before a reliable narrative history can be written. Nor can saints' *Lives* be expected to provide facts where the chronicles have failed. Above all they are texts with propaganda in mind, whether spiritual or political in the broadest meaning of the term. The extent of the difficulties involved in using the hagiography can most simply be seen through the *Life of Germanus* by Constantius. Of the major events recorded in the *Life*, one, the second visit to Britain, is thought by many not to have taken place. Further, the date of the saint's death is open to question, and indeed the saint's last actions can be dated only by reference to the *Chronicle of 452*; not the ideal supporting text (Wood, 1984: 6ff.). In addition, the date of Germanus' death is also important for judging the accuracy of the *Life of Hilary* (Wood, 1984: 14f.). The hagiography, unfortunately, does not give the narrative historian reliable dates.

Like many exercises in reconstruction, that of narrating the history of fifth-century Gaul is peculiarly difficult. The evidential problems are enormous. This is not just a matter of the detail of events. There is, of course, the more general interpretative problem posed by the contrast between the tales of disaster told by the moralists of the early fifth century and the show of continuity made by the litterati of the ensuing generations; it is not clear that the doom-laden moralists provide a less accurate reflection of their period than does Sidonius of his time. There is also the question of the implications of the tight-knit nature of the group which is responsible for almost all the surviving literary evidence. Rather than pursuing the chimera of a narrative model based on the recitation of events, it might be more profitable to undertake a history of authorial concerns, even though those concerns are not always clear. Such an approach would allow the historian access to far vaster resources, which would include not merely the material already mentioned, but also the theological works of the period, and above all the martyr acts which were being written, if not forged, throughout the fifth and sixth centuries (Dufourcq, 1900–7, with Delehaye, 1908).

Within such a context many of the staple concerns of the historian can still be explored. Thus, the fall of the western empire can be discussed from the standpoint of shifting perceptions of identity, for, although problems of interpretation make any assessment of destruction from the literary sources extremely hypothetical, responses to the rise of the barbarian kingdoms can be detected in the evidence (cf. Maas, below 283f.). Here the difficulties in penetrating beyond genre, which are presented by Sidonius' letters on Euric, cease to be a problem, but rather become an indication of the full range of cultural resources at hand for adjusting to the reality of the emergence of new power structures. Further, Sidonius not only allows us to see his own range of responses, but he also provides material for the study of those of other individuals, like Lampridius, and also Leo, who threw himself wholly into support for the new Visigothic regime (Stroheker, 1948: no. 212).

Again, the very restricted nature of the sources, limited as they are to a coherent group of writers, makes comparison between one generation and the next worthwhile. The hysteria of Orientius is scarcely to be found in Sidonius, except in his letter to Basilius. Equally the distance which Sidonius maintained between himself and the court of Euric was not possible for Avitus of Vienne, a generation later in one of the central cities of the Burgundian kingdom. The sources might be said to chart successive phases of acculturation to the fall of the western empire. For Avitus, the presence of the king or his son in Vienne was a boon (Avitus, *Ep.* 76–7). Nor did the Arianism of Gundobad make relations between the bishop and his king difficult (Wood, 1986: 75f.; Wood, forthcoming); Avitus was indeed invited to debate with the Arian clergy and to write theological tracts, by an apparently open-minded Gundobad (Avitus, *Contra Arrianos* 1–3; *Ep.* 1–4, 6, 21–3, 30). Ultimately the bishop would even, it seems, become responsible for royal correspondence with the emperor (Avitus, *Ep.* 78, 93–4). In this respect he was something of a Cassiodorus for the Burgundians. The letters to the emperor written by these two men have a very marked resemblance, one to another, suggesting that both drew upon established modes of address (compare Avitus, *Ep.* 93 with Cassiodorus, *Variae* 1.1). This is not to say that Avitus served Sigismund in the same way that Cassiodorus served Theodoric, but rather that they could draw on the same cultural resources.

For all his commitment to the Burgundian kingdom, Avitus was aware of the threats it posed to himself, his family and his class. Like his contemporary Ennodius, and like Sidonius in the previous generation (Sidonius, *Ep.* 9.3.1–2, 9.5.1) he used one further literary strategy: silence. That he did so is apparent from letters resuming a correspondence which had been interrupted because of the political situation. Thus he links the reception of greetings from friends with a period of peace (Avitus, *Ep.* 37). Equally, he did not write to Sidonius' son, his cousin, Apollinaris, in the period before the battle of Vouillé, when the latter was under suspicion of treason, since a letter from a neighbouring kingdom would only strengthen the suspicion (Avitus, *Ep.* 51). Similarly, Ennodius complained to his friend, Stephanus, that the latter had not resumed their correspondence when he was no longer under threat from treason accusations (Ennodius, 87 [*Ep.* 3.17]). In these references to and complaints about non-communication we see one of the legacies of the fall of the Empire; the ever-present possibility that relations between neighbouring kingdoms might deteriorate and the continuing connections of the senatorial aristocracy might become a liability.

Occasionally the sources are precise about the context of a particular disruption in communication; occasionally they allow us to see the exact cause for a literary strategy. Stringing these specific instances together scarcely adds up to anything more than a very fragmentary narrative, and it is important to recognize this. Nevertheless an analysis of the fall of the western empire and the creation of the successor states in Gaul is possible even when the limitations of the evidence are recognized, and indeed utilized. Looked at from the point of view of the authors of our sources, rather than from the events they recorded, the question of continuity or calamity becomes an issue of the mobilization of culture to deal with a changing world.

CHAPTER 2

From Gallia Romana *to* Gallia Gothica*: the view from Spain*

R. W. Burgess

The purpose of this chapter is to offer some insights into the problem of Roman and Gothic Gaul as seen by Hydatius, bishop of Aquae Flaviae (modern Chaves, Portugal) in Gallaecia from 428 to *c.* 469. Hydatius' chronicle is one of a very few contemporary diachronic views of the transformation of Gaul in the fifth century which we possess. That such a view comes from someone outside the province at first seems odd, but the reasons for this are simple and will be explained. My actual conclusions in this regard will not be particularly surprising or of earth-shaking importance; I find it of great interest simply to be able to examine what we see as such an important transformation through the eyes of a contemporary. What will be more surprising, I think, will be my account of the causes of the shift of Hydatius' point of view.

Because of the eastern origin of his major written source for the period to 395 – an expanded version of the *Consularia Constantinopolitana*, often called the *Fasti Hydatiani* but not the work of Hydatius (Burgess, forthcoming) – and because of his lack of a similar source for the period 395–410, Hydatius says very little about Gaul before 411. What he does have to report is of either a religious or an imperial nature, two secondary concerns of his chronicle after the barbarians. He records only two imperial events and both derive from the *Consularia*: the execution of Victor, the son of Magnus Maximus, in 388 and the death of Valentinian II and consequent accession of Eugenius in 392 (17, 20 [22]).[1] The

---

[1] All references to Hydatius' chronicle here follow the revised numbering system of Burgess, forthcoming; parallel references to Mommsen's text, where they differ from the preceding, are noted in square brackets.

19

Consularia does not report the death of Gratian at Lyon in 383 and as a result neither does Hydatius. The religious material, which may also derive from Hydatius' now-lost version of the *Consularia*, includes a floruit of St Martin of Tours, Priscillian's trip to Rome through Gaul and his eventual execution at Trier under Magnus Maximus (8, 13, 16). The only entry which can be completely attributed to Hydatius' own initiative concerns the death of St Martin and the following note on Sulpicius Severus' *Chronica* and *V. Martini* (30 [37a]). Thus for the first thirty years – the first third – of the chronicle Hydatius has very little information on Gaul, which is, as a result, of little importance for the overall theme or structure of the work thus far.

The *Consularia* covered the years 379 to 395. Hydatius' only other major written source was probably some sort of southern Gallic annalistic document which covered the years *c*. 410 to *c*. 439 and which, amidst much other non-Gallic material, offered a typically Roman view of early fifth-century Gaul successfully defended against usurpers and barbarians. From this source Hydatius learned of the usurpers Constantine III and Jovinus and Sebastian (42, 43, 46 [50, 51, 54]), and he also learned in great detail about the activities of the Goths, from their capture of Narbo in 413 to their final peace with the Romans in 439 (47, 49, 52, 61, 62, 87, 98, 101, 104, 108, 109 [55, 57, 60, 69, 70, 97, 107, 110, 112, 116, 117]). Also a part of this source was probably a reference to the eclipse of 418 (56 [64]), recorded by Hydatius because of his interest in portents of the end of the world, which he believed would occur in 482.

This document not only provided Hydatius with a fundamental source for early Gothic activity in Gaul, it also helped to shape and formalize a view of early fifth-century Gaul which he appears to have gained himself first hand, for one important block of material in this section of the chronicle on the defence of Gaul derives from his own personal researches undertaken when he was chosen to lead a delegation to Aëtius to ask him to help re-establish peace between the Sueves and the Gallaecians. While waiting for Aëtius to return from campaigning in the winter of 431–2 Hydatius learned of his victories over the Goths, Iuthungi, Nori and Franks near Arles and in northern Gaul from 430 to 432 (82, 83, 85, 86, 88 [92, 93, 95, 96, 98]). This was probably the only time that Hydatius had ever been to Gaul, though he may have used a Gallic port on his way to and from the Holy Land where he undertook a pilgrimage in 406–7 (pref. 4 [3], 33 [40]). The only other information Hydatius records about Gaul concerns portents seen in Biterrae (modern Béziers) in 419 (65 [73]). These signs were important for Hydatius' eschatological concerns and derived from a contemporary letter written by Paulinus the bishop of Biterrae.

It was also during these years that the Goths first became active in Spain, and Hydatius takes a keen interest in their successes and failures as Roman federates: from 416 to 418 he describes the first Gothic invasion of Spain and in 422 he recounts their betrayal of Castinus (52, 55, 59–61, 69 [60, 63, 67–9, 77]). In 431 he mentions, in a frustratingly vague manner, the arrival and departure of a certain Vetto, who was sent from the Goths to Gallaecia (87 [97]). These few, mostly minor, events are seen by Hydatius as a prelude to future Gothic interest in Spain.

Thus in the second third of the chronicle, from 411 to 439, Hydatius has portrayed Gaul as a province successfully defended by strong Roman generals against barbarians and usurpers (cf. Elton, below pp. 170f.). Because of what is to come, however, he is most interested in the Goths and their activities in both Gaul and Spain. What is most surprising in a chronicle written by an apparently orthodox bishop is the lack of reference to religious individuals and literature, though these are among the most notable aspects of fifth-century Roman Gaul.

The final third of the chronicle, as far as Gaul is concerned, is divided into two sections, from 440 to 455, and 456 to 468. This material is derived completely from personal and oral sources. In the period 440 to 455 Gaul is in a transitional stage (cf. Heather, below p. 91). Because of growing Gothic prominence in Spain and Gaul Hydatius begins to concentrate on the developing links between the Goths and the Sueves on the one side, and the Goths and the imperial government on the other. In 444 he recounts the flight to Theoderic of Sebastian, the exiled son-in-law of Boniface (121 [129]). In 449 he records the marriage alliance between the Suevic and Gothic kings, and the journey which Rechiarius, the king of the Sueves, made to the Gothic king Theoderic, presumably at Tolosa (132, 134 [140, 142]). He returns to his interest in the Roman defence of Gaul with the defeat of the Huns in 451 and their departure from Gaul, an episode in which the Goths play a large role as federates (142, 145 [150, 153]). Here he claims that the battle took place in the *campi Catalaunici* 'not far from Metz', though in actual fact Metz is well over a hundred miles from the scene of the battle near Troyes, proof that Hydatius knew little about Gallic geography. After the battle he reports the succession of the Gothic kings, Thorismund and Theoderic II (142, 144, 148 [150, 152, 156]). He returns for the last time to religion and literature in Gaul in 449 and 452, when he records that letters of Leo, Flavian and Cyril came to Spain by way of Gaul and that a letter of Euphronius of Augustodunum to the *comes* Agrippinus described the appearance of still more Gallic portents (137, 143 [145, 151]; cf. 100 [109]). The last episode he mentions before the Gothic invasion of Spain in 456 is the acclamation of Avitus at Toulouse and Arles by the Goths and the Gallic *honorati*, and his departure for Rome. This event is referred to again upon Avitus' death (156, 176 [163, 183]). Meanwhile, he continues his descriptions of Gothic federate action in Spain under Vitus and Fredericus in 446 and 453–4 (126, 150 [134, 158]).

The focus and climax of Hydatius' chronicle is the Gothic invasion of Spain in 456–7 (161, 163, 165–8, 169–75, 179–80 [168, 170, 172–5, 177–82, 186–7]). Hydatius expends more space, more detail and more emotion on this short sequence of events between 5 October 456 and early April 457 than on anything else in his entire history. It is this invasion which prompted him to write his chronicle, and which gives it its eschatological validity. The Goths, who had a marriage alliance with the Sueves, joined forces with an emperor who had been a Gothic nominee, to betray that alliance and destroy the Suevic kingdom. Since the establishment of peace in 433 (91 [100]; renewed in 438, 105 [113]), Gallaecia had led a generally trouble-free existence, but the Gothic invasion changed all of that. During this invasion, the Goths and their allies lost control of themselves, and ended up plundering and destroying whole Roman towns, and kidnapping and murdering Romans rather than Sueves. When they eventually retired to Gaul in 457 they left Gallaecia and Lusitania gutted and open to renewed and constant depredation at the hands of armed Suevic factions led by minor warlords. The plundering, destruction and killing had not ended when Hydatius died thirteen years later. The Gothic invasion was for Hydatius the final sign of God's wrath and the beginning of the end of the world.

In all of this Avitus is especially singled out as, at best, a Gothic dupe, at worst, a traitor: as a Gaul and a Roman he should have resisted the Goths, but not only was he their nominee, he personally desired and arranged the invasion: 'cum uoluntate et ordinatione Auiti imperatoris' (156, 163, 166 [163, 170, 173]). In the end, bereft of his promised Gothic military support because of the war in Spain, Avitus was unable to hold onto power, and lost the purple and as well as his life (176 [183]). At Avitus' first appearance in the chronicle, Hydatius stresses his Gallic origin: he is called a *Gallus ciuis* (156 [163]). The only other person described by Hydatius as a *Gallus ciuis* is the *comes* Agrippinus, who also threw in his lot with the Goths by surrendering Narbo to them (or so Hydatius had been told) (212 [217]). The only other use of *ciuis* in the chronicle comes in 468 when Lusidius, a *ciuis* of Ulixippona (modern Lisbon), surrenders that city to the Sueves (240 [246]). Each time Hydatius uses *ciuis* he is stressing the contrast between natural loyalties and the actual perverted loyalties of those involved. Avitus and Agrippinus owed their allegiance to Gaul but betrayed it, not merely by throwing in their lot with the Goths but, even worse, by assisting them in the conquest of other Romans. This was especially ironic in the case of Avitus because the invasion of 456–7 was originally launched to stop the Sueves from plundering Roman territory in Carthaginiensis and Tarraconensis (161, 163, 165 [168, 170, 172]).

And the Goths could not only destroy men's bodies, they could threaten their souls as well. For a rather different kind of invasion there is the case of Ajax, a Greek ex-catholic who had become an Arian and risen high in the Arian church (228 [232]). In late 465 or early 466, having left Gothic dominated Gaul, he appeared among the Sueves and, with the help of the Suevic king, seems to have posed a serious threat to the hitherto generally stable religious order of western Spain.

July 458 marks the beginning of a contrary, almost inexplicable and completely misunderstood period of Hispano-Gothic relations, which continued beyond the death of Hydatius. In this month a Gothic army under the command of a Gothic *dux* by the name of Cyrila moved into Baetica (185 [192]). Hydatius does not tell us what it was they were doing there. Immediately afterwards the Goths sent envoys to the Sueves (186 [192]), a most peculiar action since a year before they had been attempting to wipe them off the face of the earth. The next year Theoderic sent a detachment of his army to Baetica under the *dux* and *comes* Suniericus and had Cyrila recalled to Gaul, one assumes with his army (188 [193]). Again, what they were doing is not stated. Shortly afterwards a new supreme commander arrived in Baetica, the *magister militiae* Nepotianus, and he and Suniericus remained there from 459 until 461, when they were replaced by the *magister militiae* Arborius, probably as a result of Suniericus' hostile actions against the Lusitanian city of Scallibis in 460, the sole instance of Gothic hostility in the period (192, 196, 201, 207–8 [197, 201, 206, 212–13]). Arborius was recalled to Gaul in 465 and not replaced (226 [230]), and there is no other record of official Gothic military activity in Spain for the rest of the chronicle. The general view today is that these commanders were finishing up the conquest of Baetica, Lusitania and Gallaecia begun in 456–7, and that the Gothic presence there was continuous from 458 to 711, in spite of Hydatius' statement that the Goths left in 465 (e.g. Stein, 1959: 381, 393, 396; Demougeot, 1979: 624f., 627f., 631ff., 637; Thompson, 1982: 165, 189ff., 302 n19; Collins, 1983: 24f.; Wolfram, 1988: 179f., 182, 185f.). However, I think it highly unlikely that they were involved in conquest, or any hostile activities for that matter, in spite of the presence of the army and the military commanders. I say this because Hydatius' major purpose in writing the chronicle was to record barbarian assaults on Spain; he had many contacts with the Goths, even those in Baetica, and if there was even a hint of Gothic hostility in the south, he would have known about it and reported it. Indeed, in 468 a small, independent band of Goths, plundering for profit, entered Spain and Hydatius reports their attacks on Emerita, Lusitania and Gallaecia, noting especially that they attacked both Sueves and Romans (239–40, 244 [245–6, 250]), so there is no reason why he would not have done the same in the case of Theoderic's army if it had been involved in similar activities. The Goths do, however, appear to have been involved in establishing a sort of protectorate over western Spain, acting as a third party in an attempt to establish stability between the Romans and the Sueves. This did not involve conquest or settlement, but was mainly aimed at extending influence, power and patronage in the wake of the invasion of 456–7. The first true Gothic conquests in Spain of which we have record do not occur until 472–3 and they are in *Hispania superior* (*Chron. Gall. 511* 651–2; Isidore, *Historia Gothorum* 34).

While I am on the subject of the Gothic army in Baetica, I wish to digress slightly at this point to correct another widely accepted interpretation involving these events. Virtually every scholar accepts that Nepotianus was the father of the future emperor Julius Nepos and that both Nepotianus and Arborius were imperial *magistri militum* (*RE* XVI, 2513, *PLRE* II, 778; *RE* Suppl. XII, 1355, *PLRE* II, 129; *RE* Suppl. XII, 683f., *PLRE* II, 1289). But what is the evidence for these claims? As regards the first, Jordanes (*Romana* 338) tells us that Nepos had a father named Nepotianus. This is all he says, and no other independent source confirms or contradicts. But Nepos had marriage connections with the emperor Leo and came from a wealthy and powerful Dalmatian family (*PLRE* II, 708ff., 777f.); Nepotianus was a minor mercenary working for the Goths in Spain (see below); what possible connection could there have been between these two? There is in fact no evidence for a connection other than the identity of the names, and the two are obviously different individuals. This is a common prosopographical trap and should be avoided at all costs.

And what evidence is there that Nepotianus and Arborius were imperial commanders? The only evidence would seem to be that Nepotianus, at least, is given a Roman-sounding title – *magister militiae* (192 [197]). But surely if the Goths had armies and hired Romans to lead them, as we know they did, they would also use Roman terminology to describe them, and other Romans, like Hydatius, would also use Roman terminology to describe them. Theoderic sent *duces* and *comites* to Spain (185, 188, 192, 196 [192, 193, 197, 201]) and no one has claimed that these were in reality working for the Romans and not the Goths (cf. also *Chron. Gall. 511* 651–2: Gauterit and Vincentius), so why should one assume that the *magistri militiae* were? Besides, Hydatius always calls imperial commanders, whether they operate in Gaul or Spain, either *magistri militum* (69, 75, 102 [77, 84, 110]) or *magistri utriusque militiae* (120, 126 [128, 134]). For the latter he sometimes replaces *magister* with *dux* or *comes* to avoid the lengthy *dux et magister utriusque militiae* or *comes et magister utriusque militiae* (85, 94, 117, 214 [95, 103, 125, 218]). On the other hand, Hydatius most distinctly calls Nepotianus a *magister militiae*, a title unique in the chronicle, making it plain that he was not an imperial *magister militum* (cf. *Chron. Gall. 511* 653: Vincentius, a 'quasi magister militum'). And, as if this were not enough, he is explicitly recalled from Spain by Theoderic along with Suniericus, and his successor, Arborius, is both appointed and recalled by Theoderic (207–8, 226 [212–13, 230]). Where did a federate king ever get the right to hire and fire Roman generals? It is time that the obvious was accepted: Nepotianus and Arborius were nothing more than Romans selling their services to the Goths, like hundreds if not thousands of others at the time.

The Gothic policy instigated in 458 would seem to have continued right through the reign of Euric, and after 476 to have been extended even to capital investment and urban renewal, at least in Emerita (Vives, 1969: 363). The presence of a Gothic army in the south would appear to have been originally established to deter the Sueves from plundering. This was effective in 458 (181, 183, 185–8 [188, 190, 192–3]) but when the size of the army was reduced in 459 the plundering began again in earnest (188 [193]). Although direct punitive action against the Sueves was taken once, by a detachment of the army in response to a Suevic massacre of Romans in Lucus (modern Lugo) (194, 196 [199, 201]), the Goths usually opted for diplomatic methods of persuasion. Legates were sent to the Sueves immediately after the arrival of the army in Baetica in 458, probably to warn them off (186 [192]) and diplomatic exchanges among the Goths, the Sueves and the Gallaecians are recorded every year from 458 to 468, with the exception of 461–2, often at key moments of tension or Suevic hostility (cf. 192, 200, 215–16, 226–7 [197, 205, 219–20, 230–1]). In 463 the Goths attempted to maintain the fragile peace of 460 after the Gallaecians had sent Palogorius to them for help; in spite of repeated Gothic intervention, however, the Sueves resumed their hostilities (215–16 [219–20]). In 464 Remismund seized power after the death of Frumarius and renewed the peace (219 [223]). Theodoric enthusiastically accepted this new force for stability in Gallaecia by sending legates bearing weapons and gifts, including Remismund's wife, who would appear to have been captured and taken back to Gaul in the invasion of 456–7 (222 [226]). This situation was short-lived, however, for Theodoric received no diplomatic satisfaction after the Suevic sack of Conimbrica in 465 and he recalled Arborius and his army (225–6 [229–30]). In 466–8, the inhabitants of Aunona, a small Gallaecian *pagus*, also turned to the Goths for assistance against Suevic hostility, and repeated Gothic diplomatic intervention eventually achieved peace, at least in Aunona (229, 233–5, 243 [233, 237–9, 249]).

It is thus easy to see why Hydatius' image of Gaul changed in the last years of the chronicle. Indeed, with only two exceptions, whenever Hydatius refers to Gaul after 456 it concerns the Goths.

There does remain, however, one lone Gallic hero in the mould of generals gone by, Aegidius, who fights against the loss of Narbo and the advances of the Goths north of the Loire (212, 214 [217, 218]). However, he is assassinated and, as far as Hydatius is concerned, his death in early 465 marks the end of Roman Gaul: 'since Aegidius no longer offered his protection, the Goths soon invaded the territory which he had been guarding in the name of Rome' (224 [228]; cf. Elton, below p. 172). Gaul was now the *Gothorum habitatio* (228 [232]). Majorian had also been active in Gaul against the Goths – Hydatius knew something of a victory he had won over them in 459 (192 [197]) – but for some reason he never seems to have inspired Hydatius the way Aegidius did.

And so to sum up. For Hydatius, and perhaps the Romans of Gallaecia as a whole, the transformation of Gaul could not have been more complete nor the crisis of identity more pronounced. In the late fourth century it was seen as an orthodox Roman province suffering under usurpers like Magnus Maximus and Eugenius. The early fifth century saw the plague of barbarian invasion added to the continuing problem of usurpation by rebels such as Constantine, Jovinus and Sebastian. These early problems were dealt with by strong emperors such as Theodosius and strong generals like Constantius and Aëtius. With the death of Aëtius, however, those who should have protected Gaul, like Avitus and Agrippinus, did not, making it impossible for those who could, like Aegidius, to do so. By the mid 460s, after the assassinations of Majorian and Aegidius, the Arian Goths controlled all of Gaul. They were now the nearest great power for the Gallaecians and so could pose the greatest threat or provide the greatest assistance. Within his own lifetime Hydatius had seen the still very Roman world of the fourth century turned completely upside down by the conquests of the Sueves, Vandals and Goths, and the withdrawal of Rome. In our view he was a witness to the birth of the Middle Ages. For Hydatius it was simply another inexorable step towards the Second Coming of Christ and the *consummatio mundi*, the end of the world. And in a very real way, he was right.

CHAPTER 3

Looking back from mid century: the Gallic chronicler of 452 and the crisis of Honorius' reign[1]

S. Muhlberger

Fixing a date for the end of the Roman empire in Gaul is a task for people who, like us, can look back from a distance and see the centuries spread out like a landscape. From our vantage point, we can take in the entire history of Gaul from Caesar to Julius Civilis to Postumus to Clovis in a single glance. We can decide among ourselves which features are Roman and which are not, and based on those criteria, say authoritatively: 'There, that is the dividing line.'

Those who lived through the decline of Roman power in the Gallic provinces were not able to do this so conveniently. Forget for a moment that few of the Gauls known to us were overly concerned about the fate of the Empire, or about their country's place in it. Even those who thought about such things necessarily had a perspective much different from our own. It was difficult for them to relate recent events unambiguously to trends in the farther and sometimes poorly known past, and impossible to connect them with certainty to the yet-unknown future. Nor were contemporary views identical with each other. The shape of the recent past would change with every shift of a few years or a few miles. Yet the partial, sometimes myopic, views of contemporaries are of vital importance to us. Contemporaries knew directly what we can only poorly reconstruct: the texture of life, that real, unrecoverable world of late ancient and early Medieval Gaul. The validity of our picture of that era depends, at least in part, on

---

[1]   The author would like to thank Trent University, the Social Sciences and Humanities Research Council of Canada, and Mr and Mrs R.G. Muhlberger for making possible his participation in the conference that called forth this paper.

understanding what our witnesses thought and why they thought it (cf. Wood, Burgess, above).

We are fortunate to possess two fifth-century histories by Gallic writers that address our modern concern with the end of Roman Gaul. In 433, Prosper of Aquitaine, then resident in Marseille, issued the first edition of his well-known ecclesiastical chronicle, which included a brief description of the history of Gaul since 379 (*MGH AA*, 9: 343–5). In 452, another, anonymous, ecclesiastical writer, who also lived in or near Marseille, wrote a second chronicle (*MGH AA*, 9: 617–18). Because he, like Prosper, was continuing Jerome's very influential universal history, the Chronicler of 452 began at the same point as his older countryman, 379, and recorded many of the same events. The contrast between the accounts of these two Gauls is very marked. It is that contrast, and what it means for the history of fifth-century Gaul, that is the subject of this chapter.

The earlier of these two writers, Prosper of Aquitaine, is a not inconsiderable figure in fifth-century Latin literature. A pious layman or *conversus*, he devoted most of his life to defending Augustine's doctrine of grace and predestination, to some effect: Prosper's formulation of those doctrines helped shape the orthodoxy of the medieval Latin church (Bardy, 1936; Cappuyns, 1929; Valentin, 1900). He holds a similarly strategic place in Latin historiography. He was the first continuator of Jerome's chronicle, and a very popular one. Prosper lived through what we consider a crucial period of Gallic history, the years 406–17. Born about 395, he must have had vivid memories of the troubles in Gaul during Honorius' reign, of the invasion of the Vandals, Alans, and Sueves, the civil wars that raged thereafter, and, even perhaps, of the impact of Gothic settlement on his home province (Mathisen, 1984: 164f.; cf. Roberts, below p. 99). What Prosper wrote about these events in 433, not so long after they took place, should be of great interest.

But Prosper is a disappointment, at least at first glance. Chronicles are meant to be summaries, to include only the most important events, and summarize is what Prosper did. He has hardly anything interesting to say about the Gallic crisis of his youth. Prosper's record of political and military events before 422 is extremely brief, and may simply have been extracted from now-lost consular annals, another genre in which conciseness was the chief virtue. What distinctive material there is in the early part of the chronicle concerns ecclesiastical developments. Prosper was more interested in doctrinal strife than in conventional politics; indeed, the chronicle was probably conceived as one more volley in his long pamphlet campaign supporting Augustine's theology.

Yet if one looks more carefully at Prosper, it is apparent that he had a keen appreciation of practical politics, and a discernible opinion about the state of the Empire in the year that he wrote. He spoke mostly about developments of the period 422–33, but it is these events that shaped his evaluation of Honorius' reign.

Prosper showed his readers that since the death in 421 of the soldier-emperor Constantius III, Honorius' brother-in-law and the essential support of his throne, the western empire had been torn with dissension. Rivalries between ambitious military men had led to civil war and allowed barbarians to take advantage of Roman weakness. Prosper told his readers quite a bit about the running feud between Boniface, the chief Roman commander in Africa, and his superiors in Italy, Castinus, Felix, and Aëtius. Prosper strongly disapproved of this conflict, and seems to have blamed Boniface's enemies for it. Boniface's undoubted military talents and the resources of the state had been wasted. Worse, the war between Felix and Boniface had made it possible for the Vandals to cross from Spain to Africa and wreak devastation there. This disaster, and Aëtius' ominous use of Hunnic allies in the civil war of 432–33, were the recent political events that had most impressed Prosper (Prosper 1278, 1294, 1310).

Current difficulties strongly influenced Prosper's view of the earlier crisis in Gaul. In 433, Prosper remembered the years 406–17 mainly as years of civil war. His chronicle focussed in this period on the rise and fall of usurpers, which he systematically recorded. Barbarian activities, in Gaul or elsewhere, were treated far more casually. Prosper dispassionately preserved the date 31 December 406 for the crossing of the Rhine by the Vandals and Alans, but save for a brief, imprecise notice that 'the Vandals occupied Spain', these peoples were not mentioned again (Prosper 1230, 1237). Burgundian settlement along the Rhine was recorded in a bare sentence (1250). Only the Goths were covered in any detail, no doubt because they were central to the dynastic situation (1238, 1240, 1246, 1254, 1256, 1257, 1259; four of these entries mention either the usurper Attalus or the captive princess Galla Placidia). But even the Goths were rather on the margins of the account – indeed, Prosper put some of his barbarian entries in the margin, beside more important events, i.e., those of ecclesiastical or dynastic significance (e.g. 1237, 1246). The settlement of the Goths in Aquitania (1271) he treated as a Roman triumph, specifically, a triumph of Constantius III, who was credited for the recovery of Honorius' power and the preservation of the Theodosian dynasty (1243, 1256, 1259; cf. Roberts, below p. 100).

Whatever Prosper's original feelings about this time of troubles, by 433 he interpreted it as a dynastic crisis, one that had been successfully resolved. The activities of the barbarians were a sideshow, far less important than those of Roman leaders, good and bad. The dynasty had found its hero, Constantius, and he had saved it: once he had beaten the Roman rebels, a successful settlement of the most dangerous barbarians, the Goths, was easily accomplished. The tragedy was that he did not live longer and do more. This is a traditional view of what was important in Roman politics – imperial unity, equated with imperial strength. Prosper evidently did not think that the earlier crisis had transformed either Gaul or the Roman world as a whole (cf. Matthews, 1970, on Olympiodorus).

It might be objected on several grounds that Prosper's view is entirely too tendentious to be accepted seriously. First, he praised Constantius because he needed a stick to beat the unruly generals of his time, men who had proved inept in handling the Vandal threat. Second, Prosper wrote in the farthest southern reaches of Gaul, the area that Pliny had once called 'more like Italy than a province' (*NH* 3.31). He was in no position to see how life had changed along the Rhine and the Loire, to appreciate how limited Roman power and how weak Roman society were in those northern areas. Third, Prosper was increasingly alienated from the Gallic church. He was on the verge of leaving Marseille for Rome, never to return, and he had already adopted the values of his Roman friends and allies. For them, Rome was the world, and the Vandal threat of today of far more interest than the depredations of barbarians in Gaul twenty years ago (Muhlberger, 1990).

All of these objections have some force, and we will return to the second of them, but they do not detract from the main point. Prosper, despite his personal experience of the disasters of 406–17, despite the Gothic settlement in or very near his native province, could believe, or at least expect his audience to believe, that those events had been no turning point. Whatever the impact on Gaul, the centrality of the imperial system had not, in fact, been altered. Prosper could talk about imperial politics in a way that Ammianus Marcellinus would not have found entirely strange (Muhlberger, 1990; cf. *Narratio de*

Imperatoribus 6.10–14). Indeed, in his later editions of 445, 451 and 455, Prosper did little to alter the emphasis of his account of Honorius' reign.

Had Prosper remained in Marseille, however, he might have eventually reconsidered. By the 440s, even Marseille seemed far from safe, and Salvian, who was active there, felt compelled to answer the oft-heard complaint that God had abandoned the Romans (*De Gub. Dei* 4.12). A few years later, in 452, the second chronicle from Marseille appeared, containing the famous lament:

At this time the condition of the state appeared to be intensely miserable, since not even one province was without a barbarian inhabitant, and the unspeakable Arian heresy, which had allied itself with the barbarian nations and permeated the whole world, laid claim to the name of Catholic.

(*Chron. Gall. 452* 138)

We can say little about the man behind these words. From the contents of his work, the Chronicler of 452 must have been much the same sort of person as Prosper, though they disagreed on the doctrine of grace. It is clear that he felt himself living in a very dark time. The previous year had seen Attila invade Gaul, and Hunnic armies were rampaging through Italy even as he wrote. More interesting is that even the past – to be precise, the early fifth century – seemed very much darker to him than it had to Prosper.

One should begin by noting how the chronicle contrasts the late fourth century with the unfortunate fifth. The chronicler knew that the earlier time had not been not without its troubles, but then the state was blessed with two rulers of unusual vigor and piety: Theodosius I and his rival, the usurper Magnus Maximus. Although these men eventually came into conflict, the chronicler believed that both had conferred considerable benefits on the state, supressing heretics and defeating hostile barbarians.

The leaders of Honorius' time had not proved so useful to the state. The western emperor himself had been a nonentity. His most promising general, Stilicho, had betrayed the Romans and unleashed the barbarians on Gaul. The chronicler's characterization of the invasion of Gaul, dispassionately recorded by Prosper, is rhetorically violent: 'The madness of hostile peoples tore Gaul to pieces' (*Chron. Gall. 452* 55). Worse, this invasion was part of a general calamity that afflicted every part of the west; in the chronicler's words, 'Roman power was completely humbled by a multitude of enemies who were gaining strength' (61). The enemies referred to are the barbarians who ravaged Britain, Gaul and Spain and even 'foully devastated' Rome itself (62–5).

Rome had never really recovered from this humiliation. Since 406, the chronicler remembered few positive incidents but many defeats. Britain had been lost to the Saxons; the Sueves dominated Spain; the Vandals had taken Africa so that Carthage once again threated Rome (Muhlberger, 1983: 31f.). And the loss of provinces was paralleled by the dismemberment of Gaul. In the 430s vigorous action by Aëtius had destroyed the Burgundians and quashed a Bacaudic revolt which threatened to subvert all Gaul (*Chron. Gall. 452* 117–18), but in 440 he had returned to Italy, and begun settling barbarians in Gaul instead of fighting them (123). Alans had been given lands in 'Farther Gaul' and, more worryingly, in Valence on the lower Rhône; Sapaudia, not much further away, had been alloted to the Burgundians (124, 127, 128; on Valence, 71; on Sapaudia, Duparc, 1958). The revolt of the more distant Alans, who had quickly expelled the Roman landowners and taken full possession of the land, was an evil sign. The possibility that the revived Bacaudic movement might ally itself with the Huns, formerly Aëtius' allies but now out of control, completed Gaul's tale of woe (*Chron. Gall. 452* 133).

Thus for the Chronicler of 452, what had taken place in Honorius' time was not a run-of-the-mill dynastic crisis, which once resolved had left Gaul and the Empire much as it had been before. Rather, it was the beginning of a spiral of decline that had stripped Rome of provinces it had held for centuries, that had prostrated the Empire before the Huns, that threatened Gaul with slow dissolution. Was this all the result of a single disaster? Even for this chronicler, who tended to work with broad strokes, things were not so simple. There was at least one other element: lack of leadership.

The chronicler showed the later Theodosians as unworthy offspring of a great ancestor. His criticism of a still-reigning dynasty is subtle, as it had to be, but clear enough. Male Theodosians were inactive, females ambitious and dangerous to the state (90, 103, cf. 136 and below). Their chief servants were scarcely better. It is remarkable how much Aëtius' stock had declined over the years. Once a vigorous hero, he was in 452 held to be a failure. But most interesting is the way that Constantius III's reputation had suffered. In his own time, his victories over usurpers and his handling of barbarians had allowed him to claim the title *reparator rei publicae* (O'Flynn, 1983: 67). His accomplishments had retained some of their shine when Prosper wrote in 433. But the Chronicler of 452 was reluctant to acknowledge his prominence. If one were to believe the chronicler, Constantius did little for Gaul. For instance, Dardanus, not Constantius, was credited with defeating the usurper Jovinus and neutralizing the Goths (*Chron. Gall. 452* 69). Quite tendentiously, Constantius was reduced to a minor figure (Muhlberger, 1990).

The record was meant to show a contemporary reader that the western Theodosians were useless, and had been for decades. The chronicler felt that Rome's rulers had betrayed Gaul and brought disaster upon it. The court at Ravenna, and specifically Aëtius, had not only turned over much of Gaul to barbarians, it had failed to co-operate with Constantinople against the Hunnic threat. Only five years previously, according to the chronicler, 'not less than seventy [Thracian] cities [had been] ravaged by the looting of the Huns because no troops were brought by westerners' (*Chron. Gall. 452* 132). And the court's responsibility for the recent invasions went beyond negligence. The chronicler had heard that Honoria, the sister of emperor Valentinian III, had invited Attila into the Empire, believed the story, and dared to repeat it (139).

The chronicler's disgust with the current regime lies behind one of the most interesting features of his account, his idealization of Magnus Maximus, the famous usurper who had ruled in Gaul between 383 and 388. In general, the chronicler was a fierce legitimist, but Magnus Maximus was for him an admirable figure, a scourge to barbarians and heretics alike (7, 12). If 'tyranny', or illegitimate rule, stained his reputation, he was still the last energetic and pious ruler that Gaul had seen (Muhlberger, 1990; cf. Sulpicius Severus, *Dial.* 2.6.2; Orosius 7.34.9). The Chronicle of 452 shows the growing resentment of a feeble Italian government that would lead some Gauls to proclaim Avitus emperor in 455.

The most striking, and most important, difference between the two views of Gallic and imperial history we have been examining is in the way barbarians are discussed. For Prosper in 433, they were still quite marginal to life and history. It was only Roman dissension that made them dangerous, and one feels when reading his work that a strong hand would easily quell them. Thus Prosper concentrated on Roman leaders: their accomplishments, their virtues, their vices. Nineteen years later, the Chronicler of 452 thought that the impact of the barbarians was the most important fact of the past fifty years. The barbarians had reduced the Empire to its present sad state. There are also indications in his account that any solution to the Empire's problems would involve the proper use of barbarians against barbarians – for instance the Goths against the Huns (Muhlberger, 1990).

It would be easy to say that the difference between our two observers is simply the difference between 433 and 452, a period when Roman power visibly declined and the relative importance of barbarian peoples and their leaders greatly increased. In other words, a longer base-line made it possible for the Chronicler of 452 to estimate more accurately the long-term trend. This is partly true, and all the more congenial a conclusion because his picture of early fifth-century Gallic history is so close to the one most of us carry around in our heads. But there are two other factors that, when taken into account, qualify that preliminary conclusion.

First, we can overestimate how much the anonymous chronicler really knew about areas other than his own. The more one examines his history of Roman defeats and the loss of provinces, the more curious it looks. He was incapable, it seems, of accurately dating even so prominent an event as the fall of Carthage. He placed it not in 439, but in 444, eight years rather than the correct thirteen before his own time. He also misdated quite recent Hunnic activities in the Balkans, and rather wildly projected Suevic domination of Spain, which began no earlier than 440, back to the early 410s. His account of the dismemberment of the Roman empire is rhetorical rather than well informed or careful (Muhlberger, 1983: 30ff.; cf. Wood, above p. 15). Nor does he seem to have known that much about *Gallia Ulterior*, as he called the north and central parts of his own country. The few events he recorded from Farther Gaul were those that seemed to bode ill for his own Provence – the invasion of Attila, the Bacaudic revolts that had threatened all of Gaul, the revolt of Alanic federates in the north that suggested the dangers that might result from the Alanic presence in Valence. It is significant that he either knew or cared nothing about the Franks, and nothing about the old capital of Trier, a subject about which Salvian, active in Marseille in the same period, could have told him much (*De Gub. Dei* 6.13–15).

For the Chronicler of 452, the real Gaul, the one he really cared about, was the area around his home city. In Prosper's time, things had looked settled enough from Marseille to allow a certain complacency about northern Gaul. Whatever local conditions may have been – and Prosper too is largely silent about the north – a man in Mediterranean Gaul could feel satisfied that he was safe. Farther Gaul was performing its traditional function as a shield for the south (see Drinkwater, 1987: 255). In 452, the feeling of security had evaporated. The later chronicler was no better informed about northern Gaul than Prosper had been, but he no longer could take it for granted. The barbarian settlements were too close, the Huns too threatening. Panic, rooted in the events of the moment, inspired the Chronicler of 452 to look back to the past, where he could now see the events that had led to the current uncomfortable situation. It is in this context that the crisis of Honorius' reign became the crisis of Roman power, for Gaul and for the west as a whole.

But it was not just that the barbarians were creeping closer to Marseille. It was also that they brought heresy with them. The defeat and resurrection of the despised Arian sect is a major theme in the Chronicle of 452. The special glory of Theodosius I was that he expelled the Arians from the churches they had seized under earlier emperors, and drove them out of the Empire. But the heretics had returned with the barbarians, and it was their help that made it possible for heresy to 'permeate the whole world' – even, perhaps, southern Gaul – and '[lay] claim to the name of Catholic' (*Chron. Gall. 452* 22, 51, 138). Not only Roman order but Roman orthodoxy was threatened, and this shaped the chronicler's view as much as the mundane peril.

Comparison with Prosper is useful here, too. We can feel certain that the religious preferences of barbarians did not concern Prosper at all in 433, for the Arianism of the Goths or any other people is not even hinted at. Religiously, as politically, the barbarians remained marginal. But once their Arianism began to affect Roman Christians, Prosper made that development a center-piece of his chronicle. The evils of Vandal persecution were paraded before the reader in his edition of 445; Geiseric the tyrant is Prosper's favorite villain (Prosper, 1327, 1339, 1342, 1348). The parallel serves to remind us that these two chroniclers, among our best witnesses for the fifth century, used in part a religious test to measure the health of the Empire and the effectiveness of imperial rule. It is not a consideration we or their contemporaries would necessarily weigh equally.

No single measure of the decline of Roman power in Gaul would have won assent from all who lived in that country during the fifth century. Each inhabitant of Gaul experienced a different history, each had a different experience and different expectations of Roman power. Each passed through his or her own fall of the Roman empire – or, perhaps, missed the event entirely because it was of no personal relevance. This should be kept in mind as we explore fifth-century Gaul looking for signs of continuity and change, and make us more cautious and humble in our pronouncements.

CHAPTER 4

Old Kaspars: Attila's invasion of Gaul in the literary sources

S. Barnish

For the subjects of king Gundobad of Burgundy, the battle of the Catalaunian Plains fifty years before was an event so memorable that it gave them a time-limit on their law suits (*Lex Burg.* 17.1). Attila enjoyed an Arthurian immortality in Germanic epic and romance. His invasion in 451, the last great incursion into Roman Gaul from beyond the Rhine, achieved a legendary fame even in the eastern empire, and was recounted in the west by a host of chroniclers, historians and hagiographers from the fifth century to the eleventh. Their treatments are often related, but they look on it from many different perspectives, and describe it with different voices (Täckholm, 1969; Zecchini, 1983: ch.2.).

One of the earliest sources, Sidonius Apollinaris, epitomizes these differences. In the panegyric on Avitus, his treatment is secular and political: the Goths were awaiting the despised Huns in their own territory, until the diplomacy of the Roman whom they later made emperor brought them to the rescue of Aëtius and his handful of auxiliaries (*Carm.* 7.315–66). He may, however, have given another and holy version of the war. In 478/9, bishop Prosper of Orleans asked him for a history of the *Attilae bellum* which would star his predecessor Annianus and the siege of Orleans. Sidonius apparently began and then abandoned the task, but promised his friend a panegyric on Annianus (*Ep.* 8.15). The extant life (*V. Anniani*), which covers little more than the Hunnic crisis, may be descended from this work.

Of other sources, some chronicles and histories follow Sidonius' secular model; others – chronicle, history, or hagiology – his sacred; some straddle the gap. Within these classes, there are special lines of interest. Naturally, Sidonius, Cassiodorus, Jordanes and Isidore are concerned to stress the Gothic role; but the Goths still play an important part in Gregory of Tours, who disliked them. A surviving fragment suggests that Priscus had much to say on Frankish relations with Aëtius and the Huns (fr. 20.3). If so, little of this reached Gregory, and he and later Merovingian authors had seemingly to recreate Frankish involvement in the events of 451. This may give a clue to the politics of the lost Renatus Profuturus Frigeridus, the likeliest link between Priscus and Gregory (*MGH, AA* 5.1: xxxvif.). Prosper, Hydatius, Cassiodorus, Jordanes, and Victor Tonnonensis all seem to show what might be called a Roman approach: among them, they give some part not only to Aëtius, but to Valentinian, Marcian, and the Senate, chiefly in Italian, but also in Gallic affairs. Rather similarly, Gregory of Tours, Fredegar, the *Life of Servatius*, and the *Gesta Episcoporum Mettensium* of Paul the Deacon give varying roles not only to Gallic saints and bishops, but to the cults and relics of Roman saints.

The fullest and most dramatic account of the invasion of Gaul dominates Jordanes' *Getica* (176–228). Two characteristics are outstanding. One is the superficially old-fashioned and secular approach: bishops, saints, and Christian visions play no part. The sole supernatural element appears when, in a classical motif adapted to the Huns, Attila takes the auspices from a scraped blade bone: he discovers that an enemy leader is doomed to die, and assumes it to be Aëtius (196). A corresponding anecdote appears in Gregory of Tours, but with a Christian colouring: a vision reveals that the prayers of Aëtius' wife at the shrines of the Apostles in Rome have saved her husband from his fate (*HF* 2.7). The second remarkable feature is that Jordanes does not restrict the war against Attila to Romans and Goths: it is depicted almost as an Armageddon, though more political than religious. The invading horde of Huns, those demonic descendants of the Goths (121f.), and their terrorized subject tribes are matched (190–3, 199–201) by a free coalition of Roman, barbarian, and post-Roman peoples under the hegemony, rather than the rule of Aëtius and Theodorid (Theoderic I). Which author is responsible for this unique element, and can we see in it some wider political meaning?

Jordanes claimed to have summarized the *Gothic History* of Cassiodorus, but in his own words, and with his own additions. As a source for his material on the Huns, he six times cited Priscus, though not necessarily always or ever at first hand. The distinctive character of his Attilan narrative may, therefore, be his own work; it may be due to Cassiodorus; or to Priscus (Baldwin, 1980: 25f.; 1981). Space does not permit a detailed discussion; but I will outline my view that Cassiodorus used Priscus extensively, while significantly reworking him, and that Jordanes, despite his introductory statement, has here, by and large, reproduced Cassiodorus, so far as his abilities allowed.

In most of its Attilan material, the *Getica's* style is peculiar (see *MGH, AA* 5.1: xxxvf.): it is here less clumsy and ungrammatical than elsewhere, or than Jordanes' own writing in the *Romana*; it is marked by frequent *sententiae*, similes, and other rhetorical figures; and it gives the impression of deriving from a trained rhetorician. In general, its classicizing secularity differs from the *Romana*, a work with many Christian allusions. Is this rhetorician Priscus reproduced extensively by Jordanes? Or did Cassiodorus use him, and with some independence? Probable or possible echoes of Claudian, Lucan, and Livy suggest the latter. (With the speech of Attila, *Getica* 202–6, cf. Livy 21.40.4, 43–4, 27.18.8ff.; Lucan (quoted at 43) 7.250ff., 12.297ff.; Claudian, *De Bell. Get.* 521–49; note also *De Bell. Get.* 95–103, 468–78, 551–8, 580–97; *De VI Cons. Hon.* 127ff., 300–9, 218–22. Against Altheim's detection of Herodotean echoes (1962: 323ff.), see Täckholm, 1969: 273, n1; Zecchini, 1983: 96f.) Analysis also shows a large number of typically Cassiodorian words and phrases, paralleled in the *Variae* and speeches. (For instance, with 176 and 183, cf. *Variae* 1.4.11; with 180, 3.4.5; with 190, 3.1.1; with 193, 1.4.12 and *Or. Rel., MGH, AA* 12: 466, 1.5ff.; with 200, *Variae* 1.43.3, 11.1.19; with 217, 6.19.1, 12.25.5.) The structures and rhythms of sentences likewise recall Cassiodorus. If the style is too sophisticated for Jordanes, it also seems too florid for the 'gravitas et simplicitas' (*MGH, AA* 5.1: xxxv) shown in the Greek fragments of Priscus. We might contrast the speech of Attila in the *Getica* with Priscus' dialogue with the ex-merchant from Viminacium. Cassiodorus' use and rehandling of Priscus may be exemplified in the latter's description of Attila emerging from his palace, 'swaggering and casting his eyes around' (fr. 11.2.570f.). In the *Getica* (182; see Blockley, 1981: 169, n51), this becomes 'erat namque superbus incessu, huc atque illuc circumferens oculos, ut elati potentia ipsu quoque motu corporis appareret'. This is echoed by the description of the physiognomy of the evil-doer in Cassiodorus' *De Anima* ('oculi interdum super quam necesse est commoventur' – *De Anima* xii); it forms part of a longer portrait of Attila with other Cassiodorian echoes; and that portrait is balanced by one of Aëtius (176) recalling praise from Merobaudes and an inscription in the Forum (*Pan.* I, fr. I A, 21f., I B, 9ff; *AE* 1950, 30). Hence, it is probably at least in part the work of Cassiodorus. Finally, the absence of any significant role for the Franks contrasts with Priscus, and suggests a major pro-Gothic reshaping by either Cassiodorus or Jordanes (see Blockley, 1981: 165, n7; in general, *ibid.*, 113f.).

If, then, the *Getica's* Attila narrative is mainly Cassiodorian, what, if any, was its original significance? We cannot tell if it dominated the *Gothic History* as it does the *Getica*, but I think it very possible. The *Variae* suggest that, for Cassiodorus, to be linked with Attila, for or against him, was a touchstone of honour. The defeat of the Huns was the crowning victory of the Visigoths, of which he reminded them before Vouillé; and he recounted with pride to the Senate his own grandfather's embassy for Aëtius to the terrible king (3.1.1, 1.4.11f.). Both passages are echoed in the *Getica*. Even the subjected Ostrogoths and Gepids grow in stature through their presence on the Catalaunian Plains; and the *Getica's* portraits of their rulers again recall the *Variae*.

Did Cassiodorus have any purpose more subtle than this kind of status building? I would suggest that the figures of Aëtius and Theodorid were jointly intended to foreshadow Theoderic the Great; while, in Attila, a reader alert to official writing might have seen a precursor of Clovis. A brief word portrait of Theodorid (Jordanes, *Getica* 176) recalls language used of Theoderic in the *Variae* (10.31.5); among the allies of Aëtius, according to a likely manuscript reading, were the *Breones, quondam milites Romani* (191), who are attested in the *Variae* (1.11) as militia on Theoderic's Rhaetian frontier. At the Catalaunian plains, the Goths and their free allies avenged the destruction of Ermanaric's empire by the Huns and his own subject tribes. According to the *Getica* (120), Ermanaric had subdued the Baltic Aestii in war; *c.*525, the *Variae* (5.2) proudly tell us, that tribe entered into voluntary relations with Theoderic. The disunity of Romans and Visigoths spoiled the victory over Attila – the *humana fragilitas* blamed in the *Getica* (217) is a very Cassiodorian phrase (cf. *Variae* 6.19.1, 12.25.5). In the reign of Theoderic, however, the leadership of any similar coalition would have been united: he had improved on Aëtius and Theodorid as they had improved on Ermanaric.

Above all, Theoderic's correspondence (*Variae* 3.1–4) on the eve of the Vouillé campaign, with Alaric II, Clovis, Gundobad, and the kings of the Thuringians, Heruls and Warni, recalls 451 in the *Getica*. Alaric (3.1.1; cf. *Getica* 146) is explicitly reminded of that year. Clovis is warned 'ut gentes...subita non debeant concussione vastari'; in the *Getica*, Attila is described as 'vir in concussione gentium natus' (*Variae* 3.4.5; *Getica* 182). In the letters of 507, Theoderic tries to form a voluntary coalition against a sudden threat from a barbarian monarch in the north of Gaul, a monarch like Attila, swollen-headed, lawless, and adept in trivial pretexts for aggression. The Franks of 530 and their king are described in similar terms, in a letter written after the publication of the *Gothic History* (*Variae* 11.1.12). In many of our sources, a common theme is the sheer destructiveness of the Huns: the sack of Metz, Prosper claims, discredited Attila, and united Goths and Romans against him. For western society, forced, against all its ancient prejudices, to accept barbarians in its midst, it was useful to depict remoter barbarians as types of real savagery. In the *Getica*, a Hun is a kind of anti-Goth (see 121f.). The implication of the *Variae* that the Franks are no better matches their image of Theoderic as restorer of *libertas* and *civilitas* to the lost provinces of Roman Gaul (3.16–18, 32, 38).

If the Attilan part of the *Gothic History* was meant to have contemporary resonances, why did Jordanes reproduce it in such detail? He was probably writing in Constantinople, and twenty years or more after Cassiodorus, at a time when the political situation had altered drastically (see Croke, 1987). Three reasons seem possible. First, if the Attilan narrative was clearly the set piece of the original, it will have been natural for him to give it a similar place. Second, in both the *Getica* and the *Romana*, he deplores the damage which the Slavs, Bulgars, and Antes were then inflicting on the Empire. The Antes and Slavs had once been subdued by Ermanaric, while the Bulgars occupied the former seat of the Huns (*Getica* 37, 119; *Romana* 363, 388). For all the praise which, in both works, he gives to Justinian's reconquest, he may be indirectly criticizing an emperor who could not do what the Goths had once done; there may even be something of Procopius' view that the Gothic wars had destabilized the Danube frontier once secured by Theoderic (*Wars* 7.33; *Anecdota* 18.16–21; contrast Croke, 1987: 126ff.). Third, it may simply be that the defeat of Attila was the most exciting Gothic story known to him, and one with which he was personally linked. He was a Goth; his grandfather had been secretary to an Alan, whose race had played a major part in the action; and he himself had served a man who claimed descent from the killer of Theodorid (*Getica* 209, 265f.). Like Cassiodorus, he probably felt that any connection with these epic events was enough to ennoble.

Motives of similar complexity may appear in the narrative of Gregory of Tours (*HF* 2.5–8). Piety has some effect against Attila: from the apostles, especially Peter, the wife of Aëtius obtains her husband's life by prayer; and the prayers of Annianus, more than the leadership of Aëtius and Thorismund, are responsible for the victory at the Catalaunian Plains. However, Servatius of Tongres is unable to save his people by his pilgrimage to St Peter at Rome – he can only die before their catastrophe – while the *patrocinium* of St Stephen procures from Peter and Paul the safety of his oratory alone – Metz is doomed to destruction. In both cases, Gallic sins are too great: the saints of Rome show their love by chastening the province (contrast Van Dam, 1985: 182). There may be a lesson here for the inhabitants of Gaul in Gregory's day: impious ravaging of the churches was leading them to military disaster (*HF* 5, praef., 8.30). This was the result of avarice and the incessant civil wars which seem to be foreshadowed on the Catalaunian Plains: Aëtius there exploits the domestic suspicions of Thorismund and the Frankish king to send them home, and seize all the loot – a very Merovingian stratagem.

But should we see Gregory in careful and consistent pursuit of this moral line (see Bullough, 1986: 90f.)? His rulers, too, had their nomad enemies to face, the Avars, who are recorded under the archaic name of Huns (*HF* 4.23, 29). They were not always victorious; but he does not seem especially worried by defeat: in his day, Gallic cities were seldom threatened with sack. If there are moral and political lessons to be read in the Catalaunian Plains, they are not very obvious. Even the plot of Aëtius is recounted without evident disapproval. (On this tradition, Morgan, 1969: 440, speaks of 'heroic underhandedness' and 'a triple Themistoclean ploy'; cf. Wallace-Hadrill, 1962: 60–3; contrast Goffart, 1988: 209f., 217ff.) As in Jordanes, Attila's invasion is primarily a good story; and, as such, it brings the Franks onto the stage of Gallic history for the first time.

Fredegar (*Chronicae* 2.53) develops both themes. The duplicity of Aëtius, 'strenuosissimus consilii', is recounted with more elaboration, and again without disapproval: he promises Huns and Goths half of Gaul for defending it against each other, and then blackmails 10,000 solidi from them both. But he also pursues the Huns into Thuringia with his own troops and the Franks, using further cunning to frighten the enemy. In the end, 'Aëtius' planning laid this war to rest, and Gaul was freed from its enemies.' By implication, these are the Goths, as well as the Huns, but not the Franks: they had the credit of literally 'seeing off' Attila. Aëtius' profits eventually passed to their own treasury from the Goths (4.73). There is no subtle propaganda in all this; even Gregory's piety is almost lacking. Once again, though, a tribe is ennobled by its share in the events of 451. It may indicate the appeal of the Burgundian Fredegar's narrative that his work was copied and enlarged in mid eighth-century Austrasia, under the patronage of the historical Nibelungs, a branch of the Arnulfings (Wallace-Hadrill, 1962: 72). The glory of the Franks, and the defence of eastern Gaul against the kinsman and enemy of their legendary namesakes must have been dear to their hearts.

Saints, and sees, as well as tribes and chieftains, gained in stature from association with 451. The churches of Rheims and Arras claimed Hunnic sack (*V. Vedastis* III, 410; Heriger, *Gest. Pont. Tungr.* 173). As noted, the *Life of Annianus* is occupied almost entirely by its hero's leadership against the Huns. In this, his link with Aëtius gives rise to a significant episode. Going for help to the general's court at Arles, he finds him besieged by bishops asking favours, and wins an audience only with difficulty. Loyen (1969: 70) dates the *Life* in the sixth century; in that century, three church councils were held at Orleans under Merovingian auspices. Annianus' problems did not exist for his successors. If Cassiodorus saw Theoderic as a new and better Aëtius, did the hagiographer see the Merovingians as similar defenders, but better placed to favour the bishops of his see?

Lupus of Troyes emerges rather differently in his biography (*V. Lupi*; on date and historicity, see Ewig, 1978): not a Roman loyalist and defender of his city, but a negotiator of peace terms, and an honoured hostage with Attila. The Annianus life recounts how one captive and defeatist bishop in the Hunnic camp was justly shot down from the walls of Orleans; it may be significant that Troyes produced another Attila legend, the *Passio Memorii*, in which a party of churchmen was martyred while acting as envoys to the Huns under their bishop's orders. None the less, Lupus saved his city, and is given due credit. The *Life of Genovefa* again shows the importance to a saint of some role in 451. The Huns never reached Paris, and tradition could display the saint as neither negotiator, nor resistance leader. However, she risked lynching when she persuaded the citizens not to flee in panic, and her prayers kept the enemy far off. The biographer compares her with St Martin, who had once averted an imminent battle, and with Annianus; to the churches of the two at Tours and Orleans, she was a devout pilgrim. Martin, Annianus, and Genovefa make a remarkable trinity of saints. All three enjoyed Merovingian patronage, and the two from Merovingian capitals owed much of their repute to the Hunnic connection.

Frankish politics, saints, sees, and the Huns mingle most notably in Paul the Deacon's *Gesta Episcoporum Mettensium*, commissioned by bishop Angilramn (see Goffart, 1986, 1988: 373ff.). Metz was the home ground of the Carolingians: their ancestor Arnulf had been its bishop, with Merovingian predecessors, and he gets due space in Paul's work. He is rivalled by only two others, of whom one is Auctor, allegedly bishop when Attila sacked the city (262f.). Paul conflates two stories distinct in Gregory (*HF* 2.5–6; cf. *Liber in Gloria Conf.* 7): the vision of Servatius of Tongres at Rome, which revealed the Hunnic invasion and his own death, and that of an anonymous *fidelis* at Metz, which revealed the sack. Both are now located at Rome, ascribed to Servatius, and transmitted by him to Auctor. Auctor baptized numerous children before the sack and massacre. Enslaved with many others, he acted with heroism, and miraculously obtained their freedom. The third bishop is Chrodegang (267f.; on him see McKitterick, 1983: 44f., 56ff.; Wallace-Hadrill, 1983: 174ff.). An ex-referendary of Charles Martel, in 754 he served as the envoy of Pippin III, to escort pope Stephen II across the Alps. The Roman connection, and the cults of St Stephen and St Peter, who had long been so closely associated with the Hunnic peril, were keenly fostered by him. With Pippin's help, he remodelled the liturgy and ecclesiastical discipline of Metz on the Roman pattern. (Paul gives the see of Metz a Petrine origin.) He built shrines of St Stephen and St Peter; he founded a monastery of St Peter in the parish of St Stephen; and he procured martyrs' relics from Rome through pope Paul I, himself a devotee of St Stephen. Servatius' cult at Maastricht had also enjoyed a revival in the reign of Charles Martel. Significantly, the district was the home of Chrodegang, and also of Charles' mother Alpaida, brought with difficulty into the Arnulfing power-base by Pippin II (Krusch, 1896: 83; Gerberding, 1987: ch.7).

What did the simultaneous renewal of Roman ties and reminder of barbarian crisis imply in Chrodegang's day? Pippin III, whom he probably helped to anoint (in 751), had been fostered by Liutprand, an apparent admirer of Theoderic (see Llewellyn, 1986: 55f.). If

Charlemagne found himself, perhaps to his own surprise, a new emperor, had Pippin's more learned supporters prepared the ground by seeing him as the new Aëtius?

Paul's Attila narrative may have had contemporary resonances for its readers. He attributes the fall of the Nibelungs to Attila, following the epic tradition which had so impressed the Arnulfings. Charlemagne was the conqueror of the Hunnic Avars, 'renovator' of the Roman empire, head of a new coalition of Germanic peoples in the defence of western Europe. He removed a famous statue of Theoderic from Ravenna to Aachen (cf. Moorhead, 1983: 160ff.). In the eighth–ninth century, the *Getica* was copied near Mainz, and it was used by bishop Freculf of Lisieux, a former *missus dominicus*, in his world-chronicle of *c.* 840 (Lowe, 1934–71: no.1224; *MGH, AA* 5.1: xlvif.; Wattenbach and Levison, 1957: 350ff.). Paul himself, at Benevento, some twenty years before writing the *Gesta*, had worked its Attila narrative into his *Historia Romanorum*, stressing the coalition of 'paene totius populi occidentis' (14.4).

However, the crownings of Pippin and Charlemagne, and the victory of Aëtius, go unmentioned in the *Gesta*. In its triptych of bishops, Arnulf is the centre, with his spiritual victories, and the secular triumphs of his descendants against Basques, Arabs, and Lombards. Chrodegang restores to Metz a Roman continuity breached when the Huns submerged all Gaul (Goffart, 1986: 71ff., 91f.; 1988: 377), but his deeds and Auctor's are purely episcopal. We should remember that many Franks in Chrodegang's day, and even in Paul's, still despised or suspected the Roman connection; while anointing, perhaps an initiation for priests more than kings, was misunderstood or ignored by the laity (Llewellyn, 1986: 60ff.; Nelson, 1977: 57ff.). Charlemagne's rescue of the once imperial city is reassuringly shown by Paul as an enlargement of the Frankish empire. Avoiding controversy, he has obliquely used the church history of Metz, and especially the Attilan crisis, to affirm family ties and the bond of parallel functions between the Gallic priesthood and Gallic rulers, Merovingian or Arnulfing. Kings are linked to priests, and priests to Rome: Gaul's identity is being recreated.

The distinction conferred by the Hunnic invasion, its use in image-building for lords and churchmen, tribes and dioceses, has an interesting rival. Jordanes, and probably Cassiodorus before him, had taken pains to associate the Goths with the Trojan war – it was part of 'making Gothic history Roman' (*Variae* 11.25.5). The Franks did better: like the Arverni (Lucan 1.427f.; Sidonius, *Ep.* 7.7.2), they invented or had invented a Trojan origin for themselves. Fredegar, in whom it surfaces, and the author of the *Liber Historiae Francorum* show more interest in this Trojan past than in the Hunnic invasion; while Paul assimilates the name of Ansegisel, Arnulf's son, to Anchises. The Trojan legend had a longer and more distinguished literary afterlife than the Attilan connection: any barbarian people could use this origin; many did so, and it tied them into a remote, Virgilian past. Attila, however, had a special meaning for the Franks, as once for the Goths: he bound them into the history of Christian and Roman Gaul, a past far less remote. He also linked them with a great tradition of Germanic epic which was still living in the days of Charlemagne. (For conjectures on this tradition and the Catalaunian Plains, see Lukman, 1948; Morgan, 1969.) Probably, though, like the Tale of Troy throughout the Middle Ages, memories of the 451 invasion survived in part because they made a good story. They met the perennial demand of Old Kaspar's grandchildren, 'Now tell us all about the war/ And what they fought each other for.'

II

The Gothic settlement of 418

The settlement of Germanic peoples on Gallic soil – to protect and promote Roman interests there – was a long-standing feature of imperial diplomacy: one has only to think of the transfer of the Ubii in the first century BC; and Constantius I and Julian allowed Franks to live west of the Rhine. The fifth century saw Burgundians and Alans established over this river. However, the disaster of Adrianople, Alaric's perambulations through Illyricum and Italy, Athaulf's passage across southern Gaul, Wallia's military activity in Spain and, above all, the political successes of Theoderic I, Theoderic II and Euric have ensured that most work on barbarian settlement in Gaul in the fifth century has been directed towards that of the Goths, in Aquitania.

The details of the Gothic settlement in south-west Gaul are very obscure, and hence much debated: in this volume Wood brings even its date – conventionally agreed to be 418 – into question. In general, however, historians have concerned themselves most with the reasons behind the Roman decision to pull their recently created allies out of Spain, and the actual mechanisms by which the Goths were established in their new home.

Burns argues that the Aquitanian settlement was in accordance with current military practice. It was intended to stabilize the situation in both Spain and Gaul, following Fl. Constantius' success in dealing with the chronic instability in the Iberian peninsula that had arisen from the revolts of Constantine III and Gerontius. There Constantius had chosen to deploy Wallia's Goths, with a stiffening of Roman regulars, against the Vandal, Alanic and Suevic auxiliaries who had held the country for Gerontius, and whom Constantius had, until 416, left to do the same for Honorius. Once Spain was secure, and regarrisoned with Roman troops, the Goths could not be permitted to remain; but equally, they could not be removed too far in case their support was again needed against residual barbarian strength south of the Pyrenees.   They were therefore transferred to neighbouring Aquitania, which, now more exposed than ever before to attack, would itself benefit from their presence.   According to Burns, the Goths were settled in Aquitania principally as auxiliary frontier-troops – albeit on an internal frontier – and, as such, were maintained in the usual manner for such troops, in accordance with a system developed during the reign of Theodosius I.   Thus the *hospitalitas* that was extended to them comprised both direct monetary payments (funded by means of the re-direction of imperial taxation paid by the local provincial population) and the formal granting of land.   As auxiliaries, they were to be used in small groups, each under its own leader, independent of the king.

Nixon approaches the mechanism of the Aquitanian settlement in a somewhat different manner, taking as his main concern the apparent paradox of the Goths' moving into Aquitania in relatively large numbers (he suggests *c.* 80,000) yet failing in the long term significantly to influence the society and culture of the region.   He argues that the Goths, once removed from Spain, would need to be maintained.   However, since they were not just a war-band, but were accompanied by wives and children and possessed of a strong farming tradition, they might support themselves if given land; and land was available for them in plenty in an Aquitania that, thanks to the troubles that had beset Gaul since the invasions of 406–7 (including those brought upon it by the Goths themselves: as also noted by Burns), was fertile but conveniently underpopulated.   Aquitania was therefore settled by Gothic aristocrats and their dependants according to a system which, though based upon the standard procedures of military *hospitalitas*, was, as a result of the ready availability of *agri deserti*, probably subject to wide variations from these.   Land thus occupied by the Goths was not taxed; but that belonging to Roman citizens was, and the revenue directed towards the Gothic court (a point with which Heather would agree).   The symbiotic relationship between Goths and Gallo-Romans encouraged the continuation of Roman society and culture, the strength of which enabled them to assimilate Gothic kings and aristocrats; the Gothic peasantry, isolated in the countryside, was likewise absorbed by the local culture.

But who were these 'Goths' or 'Visigoths'?   Although Burns and Nixon come to very similar conclusions concerning the planting of

Goths under their own leaders on land throughout Aquitania, there is a clear tension between the former's analysis of the 418 settlement as an essentially military affair and the latter's characterization of it as the final stage in the migration of an unruly agrarian people, in respect of which Rome's (unfulfilled) hopes had more to do with the restoration of her Aquitanian tax-base than with the bolstering of her military strength. *Liebeschuetz* proposes that the men who followed Alaric, Athaulf, Wallia and Theoderic I should not be regarded as the *patresfamilias* of a people on the move, but as soldiers in a peripatetic mercenary army which, though it probably had a Gothic core, included warriors of widely different origins from both inside and outside the Empire. Therefore, unlike Nixon, Liebeschuetz supposes no great degree of continuity between these people and those who crossed the Danube in 376 and, above all, discounts the proposition that their ambition was always to obtain land on which to settle. On the contrary, he proposes that it was the very wanderings of these soldier-adventurers that led, in the second decade of the fifth century, to the genesis of a new 'Gothic' nation, that was born at once of common military experience and of an *esprit de corps* founded upon a particular language (Gothic) and a particular form of Christianity (Arianism). On the other hand, Liebeschuetz's views on the predominantly military character of the Goths prior to 418 sit well with Burns' proposals for their role in Spain and Gaul, and accord with the latter's thinking on the foundation of the Visigothic kingship. However, his explanation for their coming to rest in Aquitania – that essentially, as the leaders of the Goths aged, they aspired to a more sedentary way of life – is perhaps in the end not too far removed from that of Nixon.

A somewhat different issue, the subsequent development of the 'Gothic settlement' into the 'Visigothic kingdom' is investigated by *Heather*. He, like Liebeschuetz, stresses the newness of the Gothic nation. Though its basic administrative and legal framework was Roman, first and foremost it was held together by a strong dynastic monarchy, created by Theoderic I, Theoderic II and Euric. The emergence of this monarchy was not without its difficulties: to a certain extent recalling Burns and Nixon, Heather points up the potential for civil strife caused by the existence of independently minded local Gothic aristocratic leaders. Heather proposes two main phases in the evolution of the Visigothic kingdom. During the first, from 418 to *c.* 450, Theoderic I consolidated his authority within his realm, but was confined to the margin of imperial politics by the success of Roman generals (cf. King, for the possibility of the beginning of the production of gold and silver coinage by the Visigoths from this period). The second phase, from 451, saw the speedy expansion of Visigothic influence outside Aquitania consequent upon Rome's calling for Visigothic aid against Attila, and the power-vacuum that resulted from the murder of Aëtius and the extinction of the Theodosian line (see Burgess). Theoderic II and Euric thus became the main power-brokers in the politics of the continental west.

Of fundamental importance for the overall theme of this collection of essays is Heather's treatment of the Gallo-Roman reaction to the emergence of the Visigoths as a first-class power. He observes that up to *c.* 450 Gallo-Romans, especially those living within the Visigothic realm, co-operated, perforce, with the newcomers to achieve personal ends, but do not appear to have had an important place in royal councils and undertakings. The reason for this may well have been the continued attraction of imperial politics and careers, since 418 more easily accessible in Gaul thanks to the establishment of the Gallic Council at Arles (cf. Mathisen, for a more qualified view). After 450, however, we can see Gallo-Romans becoming increasingly engaged with Visigothic affairs, as generals, disaffected (or, simply pragmatic) imperial administrators (see Harries, Teitler) and, finally, even royal administrators. Heather proposes that the catalysts for change were the diversion of Roman military attention to Africa and, above all, the reign of Avitus. The latter, by creating the first political alliance between Visigoths and Romans, legitimized Visigothic power and so opened the road for others, emperors and private citizens alike, to reach their own accommodations with the new power in the land. Here, too, one might usefully refer to the defeat of Attila in 451, and Barnish's point that this marked the end of the last great Germanic incursion from over the Rhine. There were to be no new major players on the Gallic stage.

CHAPTER 5

The settlement of 418

T. S. Burns

The central theses to be advanced here are that the 'settlement' of the Goths in 418 must be understood in the general context of Constantius' plan to stabilize both Gaul and Spain, and was in accordance with traditional late Roman principles of *receptio* and recruitment then in practice along the frontiers.

SOUTHERN GAUL AND SPAIN, 409–18

Immediately following the defeat of the usurper Constantine III in 411, the two major aims of the Roman authorities in respect to the western provinces must have been the suppression of continuing political opposition in the region and the prevention of the newly arrived Goths from moving further northward into Gaul.

In Spain, the problem was not one of continuing usurpations, but of the presence of powerful barbarians, closely implicated in the most recent of the illegitimate regimes. In 409, the Vandals and their allies had concluded a peace with Gerontius, *magister militum* of Constantine III and Constans, that enabled him to take the initiative against his masters (Olympiodorus fr. 17.1). A plausible hypothesis is that this peace was in fact the 'settlement' recorded by the chroniclers that established the Asding Vandals and Sueves in north-west Spain and thereby induced them to stop their plundering. Prior to this, Gerontius, charged with the defense of the Pyrenees by Constans, had replaced Honorius' supporters and whatever remained of their defensive deployments in the passes with the *Honoriaci* and other troops brought from Gaul and placed under his command. We are told that the troops stationed in Spain requested that they be entrusted with the defense but were turned down (Zosimus 6.5.1). The new

Roman forces could not hold the passes. The *Honoriaci* reportedly turned instead to plunder (Orosius 7.40.8-10). The Vandals and their allies crossed into Spain in 409 without resistance (routes, Labrousse, 1968: 572ff.). Constantine, angered by these developments, ordered Constans back to Spain to replace Gerontius with a certain Justus. Gerontius rebelled and quickly came to terms with the barbarians. A further hypothesis is that Gerontius concluded his agreement with the barbarians not simply to buy peace but also to use their strength to replace or supplement the Roman troops in the north, help pacify the other provinces involved in the resistance of Honorius' relatives to Constans' original assumption of power in Spain, and enable him to remove substantial portions of the regular Roman garrisons to attack Constans and Constantine in Gaul (Olympiodorus fr. 17.2.14-16: at Arles his Spanish troops betrayed him).

The theory that Gerontius used the Vandals and their allies to garrison Spain helps us to make sense of subsequent developments. Gerontius' efforts to expand his power into Gaul were unsuccessful; in 411 his troops went over to Constantius without struggle. Constantius then returned to Italy, without attempting to expel the Vandals from Spain. On the present argument, he will have chosen temporarily to accept the status of the Vandals etc., recognizing that they were neither inefficient nor disloyal in executing the obligations placed on them by Gerontius: after all, he needed as many troops as possible to stabilize Italy and threaten the Goths there. Constantius' efforts in that regard bore immediate fruit when Athaulf was prevailed upon to attack and crush the usurper Jovinus in Gaul, in 413.

However, in the same year, when Honorius could not or did not provide the necessary supplies promised Athaulf, the latter marched on Marseille but failed and was wounded in the assault (Olympiodorus fr. 22). Now in open rebellion, he captured Narbonne and probably Toulouse, and took Galla Placidia as his wife (January 414) (Olympiodorus fr. 24; Orosius 7.40.2; Hydatius 57; Rutilius, *De Reditu Suo* 1.496). Confronted with this defiance, Constantius retook Narbonne and established a naval blockade, which by the end of the year had so aggravated the famine in Gaul that Athaulf had to push southward into Spain in search of provisions (*Chron. Gall. 452* 72; Prosper 1256; Orosius 7.43.1-3). Departing Bordeaux in late 414 or early 415, Athaulf's men unleashed their anger upon the city in which they had been billeted since 413. Not even the properties of former hosts were spared, despite the efforts of some Goths to protect them (Paulinus of Pella, *Eucharisticus* 285-90: it would certainly seem the billeting had been on the properties). Thanks to Paulinus, Bazas was saved when he persuaded certain Alans to break from the Goths and defend the otherwise defenseless city (Paulinus of Pella, *Eucharisticus* 386). Shortly after crossing to Spain, Athaulf died at the hands of an assassin at Barcelona, probably in August 415. Wallia succeeded after Singeric's seven-day reign. Ultimately only the Roman fleet prevented those with Wallia from crossing to Africa. The Goths then returned to plundering Spain for supplies, but that proved very difficult. They were on the edge of starvation and were blocked from returning to Gaul (*Chron. Gall. 452* 78; cf. Nixon, below p. 67), in part perhaps by the Alanic garrisons recently established nearby (Bachrach, 1969), and were hard pressed by the barbarians formerly established in Spain by Gerontius and still in place (Orosius 7.43.14). In early 416 Constantius and Wallia concluded an agreement to employ the Goths as Rome wished in exchange for the return of Galla Placidia.

The Goths received 600,000 *modii* of grain in order to supply them while on campaign (Olympiodorus fr. 30). Following the return of Galla Placidia, Constantius sent Wallia and his followers, possibly as many as 15,000 (Jones, 1964: 1109 n65), against the Sueves and Asding Vandals. It is here that attention should be directed towards an *epistula* of Honorius, addressed to Roman troops in Spain (Balil, 1970; ed. and discussed Sivan, 1985). This document may be dated either to May 416 (Balil, 1970: 618) or, rejecting the first four lines as a sixth-century addition, to the general return of peace in 418 (Sivan, 1985: 285). Together with the fact that the very same Goths who had had great difficulty just months before against the barbarian forces in Spain suddenly had no problem routing them, it suggests that Constantius strengthened Gothic forces with the addition of regular Roman troops. Rome must have simultaneously suspended her support of the Silings and Alans but not apparently of the Asdings and Sueves, who this time did not come to the aid of their former allies. Just months before, the Asdings, Silings, Sueves and Alans had together informed Honorius' government that their campaigns against the Goths were going well and that it might expect Gothic peace overtures soon (Orosius 7.43.15-16). Now, it would appear, the Romans had also successfully weakened the non-Gothic barbarian forces in Spain: their support of Gerontius had not been forgotten. Constantius allowed the Goths, perhaps strengthened by Roman regulars, to annihilate the Silings, but only to cripple the Asdings and Sueves, before recalling the Goths to Gaul.

The treaty of 416 which, on the current argument, overthrew previous understandings between Roman generals and the Vandals and their allies, was clearly a crucial transformation in Roman policy. However, it is the likely participation of Roman troops in action in Spain at this time that should not be lost sight of in any assessment of subsequent imperial treatment of the Goths. The troops mentioned in Honorius' *epistula* correspond loosely with those listed in the *Notitia Dignitatum (Occ.* 42.24-32), though this makes reference to some units doubtless no longer stationed in Spain (Balil, 1970: 611ff.) and is anyway most probably a later document (*c.* 425 or later): despite its problems, the *epistula* strongly suggests the period 416–18, and the reintegration and pacification of Spain and southern Gaul by Constantius, as the context for the re-establishing of some type of a regular Roman military presence in the Iberian peninsula. This force may have numbered *c.* 6,500 men (Sivan, 1985: 285). It was probably now seen as an extension of the Gallic army and hence assured comparable pay (*epistula* 11, attesting also to the continuance of normal payment procedures). In essence, the Goths dislodged and defeated the Siling Vandals and Alans sufficiently for them to be replaced by regular forces, perhaps those having just fought alongside the Goths under unknown command (the Sabinianus of the *epistula* 2?). However, under the current agreement with the Goths, the re-establishment of regular forces in north-western Spain would have required the placing of the Goths and Roman garrisons in the same area. This would have been risky in many ways and certainly would have placed a great strain on the local communities. By returning the Goths to Gaul and stationing purely Roman troops in such key areas as Pamplona, the location of the manuscript of the *epistula*, the Pyrenean passes could be secured and the Sueves and Goths kept isolated from each other.

The Goths returning to Gaul under Wallia's successor, Theodoric I, would hardly have discovered the opulence that so excited the wrath of Salvian (*De Gub. Dei* 7). There can be little doubt that the Vandalic raids and Gothic sieges of 407–15 had raised considerable havoc in Aquitania Secunda. The cities from Toulouse to Bordeaux had had virtually no regular Roman units, and like Bazas were essentially defenseless. The small naval garrison near Bordeaux might have been useful in Constantius' naval blockade but could not have assisted much in the defense of the towns, whose populations had suffered accordingly despite the possible efforts of a few great landlords and bishops (Rouche, 1979: 19). This point must be forcefully stressed. Aquitania Secunda had had no previous Roman troops, and the share of its taxes directed towards the military went to support troops nearer the Gallic frontier. The major condition that had changed between the death of Theodosius in 395 and the settlement of 418 was the level of unity among the Goths and their allies. In essence, Alaric had established the foundations of Gothic kingship anew over a disparate soldiery, and it was still in the formative stages as late as 418 (cf. Liebeschuetz, below p. 81; Heather, below p. 87).

THE MECHANISMS OF SETTLEMENT IN TRANSITION

In 418, the Roman aristocracy in Aquitania Secunda surely had no right to complain about the settlement of the Goths in their land, regardless of the mechanisms used. There were very good reasons to change Roman military deployment and finally assure some internal defense of this region, especially if the costs and manpower problems could be solved. Heightened civil unrest cannot be rejected totally as a motive for establishing a military presence here. The unsettled conditions in the countryside had after all forced Paulinus and others to abandon their estates. Seaborne raids also may have been considered (James, 1977: 6). But surely the most pressing need was to station support troops nearby in a cost-effective manner in order to assist Rome, if needed, against the still undefeated Asding Vandals. This is, of course, precisely what the Goths did in 422. Whatever mechanisms were used to install the Goths, the Roman government could not significantly alter the flow of tax-revenues to the highly militarized provinces nearer to the frontier, where the bulk of the Roman army was still stationed. The traditional assumption that these units had for all practical circumstances ceased to exist, except on paper, cannot be allowed to stand unchallenged (Böhme, 1985: 131f., 1988: 23f.; cf. Elton, below p. 170). By this very time, however, Rome had lowered some of the costs by employing newly recruited barbarians in the garrisons and even granting some sections of the frontier to them. These men served primarily in return for readily available land along the frontiers and Roman military benefits, probably including those conferred upon retirement (*CTh.* 7.8; cf. Sivan, 1987: 767ff., but doubting her suggestion that the Goths were settled as veterans in 418).

The sources for the settlement of 418 unfortunately do not directly support or invalidate any theory of the precise operation of *hospitalitas*, either the traditional and quite complex understanding of it as in some way a direct sharing of lands and/or their revenues, or the recent suggestion that stresses the reassignment of local tax revenues (most recently articles by Durliat and Goffart, in Wolfram and Schwartz, 1988). The latter's greatest strength is its simplicity of application. The 'guest', living elsewhere, would be told where and to whom to present himself for drawing his ration. The chief difficulties of the new theory lie in the requirement to read all texts concerning the settlement as if written in the vocabulary of tax-law and the assumption that Rome would have voluntarily assumed the incredible commitment of fiscal resources that it would have continually required: land once given, regardless of the complexity of the giving, was administratively finite (cf. Nixon, below p. 71). Both theses assume that the essentials of settlement remained unaltered for centuries, with many precedents laid down under Valentinian I. Neither hypothesis provides for a period of transition behind the legal fictions, although clearly both assume that from the beginning some creativity was indispensable. There can be no question that along the frontiers the recruitment and establishment of barbarians included the actual occupation and cultivation of the soil, which greatly reduced the direct and indirect costs of maintaining the *limes*. Nor was there a lack of available land for families to plow.

The legislation that ultimately formed the basis of what we call the *hospitalitas* system culminated in an edict of 398 (*CTh.* 7.8.5), probably designed to take care of the temporary quartering of troops either in transit or while marshalling for campaign, and still essentially in force in the *epistula* (*Ep.* 16-18), which strongly urges appropriate thanks to be given to the host when departing. Why require adieus for the re-direction of taxes? Between 398 and 411 all the so-called settlement acts of the emperors had to do with the establishment of *laeti* (as in 399), the clarification of the status of land granted previously to defenders of the frontier (as in 409), or the establishment of captured Sciri in various areas as active farmers or slaves (Ste Croix, 1981: 509f.). Only with the establishment of the Vandals in 411 is there a possible application of these procedures to the movement and recruitment of various groups of barbarians.

The case of this 'establishment' of barbarians in Spain as reported by Hydatius is the first instance in which the language of our source suggests the possible application of the law of *hospitalitas* as described in the Code: the barbarians having arrived in Spain, and now looking to establish peace, 'sorte ad inhabitandum sibi prouinciarum diuidunt regiones' (Hydatius 49). The passage then narrates the distribution of the Asding Vandals to Gallaecia, with the Sueves in the extreme west, the Alans to Lusitania and Carthaginiensis, and the Siling Vandals to Baetica. Gallaecia was already in great turmoil before the Vandals were established there. So too must have been Lusitania, which had provided loyalist troops against Constantine and Constans, ultimately including farmers and slaves (Zosimus 6.4.3). For the year 413 Prosper Tiro reports that the Burgundians 'partem Galliae propinquam Rheno optinuerunt' (Prosper 1250).

The new theory of settlement based on the diversion of tax resources, which, whether or not applicable to the barbarians as such, has certainly helped clarify aspects of the maintenance system of the regular army, is the most likely explanation of the passages dealing with Spain. The direct drawing upon local tax revenues reconciles the apparent dispersal of 'settlement' with the probable deployment of new barbarian recruits in the areas formerly garrisoned by the Roman army. That the Goths later were recalled before engaging the Asding Vandals suggests that, in fact, the Asdings were not in the same area as the Silings and were doubtless still in Gallaecia, the province Gerontius had accorded them. Only later did they move southward into Baetica, old Siling territory, perhaps as a response to the re-establishment of Roman forces in the north. Roman forces under Castinus, employing Gothic auxiliaries, attacked them in Baetica in 422. Again, the importance of the peculiar situation confronting Gerontius in 409–10 cannot be underestimated. He had to act quickly in order to engage Constans in Gaul. The easiest mechanism available was to replace the regular military units with barbarian troops and to pay them in precisely the same manner. In other words, he took the tax resources paying the Roman forces drawn from four of the provinces of Hispania and directed them to the payment of the barbarians to be stationed there.

The case of the Burgundians is surely a matter of frontier defense along the Rhine and so should have involved the actual occupation of land rather than tax re-assignment. Prosper does not mention the known Burgundian leader at this time, a certain Guntiarius (Olympiodorus fr. 18). And this is in keeping with the practice of *receptio*, in which the recruits served under new leaders. The Burgundians along the Rhine are not mentioned in the *Notitia Dignitatum*, although it was updated while they were there defending the frontier. The language in both the case of the Burgundians and that of the Vandals is frustratingly inconclusive. None the less, I suggest that two principles are operative here, noting, however, that the Romans traditionally liked to hide diversity behind as few legal procedures as possible. The first is the by now traditional system of assigning sections of the frontier to barbarian defenders. The second principle is the integration of barbarian auxiliaries within the payment system of the regular units of the Roman army based upon provincial collection and disbursement. The Silings and Alans were in place for only a very brief time before they were virtually annihilated and regular troops returned to Spain by Honorius. The Asdings ultimately crossed to North Africa. The Sueves alone remained but in the most remote area of the peninsula. As a result there is no way to test whether Rome regarded the Vandals in the same way as barbarian frontier troops in terms of status, that is, as auxiliaries serving alongside, but distinct from, the regular units. The settlement of the Goths in 418 offers an opportunity to explore the auxiliary status more fully.

As stated, the basic texts of the settlement in 418 are extremely ambiguous and defy specific analysis in terms of the theories of settlement procedures. Prosper reports that 'Constantius patricius pacem firmat cum Wallia data ei ad inhabitandum secunda Aquitanica et quibusdam civitatibus confinium provinciarum' (Prosper 1271). Hydatius relates that the Goths were recalled from Spain by Constantius and 'sedes in Aquitanica a Tolosa usque ad Oceanum acceperunt' (Hydatius 69). Philostorgius is perhaps more explicit in terms of what the Goths received by their treaty with Honorius. He states that as a condition for the surrender of Attalus and Galla Placidia, the Goths concluded a treaty 'having received a supply of grain and having been allotted a part of the land of the Gauls for farming' (Philostorgius 12.4). But which treaty is Philostorgius discussing? Galla Placidia was returned as a condition of the treaty of 416 and Attalus was abandoned to the Romans earlier, although his fall was celebrated in Constantinople in June 416 (*PLRE* II: 181).

Philostorgius must have conflated the events of 416 and 418 into one incident – the return of Roman hostages and Gothic supporters on the one hand, and the establishment of the Goths in Gaul on the other. Jones, while accepting Philostorgius, suggests that this was a one-time-only grant of *annonae* to see the Goths through to the next harvest (Jones, 1964: 1109 n65). If, however, Philostorgius is correct, in 418 the Goths under Wallia asked for and received precisely the same grant that Theodosius had accorded the followers of Athanaric in 381, when settled along the *limes*, specifically *annonae* and land (Eunapius fr. 45.3 from *Suda* Pi.2351 but rather associated with Zosimus 4.34.4–6). In the agreement of 416 the Goths had received only supplies. The source there was Olympiodorus, who would hardly have overlooked a real settlement. Unless we simply reject, as some have done (Kaufmann, 1866: 440 n1), the entire testimony of Philostorgius, there can be little doubt that the Goths as military colonists received both grain and lands in a section of Gaul for farming. According to the Latin sources, the Goths either may have received both actual land to live upon and supplies, as in the case of frontier situations, or they might have been paid through the regular mechanisms of the Roman army based upon provincial tax revenues. In short, the Latin sources remain ambiguous. The language of Philostorgius. however, seems clear enough. The purpose of the grant of land was for farming and, just as Roman frontier soldiers would have, they were also to receive supplies. The lands were simply 'a part of the land of the Gauls'. 'Land' is also a better explanation of the Latin sources, including later references in the Code of Euric to keeping to the early 'boundaries' (*Cod. Eur.* 276: Sivan, 1987: 768). The frontier-based arrangement would have more easily facilitated the establishment of farmer-soldiers, which many Goths clearly were in the Balkans and may still have been. *Receptio* had long been portrayed and conducted on the basis of families of *dediticii* (Bastien, 1972; Kraft, 1978). There is still no way to be sure of the interpretation of all the texts relevant to the general problem of barbarian settlements spanning centuries, yet, if the text of Philostorgius is accepted and compared to other texts relating to the establishment of barbarians along the frontiers, the settlement in 418 was in fact merely the transferal of the frontier program used for many generations to garrison and maintain the fortifications and agricultural systems along the *limes*. The Latin texts do not contradict this conclusion. The Romans still dictated the terms and demonstrated considerable flexibility in the application of what looks outwardly like two simple principles for maintaining troops. When the situation allowed, as in Spain in 411, the distribution system of the regular army could handle the new barbarian units. At times when this would have forced a major restructuring of the defensive system as in Gaul, Rome adapted the cheaper and less obtrusive model of the frontier.

AFTER 418

The evidence for the use of the Goths in the years immediately after 418 tends to support the thesis that they were regarded as frontier troops available for specific duties in small units. The Roman *magister militum* Castinus supplemented his army in 422 with Gothic auxiliaries (*et auxiliis Gothorum*) in his campaign against the Asding Vandals in Baetica (Hydatius 77). There is no mention of the Gothic king Theodoric I. Eight years later Aetius destroyed a body of Goths and captured their leader, the optimate Anaolsus. Again Theodoric was not mentioned (Hydatius 92). The origin of Castinus' Gothic auxiliaries must surely have been the Goths in southern Gaul. The case of Anaolsus' band reveals that the settlement had not altered the positions of the Gothic nobility at the head of their followers. The use of the Goths by Castinus and the obviously independent action of Anaolsus, both clearly without a 'royal' presence, suggest that the Romans were still able to recruit auxiliaries from among the Goths settled in Aquitania, probably by negotiating directly with the Gothic nobility, and to use them in regional campaigns.

The fact that the settlement of 418 was an experiment that in the long run failed demanded a further evolution of the settlement procedures, particularly as Rome lost the initiative. We see this with the Burgundians, who were established in Savoy in 443 by dividing up the lands and inhabitants. In 456–7 the Burgundians, this time in alliance with the Goths, who by then were truly a dominant force in southern Gaul, 'occupaverunt terrasque cum Gallis senatoribus diviserunt' (Marius Aventicensis a. 456.2). Here there is no question that the principles used along the frontier have been superseded and the legislation of 398 interpreted to implement the regular and permanent maintenance of barbarian forces by drawing upon the resources of the local elites. The barbarians were in a much better position to demand some of the best lands or their revenues, those of the senatorial class.

The Goths were thus, from 418 to the mid fifth century, the Roman military presence in south-western Gaul, maintained initially through the standard mechanisms of the frontier system. They constituted part of a new type of auxiliary force, in Roman eyes perhaps not fundamentally different from the auxiliaries of the early Principate. Moreover, like other new barbarian *auxilia*, the Goths escaped notice in the *Notitia Dignitatum*. Under certain monitored conditions the Romans believed that these forces could be trusted as much as regular units, themselves decidedly 'barbarian' in the sense of Germanic. The settlement of 418 was a stage in the evolution of Roman policy concerning the barbarians, manifested continued military flexibility, and had relatively little effect upon the civilian community.

CHAPTER 6

Relations between Visigoths and Romans in fifth-century Gaul

C. E. V. Nixon

INTRODUCTION

I deal with an intriguing puzzle: a people sweeping into Italy and the western empire, roaming around unchecked for forty years, inhabiting southern Gaul for nearly a century, yet neither leaving any trace in the archaeological record nor influencing the culture of emergent France. Were the Visigoths' numbers not so large, the impact of their invasions not so catastrophic? Did they play no intimate role in Gallic rural life, being largely confined to the towns? I don't think these are the answers, but clearly one must explain the survival of Roman culture in south-west Gaul. In this chapter I hope to provide an alternative resolution of the paradox of the undoubted military and political importance of the Visigoths, and their cultural insignificance. I shall examine the invasion period, then suggest a model of the ensuing relationship between Visigothic and Roman Gaul.

The classical historian may be forgiven for thinking that he has moved into a dark and mysterious era. Despite recent attention to the period, the pool of evidence available to him has not increased significantly. What has changed is scholarly treatment of that evidence. One such change has been to reduce the whole scale, intensity and impact of the barbarian invasions of the fifth century (Goffart, 1980). Concomitantly, the continuity of life after the barbarian invasions, particularly amongst the landed senatorial aristocracy, has been emphasized (Matthews, 1975). None the less, I wonder whether the reaction has not gone too far, and perhaps distorted the nature of the initial Visigothic settlement in Gaul and the subsequent relationship of the new settlers with the Gallo-Romans.

NUMBER AND COMPOSITION OF THE VISIGOTHS

How many Visigoths do we suppose were settled in south-west Gaul in 418? Eunapius (fr. 42) put the total number of the Goths on the Danube in 376 at 'not much fewer than 200,000'. A safer order of magnitude for Germanic numbers, it has been held (Bury, 1923: I, 105), is provided by Victor Vitensis' figure of 80,000 for the number of Vandals crossing into Africa; they had to be counted to establish how many transport ships were needed. This number is perhaps a cliché (cf. Courtois, 1955: 215ff.); but Wallace-Hadrill (1962: 25ff.) suggests 'upwards of 100,000' for the Visigoths. 'How could the numbers of Germans migrating across Europe have been as large as this?', asks James (1977: 195). We might well reply: 'how could it have been much smaller, in the light of the deeds of the Visigoths in Italy, and all that followed?'

No one can doubt that the Visigothic host that crossed the Danube comprised men, women and children (Eunapius fr. 42; Zosimus 4.20.6; cf. Ammianus 31.4, 31.6.1), and while there was considerable dividing and re-grouping in the years following, there is nothing to suggest a fundamental change in the composition of their population. An initial migration of 80,000, allowing for disproportionate losses amongst women and children, would give a minimum fighting force of *c.* 25,000. We are talking about a people which (whatever its exact composition) maintained its integrity within the Empire against considerable Roman hostility for forty years, then established itself over an area from the Loire to the Pyrenees, and after fifty years more was strong enough to expand, to invade and hold large parts of Spain and to seize Provence; and all this despite interdicts upon marriage between Goth and Roman (*Leges Visig.* 3.1.2). These facts cannot be explained by the simple expedient of postulating that the original invaders were a small group which was quickly swallowed up. Visigothic absence from the archaeological record and its ultimate cultural unimportance to the history of the developing Merovingian kingdom is a separate issue.

Acceptance of the need to sustain a large migrating people helps us to understand the pre-Gallic history of the Visigoths. In Pannonia the Goths had been starved (Ammianus 31.4.11). Later, in Italy, feeding his people had been one of Alaric's first considerations. His demands at Ariminum (in his first interview with Jovius) were for an annual supply of gold and grain, and the provinces of the two Venetias, the two Noricums and Dalmatia to live in (Zosimus 5.48). In the second round of negotiations he would settle for the two Noricums, grain, and a military alliance (Zosimus 5.50.3). After their defection from Rome in 394, Alaric's Goths had to live off the land for fifteen years. Jordanes describes some of the consequences for Italy: the ravaging of the countryside from Liguria and Aemilia to Rome; from Campania to Lucania and Bruttium (*Getica* 155–6). Zosimus has a similar tale, derived from Olympiodorus (Zosimus 5.37.2–4: 408; cf. 6.10: 410). Italy was devastated. The Theodosian Code provides dramatic confirmation[1]. Four-fifths of every class of tax payment was remitted for Campania, Tuscany, Picenum, Samnium, Apulia and Calabria, as well as Bruttium and Lucania, for five years, the period of occupation (11.28.7). Several months later Campania's total assessment was reduced to one ninth because of former heavy assessment and devastation by the enemy (11.28.12). Now all this followed the writing off of 528,000 *iugera* of *agri deserti* in naturally fertile Campania in 395 (11.28.2). Clearly, the former rulings were not the result of agrarian decline, but of recent depredations.

No wonder that in 410 Alaric tried to reach Africa, the granary of the Empire, the goal of so many barbarian invaders. His host had exhausted Italy. And shortly after his death Athaulf had to leave Italy. Perhaps Africa was denied him (cf. Bury, 1923: I, 184f.). At any rate, early in 412 he chose to cross the Alps into Gaul, presumably via Etruria, where the devastation the Goths wreaked, either now or earlier, was unrepaired in 417 (Rutilius, *De Reditu Suo* 39ff.).

There is no reason to think that Visigothic numbers were shrinking. Losses, for instance against the Huns at Pisa (1,100 men: Zosimus 5.45.6), were matched by additions of captives, slaves and deserters. Zosimus may be exaggerating when he reports that over 30,000 barbarian men in Roman service joined Alaric when they learned of

---

[1]   Here I would like to acknowledge my debt to Mr Michael Lennon, who offers a similar interpretation in his Macquarie University doctoral dissertation on the senatorial aristocracy of Italy in the fifth century (in progress).

the massacre of their women and children after Stilicho's death in 408 (5.35.5–6), but the phenomenon was real enough (cf. Ammianus 31.6.5–6). So it is not surprising that Athaulf faced the same critical problem in Gaul as Alaric in Italy: feeding the horde. And his options in Gaul after the invasions of 406–7 must have been severely restricted: 'Uno fumavit Gallia tota rogo' (Orientius, *Common.* 2.184; cf. Demougeot, 1951: 521ff.; Roberts, below).

Recovery could not be overnight. Athaulf found that he could not live off the land in southern Gaul. After the Jovinus episode (cf. Bury, 1923: I, 194ff.; Matthews, 1975: 314f.), Athaulf had negotiated with the Romans, and Olympiodorus singles out his most pressing demand as that for grain (fr. 22.1, 2). In 414, after Athaulf's wedding to Galla Placidia, Honorius' general Constantius blockaded Narbonne and the Gallic coast, and Athaulf was forced to cross the Pyrenees, after a destructive march through southern Gaul, in search of grain and land in Spain.

Athaulf's successor Wallia also wished, but failed, to cross to Africa, was plagued by famine and forced to make peace with Rome (Olympiodorus fr. 30; Orosius 7.43.12f.; Prosper 1259; Jordanes, *Getica* 165). And here, in Olympiodorus, we get a specific figure: Rome supplied 600,000 measures of grain (in the Greek, simply 'sixty myriads', presumably of *modii*), while Wallia restored Galla Placidia and undertook to fight the other barbarians in Spain (416). The figure is tantalizing. Allowing for a number of children, and the usual gap between rations for men and women, let us assume an average of two and a half *modii* per person per month (cf. Foxhall and Forbes, 1982; Garnsey, 1983: 118; 1988: 191 n26). Let us further assume, as implied above, that the Visigoths numbered at least *c.* 80,000; this would represent three months' supply. Jones (1964: 1109 n65), allowing somewhat more per person, suggests a year's supply for 15,000 men. We have no means of knowing how long the supply was intended to last, but the Goths had recently been buying grain by the scoop from the Vandals (Olympiodorus fr. 29.1); their needs were acute and immediate. Jones' 'year's supply' is too long. It is clear that the Goths came over the Pyrenees as a people: the circumstances of their passage through southern Gaul makes it certain that they did not leave vulnerable wives and children behind them. A war-band formed from a total population of 15,000 would have been helpless against fellow barbarians in Spain. And if the Goths were to remain reasonably mobile they could scarcely cope with too large an amount of grain, wagons or no. A *modius* is *c.* 2 gallons: three months' supply for 80,000 people would be about 15 gallons per person. Jones would have the Visigoths carry with them 60 gallons per man, and fight into the bargain, having precious little manpower to spare for guarding the baggage train – surely impossible.

But whatever the exact figures, enough has been said to demonstrate that the Visigoths were no mere war-band, moving at will and living freely off the land. They were a people, eating whole tracts empty, and needing sometimes to buy imported grain on a large scale unless prevented from doing so by blockades. Their movements must have disrupted farming for years.

CONDITIONS IN GAUL, 407–18

While southern Gaul had not experienced wandering hordes for as long as Italy, there can be no doubt about the destructiveness of the invasions of 406–7. It is impossible to set aside the eye-witness evidence of Salvian for the ferocity of the attacks on Trier (*De Gub. Dei* 6.82–4); and there is no reason to think that the inhabitants of the cities listed by Jerome fared any better (*Ep.* 123.16). As far as subsequent damage is concerned, Paulinus of Pella's experiences, retailed in his *Eucharisticus*, are instructive: one *domus* had been ravaged in the invasion of 407 (239), and then his house in Bordeaux was pillaged by the Visigothic *populus* in 414 (282ff.), before they fired the city (311ff.). Yet he had been *comes privatae largitionis* in Attalus' puppet regime (291ff.). There are strong hints here that, *pace* Paulinus (311: *regis praecepto Atiulfi*), the Gothic horde was out of Athaulf's control. Clearly the situation was extremely precarious. Since entering Gaul in 412, the Visigoths had been on the move, desperately seeking food, and no doubt some more permanent solution to their predicament. Their behaviour was unpredictable. Their leaders tried to stabilize matters, and arrange for the orderly billeting of their people in Bordeaux (by *ius speciale*: 285f.). But large numbers are difficult to control, and there were deep divisions of policy among their numbers, some hoping to come to terms with the Romans, and anxious to settle down, others still preferring to loot and pillage. Such a rift led shortly afterwards to the murder by his own men in Spain of Athaulf's successor Sigeric, 'created to promote peace' (Orosius 7.43.9). Wallia, elected to break it, was ordained by God to confirm it (Orosius 7.43.10): circumstances were too strong for him, as they no doubt were for Athaulf at Bordeaux.

But the firing of Bordeaux had not been the end of dislocation in Gaul in 414. The Visigothic horde besieged Bazas, in conjunction with some Alani, and the Roman defenders faced social revolution; a special assassin threatened Paulinus himself (*Eucharisticus* 334–6, 339). Roman social relations generally suggest that such disruption to Roman society in the face of a barbarian presence was widespread; in Gaul, the Bazas incident apart, numbers of small-holders and slaves fled to Aremorica. Orosius spoke before 417 of those Romans who preferred a poverty-stricken *libertas* amongst the barbarians to *tributaria sollicitudo* amongst the Romans (7.41.7). This way of thinking won't have been confined to Spain. Probably the most serious threat of Aremorica to Aquitania and its other Roman neighbours was that it acted like a magnet to peasants, *coloni*, slaves and the hard-pressed (Thompson, 1982: 23ff.; cf. Drinkwater, below p. 215). One recalls the later activities of some Bretons who had enticed away the slaves of a small proprietor (Sidonius, *Ep.* 3.9).

Another phenomenon testifies to the impact of the invasions upon Gaul – refugees (cf. Drinkwater, below p. 213; Mathisen, below pp. 228ff.). Our sources are naturally more informative about the plight of the well born. In fact we hear most about refugees from Rome and Italy after 410. None the less we do have some names of aristocratic Gallo-Roman refugees (some indeed *to* Italy), despite the patchiness of our evidence (cf. Mathisen, 1984). One is Rutilius Namatianus' friend Victorinus, ex-*vicarius*, who was forced abroad by the capture of his native Toulouse (*De Reditu Suo* 495–6). It speaks volumes about the situation in Gaul that he should retreat to devastated Etruria! He was joined there by Protadius (*Praefectus Urbi*, 400–1), a Gallic refugee who was living at Pisa when Rutilius travelled north (542ff.). And there must have been many more fugitives, like the 'sanctae et nobiles feminae' of Jerome (*Ep.* 130.4; 414), who were driven by 'a savage storm of enemies from the shores of Gaul' to Palestine. Some, like Paulinus of Pella, prepared to flee but failed to get away in time (*Eucharisticus* 408ff.; cf. Van Dam, below pp. 325f.). Certainly we find counter-examples like Rutilius himself, when chinks appeared in the storm-clouds. But one imagines more went the other way.

THE SETTLEMENT OF 418

All this I hope puts the settlement of 418 in its right perspective, and gives us a somewhat firmer foundation for reconstructing the nature of subsequent relations between Goths and Romans in Gaul. A crucial thing to recognize is that after the events of 406–7 and 413–14 there was an abundance of land available in Aquitaine – *agri deserti.* Many proprietors will have perished or fled, and those that remained may have had real difficulties finding manpower to work their land. The phenomenon of *agri deserti* of course was not new to Gaul (cf. *Pan. Lat.* 8(4).21: 297). But the invasions exacerbated the problem. We happen not to have evidence from the Codes testifying to tax relief in Gaul, but should we expect to have any? The Roman government was scarcely in a position to extract taxes, or even appraise the situation. But with the Visigoths under Wallia starving in Spain it had a bargaining counter. The Visigoths wanted a dependable source of food; the Romans wanted to end the disruptive wandering of a large host over their western domains. Aquitaine's fertility offered potential for productive settlement.

I am making two assumptions about Visigothic society. First, it had become more sharply class differentiated: the Goths had, for want of a better term, *optimates*, plus followers and slaves. This is recognizable by 376 (see Ammianus 31, *passim*, e.g. 31.12.8, 13; Thompson, 1966: 43ff.; King, 1972: 159) and observable later in the Visigothic law codes. I take it that such divisions were reinforced by the class society that they found among the Romans, and were well suited to the life that they were to lead in Aquitania. Secondly, it was to a considerable extent an agricultural society by 376. This is patent, not only from Ammianus, who reveals the Goths farming and makes it plain that the Romans counted on using them as farmers within the Empire (cf. 31.3.1, 8; 4.5, 8; 9.4; 12.8), but also from the archaeological evidence, which has become more substantial since Thompson tried to make the point (1966: 27ff.; cf. Ionita, 1975; Diaconu, 1975). That the Goths are occasionally to be seen in want of staples or importing them from the Romans (Ammianus 27.5.7; Themistius, *Orations* 10.135; Thompson, 1966: 38; 1982: 25f.) does not undermine the point; bad harvests trouble the best farmers, and within their territory north of the Danube the Goths will not have enjoyed a transport network to match that of the Romans. It might be added that the glimpses we get from the Code of Euric of the

Visigoths in the early years in Gaul are of a people intimately involved in the day-to-day life of the farmer.

So it made perfect sense for the Romans to settle the Visigoths on prime land in Gaul. Thompson (1982: 23ff.) has asked why in Aquitania, and why there were no Roman voices of protest, and answered in terms of the threat of social unrest from Aremorica. No doubt there is some force in this explanation, although others spring to mind and, while accepting the dangers of arguing from silence in a period recorded so sketchily in chronicles and hagiography, we might ask in turn how many Roman voices were left to protest, what morale and expectations were like, and whether it was thought such a blow to lose land which was officially liable for tax assessment, but which could no longer be worked effectively.

What, then, do our sources tell us of the settlement in 418? Very little, apart from the fact of it, and we are forced to turn elsewhere to find flesh for the bones. Barnish is surely right to suggest multifarious arrangements (1986: 172 and *passim*). Given the background I have sketched, there is something inherently implausible about an army of officials neatly dividing each and every estate into thirds, whether or not one restricts the process to large holdings. The tradition preserved in the later Germanic law codes, and hints in other sources (e.g. *Chron. Gall. 452* 124, 127–8; Paulinus of Pella, *Eucharisticus* 395–8, 502; Lot, 1928: 1007 n6) seem to guarantee that such a system, derived from *hospitalitas*, was utilized in Gaul, but I imagine that there were wholesale grants of *agri deserti* as well, where a Gothic leader might use his dependants as a work-force. The settlement would appear to have involved a *foedus* (Sidonius, *Carm.* 7.469; *Ep.* 7.6.4; Loyen, 1934) but the Goths' role as federates was intermittent and essentially unimportant. For long periods they disappear from history as industrious farmers are wont to do.

Goffart's (1980) notion that land was not given, but only the tax revenues, is ingenious, but apart from the problem that this is not what the sources say it seems peculiarly inappropriate to Gaul, where I contend there was available land in plenty, and where both estate supervision and agricultural labour were a crying need (see Barnish, 1986: 189). The theory also seems to saddle the Roman government with too pessimistic a view in writing off all hope of revenue from two thirds of south-west Gaul. One must accept Thompson's point that the settlement of 418 was taken on the initiative of the Roman government and not imposed upon it. It must therefore have thought that some good would come of it. It is not too cynical to assume it was looking to fiscal good.

A crucial question is whether Gothic lots were taxed. Thompson (1982: 27 n22) claims that they were not, citing *Leges Visig.* 10.1.16, which implies that if land is expropriated by Goths from Romans there results loss to the (Gothic) treasury. Though we cannot be certain that this was the situation in 418 (and for a different interpretation of the law in question, cf. King, 1972: 65f.), it seems probable. Perhaps the Romans offered an initial period of tax exemption. Certainly Rome did not give up its theoretical claims upon federate-occupied land until the days of Euric (cf. Loyen, 1934). But in fact we do not hear of any Roman tax-collector penetrating any part of Visigothic territory. Auxerre, relieved by the intercession of St Germanus of some of its tribute (*V. Germani* 4.19–24), seems to be the furthest point to which the net from Arles spread. And the taxes that we do hear of being paid within the Visigothic kingdom went to the Visigothic court. The *Vita Viviani* (4) provides evidence for Theoderic II taxing *Romans* in his kingdom (cf. Thompson, 1982: 27, n22). Salvian suggests they were lower than those levied by the imperial government (*De Gub. Dei* 4.21, 30–1; 5.17–44; cf. Ste Croix, 1981: 481). As we shall see, to judge from the evidence of Sidonius life could be very pleasant for at least some of the surviving Gallo-Roman aristocrats in the Visigothic kingdom.

But if the Visigoths were dispersed throughout the countryside, what guaranteed their security, and how could they function as federates? Lot's worries (1928: 989ff.) have been disposed of by Barnish (1986: 184f.). Not that *all* the Visigoths were scattered permanently over the land. The evidence of Sidonius reveals a substantial court by the time of Theoderic II (*Ep.* 1.2), and if we no longer believe that the city walls of Toulouse had to be extended to accommodate it (James, 1977: 198), we can at least assume the existence of some kind of standing military force, which might form the core of the Visigothic army. Court and standing army, and the obligations which attend social differentiation, cost money. Taxes, an agricultural surplus, were needed. And the Visigoths, whatever the original hopes of the imperial Roman government, were not used to paying taxes, and apparently didn't pay them. Therefore the surviving Roman landowners and tax payers were very important to the Visigothic king. Their taxes were not siphoned off to Rome or Arles. And so the Goths had a vested interest in maintaining the existing

Roman economy – and, perforce, its society and administrative structures.

VISIGOTHS AND GALLO-ROMANS

And so the Goths parasitized the exploitative Roman system as the most effective means of financing their kingdom. Hence Roman aristocratic life, provided it posed no political challenge to the Goths, could go on as sunnily in Visigothic Gaul as ever, and perhaps even more so than in Roman Gaul, which was taxed as relentlessly as the Roman government could manage it. In the circumstances, as long as there were politically harmonious relations between Roman and Visigothic Gaul, there could be an open frontier, and Sidonius could write to his peers in Visigothic Aquitaine or even visit them if he wished. In the 460s, he had several options for a bed for the night in Bordeaux or nearby (*Carm.* 22; *Ep.* 8.11.3, vv.33–9). More interestingly, perhaps, in the city of Bordeaux itself he would find Roman schools of higher education surviving, as Riché (1957) seems to have established. For Roman culture had a symbiotic relationship with Roman forms of administration and public life, and the Visigoths could not retain one without the other. So Lampridius continued to teach there (*Ep.* 9.13.2, vv.22–3), and we hear, too, of one Lupus who taught rhetoric not far away (Sidonius, *Ep.* 8.11.1–2).

Not only was Roman culture preserved in the Visigothic kingdom; Roman talent was apparently encouraged. It could be seen as a land of opportunity, and attracted the young and ambitious. Paulinus of Pella's two sons went off to Bordeaux to further their careers. Their father hoped they would recover the family's ancestral estates, but *they* were seeking freedom (*Eucharisticus* 500–2). One became a priest; the other met a sticky end (514). Certainly there was an element of gamble in this frontier land! Lampridius evidently lost his estates at a time of deteriorating relations between Euric and Rome, but he recovered them (Sidonius, *Ep.* 8.9.5, v.12; cf. 8.9.1), and gained full citizen rights in what could evidently be regarded as a separate kingdom now that Euric had broken the *foedus* (he is called *civis* by Sidonius, *Ep.* 8.9.3, but of course that may mean only a citizen of Bordeaux). Even a leader of the resistance to Euric in the

Auvergne, Sidonius himself, might hope to win the king's favour like his friend (*Ep*. 8.9.3).

At the top levels of society, any friction between Goth and Roman was usually based on political grounds, not cultural (see King, 1972: 8 n5). This is clear in the case of Theoderic I, who had his son taught Roman law and literature (Sidonius, *Carm*. 7.495ff.), and is still true in Euric's time. Visigothic Gaul, even when at war with Rome, made use of Roman notables in administration, both at the Court in Toulouse, and in the newly conquered territories. Leo, Euric's 'adviser' (*consiliarius* – GT *GM* 91; cf. *V. Epiphanii* 85: 'consiliorum principis et moderator et arbiter'), was involved in the affairs of *totus orbis* (Sidonius, *Ep*. 4.22.3). It is said that he wrote Euric's speeches for him (Sidonius, *Ep*. 8.3.3); Ennodius claims that Euric knew little Latin (*V. Epiphanii* 90). Adept in the law (Sidonius, *Carm*. 23.446ff.), Leo is naturally suspected of having helped to draft Euric's Law Code (Wallace-Hadrill, 1962: 38; Wormald, 1976: 222f.). Victorius was another Gallo-Roman appointed to high office by Euric (*PLRE* II, Victorius 4).

More and more Romans, like in the end Sidonius himself, must have come over as Euric's power increased and the imperial Roman government was seen to have abandoned Roman Gaul (see Sidonius, *Ep*. 1.7, 2.1, 4.8). While a few learned the language, no doubt the majority of Gallo-Romans shared Sidonius' contempt for their smelly and uncultivated masters (*Ep*. 7.14.10, 8.3.2; cf. *Carm*. 12) and, of course, Visigothic *optimates* had a cultural option. They could Romanize, or remain skin-clad and Latin-less, as Euric did, or affected to do. And the more advanced culture, the literate culture, triumphed in the end. The vast majority of the Visigoths remained illiterate farmers and warriors. Faceless, voiceless, they are lost to Gallic history, despite their numbers and the havoc they wreaked when they first roamed within the Empire.

CHAPTER 7

Alaric's Goths: nation or army?

J. H. W. G. Liebeschuetz

In 378 a Gothic tribe on the move, the Teruingi – generally known as Visigoths – led by Fritigern, destroyed the army of the eastern empire and killed the emperor Valens. In winter 395 a Gothic force led by Alaric set out on a succession of campaigns, of which the most sensational event was the capture of Rome in 410. Their wanderings came to an end only when the band was settled in Aquitaine in 418. It is generally thought that the wanderings of Alaric's Goths are another stage in the migration of Fritigern's Teruingi. As the events are generally described, Alaric was the chosen leader of the Teruingi settled in Moesia, who led them across the Empire in search of safer land; above all, land further removed from the Huns (Jones, 1964; most recently Wolfram, 1988: 140). The inability of Alaric and his successors to reach a lasting settlement with the imperial authorities was thus due to a conflict between *Romanitas* and a Gothic national tribal consciousness which found compromise and co-existence difficult, rather in the way that the conflicts between the nationalisms of modern Europe have been intractable (e.g. the seminal writings of Thompson: for bibliography, see Rich, 1988).

Against this I will argue that Alaric and his men started as a band of Teruingian mercenaries, who were drawn deep into the Empire by the prospect of living on the Empire's elaborate organization for paying soldiers their *annona* in kind. They realized that by exploiting this facility they would be able to live not only more plentiful but also more glorious lives. At the same time they were aware that the weakness of the Empire's native military resources gave them something like a monopoly-bargaining position (full argument and references in Liebeschuetz, 1990: ch.5).

Alaric's Goths were not the only group of mercenaries of this kind (Gainas' Goths were an unsuccessful group: Albert, 1984; Cameron, Long and Sherry, 1990; Liebeschuetz, 1990: ch.10), but they were the most successful, and their discipline and common experience eventually made a nation of them: a nation which had in common with the Teruingi the Gothic language and the Arian form of Christianity (Heather, 1986a; another view on conversion: Thompson, 1966: 103ff.), but which in respect of social institutions, and to a large extent racial and tribal origins, was a new people.

The beginnings of Alaric's career are extremely obscure. According to Isidore's *Historia Gothorum* 12, he was elected king by the Goths in 382, the fourth year of Theodosius I. This information is very unlikely to be correct, and most scholars have rejected it (e.g. Wolfram, 1988: 143ff.). One reason is that the notice is part of an extremely garbled version of Gothic history, including fundamental and demonstrable errors (Isidore, *Historia Gothorum* 12–15). How this version came into existence has yet to be explained, but it clearly will not do to believe any of it without independent confirmation. It is also the case that Jordanes dates the election to the period between the death of Theodosius I early in 395 and the consulate of Stilicho and Aurelian, that is 400 AD (Jordanes, *Getica* 146–7). What precisely this election meant in Gothic terms is debatable. But it is unlikely that Alaric held any 'king-like' position before the death of Theodosius I.

So we don't know the rank held by Alaric at the time of his earliest recorded historical action. This was when he prevented, or at least delayed, Theodosius' attempt to cross the Hebrus (Maritsa) on his march out of Thrace, presumably along the Via Egnatia (Claudian, *De VI Cons. Hon.* 107–8: 'Thracum venienti e finibus alter Hebri clausit aquas' – so M. Plattnauer in Loeb text; alternatively, if we accept the reading *aquis*, Alaric made use of the river to catch the emperor in an ambush: 'Thracum venientem e finibus alter Hebri clausit aquis'). When was this? The context in Claudian's poem suggests – but does not prove – that it was in summer 388 when Theodosius was setting out from Constantinople on his campaign against the usurper Maximus, and Gildo the commander in Africa had refused to support the eastern emperor (*De VI Cons. Hon.* 108–9). In fact this is the only *known* occasion when Alaric could have confronted Theodosius on the Hebrus while marching *away* from Thrace. If the encounter had taken place on Theodosius' return from the Maximus campaign, Alaric would have checked him coming *into* Thrace. Theodosius indeed was ambushed by Goths (Zosimus 4.49.2) on his return in the marshes of the Axios (Vardar) near Thessalonica, but this was on his way to Constantinople. Once he had returned to the capital he handed over campaigning to someone else, if Zosimus is telling the truth and the whole truth (Zosimus 5.50). The encounter between Theodosius and Alaric mentioned by Claudian is therefore unlikely to have occurred after the defeat of Maximus.

What was Alaric's position at the time of this encounter with Theodosius? Zosimus tells us that just before Theodosius set out on his campaign, an evidently considerable number of barbarians serving in Roman regular units deserted and fled to the marshes of Macedonia, that is, into what was then an area of lakes and swamps around the lower Axios and Strymon rivers (Zosimus 4.45.3, 48–9). It is possible that the engagement on the Hebrus was an incident in this episode. If this is right, Alaric would have been one of the leaders of the German (almost certainly Gothic) deserters, presumably having been one of their officers while they served in the Roman army: one of the very many Roman officers of German origin in the Roman army at that time (Waas, 1965).

This view of the start of Alaric's career must remain tentative because it is argued on the assumption that Zosimus gives a complete account of the campaigns of Theodosius I. This may well not be the case. It is for instance possible that, contrary to the information of Zosimus, Theodosius set out from Thrace to campaign once more after he had returned to Constantinople in November 391, and that the incident on the Hebrus occurred then (Wolfram, 1988: 136). In that case Alaric was probably the leader not of the deserters on the way to the marshes, but of one or several of the numerous bands of barbarians who had exploited the absence of Theodosius and his army in the west to raid Thrace (Claudian, *In Rufinum* 1.308–22, 332–3; *De Cons. Stil.* 1.94–115). These probably included considerable numbers of the Teruingi-Visigoths settled along the Danube (*De Cons. Stil.* 1.945–6).

If Alaric was leader of a group of Goths who had broken loose in 391 it is unlikely that he occupied the position by virtue of a hereditary king-like role among the Teruingi. Two arguments strongly suggest that he was no more than the successful leader of a war-band. First there is the fact that the historians who report the beginning of the long series of campaigns of Alaric's Goths in winter 394–5 evidently knew nothing about his past (Zosimus 5.5.3; Socrates 7.10). If Alaric had been really prominent before 394–5, Eunapius, or whatever other contemporary writer furnished information for Zosimus and Socrates, would surely have mentioned it. It is also significant that we are nowhere told the name of Alaric's father. According to Jordanes, Alaric's family, the Balthi (see stemma *PLRE* II 1332 no. 40), was the second noblest among the Goths (Jordanes, *Getica* 146). It is all the more remarkable that neither Jordanes (who was of course primarily the historian of Theoderic's family, the Amali (stemma: *PLRE* II 1330 no.37), nor Isidore, the historian of Alaric's descendants, the Visigothic kings of Spain, reports Alaric's pedigree. It looks as if Alaric was a *novus homo*, and that the Balthi became outstanding only through his own heroic achievements.

The next occasion we hear of Alaric, he has been transformed from an enemy into an officer of the emperor Theodosius. In 394 he commanded a force of Goths in the army that Theodosius led to Italy in order to overthrow the usurper Eugenius (Socrates 7.10; Zosimus 5.4). Alaric was not commander of all 20,000 Gothic federates – that was Gainas (Zosimus 4.57; Eunapius fr. 60; Jordanes, *Getica* 145). This meant that he commanded no more than a regiment, perhaps not much more than a few thousand men. Alaric (Zosimus 5.57; Eunapius fr. 60) did not have that command as a result of tribal rank: we are told that he had been appointed by Theodosius (Zosimus 5.4). In other words he served – possibly a second time – as a federate officer of Gothic origin leading a federate unit of Goths. It would be a plausible conjecture that Theodosius had finally come to terms with the barbarians in Thrace and the Macedonian marshes by incorporating many of the guerillas and their leaders into the Roman army.

Eugenius was duly defeated, and Alaric and his men – but not all the Gothic troops – were sent back to the east early in 395 (Zosimus 5.5; Claudian, *In Rufinum* 2.36ff.). This is the beginning of the continuous story of *Alaric's Goths*, and it is worthwhile to look at the event more precisely. Alaric's service in the war had been rewarded with a 'Roman dignity', but he was not satisfied (Socrates 5.10). One grievance was that he wanted to have regulars as well as federates under his command (Zosimus 5.5.4). Perhaps he was jealous of Gainas, who became commander-in-chief of the eastern units. The outcome was that Alaric and his men mutinied and invaded Thrace, threatening Constantinople (Zosimus 5.5.5). This invasion marks the beginning of the continuous history of Alaric's Goths. It is significant that, according to the sources, this mutiny was caused by the grievance of a federate officer in Roman service. There is no hint that Alaric was a tribal leader, or that he appealed to Goths settled in

Moesia. It is clear that this was a chaotic period in the eastern Balkans. Once more barbarians had made use of the absence of the imperial army – and also of the freezing of the Danube – to invade the Empire (Claudian, *In Rufinum* 2.27 ff.). Of Alaric it is said that he led the forces he had brought from Italy together with 'additional riff-raff' (Zosimus 5.5.4). None of the sources implies that Alaric's invasion of Thrace and Thessaly involved a breach of the treaty which Theodosius had made with the Goths in 382, and which had resulted in the settlement of at least some of them in Moesia.

So I would argue that what Alaric led into Thrace was essentially his regiment, enlarged by whatever individuals, irrespective of their origin, would join him, but not the mass of Goths settled in Moesia. Wolfram suggests that the Goths in Moesia might well have felt exposed and insecure, and thus have had a motive to abandon their settlements (Wolfram, 1988: 139f.), but neither he nor anybody else can produce positive evidence that they did abandon their settlements.

I have argued that the sources recording the start of Alaric's operations do not suggest that he was the leader of a people. The subsequent behaviour of him and his band during the next twenty-three years of adventures within the Empire is difficult to reconcile with the view that he was leading a people in search of lands. The story is a complicated one, a succession of military episodes interrupted by negotiations (Matthews, 1975: 284ff.; Liebeschuetz, 1990: 57ff.). But what to my mind is significant is that at no time before 418 is there unambiguous evidence that the Goths were seeking farm land. There is no space to go through the abortive diplomatic activity, but it is I think fair to say that what was discussed between Alaric and Roman leaders was that the Goths should be given a reward in corn or money, or both, in return for military service; i.e. discussion was about the conditions of service of a mercenary army (e.g. Zosimus 5.29.5, 36.1, 42.1, 48–51).

Negotiations involved the question of where the Goths were to be stationed (Zosimus 5.36.1, 48.3, 50.3). But this does not mean that there was a question of them settling on land which they would farm permanently. Zosimus here employs the word *oikein*, 'to dwell', and seems to use it in its narrowest sense of having somewhere to live. On two occasions we get brief glimpses of the Goths as it were 'dwelling' in garrisons rather than on the march, first in 398 in Epirus (Zosimus 5.26) or Macedonia (Claudian, *De Bell. Get.* 497: *Eumathia tutus tellure*), and later, in 414, at Bordeaux (Paulinus of Pella,

Eucharisticus, 285–90). During the first period they evidently did not farm land (they are contrasted with the Greutungi in Phrygia who did), but received arms from the arms factories in Thrace (Claudian, *In Eutropium* 2.196ff.). During the latter period they were billeted in houses. On both occasions they were treated not as a wandering peasant people, but as an army.

Similarly, what we learn about successive negotiations seems to be about pay and conditions of service, with the terms varying according to the relative strengths of the two parties at the moment. In 401 the Goths invaded Italy because the eastern government had stopped their customary *dona* (Jordanes, *Getica* 146). We don't know on what terms, if any, the Goths eventually withdrew from Italy. In 404 Stilicho made an alliance with Alaric, the terms of which stipulated that Alaric and his Goths would conquer eastern Illyricum for the west in return for pay. Alaric's Goths moved into Epirus to wait for the start of a campaign which, in the event, never took place, with the result that the Goths received no pay. In 408 Alaric demanded heavy compensation, threatening Italy (Zosimus 5.29.5). Stilicho, against heavy opposition, insisted that Alaric's terms should be accepted; he was going to use Alaric and his men to put down the usurper Constantine in Gaul. There followed the fall of Stilicho, which resulted in a great weakening of the Empire and strengthening of Alaric. Alaric moderately offered to continue the agreement made with Stilicho – only asking for a little more money.

There is no space to go through each of the succession of negotiations in detail. It is enough to list the points over which negotiations broke down. The emperor refused to hand over hostages (Zosimus 5.44.1). He agreed to make payments but refused to make Alaric a *magister militum* (Zosimus 5.48.4; Sozomen 9.7). He had sworn an oath not to make peace with Alaric (Zosimus 5.51.1). The puppet-emperor Attalus refused to send Goths as part of an expeditionary force to Africa (Zosimus 6.12). In fact the first time that land *for farming* was mentioned was in the course of negotiations in 416 (Olympiodorus fr. 26.2 = Philostorgius 12.4–5).

If the objective of the Goths had simply been to receive a settlement on safe land of the kind they eventually obtained, one wonders why the wanderings took so long. After all, the Romans had frequently settled large numbers of barbarians on land within their Empire. The long delay does call for explanation. Wolfram is forced to resort to such intangibles as the problems of how the imperial powers and a barbarian kingship could be reconciled on Roman soil (Wolfram, 1988: 160f.). There is something in this. But a simpler explanation would be that settlement had a very low priority for Alaric and his Goths. Their mobile existence – earning a living by the sword rather than the plough – was congenial and honourable (see Tacitus, *Germania* 14). Of course, it was an existence more enjoyable for young men than for men in late middle age. One suspects that the Goths agreed to be settled when their veteran leaders were beginning to feel too old for that kind of life. Twenty-three to twenty-five years is not too far from the period of service of a legionary.

Of course the number of men who served through the whole period of waiting will have been very small. Alaric's band must in any case have had a changing composition, growing in periods of success, shrinking after defeats or in famine. When he returned from the Eugenius campaign he presumably had not much more than a thousand. Clearly his band gained in strength during his successful march through Greece, and during the time when he was *magister militum per Illyricum*. He had heavy losses in battle and through desertion during his invasion of Italy (Claudian, *De Bell. Get.* 87–90; *De VI Cons. Hon.* 129–30, 309–15). The second invasion produced an enormous increase in numbers. He is said to have been joined by 30,000 federates of Stilicho (Zosimus 5.35–6), by fugitive slaves from Rome (Zosimus 5.42), and by a second large war-band under the leadership of Athaulf, his brother-in-law. His total strength is said to have gone up to 40,000 (Zosimus 5.42.3). After the sack of Rome, chronic supply difficulties in Italy, Gaul and Spain are likely to have reduced the force again. The 600,000 *modii* of corn promised to Wallia in 415 might have fed 20,000 for a year (Olympiodorus fr. 30). Quite apart from the losses through battles, desertion and shipwreck, Alaric's band must have had high casualties from disease, probably 3 per cent per year or more (see statistics of mortality in French, British and Russian armies in the eighteenth and nineteenth centuries in Urlanis, 1971: 229f., 233). The band must have had a very high turnover. But time, and danger jointly faced and Alaric's leadership made a nation of them.

Wolfram described the making of the new Gothic nation as 'ethnogenesis'. Of course this process did not start from scratch. Alaric's band possessed a sense of ethnic unity from the beginning. This was certainly deliberately cultivated during the period of wandering and subsequently. The group always thought of themselves as Goths, more precisely as *Vesi* (Sidonius, *Carm.* 2.377, 5.476ff., 7.399, 431), and Romans thought of them as descendants of the tribe that had been led into the Empire by Fritigern in 376 (Claudian, *De Bell. Get.* 166ff.). The tradition of common origin was confirmed by the preservation of Gothic as the national language, which was greatly helped by the fact that, thanks to Ulfila's translation of the Bible, it was the language of their version of Christianity (Thompson, 1966; Schäferdiek, 1970, 1976). Nevertheless, for many of Alaric's Goths the tradition of a common origin must have been a myth.

As we have seen, there is quite a lot of evidence that Alaric's Goths were able to absorb large numbers of outsiders, certainly Goths and other Germans but also – I would argue, though I cannot prove it – even Roman provincials (Fritigern's Goths were joined by slaves, miners and others: Ammianus 31.6.4–7, 7.7, 15.2). The absorption of outsiders into the 'tribe' must have been facilitated by the institution of the personal following (see regulations for *bucellarii* and *saiones* in *Leges Visig.* 1.3.1–4). It must also have been assisted by the fact that the Goths and other Germans had long been neighbours of the Roman empire, and subject to its cultural influences. Trade over a long period and, during the fourth century, recruitment into the Roman army had narrowed the cultural gap between the different barbarian tribes and between them and Romans (Scardigli, 1973; 1976). One wonders how much difference there was between peasants on the Roman and barbarian sides of the Danube.

Clearly the Romanization of the Goths and others intensified as they wandered through the Empire. And it is not surprising that the institutions created to hold the warrior-band together had a strong Roman element. It is certainly the case that the law code which Euric issued for his Gothic subjects contains a very strong infusion of vulgar Roman laws (Nehlsen, 1984; Wieacker, 1963, 1964) and must have been very different from the customs that had governed their lives east of the Danube.

The view of the ethnogenesis of Alaric's Goths put forward here has historic parallels. To cite J. M. Wallace-Hadrill: 'Warbands are tribes in the making' (Wallace-Hadrill, 1971: 11). The Normans, as a separate people distinct from Danes, Norwegians and Franks, date from Rollo's settlement in Normandy. The Normans were extremely mixed but the myth of common descent helped to make them into the formidable people that they became (Loud, 1982). It has recently been argued that the Ottoman Turks similarly grew out of multi-confessional polyglot war-bands, composed of an unlikely mixture of Turkish pastoralists and Byzantine peasants which crystallized around Osman, a great warrior and leader, who played a role like that which I have suggested for Alaric (Lindner, 1983: 32ff.)

Ibn Khaldun (1332–1406) observed the process of ethnogenesis among the tribesmen of Arab North Africa:

It is clear that a person of a certain descent may become attached to a people of another descent, either because he feels well disposed towards them, or because there exists an old alliance or client relationship, or yet because he has to flee from his own people because of a crime he has committed. Such a person comes to be known as having the same descent as those to whom he has attached himself, and is counted as one of them with respect to all things that result from common descent.

(Muquaddimah 267)

The time had been when Roman citizenship was so attractive that the inhabitants of the Empire, whether Gauls, Britons, Illyrians or North Africans, were eager to accept all the privileges and duties and patriotic emotions that went with it. In our period, Roman civilization, especially its language and Christian religion, still exerted great attraction, but Roman citizenship had ceased to do so entirely. If Roman citizenship had retained its attraction, the Goths and other Germans would after a few decades have become patriotic Romans, and the Empire would have re-emerged after a time, even in the provinces flooded by barbarians. Instead, patriotic community-building forces radiated from Germanic war-bands and emerging Germanic kingdoms, and the political unity of the Roman world was irreversibly broken.

CHAPTER 8

The emergence of the Visigothic kingdom

P. Heather

The Visigothic kingdom from Theoderic II and Euric onwards was a quite different entity from the allied army settled in south-west Gaul in 418. This chapter will attempt to explore how one evolved into the other.

FROM SETTLEMENT TO KINGDOM

Precisely what changed, then, between 418 and the emergence of a Visigothic kingdom? By war and diplomatic negotiation, an area of territory was defined over which the Visigothic monarch held sway from Toulouse (e.g. Wolfram, 1988: 173ff.). At least partly because of the available source material, an account of the military and diplomatic activity which defined the Visigothic kingdom tends to divide itself into two phases, the second of which begins with the 'great alliance' which defeated Attila in 451. Up to *c.* 450, we have little more than a few chronicle entries, which show the Goths active in two directions. Occasionally, Goths are found in Spain, where they tended to operate on the orders of the Roman state (Hydatius 77, 134). In southern Gaul, however, Goths attacked Arles in 425 and 430 (Prosper 1290; Hydatius 92), and between 436 and 439 there was a longer and seemingly more serious confrontation with the Empire. Arles was again attacked and Narbonne besieged in 436–7, but the Goths were then driven back to Toulouse by Litorius operating under the command of Aëtius. Litorius having been captured, an agreement restored peace (e.g., Wolfram, 1988: 175f.). We hear of no further trouble before 451.

We do not know precisely what was at stake in these disputes, although the Goths presumably wanted in some way to change the terms of their settlement. Merobaudes' second panegyric on Aëtius would imply that the Goths wanted extra territory (Clover, 1971: 50f., 56ff.), but panegyrics in favour of a particular protagonist are not a reliable guide to his opponents' motives. Nor is the fact that the Goths sometimes aimed for Arles a clear sign that they wanted access to the Mediterranean. Arles was the capital of the Gallic prefecture, and the Goths may simply have aimed to pose such a threat to the jugular of Roman administration in the area that the Empire would be forced to concede their demands. This had been Alaric's strategy in front of Rome (Matthews, 1975: 286ff.). Unfortunately, because we are ignorant of what the Goths were actually granted in 418 (cf. above, Burns, Nixon), it is hard to know what they may have felt themselves deprived of.

Whatever else they may have gained from these struggles, it was not extra land; nor, seemingly, was the Goths' ability to influence imperial politics increased. Theoderic I remained, without a generalship, perched on the edge of Roman territory beside the Atlantic ocean. Matters were transformed after 450, however, when the great alliance against Attila brought the Goths once again into the centre of imperial affairs. The subsequent end of the Theodosian dynasty in the west then left a power vacuum, and, as one of the major military forces on imperial soil, the Goths were an obvious potential ally for any pretender. As such, they could demand concessions as the price of their support.

Petronius Maximus was the first to approach them (Sidonius, *Carm.* 7.392ff.), they were major sponsors of Avitus (*Carm.* 7.508ff.), and Majorian felt it necessary to integrate them into his regime (Mathisen, 1979b: 618ff.). In return, the Goths seem to have extracted the right to intervene more freely in Spain; after 455, seemingly in co-operation with the Empire since Hydatius records armies with joint commanders (one Goth, one Roman; cf. Burgess, above pp. 24f.), the Goths destroyed the previously stable kingdom of the Sueves, conducting widespread and no doubt profitable warfare (Hydatius 170).

The reign of Libius Severus saw further advances. As the price of their support, they gained Narbonne in 462/3 (Hydatius 217). Severus' decision to cede Narbonne seems to have caused the Gallic army under Aegidius to revolt, affording the Goths further opportunities. Despite initial setbacks, they were able to move into the Loire valley after Aegidius' death (Wolfram, 1988: 180f.). At this point, Euric assassinated Theoderic II, but trod carefully until Anthemius' regime was emasculated by the fiasco of its Vandal expedition, and then dropped all pretence of obedience. By the late 470s, Euric had consolidated the vast majority of Spain, Provence, the Auvergne, and areas as far north as the Loire (Wolfram, 1988: 182ff.). A large territory had been carved out since *c.* 450 and independence asserted.

This brief sketch is not the full story of the emergence of the Gothic kingdom; the territory acquired had also to be governed, and the basic system closely followed its Roman predecessor. The pattern of provincial administration was retained, each province having its *rector* or *iudex.* These officials continued to occupy *praetoria,* and each employed bureaucratic assistants organized in *officia.* Within the city, most governmental business was the responsibility of the *defensor,* who was, at least notionally, elected by his fellow citizens (Jones, 1964: 257ff.). The Roman tax system, similarly, was left untouched, with specific reference in the sources to the land tax, customs tolls, and the *collatio lustralis;* money was delivered, of course, to the Visigothic court (Jones, 1964: 257ff.; cf. Nixon, above p. 72). In law too, the holdover from the Empire is very marked. Throughout Euric's reign, his non-Gothic subjects retained the Theodosian Code as their basic, or, at least, most up-to-date legal reference work. In 506 it was replaced by the Breviary of Alaric, but this was closely modelled on the Code. Much of the actual legislation, legal practice, and the legal principles it embodied were indistinguishable from Roman predecessors.

The origin of these sophisticated methods of government is Roman, and Romans continued to operate them for Gothic kings. The Preface to Alaric's Breviary, for instance, mentions the roles played in its formulation by Timotheus and Anianus (*PLRE* II, 90 and 1121). Again, Ruricius of Limoges mentions various Romans who were men of influence within the Visigothic kingdom after *c.* 480 (e.g. Elaphius, Praesidius, Rusticus and Eudomius: *Epp.* 2.7; 2.12; 2.20; 2.39 – cf. Caesarius of Arles, *Ep. ad Ruric.* 7). Men such as these were *iudices* and *rectores,* providing administrative know-how for Gothic kings (see Elton, below p. 174). The Visigothic kingdom had essentially two component parts, therefore: Gothic warriors and Roman administrators. The contribution of both requires further investigation.

THE GOTHS

Based on the sixth-century account of Jordanes' *Getica*, historians have seen the Visigoths as an ancient subdivision of the Gothic people. Jordanes, however, is deeply misleading, and more-contemporary Greco-Roman sources allow us to see that the Visigoths of 418 (more accurately the Visi or Vesi) were the product basically of an amalgamation of three previously independent Gothic groups: part of the so-called Tervingi, some Greuthungi (both of these had entered the Empire separately in 376), and a number of survivors from the force that Radagaisus had led to Italy in 405–6 (Wolfram, 1988: 117ff.; Heather, 1986a: 13ff.; Liebeschuetz, above – there are differences among these accounts).

Correspondingly, there was no direct continuity between the leaderships of these three major contributors and the dynasty which ruled in Gaul. None of those who led the three groups across the frontier managed to retain control in the first shock of contact with the Empire, and Alaric's extended career stabilized matters only in part. He definitively united the three groups contributing, and handed the leadership on to a designated and related successor: his brother-in-law Athaulf. Between them, these two leaders ruled for twenty years. In 415, however, opposition to Athaulf surfaced in a successful assassination attempt, probably organized by Sergeric, who slaughtered Athaulf's children. Sergeric in turn failed to retain power, and was murdered after only seven days, but his intervention had effectively destroyed nascent dynastic continuity (Olympiodorus fr. 26.1; cf. *PLRE* II, 978f.; Heather, 1986a: 28ff., 213ff.). He was succeeded by Wallia, who has no recorded family ties with preceding leaders. Only the thirty-three-year reign of Theoderic I finally established a Visigothic ruling dynasty. In part, Theoderic built on the legacy of Alaric and Athaulf because he married Alaric's daughter. But the reigns of Sergeric and Wallia had broken the dynastic pattern, and there is no reason to think that Theoderic was elected because he married Alaric's daughter (*PLRE* II, 1070f., 1332; cf. Claude, 1971: 35f.).

Against this background, the unity of the largely Gothic warriors who founded the kingdom is not the historical certainty it might at first seem. Paulinus of Pella, for instance, records that some Alans formed part of the force at one point, but eventually preferred to attach themselves to the small town of Bazas instead (*Eucharisticus*

377ff.). Possidius' *Life of Augustine* reports that some Goths accompanied the Vandals to North Africa (28.4), and it seems likely that they had originated with the Visigoths, but decided that life with the Vandals looked more promising. We also hear of a man called Vetericus, probably a Goth, who fought with the Romans against Theoderic I in 439 (Prosper 1337). In fact, one of the prime reasons for leading Gothic nobles to appear in Roman society was that they had had to flee the results of leadership struggles. This is true of Fravittas and Sarus, of the family of Aëtius' Gothic wife – since, although of royal stock, her son was 'barred from the Gothic throne' (Sidonius, *Carm.* 5.203f.; cf. Clover, 1971: 27ff.); and it may also have been the reason why Ricimer, grandson of the Visigothic king Wallia (Sidonius, *Carm.* 2.361f.), pursued an entirely Roman career. In talking about a band of Goths under one Anaolsus rampaging in the vicinity of Arles in 430 (92), Hydatius may thus be indicating that this was the independent action of a sub-group, rather than a confrontation between the Visigoths and the Roman state.

Correspondingly, the fact that Theoderic I reigned for an exceptional period and passed on power to his sons must not mislead us into thinking that internal politics were anything but unruly. Theoderic's sons succeeded to the throne by murdering one another (refs. in *PLRE* II, 1072 and 1116). The political experiment of Theoderic II is also relevant. In this, another brother, Frederic, was given a recognized share of power (e.g. Sidonius, *Carm.* 7.431ff.; cf. Harries, 1981: 188ff.; Wolfram, 1988: 178f.), surely in an attempt to forestall any fraternal resentment which might have led to Theoderic's murder. He would have been well-advised to extend this to his other brother, Euric, who eventually murdered him.

These royal murders involved something more than fraternal rivalry. A century later, when the centre of Visigothic power had shifted to Spain, a powerful and fractious Gothic nobility was the main cause of intense dynastic instability (Claude, 1971: 36ff.). Less is heard of Gothic nobles in the fifth century, but this is primarily the result of a paucity of sources, and they clearly did exist. Non-royal Goths commanded in Spain (e.g. Suniericus, Heldefredus, Gauterit: *PLRE* II, 1040; 529; 496), Merobaudes describes Goths fighting without their king between 436 and 439 (Clover, 1971: 32ff.), and Sidonius indicates that important non-royal Goths were consulted by the king and exercised patronage (*Carm.* 7.441ff., *Ep.* 1.2.9). It seems probable, therefore, that behind the murders of Thorismud and Theoderic II lay the factional divisions of important Gothic nobles.

Both the Visigoths and their ruling dynasty were recent creations. This combines with the plentiful evidence for dispute and division among the Goths to make it clear that their allegiance to the kingdom cannot simply be taken for granted. The same is even more true of the second major group of contributors to the Visigothic kingdom: Roman administrators.

GOTHIC KINGS AND ROMAN ADMINISTRATORS

It is remarkable that educated Romans should have played a major role in the creation of the Visigothic kingdom. The general attitude of Roman culture before *c.* 400 towards tribal peoples was far from welcoming (e.g. Teillet, 1984: 47ff.; cf. Dauge, 1981: esp. 677ff.).

For the earlier phases up to *c.* 450, the sources prompt a number of observations on how the Gallo-Roman elite came to be involved with Goths. Some sought to use the Goths as a weapon in their political disputes with the central imperial authorities. Thus the 'Gothic usurper' Attalus, when his cause was revived by Athaulf in the 410s, attracted the support of a section of the Gallo-Roman aristocracy. A certain Ingenuus hosted Athaulf's marriage to Galla Placidia (Olympiodorus fr. 24); Orosius reports his conversation with another Gallic aristocrat who, perhaps to avoid the political fall-out, left for the Holy Land when the usurpation collapsed (7.43.4; cf. Hunt, below p. 273); and Paulinus of Pella held office (*Eucharisticus* 290ff.). Men such as these saw the Goths as a bulwark for a regime that would propel them into power, although mixed motives must have operated. Paulinus of Pella is not necessarily lying when he claims that he became involved with Attalus because he thought it overridingly important to make peace with the Goths.

After 418, economic reasons dictated that any Gallo-Roman with estates in the Garonne had to enter into relations with the Goths or leave (cf. Mathisen, 1984: 159f.; below p. 229). Much of Paulinus of Pella's patrimony, for instance, was situated in areas around Bordeaux that were now dominated by the Goths, and this was perhaps the primary reason why his sons migrated to the Visigothic court (*Eucharisticus* 499ff.). The unexpected arrival of payment from a

Goth for one of Paulinus' former farms may have been the result of some successful lobbying (Paulinus reports that one of his sons experienced both the good and bad side of the Visigothic king: *Eucharisticus* 570ff., cf. 514f.). Salvian, perhaps not very trustworthily, claims that many, including even educated men, had moved to the Visigothic court because of financial pressures (*De Gub. Dei* 5.5ff.). Sidonius also carefully emphasizes that Avitus, while well received at the court of Theoderic I, behaved like a proper Roman, and rejected financial inducements to become too closely associated with the Gothic king (*Carm.* 7.213–29).

Another kind of involvement was quite involuntary; hostages were exchanged. We know of only one Gallo-Roman hostage at Theoderic's court – Theodorus, a friend of Avitus – and it is not certain when precisely he was at Toulouse (Sidonius, *Carm.* 7.213ff.; cf. *PLRE* II, 1087). Yet Theodorus' predicament is symbolic of the whole situation in the Garonne valley and adjacent areas of south-west Gaul. Whether local Gallo-Romans liked it or not, Goths had been planted upon them, and they had to preserve themselves in this new situation. Again Paulinus of Pella illustrates the point; when the Goths evacuated Bordeaux, his house was sacked because he had no Goths billeted on him to provide protection (*Eucharisticus* 285ff.). The lands of Roman aristocrats were henceforth the battlefield in Gotho-Roman disputes, and they had every interest both in conciliating the Goths and preventing further disputes. Thus we find bishop Orientus of Auch acting for Theoderic I before Roman generals in the 430s (*V. Orientii* 3, 5).

Between 418 and 450, some relationships grew up of necessity, but we do not hear of important Romans acting as the king's close advisers, or serving him in military capacities as they were to do later. In part, this may be due to the paucity of sources, but there is some fragmentary evidence which might suggest that the silence is significant, and that before *c.* 450 there was no close alliance of Goth and important Gallo-Roman. For Pontius Leontius, the leading aristocrat of the Garonne valley, Sidonius gives no indication that he moved in Visigothic court circles (*Ep.* 8.11, 12; *Carm.* 22). That he continued to live in the luxury of his castle villa suggests that he may have reached an accommodation with the Goths, but he is not found actively involved in their cause. Second, Sidonius' description of Theoderic II's court in *c.* 455 does not hint of a major Roman presence, although his focus was admittedly on the Gothic king himself (*Ep.* 1.2). Third, men who were later to figure at the Visigothic court are still to be found active in Roman circles in the 450s. In 458, for instance, Lampridius from Bordeaux, actually in Gothic territory, attended a gathering at Lyon where Majorian seems to have been trying to conciliate former supporters of Avitus (Mathisen, 1979b: 611ff.). He was still in Majorian's entourage in 460, and appears among the Goths only in 476. Similarly, Leo of Narbonne, later to be Euric's chief adviser, continued to live in Narbonne in the 460s (Sidonius, *Carm.* 23.446), and is recorded among the Goths only later (*PLRE* II, 662f).

If this evidence is significant, then a likely cause of the lack of closer relations is that the annual *Concilium* of the Gauls had continued to function. As many have remarked, it can be no accident that this council was given new life at precisely the moment the Goths were settled in Gaul (cf. Wood, above p. 15). Apart from conciliating Gallo-Roman opinion (Matthews, 1975: 333f.), the council was probably also designed, more generally, to keep loyalties firmly focused on the Empire. I would suggest that its specific aim was to counter the dangerous phenomenon witnessed in Gaul in the 410s when Roman aristocrats had combined with Gothic soldiers to create alternative imperial regimes. This happened not only in the case of Attalus; Athaulf had also supported the usurper Jovinus in 411–12 (Olympiodorus fr. 18, 20.1). This is the most obvious kind of threat that an institution such as the Gallic council was suitable for preventing. It demanded representatives from every class of political importance in the region: governors, decurions and ex-officials. The lack of any further Gallic usurpers basing themselves on Gothic military support between 418 and 450 may be a sign that it kept the minds of these men firmly concentrated on Rome.

After 450, the writings of Sidonius illustrate how an ever-larger proportion of the political classes of southern Gaul was drawn into the Gothic orbit, as the Goths participated more centrally in imperial politics (cf. Mathisen, below p. 232). The basic process is well known, and I will therefore just highlight some major developments. First, from the early 460s, we find Romans holding military offices to which they had been appointed by Gothic kings. Arborius, for instance, was appointed by Theoderic II to replace Majorian's nominee, Nepotianus, in Spain after the emperor's assassination (Hydatius 213; cf. Harries, 1981: 4f.). From the 460s a succession of Romans entered Gothic military employ (cf. Burgess, above p. 25;

Elton, below p. 174; Teitler, below p. 317). Vincentius, perhaps an imperial *magister militum* in 465, was by 477 Euric's *dux Hispaniae* (*PLRE* II, 1168). Victorius was Euric's commander in Gaul in the early 470s (*PLRE* II, 1162–4), when Calminius also served with Gothic forces (Sidonius, *Ep.* 5.12). By the late 470s, Namatius was likewise commanding forces designed to counter Saxon pirates (Sidonius, *Ep.* 8.6).

Second, we hear of disaffected Roman officials negotiating with the Goths (cf. below, Harries, Teitler). In 468, the newly reappointed praetorian prefect of Gaul, Arvandus, wrote to Euric telling him to throw off the rule of Anthemius and divide up Gaul with the Burgundians (Sidonius, *Ep.* 1.7.5). Disenchantment with the central imperial regime seems to have been the motive here, but it has also been suggested that Arvandus' move was part of an abortive plot hatched by Ricimer (Stevens, 1933: 106ff.). Shortly afterwards, Sidonius' correspondence records outrage at another imperial official, Seronatus, possibly *vicarius* to the Gallic prefect, who visited Euric on several occasions, encouraging him in the same direction as Arvandus (*PLRE* II, 995f.). The final stage of development came with Romans holding high civilian appointments under Gothic kings. The first known from the sources is Leo of Narbonne, Euric's chief adviser by the mid 470s (*PLRE* II, 662f.).

The brief reign of Avitus, it seems, was a crucial catalyst. Avitus was from a distinguished Gallo-Roman family and held commands under Aëtius, culminating in the Gallic prefecture in 439. He returned to public life in the 450s, and was sent on a mission to enlist Gothic support for Petronius Maximus. The latter died, however, while Avitus was still at the Gothic court, and his elevation to the purple took place first among the Goths, before being confirmed by leading Gallo-Romans at Arles on 9 July 455 (*PLRE* II, 196–8). His regime was thus an alliance of Goths and Gallo-Roman aristocrats. It was at this point that Sidonius wrote his favourable description of Theoderic II and the panegyric of Avitus, which allocates much praise to the Gothic king (and his brother), and he also went on missions to the Gothic court (*Ep.* 1.2, *Carm.* 7; see also Mathisen, 1981a: 233f.). Short-lived as it was, the regime of Avitus brought Goth and Gallo-Roman together again in political alliance for the first time since the 410s. As other imperial regimes bought Gothic support, they further legitimized the Goths' position: Majorian sanctioned joint campaigns, and Libius Severus ceded them Narbonne (above). This greatly eased the transition of Romans into Gothic service.

Unlike the 410s, furthermore, no Fl. Constantius was able to check the Empire's political fragmentation, so that, as Gothic influence continued to increase, more Romans were encouraged to take up service with the Goths. Sidonius is surely hinting at this kind of development when he comments, perhaps ironically, on how sensible it is of Namatius (Gothic commander against the Saxons) to follow 'the standards of a victorious people' (*Ep.* 8.6.16). In addition, recent studies have stressed how competitive were the lives of Gallo-Roman aristocrats; that is, they were constantly in dispute with one another for prestige and financial gain (Van Dam, 1985: 57ff.; Brown, 1982; Harries, 1981: 77ff.). In circumstances in which Gothic power was increasing, and had, to an extent, been legitimized, it was natural to look to the Goths for assistance (cf. Harries, 1981: 184ff.).

While some were willing to work with Gothic kings, however, others were not, especially if the Goths threw off their allegiance to the Empire. Sidonius is representative of this strand of opinion. He was happy to work with and even praise the Goths when they were a plank of Avitus' regime, and was willing to accept Gothic territorial extensions, such as the ceding of Narbonne, if they were legitimized by the Empire, but when the Goths took over southern Gaul without authorization, he resisted. His chief collaborators were Ecdicius, son of Avitus, and Eucherius (*PLRE* II, 384; cf. Sidonius, *Ep.* 3.8; Harries, 1981: 197ff.). For these Romans the Goths were acceptable as allies but not an alternative to the Empire (cf. Mathisen, 1984: 166ff.).

These men had counterparts before 450. Rutilius Namatianus mentions Protadius and Victorinus, who abandoned estates in southern Gaul altogether rather than accommodate themselves to the Goths, Protadius, at least, accepting a drop in income (*De Redito Suo* 1.495f., 542, 551–8; cf. Mathisen, 1984: 161f.; below, pp. 229f.). In the Holy Land, Jerome knew a lady called Artemia, whose estates had been devastated by barbarians, and who wanted her husband Rusticius to join her, abandoning his attempts to reclaim their lands (Jerome, *Ep.* 118, 122; cf. Mathisen, 1984: 162ff., Hunt, below p. 271). Even in 417, Rutilius Namatianus hoped to see the Goths bow their heads and pay tribute in servitude to Rome (*De Redito Suo* 1.141ff.). This kind of sentiment balances more recent accounts which have stressed the smoothness of the process by which 'barbarians' occupied former imperial territories (e.g. Goffart, 1980: 3ff.; Geary, 1988: 5ff.).

CONCLUSION

Tracing some of the means whereby partly legitimized Gothic power insinuated itself into the lives of the Roman aristocracy of southern Gaul explains the 'when' and the 'how' of the alliance which created the Visigothic kingdom. It does not explain 'why'. The Roman aristocrats of southern Gaul – even Sidonius himself it seems after his brief, enforced exile – were willing to accommodate themselves to Gothic power if they had to, but why did they have to? The answer, of course, lies in the worsening strategic situation of the western empire which made it no longer willing or able to defend Gaul. Left to itself, the local nobility simply had to accommodate itself to Gothic power.

Thus Gallic events can be understood only in a much broader context, and the political disintegration of the western empire after *c.* 450 must not be taken for granted. The propaganda of the regimes of both Majorian (Sidonius, *Carm.* 5, esp. 53ff., 305ff., 385ff., 510ff.) and Anthemius (Sidonius, *Carm*, 2.478ff.) declares that they will address themselves to the reconquest of Vandal Africa, and both, particularly Anthemius in alliance with Constantinople, made major efforts to achieve precisely that (e.g. Courtois, 1955: 98ff.). They failed, but Justinian shows that reconquering Africa was not impossible. Had Anthemius defeated the Vandals, as well he might with eastern help, then could a western empire, reinvigorated with African revenues, have reasserted itself in Gaul? I can see no obvious reason why not.

III

The immediate crisis: 406–418

The barbarian invasions of 406–7, Roman civil wars from 406 to 413, and the movement of the Goths across the south of the country into Spain and back again could not have left Gaul and its population unscathed. Confirmation of Gallic suffering, and an insight into local reaction to it, is offered by *Roberts'* study of three Christian poems, all probably composed in south-western Gaul in the period *c*. 409–16 and all of which therefore predate and provide the literary context for Orientius' more famous *Commonitorium*. They present a very sorry picture of the condition of Gaul in the decade or so after the Alanic, Suevic and Vandal incursion, for they describe a society completely traumatized by the wholesale and indiscriminate destruction of its human and material resources; we read of fortunes lost, villas ruined, fields empty and urban settlements captured, sacked and put to the torch. War, disease and famine have already caused the deaths of many; and no one can be sure that the troubles are over.

We cannot, of course, unthinkingly accept the complete reliability of this tale of disaster. Apart from the natural human propensity to exaggerate distress, and the fact that the three writers concerned here could not have known of the partial recovery to come (an observation of some pertinence if the composer of the *Carmen ad Uxorem* really was the same Prosper who would later give a much more positive account of early fifth-century history: see Muhlberger), these three, closely related poems must be recognized as unashamedly moralizing works, which sought to remind Christians of the vanity of human ambition in a transient world. As Wood has pointed out, Gallic Christian writers of the first half of the fifth century shared a common ascetic tradition, which inclined them to emphasize contemporary misfortunes in order to point up contemporary moral decay. Nevertheless, their general message of unhappiness rings true – and the more so because the *Epigramma Paulini* contains a passing reference to efforts already being made to repair the material damage (cf. Drinkwater).

This last point brings us to the strategies that the Gauls adopted in response to a changing world, which are of course particularly significant for any consideration of whether the fifth century saw these people undergoing a 'crisis of identity' in respect of the Roman empire. In this regard, Roberts identifies two further aspects of great importance to this theme. He observes that there are strong hints that the writers of both the *Epigramma Paulini* and the *Carmen de Providentia Dei* shared a local patriotism. We find them urging that, having morally re-armed themselves, the Gauls could and should take a more direct responsibility for their own defence against the detested barbarians; and that, properly supported by its inhabitants, Gaul would rise again. On the other hand, Roberts notes the more negative view of the *Carmen ad Uxorem*, which preaches that the most prudent response to the troubles of the age is, if possible, to distance oneself from them but, if they happen to befall one, to endure them in the manner of a latter-day martyr. The phenomenon of aristocratic rejection of the world, in favour of a life of Christian devotion, is examined later in this volume by Wes, in a section where the early fifth-century options of 'self-help' and flight are addressed directly.

CHAPTER 9

Barbarians in Gaul: the response of the poets

M. Roberts

'All Gaul was filled with the smoke of a single funeral pyre.' This line from a poem of Christian moral exhortation, the *Commonitorium* of Orientius (2.184), is the best-known poetic response to the invasions of the fifth century (cf. Hunt, below pp. 266f.). It is a favorite quotation in modern histories of the period. Less well known are three poems which predate the *Commonitorium* and provide the literary historical context for Orientius' work. They are the pseudonymous *Epigramma Paulini*, written after the initial invasion of Suevi, Vandals and Alans in 406–7 but before the coming of the Visigoths, the *Carmen ad Uxorem*, generally attributed to Prosper of Aquitaine and also probably early, and the *Carmen de Providentia Dei* (hereafter *CPD*), a larger work of Christian didactic, which must date to the second half of the second decade of the fifth century (Courcelle, 1964: 85ff., 96ff.; Fontaine, 1981: 230f., 238ff.). All three poems provide an immediate Christian response to the disturbed circumstances of early fifth-century Gaul. They constitute, along with the *Commonitorium*, a self-contained corpus, addressing similar issues and probably written in the same milieu and for similar audiences (cf. Wood, above p. 10).

The *Epigramma Paulini* is probably the earliest of the poems under discussion. It was written in the immediate aftermath of the invasion of Alans and Vandals, who are referred to by name in the poem (19). The *Epigramma* is in dialogue form, and has a monastic setting. The bulk of the text is made up of two speeches by a certain Salmo, who has returned to the community of which he was once a part, to be welcomed by the head of the monastery (unnamed) and his companion, Thesbon (1–5). Salmo denounces the degeneracy of the secular world in which he now finds himself (10–51 and 55–95). Although the literary fiction is that Salmo's speeches are addressed to the two monks, the readership intended for the poem presumably includes those *saeculares* whose degeneracy Salmo describes, as well, no doubt, as the many pious lay Christians who can still be found, he admits (98), among so much decadence (cf. Salvian, ed. Lagarrigue, 1975: 17).

What is the relevance, then, of the invasions to this denunciation of immorality? In the main, 'Paulinus' uses contemporary events as a foil to intensify the force of his preaching rather than accommodating his message to make recent experience intelligible in Christian terms. His argument depends on the comparison between the recent warfare with the barbarians and the spiritual warfare every Christian must wage with the forces of sin. It is developed antithetically, in three stages: (i) 10–17, only recently (*nunc primum*, 11) have solidly constructed villas been destroyed, but the assaults of the enemy within are of long standing (*olim*, 16); (ii) 18–25, despite the uncertain future and difficulty of the task, we strive to repair the damage caused by the invasions, but our spiritually derelict state is entirely neglected and in defeatist mood we readily surrender ourselves into captivity, as sin's prisoners; and (iii) 26–9, a repetition of the previous point exploiting the metaphors of spiritual husbandry and architecture: though we clear overgrown vineyards, restore doors and replace windows, the 'broad plains of the soul' (28) and 'palaces of the heart' (28) receive no cultivation or repair. 'We are, as we always were', 'Paulinus' concludes, 'subject to the same faults: neither sword, nor the threat of famine, nor disease has made any difference' (30–1).

This final statement returns to the point of the first antithesis. Barbarian invasions and the accompanying material destruction are recent events; neglect of spiritual welfare is of long standing. Efforts to re-build after the invasion are further evidence of the preference for the material and perishable over abiding spiritual values. From this perspective, invasion has indeed made no difference to the underlying moral condition of Gaul. There is no suggestion, as there is in Salvian, that the invasions are punishment for sinfulness. But it is implied that recent events should provide an incentive to moral improvement by demonstrating the transience of material possessions (12–13). Salmo's second speech ends with a description of the benefits to be won from such a change of heart: 'if we changed our ways and adopted a healthy cast of thought, if our mind was freed of dark mists and was cleared and open to Christ, if we put the scythe of the Word to the heart and were ready to cut from there the entanglements of ancient faults, no force could prevail against the servants of Christ'. He goes on to be more specific about the advantages of such spiritual health. Unfortunately, the text here is lacunose. There can be little doubt, however, that among the forces rendered ineffectual by such a change of heart are the invading Alans and 'those who now behave lawlessly, made arrogant by our disaster' (95). The point may be purely otherworldly: spiritual regeneration deprives suffering in this world of its power to hurt. But the passage would certainly bear the interpretation that such a moral revival will also bring real success in this world in resisting the barbarians and those who have benefited from their invasions. The language of moral husbandry and cultivation used in this passage to describe the achievement of mental health intentionally recalls the beginning of Salmo's first speech. There the speaker protests against the defeatist passivity (24) with which his fellow countrymen surrender their necks to chains and their hands to fetters as spoils of sin (25). The passage overtly describes the mental health of the society in which Salmo moves. But the language used reflects and derives its emotional force from the poet's reaction to the real failure of his native Gaul to resist the barbarians. The main force of the *Epigramma* is moral and spiritual. Not far below the surface, however, is a strain of Gallo-Roman patriotism that calls for resistance in this world to the recent onslaught and its effects.

Prosper's poem to his wife, probably roughly contemporary with the *Epigramma*, is very different in tone from the poem of 'Paulinus'. It is a poetic epistle with a strong element of personal confession, announcing the poet's determination to devote his life to Christ and urging his wife to join him in that undertaking. The life he anticipates is that of the *conversus* (Griffe, 1964–6: III, 128ff.), the lay convert to an ascetic lifestyle, who, like Sulpicius Severus, might withdraw to his own estate to practise his new manner of life, and, like Paulinus of Nola, might continue to live with his wife in continence. Much of the poem would be applicable to any period. Contemporary events, however – the invasions – provide the immediate impulse to conversion and give special urgency to Prosper's confession of faith. The poem begins with a lyric declaring the collapse of 'the frame of the fragile world' and the fugitive nature of wealth and power, followed by a fuller tableau of contemporary conditions (17–30), composed in elegiacs, the metre of the rest of the poem:

He who once turned the soil with a hundred ploughs, now labors to have just a pair of oxen; the man who often rode through splendid cities in his carriages now is sick and travels to the deserted countryside wearily and on foot. The merchant who used to cleave the seas with ten lofty ships now embarks on a tiny skiff, and is his own helmsman. Neither country nor city is as it was; everything rushes headlong to its end.

Prosper's categorization of the ranks in society affected by the invasions follows the standard categories of Roman moral philosophy (e.g. Horace, *Sat.* 1.1.4–12). His main point is that made in the preceding lyric: the emptiness of worldly show (12). Like 'Paulinus', he sums up his tableau of decline in an enumerating generalization: 'with sword, plague, starvation, chains, cold and heat – in a thousand ways – a single death snatches off wretched humankind' (25–6). The language is exaggerated, but is evidence of the powerful effect recent devastation has had on the minds of the Gallo-Romans. War is everywhere, war-frenzy grips everyone (27), and then a specific detail: 'with countless weapons kings fall upon kings' (27–8), a reference to fighting between barbarian kings. The spectacle of warfare and its attendant evils, in particular of the mutability of human prosperity, becomes the impulse for the poet's conversion. By adjusting his spiritual horizons the poet is able to transcend the sufferings of this world: exile and starvation are no longer causes for fear (97–8). Indeed, the experience of exile can stand by metaphor for the real situation of the Christian in this world. He is a 'citizen of another country' (104), a 'soldier in the service of Christ, bidden to pass as alien through this world in decline' (105–6; cf. Fontaine, 1981: 233). If 'Paulinus' aspires to a patriotic revival in this world, all Prosper's hopes are transferred to the world to come. The patience to endure suffering becomes, in this scheme of things, a positive value, evidence of an individual's devotion to the standard of Christ. It is scarcely surprising that Prosper represents his new resolve in terms of martyrdom, the exemplary Christian instance of the transcendence of earthly suffering by mental adherence to heaven (94). The punishments enumerated, torture, dismemberment, imprisonment, execution, are the standard constituents of the late antique martyr narrative. We need not assume, with Courcelle (1964: 86), that Prosper is anticipating the same punishments from the barbarians. Such sufferings are to be understood figuratively. They stand metonymically for any and all physical sufferings incurred in the service of Christ. Again, Prosper has spiritualized contemporary experience. The Christians of his own day re-enact in their tribulations the experience of the great heroes of the post-Biblical world, the martyrs, just as in their exile they repeat the exiles of the Jewish patriarchs described in the Old Testament (105).

The *Carmen de Providentia Dei* is a lengthy didactic poem treating for the most part the question of God's providential care for humankind, which the events of the early fifth century in Gaul had called into question. The poem has been attributed to Prosper of Aquitaine, but, because of some suggestions of semi-Pelagianism, this attribution has been doubted and its authorship remains an open question. The date of the *CPD* is easier to establish. In verses 33–4 there is a reference to 'ten years of slaughter' by the swords of Vandals and Goths, which would give a date in 416, or soon thereafter. Probably, like the two shorter poems already discussed, the *CPD* was written in south-west Gaul, though there are no precise geographic references (McHugh, 1964: 19).

Many of the themes already encountered recur in the *CPD*: the contrast between the eternal and the transitory (10), and the picture of a broken world (7). In describing 'the image of a smoking homeland' ('patriae ... fumantis imago', 17), the poet of the *CPD* has coined a phrase that Orientius was to improve on in the *Commonitorium*. The Gallic countryside, we are told, has been devastated by 'fire and flood' (14, 29–32). When it comes to the 'ten years of slaughter' of the Vandals and Goths, however, it is the urban, human side that is emphasized: 'fortresses on crags, towns on lofty mountains, cities on rivers that lead to the sea', all are unable to resist the onslaught; 'the suffering is extreme'. This is hyperbole, but not without historical basis, for all that. The impression that the destruction is universal is created by describing the effect of the barbarian onslaught at two geographical extremes: the heights of mountains and the depths of valleys. The implication, i.e. the rhetorical meaning, is that all sites between the two extremes are captured. The historical foundation for this is that instances must be known to the poet of hill-top fortresses and towns, and of cities in river valleys which had fallen to the barbarians. The rhetorical reading of the passage conveys the mood of Gaul's beleaguered inhabitants, the historical the facts that gave rise to this mood.

What, however, is particularly disturbing to the Gallo-Roman observer, and gives rise to the questioning of divine providence, is that the misery is indiscriminate (39); the suffering was 'confused and without order' (62). Between these introductory and concluding statements is a roll-call of elements in society affected by the invasion, arranged according to degree of holiness. Those of more advanced years might have done something to merit punishment from God, but innocent boys and girls? What crime had they committed (41–4)? And, if the suffering of secular society could seem undeserved, how much more would this be true of the religious realm? Churches are burnt and liturgical vessels desecrated (45–6); virgins and widows find no protection in their special status (47–8); hermits lose their lives in the general slaughter; and bishops suffer beatings and imprisonment (49–56). The passage ends with the particular case of an unnamed bishop who had been forced to abandon his burning city with his flock, a homeless refugee (57–60). The story would presumably be known to the *CPD*'s readers – though modern historians have disagreed about the identity of the bishop (Courcelle, 1964: 97; Griffe, 1964–6: II, 23). It provides a fitting vignette to fix in the mind and make memorable the point of the preceding development. The social hierarchy, secular and especially religious, attested by the passage is contradicted by the experience of suffering under the barbarian invasions: all now is confusion and without order.

This apparent disorder gives rise to the question that the poet of the *CPD* proposes to address. At the end of the poem he comes back to the conditions of fifth-century Gaul, thereby returning also to the considerations which gave rise to the poem's composition. In the process many of the themes occur which we have already identified in 'Paulinus' and Prosper. The contrasting of the perishable (*CPD* 870 and 938–9) and the eternal is found in all three poems and is a natural Christian reaction to the spectacle of destruction which confronted the Gallic poets. Like Prosper, the *CPD* poet assimilates the experience of contemporary Christians to that of the martyrs: life in fifth-century Gaul is a contest (912) that leads to the heavenly reward of crown (*corona*, 852 and 900) or palm (873). In this respect it is analogous to the struggle with sin and temptation which every Christian must undergo in this world – the 'daily martyrdom' of Christian homiletic – which continues irrespective of external historical circumstances and which is described in the *CPD* in similar language: the Christian must 'fight the contest of virtue' (605) to win 'the crown above' (604–5).

The most striking coincidences in this concluding section of the *CPD*, however, are with the *Epigramma Paulini*. The poet elaborates on the contrast between the transitory and the eternal by imagining the reaction various individuals would have to material loss: 'one laments the loss of gold and silver; a second is tortured by the carrying off of furniture [*suppellex*, i.e. movable property] and necklaces that have now been shared among Visigothic brides; a third is moved by the appropriation of his livestock, the burning of his houses, the drinking of his wine, the tears of his children and the shabby state of his servants' (903–7). The passage enumerates the property and personnel of a rich Gallo-Roman estate in the early fifth century, of the kind, perhaps, that Paulinus of Pella was so reluctant to abandon to the Visigoths (*Eucharisticus* 202–19). In contrast, 'the wise servant of Christ has lost none of these things, which he scorns; his riches are already stored up in heaven. Whatever befalls him in the storms which beset the world, he will undergo it fearlessly' (908–11).

The passage goes on as follows:

But you, who weep over overgrown fields, deserted courtyards and the crumbling terraces of a burnt-out villa, shouldn't you rather shed tears for your own losses, when you look at the desolate recesses of your heart, the beauty covered over with layers of grime, and the enemy rioting in the citadel of your imprisoned mind? If that citadel hadn't been surrendered, with every door opened wide, and hadn't provided kindling for the torches that wreaked its own destruction, these beauties created by the hand would still remain to bear witness to the virtue of a holy people. But since they lie prostrate in shapeless ruin they represent to us our misfortune as well as theirs. And so let us, a captive band, lament in the hall of the devastated heart these ruins of churches and graves of the powerful, which lie in random array, we who once were the brilliant vessels of God and the holy altars and shrines of Christ. (913–28)

The passage follows a development very similar to the beginning of Salmo's first speech in the *Epigramma Paulini*. The desolation of the Gallic countryside is described, overgrown fields, abandoned and destroyed buildings (913–14). The argument is an *argumentum ex minore*: 'if you weep for these, how much the more should you weep for your inner desolation of heart?'. The same point is made, in the same way, in the *Epigramma*, except that there the poet is able to cite the rebuilding activities taking place on the Gallic properties. There is even a striking coincidence of wording. McHugh (1964: 376) notes that the sense 'terrace' for *proscaenia* in the phrase *exustae proscaenia diruta villae* (914) occurs nowhere else in Latin literature. This is not quite accurate. The *Epigramma Paulini* has the following pair of lines:

[nec ...] nunc prosunt structae solido de marmore villae
absumptaeque omnes vana in proscaenia rupes (13–14).

Griffe (1956: 190) translates line 14: 'bien inutiles aussi ces blocs de roche employés à bâtir les frivoles théâtres', that is, he gives *proscaenia* its normal theatrical sense. While the Latin in isolation could certainly have that sense, I think in context it is better to take *proscaenia* as 'villa-terraces' and understand the two lines as an example of theme and variation. Both refer to building material (*solido de marmore, rupes*) and structure (*villae, proscaenia*). The rare word is, as often in such cases, explained by a word in the same context that is closely related to it in sense. In this case *proscaenia* bears a synecdochic relationship to *villae*. The author of the *CPD* must have understood *proscaenia* in the *Epigramma* in this way. He incorporates into a context which shows other parallels in sense with the earlier poem the unambiguous phrase *proscaenia ... villae*. In the *Epigramma* we are perhaps to think of villas built into or on mountain sides, where the mountain acts as backdrop (*scena*) for the villa buildings.

Like 'Paulinus', too, the author of the *CPD* exploits various metaphors for the spiritual life to elaborate on the parallels between the state of the world and the state of the soul. Both speak of a captive mind (*Epigramma Paulini* 29; *CPD* 918); 'Paulinus' talks of the 'palaces of the heart' (28), the *CPD* of 'the hall of the devastated heart' (926). The metaphor of spiritual architecture, present in subdued form in the earlier poem, receives ample treatment in the *CPD* (Lagarrigue, 1983: 138f.). Because the soul can be described as a temple or hall, the presence of ruined buildings in the Gallic countryside can bear a spiritual interpretation; such ruins are evidence not just of the material decline of the Gallo-Roman world, but also, understood metaphorically, are a reminder of similar desolation of the soul. In the language of lines 919–26 it is often difficult to distinguish when the poet is talking of literal and when of metaphorical building. The city that is surrendered to the enemy by the throwing open of all its gates (919) is presumably the 'citadel of the mind' of the previous line, though the language undoubtedly gains force from recent experience of real cities being surrendered in this way. On the other hand, the beauties created by the hand (921) must refer to man-made constructions. The poet is thus committing himself to the proposition that, if the citadel of the mind had not been surrendered to the assaults of the enemy (i.e. to Satan), Gaul would not have suffered literal material destruction. The persuasiveness of this argument depends on the elusiveness of the language, which is able to accommodate two different levels of meaning.

By committing himself to the proposition that material decay is consequent on spiritual decay, the poet also implies that the reverse is true: spiritual regeneration means material and political regeneration. In this, too, he follows the line of the *Epigramma Paulini* (89–95). The implications already present in the passage just quoted soon become more pronounced:

If any mental energy remains, let us shake off the servile yoke of sin, break the chains, and return to freedom and the glory of our native-land. Pacts made with a cruel tyrant will be no hindrance, for they were written by a hand held captive. This treaty can be dissolved by Christ; he can overturn it with justice and right, calling back those who have turned away and welcoming those who convert, whom he, an extravagant purchaser, sought with his own blood. (941–48)

While the passage contains some language that is unambiguously spiritual, other phrases evidently derive special force from the condition of contemporary Gaul: the language of mental imprisonment, for instance (941–3; cf. *Epigramma Paulini* 24–5). Moreover, as Lagarrigue (1983: 141ff.) has persuasively argued, the reference to a treaty that the reader is urged to break takes on added significance in the light of the *foedus* struck with the Visigoths, that led to their occupation of Aquitania in 418. The *CPD* ends with a ringing apostrophe: 'Let us not fear, because we have collapsed in flight in a first contest, to take a stand and embark on a second battle' (958–9). As the passage continues, it soon becomes clear that the primary referent is to warfare with Satan, the already conquered enemy (962). But at a certain level the distinction is a meaningless one, for, if the poet is right, victory in spiritual warfare and resistance to the real enemies in Gaul go hand in hand. In the context of the times the poem's words could scarcely have failed to evoke a political as well as a spiritual response, however circumspect the language.

The *CPD* is a more complex poem, especially in its theology, than the others we have discussed. But in the reactions it expresses to contemporary circumstances in Gaul, it has much in common with Prosper's poem to his wife, and especially with the *Epigramma*. Like the *Ad Uxorem*, the *CPD* seeks consolation for and escape from present troubles by adopting a field of vision that takes in the celestial and eternal, not just the earthly here and now, and sets current events in the context of the history of salvation. But like 'Paulinus' and unlike Prosper, in the *Ad Uxorem*, who imagines the Last Judgement to be imminent, the poet of the *CPD* carefully chooses his language to suggest that spiritual and political battle against the occupiers of heart and of country go hand in hand. With the pagan poet, Rutilius Namatianus, in the nearly contemporary *De Reditu Suo*, the Christian poet is the last to express belief, however qualifiedly, in the possibility of a Gallo-Roman resurgence. While Rutilius' vision is political, social and antiquarian, the *CPD* poet's is religious. Rutilius appeals to the examples of Roman history, the Christian poet to the martyrs.

IV

Recovery: social and economic

That the culture and society of Roman Gaul did not undergo radical change in the early decades of the fifth century, but rather enjoyed something of a revival, emerges from both the literary and archaeological evidence. In respect of the former, Wood has already commented upon the continuity of southern Gallic aristocratic families from the fifth into the sixth century, as revealed by prosopographical studies. His general observations are confirmed by *Mommaerts* and *Kelley* in their analyses of individual genealogies, which identify the complex family relationships that linked leading Gallic clerics and lay-people to each other and to members of the high Roman nobility throughout this period (though for doubts as to the practical importance of the latter, see Mathisen). Especially remarkable are their proposals that Eparchius Avitus was the brother-in-law of his immediate predecessor as emperor, Petronius Maximus; and that, through the marriage of Avitus' sister to Petronius Maximus, subsequent generations of Avitus' family were able to claim descent not only from the Roman Anicii but also from the fourth-century usurper, Magnus Maximus.

With regard to archaeology, *Hitchner*'s study of various objects of trade demonstrates that goods from the Mediterranean littoral continued to be imported into southern Gaul during the fifth century and later. These goods included those produced in the east, though, as the century progressed, African products increasingly tended to predominate: a phenomenon that may plausibly be associated with the Vandal conquest of North Africa, and the subsequent freeing of this country from its long-standing tax obligations to Rome. Thus, down to the seventh century, southern Gaul remained part of the Mediterranean economy.

The impression of uninterrupted commerce in the south and south-west is confirmed by *Sivan's* survey of the archaeology of Bordeaux and its region. Here, in the heart of an area that had suffered badly from the troubles of the early fifth century and which, from 418, had fallen under Visigothic rule, we see clear signs of strong economic and social continuity. Though much reduced in area by its new fortifications, late third- and fourth-century Bordeaux had retained and profited from its central harbour. It sprouted extensive suburbs, and the density of building within its walls is suggestive of a high level of population. Its inhabitants were engaged in a variety of activities, both commercial and industrial. There is no sign that this city business was dislocated by the Visigothic occupation; indeed, the Visigothic administration, like its Roman predecessor, took care to ensure its well-being, in particular through the provision and maintenance of flood defences. The economic life of Bordeaux was sustained by its continuing role both as the main market for the produce of the villa-based estates of the region and the place that provided the goods and services on which the profits from this trade might be spent. Indeed, the archaeological evidence strongly suggests that the late Roman aristocratic lifestyle, founded on the possession of large rich villas (identified as such by their being provided with elegant mosaics and extensive bath-houses) lived on in Aquitania after the establishment of the Visigothic kingdom; and that, at least to judge from the similarity in decorative styles between rural mosaics and urban sarcophagi which it is plausible to assume were commissioned by rich Visigothic clients, this lifestyle was practised by Gallo-Roman and Visigoth aristocrats alike. As Nixon has already suggested, the newcomers were assimilated into the local culture.

Sivan noted that the suburbs of late Roman Bordeaux were enlivened by the presence of centres of Christian worship. The connection between religion and urban vitality in southern Gaul in the fifth century is examined in more detail by *Loseby*, through a study of the development of the region's episcopal hierarchy. Loseby maintains that variations between the pattern of local centres of secular administration and that of known sees are authentic differences, which arose from changes in the importance of communities within the urban network. These changes included the rise to prominence of a number of secondary centres. The Christian church adapted itself to such circumstances and may even have had a hand in forming them: the cut-and-thrust of ecclesiastical politics led to the establishment of new sees, and any community that managed to attract episcopal residence enjoyed enhanced status and the stimulation of its economy. More important, however, is Loseby's argument that these changes in no way reflect any chronic weakness or instability in the main urban framework, which, in terms of size and vitality, was increased rather than diminished by them. On the local level, Loseby observes that, wherever it came to be situated, episcopal residence, by creating a demand for new buildings for worship and accommodation, profoundly affected a town's land market and, depending on where land could be acquired, its topography. The preferred location for episcopal complexes was in the centre but, given the high density of urban population usually to be found there (a point already graphically demonstrated by Sivan), without generous patronage, either private or imperial, this was not always possible.

So far this Section provides a positive view, but we should not assume that Gaul's recovery from the misfortunes of the early fifth century was total. Consideration of the role of Christianity in a somewhat different context allows *Percival* to strike a more cautionary note. In his examination of the fifth-century villa he frequently draws upon much the same evidence as Sivan, and is prepared to admit that in Aquitania the rural situation may have been as she describes. On the other hand, while conceding that there is a case for the survival of a few traditional – open and sprawling – rich villas in Gaul into the fifth century, he maintains that the contemporary trend, in Aquitania and beyond, may have been towards stronger, more secure and military-looking establishments, perhaps the preserve of the very wealthy. On this basis, Percival argues that the majority of the older villas had probably disappeared and that, even in those cases where archaeological excavation would seem to suggest continued occupation of a site, we should be alert to the operation there of forms of activity quite different from those of the previous century. In brief, most 'villas' were no longer the residential or agricultural bases of great land-owning aristocrats, but rather the preserve of squatters or, most likely, new *foci* of Christian worship. In both cases, we may see the origin of the Medieval village.

This potential for significant change in Gallo-Roman society is also demonstrated by Hitchner, albeit in a somewhat different way from Percival. He draws attention to the fact that, as far as can be seen, the southern Gallic economy was never as robust as that of other areas on the western Mediterranean seaboard. In the fifth century, as in both earlier and later periods, it may be characterized as a regional economy: it produced few exports, and the level of its imports was, in absolute terms, never very high. This leads Hitchner to make a point of no small significance to the theme of a Gallic 'crisis of identity', namely that, despite its continuing external links, when uncertain times returned such an economy would have offered few real countervailing tendencies to the emergence of a shift in local political allegiances – away from an increasingly weak and repressive imperial government and towards the more efficient yet less-demanding rule of the barbarian monarchs.

CHAPTER 10

The Anicii of Gaul and Rome

T. S. Mommaerts and D. H. Kelley

This chapter draws heavily upon data summarized in *PLRE* II, and to some extent on data from *PLRE* I. They are supplemented occasionally by other information, and interpretation is sometimes quite different.

Among the members of the family for whom we have early direct testimony are Ruricius, bishop of Limoges from about 485 to 507, and his grandson of the same name and position, honored by Venantius Fortunatus: '[the] Ruricii, twin flowers, to whom Rome was linked through the peak of the family tree of the Anicii' (*PLRE* II, Ruricius; Fortunatus, *Carm.* 4.5, 7–8.). (See Fig. 10.1.) According to Gregory of Tours, whose family came from Clermont, the family of Ruricius was also of Clermont, as Ommatius, a son of Ruricius, came from Clermont to be bishop of Tours. Gregory mentions that Ommatius was 'of senatorial family' but says nothing of the Anicii. Another son of Ruricius was Eparchius. Most names were hereditary in Gaul and throughout much of the Empire, and thus are often good indications of kinship (Mathisen, 1979d). Here, then, we have an indication of a relationship to the emperor Eparchius Avitus (Augustus 455–6, b. *c.* 400: *PLRE* II, Avitus 5), whose family came from Clermont. Another Eparchius was bishop of Clermont from *c.* 462 to 472, and was the immediate predecessor of Sidonius Apollinaris as bishop of Clermont. Sidonius had a school-mate and relative named Avitus. They were apparently *consobrini* – Sidonius to Avitus (Sidonius, *Ep.* 3.1): 'closest connection of blood, related through our mothers'.

A close relative of Ruricius of Limoges was probably Papianilla (*PLRE* II, Papianilla 1), wife of Tonantius Ferreolus, praetorian prefect of Gaul, 451–2. Sidonius, on a visit to the neighbors, Apollinaris and (Tonantius) Ferreolus, says that he was, himself, related to the one, and, through his wife, Papianilla, daughter of the emperor Eparchius Avitus, to the other. Since he was called Sidonius

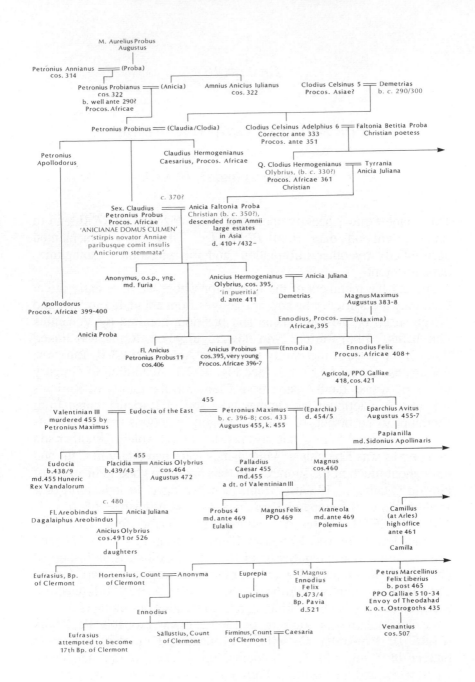

Fig. 10.1 The Anicii of Gaul and Rome: postulated relationships

The Anicii of Gaul and Rome

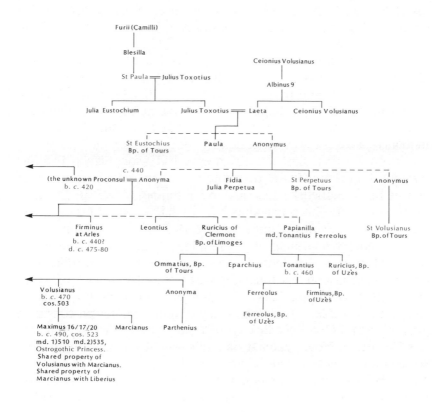

Faltonius Probus Alypius

Adelfia
Christian
buried in Syracuse
md. Count Valerius

Furii (Camilli)

Blesilla

St Paula ═══ Julius Toxotius

Ceionius Volusianus

Albinus 9

Julia Eustochium

Julius Toxotius ═══ Laeta

Ceionius Volusianus

St Eustochius
Bp. of Tours

Paula

Anonymus

c. 440

(the unknown Proconsul ═══ Anonyma
b. c. 420

Fidia
Julia Perpetua

St Perpetuus
Bp. of Tours

Anonymus

Firminus
at Arles
b. c. 440?
d. c. 475-80

Leontius

Ruricius of
Clermont
Bp. of Limoges

Papianilla
md. Tonantius Ferreolus

St Volusianus
Bp. of Tours

Ommatius, Bp.
of Tours

Eparchius

Tonantius
b. c. 460

Ruricius, Bp.
of Uzès

Volusianus
b. c. 470
cos. 503

Anonyma

Ferreolus

Firminus, Bp.
of Uzès

Maximus 16/17/20
b. c. 490, cos. 523
md. 1)510 md.2)535,
Ostrogothic Princess.
Shared property of
Volusianus with Marcianus.
Shared property of
Marcianus with Liberius

Marcianus

Parthenius

Ferreolus, Bp.
of Uzès

Apollinaris, and his grandfather, uncle and son all had the name Apollinaris, it is clear that he was related to Apollinaris, while his wife, Papianilla, was related to Papianilla, the wife of Tonantius Ferreolus. At about the same time of the visit, Tonantius, son of Ferreolus and Papianilla, was still 'youthful', and a birth date of about 450 seems likely.

PLRE II has entries for Ferreolus, Tonantius and Papianilla. No mention is made of her son, Ruricius, bishop of Uzès. Ruricius of Uzès was the uncle (Duchesne, 1907; Balon, 1963) of Firminus, bishop of Uzès, son of Tonantius (the son of Papianilla), which Firminus was the uncle of Ferreolus, bishop of Uzès. (For these and other descendants of Papianilla, including the Carolingians and Capetians, see Kelley, 1947.) The name Ruricius suggests that Papianilla was related to the Ruricii of Limoges, while her relationship to the daughter of Avitus is attested. With Ruricius' son, Eparchius, cited above, we now have another suggestion of the marriage of an ancestor of Ruricius (an Aniciid), and a close relative of the emperor Avitus.

At Arles there was also a family of Anicii, of whom the most famous member was Magnus Felix Ennodius, bishop of Pavia *c.* 514–21 (*PLRE* II, Ennodius 3; Llewellyn, 1970). Ennodius claimed, in his letters to them, to be related to a large number of individuals. Unfortunately, he seldom specified the nature of the relationship. Ennodius' parentage was suggested by Vogel, who edited his works (*MGH, AA* 7). Ennodius' sister, Euprepia, had a son, Flavius Licerius Firminus Lupicinus (*PLRE* II, Lupicinus 3), who was named after both of his grandfathers, Licerius and Firminus (*PLRE* II, Licerius, and Firminus 3). Since Ennodius had a relative named Firmina, and another at Arles named Firminus (*PLRE* II, Firmina, and Firminus 4), and there are no indications of any relationship to a Licerius, it seems clear that it was Firminus 3 who was the father of Ennodius. Sirmond's suggestion that Ennodius was a son of Camillus, of Arles, whose father was a proconsul and a brother of the consul Magnus, of 460, is not tenable. The further suggestion that the proconsul in question was Felix Ennodius (*proconsul Africae* 408/423) is not possible for, as Vogel pointed out, this would put too long a time between the proconsul and his brother. It is equally an objection to making Felix Ennodius a grandfather of Ennodius of Pavia. Ennodius' parents died while he was still young, and he went to live with a paternal aunt in Liguria. Hence he sometimes referred to Liguria, and sometimes to Arles, as his home country.

Among Ennodius' relatives was a certain Camillus, living at Arles (*PLRE* II, Camillus). This Camillus had already held high office before 461, although still young at the time. Ennodius, who had three older sisters, was not born until 473/4, so that Camillus was of the generation of Ennodius' father (Firminus, see above). This conclusion is reinforced by the fact that Camillus had first cousins, Magnus Felix, Probus, and Araneola, of about the same date (*PLRE* II: Felix 21, Probus 4, and Araneola). Magnus Felix was a school-mate of Sidonius Apollinaris, who was born *c.* 430, and was already urban prefect in 469. Both Probus and Araneola were married between 461 and 469. Probus, like his brother, was a school-mate of Sidonius Apollinaris. Magnus Felix was of Narbonne, son of Magnus, consul in 460 (*PLRE* II, Magnus 2). The brother of Magnus, the consul of 460, was an unnamed proconsul (*PLRE* II, Anonymus 42), the father of Camillus. The directly attested relationship of Ennodius to Camillus, of Arles, and the relationship of the names of Magnus Felix, of Narbonne, and of Magnus Ennodius Felix suggest that Ennodius' father, Firminus, of Arles, was a close relative of the Camillus that Sirmond mistook for Ennodius' father – probably a brother.

Magnus, consul of 460, was a grandson of Agricola (*PLRE* II, Agricola 1), and a descendant of Philagrius, who was also the ancestor of the emperor Avitus. This last had a son named Agricola. On this basis, it has been widely accepted that Avitus was a son of Agricola. If one accepts that Ennodius was an Anicius, and that Magnus was a great-uncle (likewise an Anicius), we have yet another suggestion that Magnus' Anician father married a sister of Avitus. The suggestion of *PLRE* II (Stemma 15) is that Magnus' father might have been Nymphidius 1, indicated as a possible brother of Avitus. However, the reference is to a poem of Sidonius Apollinaris, on the occasion of the marriage of Araneola, Magnus' daughter, to Polemius. The poem is ambiguous, and refers to a grandfather, Nymphidius. He may belong equally well to Polemius or to Araneola. *PLRE* admits of both possibilities, and we suggest that Nymphidius is the grandfather of Polemius (*PLRE* II, Nymphidius 1; Sidonius, *Carm.* 15.200).

Further examination of the family of Felix Ennodius sheds additional light on some of his relationships. The sons of Cynegia and Fl. Anicius Probus Faustus iunior, Niger, *cos.* 490, were Rufius Magnus Faustus Avienus and Fl. Ennodius Messala. Here one has the name Magnus, while the other has the name Ennodius, both names of our bishop of Pavia. The name Ennodius seems to derive from Felix Ennodius, proconsul of Africa at some time between 408 and 423 (*PLRE* II, Ennodius 2; *RE* V, 2629, lists an earlier Ennodius, proconsul of Africa in 395). Some suggest that Felix Ennodius was a direct ancestor of Ennodius, bishop of Pavia; but if Magnus Felix got his name, Felix, from the same source, the shared ancestry of Ennodius and Magnus Felix comes no later than the marriage of an Anicius and a sister of Avitus, which means that a marriage to bring in the names Ennodius and Felix must precede the generation of Avitus. Given Avitus' birth about 400, it looks as though the name is more likely to come through a sister rather than a daughter of Felix Ennodius. The distribution of the name Magnus in the family seems to suggest that it derives from the same source since we suggest that Magnus Felix was a first cousin of Firminus, father of Magnus Felix Ennodius, and since Cynegia included the names Ennodius and Magnus among her children's names (Arnheim, 1972) rather than Agricola, the name of Avitus' father, who was connected essentially with Gaul. Descent from an Anicius who was proconsul of Africa and married to a sister of Felix Ennodius seems likely. Cynegia's name is that of the Cynegii, one of the Spanish families who became prominent in the Empire as followers of the emperor Theodosius I (Matthews, 1967; 1975).

Additional light is thrown on the family by the fact that Venantius (*cos.* 507, with the emperor Anastasius, and son of Petrus Marcellinus Felix Liberius – *PLRE* II, Venantius 2; Liberius 3) is described by Ennodius as 'near in blood' to him, a description not applied by him to any other. Venantius was still young when he held the consulate, and must have been a generation younger than Ennodius, who was 34 in 507. The father of Venantius, Liberius, was identified by Ennodius as a relative of Rufius Magnus Faustus Avienus, who was son of Ennodius' relative, Cynegia (see above). 'Near in blood' seems a strong description to apply to the son of a first cousin, so it seems to us that Venantius was a nephew of Ennodius. Liberius, who shared the name Felix with Ennodius, and was, like Ennodius, a relative of Rufius Magnus Faustus Avienus, is likely to have been Ennodius' own older brother, rather than a brother-in-law. Liberius was born somewhat after 465, and so might have been as much as eight years older than Ennodius.

This identification of Liberius, in turn, tends to suggest the identity of Maximus 16 and Maximus 20 (*PLRE* II). Maximus 16 was a relative of Ennodius, Maximus 20 one of the Anicii. Since Liberius was an Anicius, it is expected to find Liberius associated with a specified member of the Anicii. Both Liberius and Maximus 20 were in high favor with the Ostrogothic king, Theodahad, who, in 535, sent Liberius on an important mission for him, and, in the same year, married an Ostrogothic princess to Maximus. Theodahad, furthermore, gave the estates of a certain Marcianus to Maximus. Justinian subsequently divided these estates between Liberius and Maximus. This Marcianus suggests, further, an identification of Maximus 16/20 with Maximus 17. Properties of Volusianus 5 were restored to his sons, Maximus 17 and Marcianus (*PLRE* II, Marcianus 14) by Theodahad's uncle, Theoderic the Great, in about 510/11. It is suggested that Marcianus' share was awarded to his brother, Maximus 16/17/20, and later divided between this brother and their uncle, Liberius. The name Volusianus is discussed below.

Two arguments against this series of identifications can readily be dismissed. The first is the marriage of Maximus 16 in 510 put against the marriage of Maximus 20 in 535. At first glance, it should be clear that Maximus' first wife (of 510) could easily have died in the twenty-five-year interval between the two marriages. Additionally, since Maximus 20 (m. 535) is known to have been consul in 523, it is quite unlikely, given marriage patterns of the time, that the marriage of 535 would have been his first.

The second argument against this identification is the fact that before the division of Volusianus' property between Marcianus and Maximus (*c.* 510/511), and almost certainly before the reassignment of part of that property to Liberius (maybe 535), Maximus 16 is described by Ennodius (*Carm.* 1.4.87) as 'generis spes unica summi', which *PLRE* interprets as 'the only one left to continue the line' (*PLRE* II, Maximus 16) and therefore not possessed of a brother (i.e. Marcianus). There are any number of reasons why Maximus should be the unique hope for the survival of his family while still having a brother.

This Maximus, then, is he who is identified as a descendant of the usurping emperor of 455, Petronius Maximus (*PLRE* II, Maximus 22), an Anicius. The Petronii identified themselves as Anicii. Petronius Probus was called 'Anicianae domus culmen' and his children were all given the name Anicius. The identification of the noble Petronius

Maximus with this family has for long been widely recognized. He was born *c*. 396–8, and was a close contemporary of Avitus, born about 400. Petronius Maximus became emperor 17 March 455, and was killed 31 May the same year, when he was succeeded by Avitus. In this situation the succession of a brother-in-law is not unexpected. Evidence that Petronius Maximus is the Anicius who married a sister of Avitus is quite clear. Another piece of evidence is the name of his son, Palladius, who was named Caesar in 455 (*PLRE* II, Palladius 10). The Palladii were a noble family, primarily of Bourges, where several of them were bishops (Duchesne, 1910; *PLRE* II, Palladius 13 and 14). (Also of this family may be nos. 1, 2, 4, 11, 12 and 19.) We would suggest that the Palladii were related to Agricola, the father of Eparchius Avitus, and probably to Avitus, bishop of Bourges at about the same time. This would, then, explain how the name Palladius, heretofore not evidenced among the Petronii-Anicii, came to Petronius' son.

If our reconstruction is correct, Petronius Maximus was the father of Magnus, the consul of 460, and the grandfather of Probus. The name Probus is not restricted to the Petronii, but was important in that family, and rather suggests descent from Sex. Claudius Petronius Probus himself, the 'peak' of the Anician house. Petronius Maximus is said in a number of late sources to have been descended from the usurping emperor, Magnus Maximus, although this assertion is dismissed in *PLRE* as 'untrustworthy and improbable'. If we are correct in thinking that Magnus, the consul of 460, is a son of Petronius Maximus, the probability of such a descent is enhanced. We have previously suggested that the name Magnus may have come into this family through the mother of the Anicius who married the sister of Avitus, which Anicius we would now identify as Petronius Maximus. We know little of the Ennodii, but we do know that there was some intermarriage with the Cynegii, as pointed out previously, and that they were among the Spanish followers of Theodosius I, and perhaps related to the imperial house. Magnus Maximus was also a Spaniard, among the early followers of Theodosius I, and himself said to be related to the emperor, although his own proclamation as emperor naturally put him on the other side from the loyal supporters of the Theodosian house (including Petronius Probus, who staunchly opposed Magnus Maximus). (Maximus is called an affinal relative. He seems to have served under Theodosius [father of the emperor] in Britain, and in an exalted position [because of his relationship to the family of Theodosius?]. It would therefore appear that Magnus Maximus was married to a relative of Theodosius I, rather than that Theodosius' wife, Flavia Aelia Flacilla, was a relative of Magnus Maximus.) Magnus Maximus is known to have had a daughter, and we think that she may have been the wife of Ennodius, the proconsul of Africa in 395, and the mother of a daughter (whom we might call Ennodia), mother of Petronius Maximus.

Olympiodorus is said by some to have reference (fr. 41.2) to Petronius Maximus' family in a statement that would make the name of Petronius' father Maximus. There is nothing to suggest, however, that this passage applies to the family of Petronius Maximus.

If we turn back to the events of 455, we see that Petronius Maximus was allegedly responsible for the murder of Valentinian III. The murder of Valentinian was followed by the marriage of his widow, Licinia Eudocia, to the new emperor, Petronius Maximus (whose first wife, Avitus' sister, had earlier committed suicide), the marriage of her elder daughter, Eudocia, to Palladius, the son of Petronius Maximus, and the marriage of the younger daughter, Placidia, to Anicius Olybrius. (It seems very unlikely that the marriage occurred before the death of Valentinian; yet the marriage had to have occurred before the Vandal sacking of Rome and carrying off of the empress and her two daughters.) Hence three Anicii married three princesses of the Theodosian imperial house in the spring of 455.

It seems to us highly unlikely that Petronius would be setting up a potential claimant to the throne from any distant branch of his own family. The historical situation indicates that Anicius Olybrius, whose parentage is not attested in any of our sources, was, himself, a younger son of Petronius Maximus. Since he later became emperor, through the support of Eudocia's second father-in-law, the Vandal Geiseric, and was recognized as legitimate because of his marriage to Eudocia's sister, the daughter of Valentinian III, it is understandable that the sources gloss over the identity of his father if Olybrius were son of Petronius Maximus, the man that had had Valentinian murdered. It is often said that Anicius Olybrius was a grandson of Anicius Hermogenianus Olybrius, consul in 395, by his cousin-wife, Anicia Juliana; and this is almost always supported by the fact that the daughter and heiress of the emperor, Anicius Olybrius, and of Placidia was also named Anicia Juliana. However, this point is inconsequential, because Julianus/a, was a name commonly used among the Anicii from a much earlier date, and any descendant of the Anicii might have been called Julianus/a. Moreover, it has been a problem that Anicius Hermogenianus Olybrius appears to have had only one child (at least that survived childhood), a daughter, Demetrias, his heir, who dedicated herself to a religious life and remained a virgin. We think that Anicius Olybrius was a great-nephew of Anicius Hermogenianus Olybrius and that Petronius Maximus was a son of Anicius Probinus, consul, like his brother, Anicius Hermogenianus Olybrius, in 395, but apparently somewhat older, although still very youthful. This would seem chronologically necessary, since Petronius Maximus was apparently born about 396–8. In the year in which Anicius Probinus was consul, Ennodius was the proconsul of Africa, and, in the following year, Anicius Probinus himself became proconsul of Africa, the only son of Sex. Claudius Petronius Probus to hold that office. We know nothing of a wife for Anicius Probinus, but our postulated sister of Felix Ennodius is not precluded. She could not be the wife of Anicius Hermogenianus Olybrius, as we know his wife to have been Anicia Juliana. If Petronius were, indeed, a grandson of Petronius Probus, this would seem to be his parentage, for Probus' son, Fl. Anicius Petronius Probus, did not become consul until 406, and was clearly still younger than Olybrius.

We return to Volusianus. Another Volusianus, besides the father of Maximus and Marcianus, is known to us as a relative of Ruricius, the Anician bishop of Limoges. This Volusianus is St Volusianus, seventh bishop of Tours (Ruricius, *Ep.* 2.64; Stroheker, 1948). St Gregory, nineteenth bishop of Tours, tells us that St Volusianus was of the same family of his predecessor, St Perpetuus, sixth bishop of Tours. Both were closely related to St Eustochius, fifth bishop of Tours (GT *HF* 10.31; Duchesne, 1907). All are stated to be senatorials. The relatively rare name of St Eustochius suggests Julia Eustochium, daughter of St Paula and Julius Toxotius the elder. What strengthens this connection is Julia Eustochium's brother, Julius Toxotius the younger, being married to Laeta, daughter of Publilius Ceionius Caecina Albinus, son and brother of Volusiani. The Ceionii Volusiani were second only to the Anicii in power and prestige. Taken as a whole, these three saints suggest a descent from Julius Toxotius and Laeta to the bishops of Tours. While Julius Toxotius and Laeta had an only daughter, Paula, the phrasing in Latin, unlike its modern Romance descendants, would not preclude Paula's having had brothers. By dates, St Eustochius would be a nephew or brother of Paula the younger. A niece of Paula's would have been of the right age to marry our anonymous proconsul, thus bringing the name Volusianus into the line, as well as the name of her apparent son, Camillus. Camillus was a *cognomen* of the Furii, the family of St Paula's mother, Blesilla (*PLRE* I, Paula 1, Toxotius 1 and 2, Blesilla 1, Eustochium, Laeta 2, Albinus 8, Volusianus 3, Lampadius).

Finally, we would see Ruricius of Limoges as brother of Camillus of Arles, and as uncle of Ennodius of Pavia.

Unfortunately, the constraints of space preclude a discussion of the social, cultural, political, economic, or religious ramifications of the hypothesis here presented. We must leave these conclusions for other researchers to elucidate.

CHAPTER 11

Meridional Gaul, trade and the Mediterranean economy in late antiquity[1]

R. B. Hitchner

INTRODUCTION

Over the last two decades our understanding of the Mediterranean economy in Late Antiquity (*c.* AD 300–700) has improved considerably, thanks to archaeology. The results of excavations and surveys conducted in, in particular, Italy, Spain and North Africa have shed new light on the character and organization of trade, both tied and untied, and its relationship to regional economies (see Giardina, 1986; Fulford, 1987). If, however, we hope to advance knowledge on these matters, it is essential to extend systematic archaeologically based investigation to less well-known regions of the Mediterranean (Wickham, 1988: 193). There are, admittedly, significant impediments to the achievement of this end, not infrequently of a

[1]   My research for this paper was supported by generous grants from the Society for Libyan Studies and the American Philosophical Society, which allowed me to travel to southern France. There I was able to make use of the resources of the library of the Centre Camille Jullian, Université de Provence, and to visit archaeological depots. Jean-Pierre Brun and Michel Bonifay deserve special thanks for giving of their time to discuss with me various aspects of my research and for providing me with copies of related articles and (as yet) unpublished papers, without which this chapter could not have been written. I am also grateful to Philippe Leveau, David Mattingly, and Sylvie Sempere for their assistance in various ways in assuring that my research in Provence would be successful. My wife, Becky, also deserves a word of gratitude for tolerating my seemingly endless commentary on this piece of work.

political nature. At the same time, there are some areas where on-going archaeological research has been overlooked. A good case in point is Provence where, over the last quarter century, much new archaeological evidence has been accumulated on the late antique period (see Février, 1988). In this chapter I intend to use some of this evidence to explore trade relations between meridional Gaul and the rest of the Mediterranean in the fourth through seventh centuries and to construct, if possible, a very general model of the southern Gallic economy in the period. I shall draw primarily on the published record of pottery, amphorae, and, to a lesser degree, shipwrecks, coinage, and imported stone. The documentary record on late antique commercial relations between southern Gaul and the rest of the Mediterranean is wholly inadequate, largely comprising isolated and highly anecdotal statements in writers such as Salvian, Sidonius Apollinaris, and Gregory of Tours: it is only through the material evidence that we are able, at present, to build practicable hypotheses regarding the organization of the late antique economy. There are, however, obvious limitations to drawing historical conclusions from primary evidence (see, e.g., the remarks of Bonifay, 1986: 295f.); of necessity, therefore, the findings of this chapter ought to be viewed as highly provisional.

THE EVIDENCE

Pottery

African Red Slip ware (ARS), including lamps, predominates in the assemblages of imported wares (fine and common) at both urban and rural sites along the Mediterranean littoral of Gaul between the late fourth and seventh centuries (Février, 1988: 182). However, with the exception of lamps (generally Hayes types I and II: Bonifay, 1983: 324; Deneauve, 1972), within this period, it is possible to discern some fluctuations in the amount of African pottery being imported. Excavations at the Bourse in Marseilles, for example, suggest that the volume and range of ARS forms (including Hayes 56B, 61B, 64, 67–8, 81, 91A or B) were lower in the late fourth to mid fifth century by comparison with later periods (Bonifay, 1983: 306, 324; Février,

1988).   A similar trend is evident at Arles, Narbonne, and Toulon (Conges, 1980; Berato *et al.*, 1986: 143, 146; Bonifay and Villedieu, 1988; Raynaud, forthcoming). This situation cannot be explained as the result of a supplantation of ARS by other imported wares, most notably late Roman C and D wares from the eastern Mediterranean, for the latter show no indication of competing seriously with African imports anywhere in the Midi. Indeed, though some C ware examples have been recovered at various sites extending from Port Vendres to Fréjus, and a few sherds of D ware have been found at Saint Blaise (Bonifay and Villedieu, 1988), there is a virtual absence of eastern wares in the mid fifth-century phases at the Bourse (Bonifay, 1983: 322ff.; 1986: 298f.). Sondages conducted at Toulon also failed to turn up examples of late Roman C or D wares (Berato *et al.*, 1986).

As alluded to above, an increase in the importation of ARS is evident from the second half of the fifth century. At Marseilles, again our best source of information, both the range and quantity of ARS forms rise between the mid fifth and mid sixth centuries before declining slightly in the late sixth and early seventh century (Bonifay, 1983; a similar increase in imports of African tableware in this period has been noted at Porto Turres in Sardinia: see Villedieu, 1986: 328ff.). A similar trend is apparent at Toulon at least through the sixth century (Berato *et al.*, 1986: 146).

Amphorae

Amphorae carried foodstuffs. This fact alone makes them a better indicator of commercial activity than pottery in that foodstuffs are frequently imported from a wide range of sources at different times of year to offset shortage problems posed by seasonality and changes in consumer demand. These factors were certainly at work in late antique southern Gaul, to judge from the presence of not inconsiderable numbers of eastern Mediterranean, North African, and Spanish amphorae at many sites (Bonifay and Villedieu, 1988). Although the number of published reports on amphorae is still too low to venture a definitive statement on their import history, it appears that eastern amphorae arrived on a substantial scale in the late fourth and early fifth centuries (for a similar pattern in Africa, Italy and Spain see Fulford, 1980, 1983: 9ff.; Riley, 1982; Panella, 1983,

1986; Arthur, 1985; Whitehouse *et al.*, 1985). In fact, at Marseilles, Arles and Beaucaire, eastern examples (generally LRA 1, 3, 4, Keay LIV, but also LRA 5, 6, Keay LII, and Robinson M334) constitute the largest percentage of imports in the period. (Marseilles, 37–40 per cent eastern:20–22 per cent African; Arles, 40 per cent:30 per cent; Beaucaire, 48 per cent:42 per cent; for deviations from this pattern west of the Rhône and at Lyon see Bonifay and Villedieu, 1988; Brun, 1988: 143ff.). Although African amphorae form the second largest group of imports in this period, it is important to note that at Marseilles the smaller number of examples of African amphorae by comparison with those from the east was offset by the larger capacities of the former (Bonifay, 1986: 300; Bonifay and Villedeau, 1988).

Significantly, all period 1 oriental amphorae and all African spatheia and Keay XXXV, as well as two of the Keay XXXVI and one Keay XXVII, found at Marseilles were tarred on their interiors. According to Bonifay, this would seem to exclude oil 'among the products most frequently imported at Marseilles in the fifth century' thereby modifying the 'assimilation which is often made between African amphorae and oil'. Bonifay offers four possible explanations for this phenomenon: (i) oil occupied a less important place in the alimentary and other needs of Marseilles and its hinterland; (ii) local production of oil was sufficient to limit demand for import supplements; (iii) oil imported in amphorae may have come through other ports; and (iv) tarred amphorae may be restricted to the group of examples being considered (Bonifay, 1986: 300f. – later period amphorae were not analyzed). Whatever the explanation, the presence of tarred African amphorae indicates that wine was being imported from that region and potentially in enough volume to compete rather evenly with eastern wines. Unfortunately, detailed publication of amphorae recovered at other sites is lacking, though reports on the amphorae found at Narbonne and Beaucaire are forthcoming. African amphorae of the fifth century are found at sites throughout Provence and Languedoc, though in what percentage in comparison with oriental examples is unclear.

Quantitative evidence for amphorae imports from the late fifth through seventh centuries in meridional Gaul is restricted to Marseilles, and there the published data are presently limited to selected phases dating to the late sixth and early seventh centuries at the Bourse excavations (Bonifay, 1986; Bonifay and Villedieu,

1988). The evidence shows African amphorae (Keay LV, LXI/LXII, spatheia) constituting roughly 50 per cent of total imports, as opposed to 25 per cent for eastern amphorae (LRA 1, 2, 4, 5 and 7), in the late sixth century. By the seventh century African imports account for more than 90 per cent of the total, with less than 10 per cent coming from the east (Bonifay, 1986: 286ff.).

Shipwrecks

Twenty-one shipwreck sites dating to between the third and seventh centuries have been identified off the Mediterranean coast of Gaul, all but two between Monaco and the mouth of the Rhône (Février, 1988: 186f.). Of these, two or three date to the third century, eight or nine to the fourth century, five or six to the fifth century, and one or two to the seventh century. The cargoes, where ascertainable, comprised tableware and amphorae. Four of the six ships in which coins were found belonged to the early fourth century. Three of the fifth-century ships were transporting African tableware and/or amphorae, though it appears that at least three other ships were carrying cylinder amphorae of African origin. Only one wreck, possibly of the third century, contained Spanish amphorae. In so far as one can conclude anything from the shipwreck information, it is that the fourth and fifth centuries for meridional Gaul were a period of greater long-distance commercial activity than either the third or seventh century. African products also appear to dominate among the goods being carried by these ships, most of which were headed for ports between the Ligurian coast and the Rhône mouth. The apparent absence of wrecks carrying eastern products is curious, but again the small number of examples prohibits firm statements one way or the other. In general, the patterns observed in the shipwreck evidence parallel those of the ceramic record in showing the overall strength of African imports in the late antique period.

Coinage

The absence of a Gallic or proximate Italian mint emitting bronze coinage after *c*. 423–5 (cf. King, below p. 185) contributed to a considerable shortage in specie in southern Gaul in the fifth and early sixth centuries. One response to this problem was, evidently, the continued circulation of the ubiquitous *AE*3 and *AE*4 of the fourth century. Denominations of this and earlier centuries were, not infrequently, cut into halves, thirds, and quarters, or simply reused if they corresponded to some denominations currently in use (Morisson, 1983; Février, 1988: 197). Of greater interest for our purposes was the apparent employment of Vandal *nummi* emitted in the late fifth and early sixth century, reformed Byzantine bronze denominations of the same period, and even Ostrogothic bronze and silver pieces (Février, 1988: 197, 199) for small-scale commercial transactions until the second quarter of the sixth century, when the Franks began minting copper coinage locally (Brenot, 1980).

Marble

The marble trade in late antique southern Gaul has not been the subject of detailed scrutiny, but, to all indications, marble imports from Carrara, Asia Minor, and the Pyrenees ceased in the fifth century. However, a late antique marble capital in the Lapidary Museum at Arles has been identified by Février as an import from Proconessus, suggesting that some marble from the east continued to find its way to the west in the late fifth and early sixth centuries (Février, 1988: 166, 170ff.).

SYNTHESIS

Although the evidence presented here is quite limited and restricted to urban contexts, the following seems to be clear regarding meridional Gaul's links with the larger Mediterranean economy:
(i)   Goods from Africa, as evidenced by ARS ware and amphorae (the latter carrying oil, fish products, and wine) seem to have

dominated the import market in meridional Gaul between the fourth and seventh centuries.

(ii)   The importation of eastern amphorae, carrying mostly wine, was greater in the late fourth to mid fifth centuries than in the late fifth to seventh centuries. In the former period, eastern wine imports may have competed on a roughly even basis with wine(?) imported in larger amphorae containers from Africa, though it is the apparent export of African wine which is perhaps the more interesting discovery.

(iii) The import of goods from both Africa and the east was greater along the coast between Liguria and the mouth of the Rhône than between the Rhône and the Spanish coast. In the latter region, Spanish imports continue, though evidently in much reduced volume, into the fifth century.

These observations fit well into the larger picture of Mediterranean economy, society, and politics in the late antique period. Perhaps most striking in this regard is the evidence for continued and even increased levels of African imports from the second half of the fifth century, precisely the period of Vandal control in Africa. This not only confirms a pattern observed by a number of scholars, namely that African goods freed from the *annona* were redirected to other markets, but reveals meridional Gaul to have been one of those markets (Spain: Keay, 1984: 420ff., 434f.; north-west Italy: Barnish, 1987: 180; Sicily: DeMiro, 1980–1: 578f., Fulford and Peacock, 1984: ch. 12; the east and Vandal trade generally: Giardina, 1986, with Fentress and Perkins, 1988: 213f.). The strength of the late fifth-century Africa-Gaul trade connection may be rooted in the brief alliance struck up between the Vandals and Ostrogoths who controlled Provence as a result of the marriage of Thrasamund (496–523) to Theodoric's sister (see Barnish, 1987: 181).

The continuing dominance of African exports to meridional Gaul in the sixth and early seventh centuries is, however, something of a surprise since elsewhere in the Mediterranean the level of imports from Africa seems to have been in decline (Fulford, 1980: 75f.; Keay 1984, 427f.; Arthur, 1985: 256; Barnish, 1987: 181; Wickham, 1988: 192). One explanation for this seeming anomaly may be that some form of tied trade involving ecclesiastical properties in Africa and the Church in southern Gaul may have grown up at about this time, the parallel for this being the Sicilian papal estates' exports to Rome, which began in earnest under Gregory the Great. Gift exchange between Byzantine, African and Gallic nobles may also account for some of this activity. (On the continuing demand for African oil in Gaul during the sixth century see GT *HF* 5.5.) It is also important to note that Africa from the mid sixth century, unlike many other regions of the Mediterranean, was relatively peaceful and thus in a more favorable position to conduct long-distance commerce without serious interruption: recent survey evidence from central Tunisia shows continued olive-oil production on a substantial scale into the seventh century (Hitchner, 1988).

A similar tranquility in the east during the fifth century may account for the percolation in exports from that region to southern Gaul in the first half of the century (Patlagean, 1977: 281, 419, 426). It has also been suggested that the increase in eastern amphorae at this time may stem from 'attempt[s] by east Mediterranean entrepreneurial traders to take advantage of the lack of central [i.e. imperial] control in the west Mediterranean' (Keay, 1984: 429); but this is difficult to prove. The subsequent decline in oriental imports in the sixth century was probably a consequence of not only increased insecurity in the east, but also the long and disastrous Gothic wars in Italy, which can only have impeded regular shipping and cabotage along the Italian and Ligurian coast, the primary route by which eastern goods reached Gaul.

The presence of Spanish amphorae along the Languedocian coast and even at Marseilles through the early fifth century should perhaps be viewed as a remnant of the non-tied coastal trade which emerged as an offshoot of Spanish metal and *annona* exports to Rome between the first and fourth centuries (Mattingly, 1988: 52f.). Archaeological evidence from Lyon (Bonifay and Villedieu, 1988) and a passing reference to the regular shipment of Spanish goods to Marseilles in Gregory of Tours (*HF* 9.22) suggest that trade with Spain continued into the sixth century.

But what does all of this tell us about the economy of meridional Gaul in the late antique period? To begin with, it must be stated that southern Gaul probably never played the central role that Spain or Africa did in the state- and elite-sectors of the Roman economy. Accordingly, it will not have yielded the same high levels of tax- and rent-driven surplus production as did those two regions, the virtual absence of south Gallic exports on any scale after the first century serving as clear if negative testimony to this. The economy of meridional Gaul will therefore have been essentially regional in nature, i.e. producing sufficient surpluses to meet tax- and rent-demands as well as local requirements, but not enough to export locally produced goods on a substantial scale and thus restricted in its imports to luxury items or goods designed to supplement local production. For the late antique period the picture, as we have seen, is more complicated. Imports of African and eastern products point to the existence of long-distance commercial activity between southern Gaul and the southern and eastern Mediterranean, but whether this represents a change from the previous period remains uncertain. Other indicators, however, suggest that the south Gallic economy remained essentially regional in scope. TS Gris ('grey ware'), for example, though influenced by African Red Slip ware, and produced in great quantities, is essentially a local product intended to meet local demands. There is also evidence for continued olive-oil production in Provence, but on a reduced scale by comparison with the first to third centuries (Brun, 1987); and villas continue to be inhabited, but on a more modest scale (Février, 1978; 1988: 110ff.; Brun *et al.*, 1985: 243ff.). The presence of such markets would also account for the maintenance of a monetized economy as evidenced by the enormous quantities of small bronze flans even after imperial mints at Trier, Arles, and Aquileia shut down in the early fifth century. In political terms, the historic regionalism of the south Gallic economy contributed, in the less secure conditions of the fifth century, to a weakening of allegiance to Roman government on the part of both curial and senatorial aristocrats, the primary landholders in the region. That is, in the face of increased Roman taxation and erosion of customary property and labor relations, the benefits of a less complicated economic life under peaceful barbarian rule may have been very attractive (cf. Drinkwater, below p. 212). Such economically motivated secessionist tendencies certainly emerge in the pages of Salvian (cf. Drinkwater, below pp. 214f.) and may explain the ease with which the region eventually fell under barbarian control. At the same time, the continued viability of the local economy under Visigothic, Ostrogothic, and finally Frankish rule may have helped sustain long-distance Mediterranean trade through the seventh century, and with it the continued political, social and cultural contacts, evidenced in the secular and ecclesiastical sources, between Gaul, Africa, and Constantinople. In terms, then, of its economy, meridional Gaul suffered no crisis of identity before the seventh century: it still belonged soundly to the Mediterranean economic system created by Rome (cf. Van Dam, below pp. 331f.).

CHAPTER 12

Town and country in late antique Gaul: the example of Bordeaux[1]

H. Sivan

The general picture of urban decline in Late Antiquity is familiar and has been recently reinforced by Fergus Millar in an article on the negative effects of imperial legislation on urbanism (Millar, 1983: 76ff.). Similarly, any reader of the Gallic reports on the invasions of the early fifth century is acquainted with the dark and somber hues in which the destruction of the Gallic countryside was described (Courcelle, 1964: 79ff.; Roberts, above). Thus, ruined cities and deserted lands appear to characterize Gaul of the fifth century. Yet, modifications have already been introduced. In a study of the North African cities of the late Empire, Claude Lepelley demonstrated the vitality of urban life as seen, in part, through the traditions relating to acts of private generosity maintained well into the fourth and fifth centuries (Lepelley, 1979–81: *passim*, esp. I, 304ff.). No parallel study exists as yet for Gaul (Février, 1980: 397ff., for a brief sketch), but Lepelley's conclusions should alert us to the possibility of significant deviations from the standard.

This chapter would not have been possible some twenty years ago. The rapid pace of environmental change of the last two decades and the merciless advance of bulldozers over ancient urban sites gave impetus to urban archaeology and brought the archaeologists hot-footed to many areas where salvage operations needed to be conducted. Bordeaux is a case in point, for since 1970 the number of excavations there has multiplied and with it our understanding of the

---

1   My thanks to J.-P. Bost, Centre Pierre Paris, Université de Bordeaux III, for taking me to Plassac; to C. Balmelle and M. Gauthier for showing me around St Emilion, and to D. Barraud, J.-F. Pichonneau and M.-A. Gaidon of the Direction des Antiquités at Bordeaux for their kind help and information.

Roman and Medieval city (*Gallia*, Informations, annually, for brief reports; *Bulletin de Liaison*, 1982+; *Chronique d'archéologie bordelais*, annually). In addition, recent studies of the mosaic decoration of rural establishments have significantly contributed to our understanding of the Aquitanian countryside in the late antique period.

BORDEAUX

An image of the city in Late Antiquity is determined in the first place by its walls. These changed not only the city's outward appearance but also the tenor of urban life both within and without their protection. In Bordeaux, the 400 x 700 meter wall circuit enclosed an area of some 32 hectares, which represents about one quarter of the territory of the open city of the early Empire. Several important monuments were left outside the walls, including the only two to survive into the modern period: the so called 'Palais Galien', once the amphitheatre, and the 'Piliers de Tutelle', a structure the function of which is still uncertain. While the precise location of the forum is unknown, several foci of urban life, like the amphitheatre, were left outside the walls. Other monuments, public and private, were used as a source of material for the walls. Indeed, most of the funerary *stelae* erected in Bordeaux in the course of the first three centuries were re-used as construction blocks by the builders of the late rampart. Yet, the living quarters of the city extended well beyond the limits of the walls, and recent excavations point to a pattern of houses, industrial quarters and agricultural plots intermingling outside the ramparts (Gaidon, *pers. comm.*). The earliest Christian edifices, lively centers of worship during religious festivals, were built outside the walls, including the famed St Seurin (Maillé, 1959: 109ff.; Duru, 1982: 57ff.; cf. Loseby, below p. 149).

To date, the most ambitious program of digs has been carried out on a vast area in the heart of the enclosed city. Three campaigns conducted on the site of St Christoly between 1973 and 1983 had the singular merit of clarifying for the first time details of urban life *intra muros* during the fourth and fifth centuries (*Gallia* 33, 1975: 461ff.; 41, 1983: 450ff.; Bordeaux, St Christoly, 1982; Bordeaux, St Christoly Reports). (Perhaps one should add that the story of St

Christoly is also the story of the vicissitudes of urban archaeology at the end of the twentieth century. Not only did the archaeologists plow their way through water and mud but the end result was that all the ancient layers uncovered are now buried for good underneath an imposing white structure which serves as a shopping center, while the items found in the course of the digs were indeed removed but are still awaiting display in the newly reconstructed Musée d'Aquitaine.)

Already, in 1877, a polychrome mosaic depicting a vase with vine leaves emerging from it had been found in the St Christoly area, affording a hint of the wealth buried underneath later constructions (Girault, 1878: 131ff.). Nearly a century later, when an area of no less than 8,000 square meters was allotted for the construction of a new shopping center, archaeological works were resumed. St Christoly is located in the heart of the ancient *castrum*, just off Rue Ste Catherine, the Roman *cardo maximus* and even now a major shopping street (Fig. 12.1). Moreover, the area of the excavations bordered on the ancient river-bed of the Devèze (now completely dry) which, throughout antiquity, flowed into the harbor. A preliminary dig in 1973 brought to light a considerable number of late Roman vestiges of exceptional density, a fact which inspired hopes of finding there the most elusive ancient monument of the city, the fountain of Divona described in loving detail by Ausonius in his *Ordo* (20.30ff.). More significantly perhaps, this initial probe held out the further hope of clarifying for the first time the precise relation between the ancient harbor and the river Devèze. The end of 1973 saw the first planned dig in the area, terminating a year later on account of an acute danger of flooding. Between December 1974 and May 1981 no further works were undertaken; the initial dig had to be covered, and the site was turned into a parking lot. A second campaign finally began in 1981, limited in its area and depth, and followed as before by a parking lot. The last campaign took place from April 1982 to the beginning of 1983 and completed the unearthing of late Roman Bordeaux in that section. It appears that, prior to the construction of the walls (late third/early fourth centuries), the *quartier* of St Christoly consisted of public and private buildings as well as of artisan workshops, all located along the banks of the Devèze at some distance from one another. The river, at that time supplemented by the water of the river Peugue, served to transport goods to and from the harbor, as the existence of storage rooms along the river banks

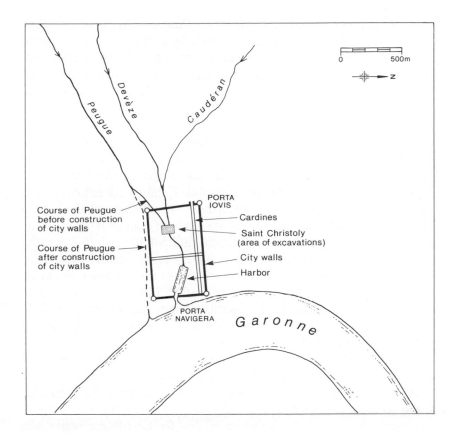

Fig. 12.1 Town and country in late antique Gaul: late Roman Bordeaux

show. In the course of the construction of the walls, the Peugue was
diverted away from the Devèze, directly into the Garonne (Fig. 12.1).
Both the Devèze and the harbor were included within the narrow
space of the walled city. Their inclusion demonstrates the solicitude
of the city-planners to ensure the continuity of the city's commercial
viability. Paradoxically, the gradual rise of the water level of the
Devèze, and the silting up of its bed, rendered the water channel
impassable in the long run. By the sixth century, the harbor had to be
abandoned (Debord and Doreau, 1975: 5ff.). There are two
references, one from the late fourth, the other from the mid fifth
century, to the internal harbor. Ausonius (*Ordo* 20.18–20) implies
that access to the harbor was limited to the period of high tide; this

observation is confirmed by a text of Paulinus of Pella (*Eucharisticus* 44–6: 'Burdigalam veni, cuius speciosa Garumna / moenibus oceani refluas maris invehit undas / navigeram per portam'). The importance of rivers in the scheme of transport in late antique Aquitaine cannot be doubted, and prompts reflection on the fate of the road system in the fifth century.

Another result of the replanning of the city in Late Antiquity was a growing demand for space within the *castrum*, a situation which must have been responsible for the recovery of every available piece of land, including marshy areas. At the confluence of the Devèze and the Peugue, an area previously uninhabited, industrial constructions, shops and private houses were unearthed. The density of the habitat seems exceptional, and the numerous finds of faunal remains in an excellent state of preservation reveal the vitality of this section throughout Late Antiquity. Among the domestic animals which the Bordelais kept in their houses or ate were cats, dogs, horses, donkeys, pigs, boars, stags, deer, goats, lamb, cattle and hares. Late Roman Bordeaux, then, to judge by St Christoly, witnessed an intensification of construction inside the walls, coupled with a conscientious use of all the urban space in the *castrum*.

A constant source of anxiety for the ancient inhabitants of that area were the periodical inundations which threatened to flood the buildings. The most important public monument of the early Empire in the area of St Christoly, a market-place with a central courtyard, had been supplied with a complex system for evacuating water into the Devèze. With the diversion of the Peugue to accommodate the plan of the city walls, and the general rise of the level of the water, the builders of late Roman Bordeaux were forced to devise other solutions to the problem of inundations. Elaborate wooden constructions were designed to raise the banks of the Devèze and to ensure regular canalization of water. It may be well to remember that works on such a scale, combined with the costly construction of walls, must have mobilized considerable economic resources, and required a high degree of maintenance. Between the fourth and the seventh centuries the constructions along the river-bed in that area underwent numerous modifications, designed, presumably, to supply contemporary needs. In short, excavations of this part of late Roman and Visigothic Bordeaux and their finds (below) indicate that, if the image of urban life is to be based on economic activities rather than on the traditional concept of the city as a civic center, then the fifth century represents for Bordeaux a period of significant efflorescence.

Vast quantities of pottery shards were assembled from the various stages of the excavations at St Christoly. They belong to the group known as 'céramique estampée tardive du Groupe Atlantique' or, more generally, as 'late Roman ware' (Rigoir, Rigoir and Meffre, 1973: 207ff.; Gauthier, 1975: 19ff.; Marmion, 1984–5). Among the decorated shards, some bear symbols of Christian religious affiliation (crosses, etc.), and could have been used by members of a lower-middle class, such as the family of Maurisius and Ursa, who commemorated the death of their infant son in 405 on an inscription engraved with uneven characters and disordered lines and bearing the Christogram (Jullian, 1887–90: 945; Bordeaux 1973: no. 130). Thus visual testimony to the presence and diffusion of Christianity is provided not only through the existence of churches and cemeteries but also on instruments of daily life. Of interest also is the widespread employment of geometrical, floral and vegetal motifs, engraved on a large sample of the shards, and resembling the decoration of some of the carved stones found on the site, such as columns and capitals (Bordeaux, St Christoly 1982: 27, 47, 50).

Both the number of the pottery shards and their distribution in the Aquitanian countryside have led scholars to regard Bordeaux not only as a center of diffusion but also as a major center of production. In fact, no other urban site in Aquitaine has produced such quantities of late Roman pottery. While its precise chronology has not yet been established, the period of production of this type of grey and orange pottery falls within the period between the late fourth and the sixth centuries. The type of pottery with which Bordeaux has been associated is found primarily in rural sites in the modern department of the Gironde, as well as in sites along the Garonne and as far north as Nantes, the valley of the Loire, and Britain. Many of the Aquitanian find-spots correspond to known late Roman villas, which were situated along major rivers. This pottery distribution confirms the conclusions regarding the importance of the harbor in late antique Bordeaux as a focus of commercial navigation by sea and river.

Among the most important finds of St Christoly were several mosaics which display a marked similarity of artistic concept and execution (*Gallia* 33, 1975: 465 = Bordeaux, St Christoly, 1982: 49; Balmelle, 1983: 21ff.; Balmelle, in preparation). On stylistic grounds they appear to date to the fifth century, and the two which were restored to their original dimensions (8.0 x 5.2 meters and 8.5 x 3.1 meters respectively) were decorated with geometrical, floral and vegetal patterns. Some of the decorative schemes may have been brought to Aquitaine from North Africa where they had originated. This type of geometrical/floral decoration appears on numerous mosaics of late antique Aquitaine and constitutes the most important single common denominator of urban and rural settlements at that time. The close artistic ties between urban mosaics, such as those discovered in Bordeaux, and those unearthed on numerous rural sites in Aquitaine, imply the existence of a constant exchange between the city and the countryside throughout the period and of an important school of mosaicists which supplied local demands.

THE AQUITANIAN COUNTRYSIDE

In a poem dedicated to Pontius Leontius, foremost among the Aquitanians in the fifth century, Sidonius Apollinaris supplies a detailed description of Leontius' fortified villa (*Burgus* = Bourg-sur-Gironde, *Carmen* 22.101ff.; cf. Percival, below pp. 158f.). At the very entrance to the estate an inscription proclaiming its ownership met the visitor's eye and beyond it the reception court with probably a fountain. The vast complex was oriented to meet the exigencies of changing seasons while its topography was carefully planned to introduce a distinction between the *pars rustica* and the *pars urbana*. Among the more memorable parts of the villa were bath-houses and weaving-chambers. Equally remarkable was the monopoly which the owner held over sources of water on his domain, diverted to the exclusive use of the estate and its residents. This aspect of the extent of the influence of local landowners over their surroundings is familiar from Aquitanian estates like Montmaurin and Valentine, where such monopoly over curative waters generated a not inconsiderable income (Fouet, 1972: 83ff.; 1975: 128ff.). The decoration of Leontius' *Burgus* included mosaics depicting subjects of Roman history for which no parallel has ever been found in the course of digs conducted in Aquitaine. Finally, the villa boasted, it seems, a private chapel, whose walls were covered with illustrations of themes from the book of Genesis.

The existence of big estates in Aquitaine throughout the first five centuries of our era is known particularly through the rather spectacular, if perhaps atypical, villa of Chiragan (Grenier, 1934: II, 884ff.). But, in recent years, the exceptional density of estates of various sizes, all dating to the fourth and the fifth century, and each provided with a series of mosaics with an unusual degree of uniformity, has contributed to an impression of great prosperity of the Aquitanian countryside in Late Antiquity (Fig. 12.2 for some examples; Raguy, 1978–9 for a partial survey; Balmelle, 1980 and 1987 counts some 300 sites). Although none of the rural estab-

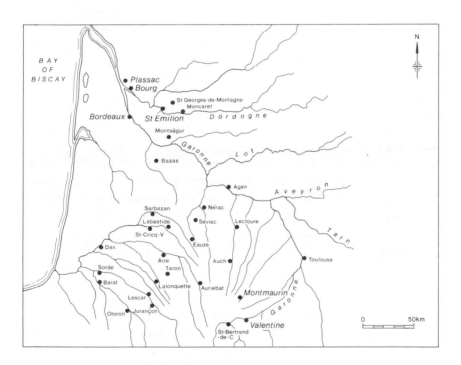

Fig. 12.2 Town and country in late antique Gaul: late antique Aquitaine. Major urban and rural sites

lishments so far surveyed or excavated yielded fortifications of the sort described by Sidonius in respect of *Burgus*, many residences reveal components which can be compared with those he enumerates. On the basis of archaeology alone, it is possible to observe that most rural estates can be noted for two prominent features: their bath-houses and their mosaics. The baths, usually decorated with Pyrenean marble and mosaics, were at some distance from the main building and included a *frigidarium*, a *tepidarium* with a hypocaust, and a *caldarium* (Monturet and Rivière, 1986 for the most comprehensive analysis to date). Most, if not all the villas were decorated with mosaics (Balmelle, 1980; 1987). Two examples of rural establishments in late antique Aquitaine may be cited here, both subjects of recent excavations.

Just north of Bordeaux, not far from Bourg-sur-Gironde, the estate of the Leontii, a villa, founded some time in the first century and abandoned in the sixth or early seventh, has been unearthed at Plassac (*Gallia* 31, 1973: 455f; 33, 1975: 468ff.; 35, 1977: 452; 37, 1979: 496f.; 39, 1981: 480; Premiers, 1986: nos. 270–5; Bost *et al.*, 1987; cf. Percival, below p. 160). Plassac has the unique advantage of being mentioned in a will of the early seventh century composed by Bertchramnus, the later bishop of Mans. Its excavators point to construction and reconstruction in the course of its 500 years' existence, but the extent of the late Roman modifications needs further research. In spite of what appears as a considerable expansion of the existing plan in the fifth century, the material resources of the then owners may have fallen short of the wealth of Plassac's earlier masters, who were able to furnish their residence with a series of high-quality wall paintings (Savant, 1985: 113ff.). Be that as it may, the fifth-century phase of Plassac is further connected with a polychrome mosaic decorated with geometrical and floral patterns which recall the mosaics found on the site of St Christoly in Bordeaux.

Rather spectacular is the series of mosaics unearthed in the course of excavations in the late 1870s in the town of St Emilion (Gironde), east of Bordeaux (Balmelle, Gauthier, and Monturet, 1980: 59ff.). The villa of Palat is a good example of the type of estate established in the course of the fourth or the fifth century on a previously unoccupied territory (at least no earlier layers have been found to date). Its layout – a large basin in front, a reception court with a fountain in the center, and two symmetrical wings of chambers –

recalls the importance of hospitality in the life of estate owners. The mosaics of villa Palat contain different schemes of decoration. One, unique within the context of late antique Aquitanian mosaics, displays human figures bent on a hunt, a popular aristocratic pastime all over the Empire but one which is altogether absent from the mosaic floors of Aquitaine. Very popular are the familiar motifs of geometrical, floral and vegetal patterns, which find echoes both in Bordeaux and in many rural sites of the region. Above all, such patterns recall the decorative schemes of the numerous sarcophagi which have been found primarily in urban cemeteries in Bordeaux, Toulouse and Narbonne.

TOWN AND COUNTRY: VISIGOTHIC INTEGRATION?

One of the most important criteria currently at our disposal by which to evaluate the type of relations between country and town in the area under discussion is the artistic affinity between certain urban and rural monuments, namely sarcophagi and mosaics. The mosaics of late antique Aquitaine remain unique in this period, for no other Gallic region has yielded a comparable quantity of so late a date. Most of these mosaics were found within a rural context, adorning one part or other of a country estate. Only a few were found in an urban milieu like Bordeaux, a fact which may be due to the hazards of survival rather than to the extent of their use in the city.

In her studies of the Aquitanian mosaics Catherine Balmelle draws attention to the similarities between the decoration of the mosaics and that of the sarcophagi (Balmelle, 1980, 1987: *passim*). Although a detailed study of the two groups together has never been done (Sivan, 1983: ch. 5 for some preliminary observations), some salient features emerge. In the first place, their striking anonymity is expressed in the absence of inscriptions on both mosaics and sarcophagi, and of clues to the identity of the owners and their daily routine. The one exception to this rule, an inscription in honor of Nymfius, the owner of Valentine near St Bertrand de Comminges, points to close relations between estate owners and the nearby urban community (*CIL* XIII, 128; Sivan, 1989a). Both the mosaics and the sarcophagi used local materials, including calcaire, marble and limestone in different colors. Both display similarities of artistic concept and execution. Basically, the decoration of the mosaics consists of schemes of geometrical compositions of repetitive structure into which the artists fitted vegetal and floral motifs, which include floral pyramids, baskets of flowers, scrolls growing out of vases, laurel wreaths, ivy and vine scrolls. All these motifs are familiar from the repertory of the Aquitanian sarcophagi, which have been dated in the main to the fifth century (Ward Perkins, 1938: 79ff.; James, 1977 for a fifth-century date; Fossard, 1957: 323ff.; Briesenick, 1962: 79ff. for a sixth/seventh century date; Boube, 1984: 175ff. for a late fourth-century date).

Human figures are rarely employed, a characteristic which prompted Demougeot to suggest a link between the sarcophagi and Arianism and, by implication, between these funerary monuments and the Visigoths, the rulers of Aquitania in the fifth century (Demougeot, 1965: 491ff.). While the religious message, if any, of the sarcophagi remains an open question in the absence of established Arian iconography, what appears as a preference for certain motifs over others within the context of both funerary monuments and mosaic pavements may not have been a coincidence. If both were made at one time for the same clients, these similarities are easily accounted for.

Estimates relating to the survival of the Gallic aristocracy in fifth-century Aquitaine (Mathisen, 1984: 159ff.) point to considerable decrease of senatorial population. We may then be justified in looking elsewhere for the patrons who commissioned the mosaics and the sarcophagi in that period. Throughout the fifth century, the Visigothic nobility lived in close proximity to members of the Gallo-Roman aristocracy who elected to remain or return to Aquitania. An exchange of influences, if not deliberate imitation on the part of the newly settled Gothic aristocrats, cannot be discounted. While the owners of fifth-century country estates in Visigothic Aquitania may not all have been of Gothic origin, the artistic affinities between rural mosaics and urban sarcophagi suggest that many were commissioned by Gothic patrons (Sivan, 1986: 339ff.). Perhaps herein lies the truth in the statement that 'the failure of the Visigoths to leave much impression on the archaeology and toponymy of south-western Gaul is arguably a more probable consequence of rapid integration than of relative isolation' (Wormald, 1976: 223). The monuments which the inhabitants of the Gallic south-west left in great abundance may have been the result of just such a process: corroboration of the rapid assimilation of the Visigoths into the Aquitanian landscape in the fifth century.

CHAPTER 13

Bishops and cathedrals: order and diversity in the fifth-century urban landscape of southern Gaul[1]

S. T. Loseby

BISHOPS AND THE URBAN NETWORK

The third to fifth centuries saw the evolution of a network of episcopal sees across southern Gaul (here, the late antique provinces of Narbonensis Prima and Secunda, Viennensis and Alpes Maritimae: see Fig. 13.1). Although the lists of bishops attending church councils provide only an arbitrary and imprecise chronology for the development of sees in this area, they show that the process was virtually complete by the end of the fifth century. In general, the episcopal organization mirrored the existing secular administrative set-up, and bishops were installed in *civitas*-capitals. Some differences between the secular and ecclesiastical urban hierarchies are nevertheless revealed by comparing the recorded seats of bishops with the *civitas*-capitals listed in the original version of the *Notitia Galliarum*, drawn up around 400 (a secular document: Harries, 1978; *contra* Rivet, 1976). Five centres in southern Gaul which do not appear as *civitas*-capitals in the *Notitia* receive a bishop before 450: Nice, Carpentras, Toulon, Uzès and *civitas Eturamine* in Alpes Maritimae (cf. Heinzelmann, below p. 248).

---

[1]   I would like to thank Ruth Featherstone, Jill Harries and Bryan Ward-Perkins for their generous help with this chapter. Any errors which remain are of course my own.

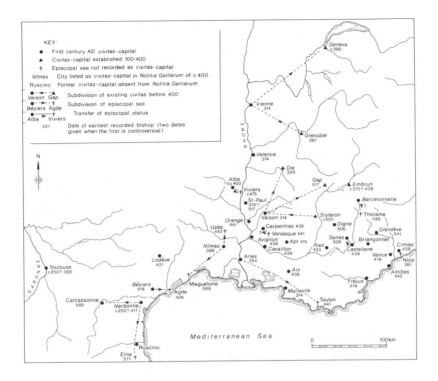

KEY:

● First century AD *civitas*-capital

▲ *Civitas*-capital established 100-400

+ Episcopal see not recorded as *civitas*-capital

Nîmes City listed as *civitas*-capital in *Notitia Galliarum* of *c.*400

Ruscino Former *civitas*-capital absent from *Notitia Galliarum*

●--►--▲
Vaison Gap Subdivision of existing *civitas* before 400

●--►--+
Béziers Agde Subdivision of episcopal see

●——►——+
Alba Viviers Transfer of episcopal status

421 Date of earliest recorded bishop (two dates given when the first is controversial)

Fig. 13.1 Bishops and cathedrals: *civitas*-capitals and episcopal sees in southern Gaul from the early Empire to *c*. AD 600

The last of these can probably be identified with Thorame, and should therefore be considered in relation to the only *civitas*-capital recorded in the *Notitia* which never produces a bishop, *civitas Rigomagensium* (*Not. Gall.* XVII, 3). They could be identical, but it seems more likely that Rigomagus should be identified with Barcelonnette (Griffe, 1964–6: II, 120f.; Rivet, 1988: 338, 344), in which case this anomaly is most likely to derive from a transfer of secular status from Barcelonnette to Thorame early in the fifth century. This would explain why Thorame is qualified as a *civitas* in the bishop list (at Vaison in 442: *Conc. Gall.* I, 102), whilst none of the other sees absent from the *Notitia* is (except Carpentras, which, as we shall see, is a special case). Excluding *Rigomagus*, I would emphasize that every *civitas*-capital listed in the *Notitia* became an episcopal see.

The early but, in terms of urban status, anomalous appearance of a bishop at Nice (by 381: Duchesne, 1894: 286) must be connected with its exceptional position in the secular organization of the province as a tiny coastal enclave pertaining to Marseille (Rivet, 1988: 65ff., 222; *CIL* V, 7914). A Christian community was established there by 314 (*portu Nicensi: Conc. Gall.* I, 16) and at some point in the fourth century the bishopric presumably developed independently of the *civitas* structure to serve it. This caused problems later, for by 439 a bishop was established in the immediately adjacent *civitas*-capital of Cimiez (Duchesne, 1894: 285). The pope intervened in 465, but his letter does not make it clear whether he sought to combine the two sees or simply to put them under the authority of a single metropolitan (Hilary, *Ep.* 4: *PL* 58.20–2; Duval, Février and Guyon, 1986: 85). At Orleans in 549 a priest subscribes on behalf of bishop Magnus of Cimiez and Nice, which certainly suggests the sees were amalgamated (*Conc. Gall.* II, 160). Magnus and his successors sign thereafter as bishops of Cimiez or Nice, but not both (Cimiez in 554, *ibid.*, 172; Nice in 585 and 614, *ibid.*, 249, 282, cf. GT *HF* 6.6). However they chose to describe themselves, bishops never appear simultaneously at both centres, which makes it likely that the two sees had been combined at some point. The emergence of a bishopric at Nice was therefore a response, which proved inappropriate in the long term, to an anomalous secular administrative arrangement.

Uzès, *Eucesia oppido*, does figure in the *Notitia*, but as a *castrum* (*Not. Gall.* XV, 6). The *castra* of the *Notitia* are difficult to interpret, but they seem to be later accretions to the *Notitia* made on ecclesiastical grounds (Harries, 1978: 35f.; also Rivet, 1976: 121f., 134f.), and therefore give no necessary indication of prior significance. But Uzès was probably already an important secondary centre, as the *locus* of Toulon certainly was (e.g. *CIL* XII, 3362; *Not. Dig. Occ.* 11.72), and their acquisition of bishops (*Conc. Gall.* I, 87, 102) can conveniently be considered together. The claim that they were respectively the alternative seats of the bishops of Nîmes and Marseille, who were not present at the councils in question (Rivet, 1976: 122), does not hold water. Toulon was in the city-territory of Arles, not Marseille; the absence of the bishops of Marseille and Nîmes from councils presided over by Hilary of Arles is hardly surprising given the ecclesiastical politics of the time. The presence of a bishop from Uzès, the only prelate from Narbonensis Prima, is the real anomaly (see below). It is only an accident of the evidence that the next bishops of Uzès and Toulon are not recorded until the sixth century (*Conc. Gall.* I, 213; II, 45, 82), for we have no further fifth-century lists in which their presence might reasonably be expected. These centres are therefore best regarded as permanent episcopal seats from the mid fifth century onwards.

The absence of Carpentras from the original *Notitia* is something of a mystery. Since it was an early imperial *civitas*-capital, and has a bishop by 441 when it is again qualified as a *civitas* (*Conc. Gall.* I, 87), it has been suggested that its omission is a blunder by the compiler of the *Notitia* (Rivet, 1988: 100), later corrected. While this is plausible, there could be another explanation. First, there is no late antique evidence which contradicts the *Notitia* by showing the continued status of Carpentras as a *civitas*-capital. Secondly, it appears that the bishops later abandoned Carpentras, on the open plain, for the naturally well-defended site of Venasque, 10 kilometres away. Whilst the titles of the sixth-century bishops of the see vary, the two recorded in seventh-century lists both subscribe as bishops of Venasque (*Conc. Gall.* II, 281, 309; Duchesne, 1894: 263ff.). The curious lack of information about the continued status of Carpentras in the imperial period and the subsequent movement of the bishopric to a nearby site suggest that Carpentras was not a notably successful centre. I would therefore speculate that its omission from the *Notitia* reflects a real decline in the city's status, which was temporarily arrested by the consecration of a bishop to Carpentras early in the fifth century.

It is possible that the emergence of bishops at Toulon, Uzès and Carpentras is connected with Hilary of Arles (cf. Heinzelmann, below pp. 243, 248). Harries has observed that the emergence of bishops for the first and only time from cities like Castellane and Thorame at the councils convoked by Hilary may reflect his 'need of men to toe his party line' (1978: 33). For the same reason, Hilary could have created sees in centres which were not *civitas*-capitals. There is nothing specific to suggest this for Carpentras, but the potential link between the bishops of Arles and the establishment of a see at Toulon is obvious, since it lay within their *civitas*. The first bishop of Toulon, Augustalis, is assigned to *Arelato civitate* in an early martyrology (*Mart. Hieronym.* VII id. sept.; Duchesne, 1894: 269). Its next recorded bishop, Cyprianus, represented Caesarius of Arles at a council in 529 and co-wrote his *Vita* (*V. Caesarii* 1.1, 60), so close relations between the sees continued. As for Uzès, its first known bishop, Constantius, was certainly close to Hilary. As noted above, he was the only bishop from Narbonensis Prima to attend any of Hilary's councils. And after the pope had acted to stop the supra-provincial activities of the bishop of Arles, Constantius was the bearer of one of Hilary's letters to Rome (*V. Hilarii*, 22). He appears again in 450 among the suffragan bishops seeking the restoration of metropolitan rights to Arles after Hilary's death (Leo I, *Ep*. 66: *PL* 54.884). His see remained in Narbonensis Prima (Hilary, *Ep*. 8: *PL* 58.24ff.) but its association with Arles is unquestionable.

New centres were therefore emerging in the fifth century alongside existing *civitas*-capitals as episcopal seats. The continuation of this process is marked by the appearance at sixth-century councils of bishops from Agde (506), Elne (a see by 571), Maguelone and Carcassonne (589) (*Conc. Gall.* I, 213; John of Biclarum: *PL* 72.865c; *Conc. Gall.* II, 257), none of which appears in the original *Notitia*. With the exception of Nice and Arisitum, a temporary (*c.* 570) creation in response to political circumstances (GT *HF* 5.5; Duchesne, 1894: 305f.), these are not fortuitous, unsustainable developments necessitating later correction, but continuing modifications of the urban network begun in Late Antiquity with the rise of secondary centres like Geneva, Grenoble, Gap and Sisteron to the status of independent *civitates*. Like these cities, established in the anomalously large *civitates* of Vienne and Vaison, almost all the new sees were carved out of large city-territories which could readily support more than one bishop. All were already significant secondary centres, or ports and centres of economic activity, or naturally well-defended strategic sites, and often combined these attractions. The appearance of bishops at new centres does not therefore represent the breakdown of the old urban order, but its continuing evolution under the new impetus provided by the Church.

The unique example of a *civitas*-capital listed in the *Notitia* which gained and lost its bishop before the end of the fifth century is Alba, whose bishops moved to Viviers, 10 kilometres away, a strategic well-fortified Rhône-side site, with consequent economic advantages (Esquieu *et al*, 1988: 8ff.). The *Dotatio*, a (?)seventh-century inventory of donations made to the church of Viviers later incorporated into a tenth-century cartulary, begins with a bishop list. This gives five bishops of Alba, before the see was moved to Viviers by a bishop 'qui de Albense Vivario contulit et Alba vicum appellari voluit'. It goes on to state that the second bishop of Viviers held the see in the reign of Alaric (484/5–507), so the shift probably dates from around 475 (*Dotatio*, 414–15; Duchesne, 1894: 229ff.; Lauxerois, 1983: 190ff., 223ff.).

There is no reason to assume that the move to Viviers was caused by the destruction of Alba suggested by legend, since church buildings excavated there continued in use well into the sixth century (Esquieu and Lauxerois, 1975: 22). Indeed, an archdeacon subscribes at a council in 549 on behalf of bishop Melanius of Alba (*Conc. Gall.* II, 160), who is listed in the *Dotatio* among the bishops of Viviers (*Dotatio*, 415). This may reflect a conservatism in the use of episcopal titles, or a real duality such as could also have existed between Carpentras and Venasque, or Cimiez and Nice. These examples suggest a conflict between adherence to the urban network inherited by the Church from the secular administration, and the perceived reality that the bishop now embodied civic status, and that if he moved, that status moved with him. But such transfers occur very rarely and, when they do, close links with the original episcopal seat or outmoded episcopal titles are retained. This emphasizes the extent to which the bishop was constrained by fidelity to the existing urban network. This fidelity guaranteed the enduring significance of the vast majority of *civitas*-capitals in the south: as in earlier centuries, additions to the urban network were far more common than transfers or removals of civic status.

THE SITING OF CATHEDRALS

The coming of Christianity had a dramatic impact on the particular topography of each individual city. The fifth centurys witnessed a public building explosion; a great number of Christian buildings were erected in and around cities (see Sivan, above p. 133). Here I will consider only episcopal groups. These varied considerably in plan and scale. Two or more churches were frequently included, whether unitary as at Trier (Gauthier and Picard, 1986: 21ff.), or physically distinct as at Geneva or Lyon (Beaujard *et al.*, 1986: 22ff.; Biarne *et al.*, 1986: 44ff.). The associated baptisteries could be separate buildings or could be attached to other elements of the complex.

Where detailed excavations have been carried out, a plethora of ancillary buildings of uncertain function have been revealed, as at Geneva where, by the sixth century, the episcopal complex had evolved to encompass a quarter of the intra-mural area (Biarne *et al.*, 1986: 42). At Cimiez, by contrast, the episcopal group established in the ruins of part of a third-century bath-suite formed an extremely compact unit (Benoit, 1977: 89ff., 137ff., plate 31).

I would suggest that the siting of these complexes within the existing urban landscape also varied considerably. The relationship between the sites of the earliest cathedrals in Gaul and late antique city-walls has long been debated. Some have argued that cathedrals were originally established in suburban cemeteries and only later moved within the walls (e.g. Hubert, 1958: 540f.; Griffe, 1964–6: III, 12ff.). Others have asserted that they occupied an intra-mural site from the outset, a view which has recently tended to predominate (e.g. Février, 1974: 118f.; 1980: 424; and most categorically Brühl, 1988: 45). However, in southern Gaul this approach is not helpful because there are very few well-defined and dated reduced enceintes of late antique type and the question is further complicated by the continuing existence of early Roman wall-circuits at some cities (e.g. Aix, Fréjus) and the apparent absence of defences at others (e.g. Alba, Vaison). This forces us to consider other associated factors – patronage and the availability of urban space – which were crucial to the siting of episcopal groups and which are apparent in well-known examples from central Gaul, where the emphasis has hitherto been laid on the role of late antique walls.

At its early imperial peak, Clermont sprawled over some 200 hectares, but by the mid third century was contracting rapidly (Fournier, 1970). Its late antique rampart delimited a mere 3 hectares, although suburban settlement continued. Gregory of Tours states that the (intra-mural) cathedral in use in his day had been built by bishop Namatius around the middle of the fifth century (GT *HF* 2.16). Eparchius, who succeeded Namatius, had to live in the cathedral sacristy because at that time the church had little property within the city-walls (GT *HF* 2.21). But a suitable episcopal residence could well have been acquired under the next bishop, Sidonius, whose own house may have passed to the Church (Prévôt, Barral and Altet, 1989: 33). The difficulty of obtaining intra-mural space might explain why the baptistery was still outside the walls in Gregory's day (GT *HF* 5.11). Fournier showed that this building stood over 600 metres from the cathedral in an area crowded with funerary basilicas (1970: 289ff.). This is an extraordinary separation between cathedral church and baptistery: it seems far more likely that the baptistery had formed part of an earlier episcopal complex than that it had been built so far from the cathedral in the sixth century (*contra* Pietri, 1980: 198ff.). In a city where space was clearly at a premium, the siting of Namatius' cathedral would have been determined not only by the status and security conveyed by an intra-mural site, but by the availability of intra-mural space.

A second example shows patronage solving this problem of the availability of space. The late sixth-century Life of Amator, bishop of Auxerre, states that in Amator's day the cathedral stood outside the late antique ramparts. But Amator's preaching brought so many to the Christian faith that this church was no longer big enough, and there was no room to extend the existing building. So Amator went in search of a *latior locus* on which to build a new cathedral. He sought out Ruptilius, a 'vir clarissimus', who had inherited an 'amplum et excelsum domicilium' within the walls, and told him that God's house was too small and that his dwelling was required for conversion into a church. Ruptilius was, understandably perhaps, not impressed and roundly told the bishop so. Amator prayed; Ruptilius fell seriously ill and, commanded by God, hastened to comply. Lest we feel too sorry for Ruptilius, it seems that he gave only part of his house to the bishop and that this was in a semi-ruined state. Nevertheless, Amator's new intra-mural cathedral was duly erected to serve the ever-expanding Christian community (*V. Amatori* 18–21; cf. GT *HF* 1.31 for a similar example of private patronage determining the site of the cathedral at Bourges).

While we can accept that where there were walls bishops were eager to build within them, they had to wait until patronage provided the necessary space. In the absence of a benefactor or where the intra-mural area was particularly cramped this could take time. The longer it took, the more likely it is that an extra-mural focus of episcopal activity would develop to serve as an *ad hoc* cathedral.

The above examples have shown the potential difficulty for the early Church in acquiring intra-mural space, and how this problem was gradually resolved through the rise of Christian patronage, which in Gaul, as elsewhere (e.g. in Italy: Ward-Perkins, 1984: 51ff.), came not only from individuals but also from the state. The combined role of public and private patronage in the building of a cathedral is illustrated in an inscription of 445 from Narbonne (*CIL* XII, 5336; Marrou, 1970). It lists the contributors to the work and the sums they donated. Part of the list is missing, but the main benefactor was clearly Marcellus, praetorian prefect of the Gauls, who had asked the bishop to undertake the work, and who had underwritten it with 2,100 solidi. His generosity was supplemented by much smaller donations from bishops and others, presumably members of the landed civic elite. The specific emphasis on the timing of Marcellus' contribution *per biennium administrationis*, his role in commissioning the building and his large share of the costs all suggest that the prefect was acting in an official capacity and contributing the money out of public funds.

The state had another asset of great value: land. The problem of the availability of urban space could have been most readily resolved with the active support of the imperial administration, as at Trier, where a vast double cathedral was erected *intra muros* in the fourth century, commensurate with the status of an imperial capital (Gauthier and Picard, 1986: 21ff.). It is surely no coincidence that the movement of the cathedral at Arles from an intra-mural but peripheral site to a central position in the immediate vicinity of the forum seems to have taken place in the first half of the fifth century, when Arles supplanted Trier as capital of Gaul and became an occasional residence of the emperors (Février, 1964: 51ff.; Biarne *et al.*, 1986: 80). It seems likely that the presence of the emperor could facilitate and accelerate the provision of large tracts of land for church use at the heart of the urban area.

But this land was occupied by existing buildings. Just as a private patron like Ruptilius made over his house to the Church to be turned into a cathedral, so the state made over public buildings. The traces of Roman structures found beneath cathedrals are generally not pagan temples, as traditionally assumed (see Ward-Perkins, 1984: 91f. and Brühl, 1988: 44f.; Avitus, *Hom.*, 20, provides the earliest conversion known to me of a temple into a church in Gaul, in 515). Where extensive excavations have taken place beneath known early cathedrals, the evidence is generally too meagre to determine whether the underlying Roman structures are public or private in character (e.g. at Geneva, Biarne *et al.*, 1986: 41f.). The conversion of public buildings into cathedrals has, however, been confirmed archaeologically in at least two cities in southern Gaul.

As already mentioned above, a complete episcopal group was established at Cimiez in the fifth century in the four main rooms of a public bath-suite. But this bath-suite was already in ruins when the cathedral was built (Benoit, 1977: 158ff.) and it has been claimed that it lay outside the late antique urban area (Benoit, 1977: 96; *contra* Février, 1964: 50). I will therefore concentrate here on the recent excavations at Aix-en-Provence in and around the cathedral of Saint-Sauveur (Guild, Guyon and Rivet, 1980; 1983; Guild *et al.* 1988; Duval, Février and Guyon, 1986: 24ff.). These showed how the north-west corner of the forum had been in-filled to bring it up to the level of the *podium* which dominated it to the north. Partly on the *podium* and partly on the in-fill was built the surviving early Christian baptistery. This baptistery lay immediately south of a contemporary cathedral, still little known but clearly implanted on the site of a major public building dominating the forum, probably a basilica, possibly a temple. Further elements of this episcopal group have been revealed, showing that wherever possible the builders of the early episcopal group had retained the walls of the forum complex in foundation or elevation.

The date of this transformation still remains to be settled, but the excavated pottery suggests a date around the very end of the fifth century (Guild *et al.*, 1988: 18; Duval, Février and Guyon, 1986: 24). This leaves a series of questions to which the answers are at present unclear. First, who was responsible for such a fundamental change? Secondly, had the forum already been abandoned, and, if so, for how long? There is some evidence to suggest it was in a sorry state, but we cannot be sure whether this reflects loss of function or the desolation typical of any building site when work is in progress (Guild, Guyon and Rivet, 1983: 184f.). Finally, the origins of the see of Aix are obscure, but its first well-attested bishop appears in 408 (Duchesne, 1894: 271ff.). If the proposed date for the excavated complex is approximately correct, where was the cathedral before *c.* 500? These excavations have given fresh impetus to the question of whether Aix's earliest cathedral lay beneath St Sauveur, or whether it occupied the site of the Medieval church of Notre Dame de la Seds, more than 500 metres away to the west (Février, 1964: 53f.; Duval, Février and Guyon, 1986: 26). Excavations planned for the latter site may bring some clarification: meanwhile it seems probable that this is an example of the development of an episcopal group at the heart of an urban area in which the necessary space was provided through the patronage of the state, and not of a private individual.

The example of Aix shows how difficult it is to determine the spatial relationship between an episcopal group and a contemporary wall-circuit. If the cathedral was indeed originally sited at Notre Dame de la Seds, then this lies within the early imperial wall-circuit. But excavations in the 1950s showed that this area of the city was in ruins by Late Antiquity, and that burials were beginning to penetrate the former intra-mural area (Benoit, 1954: 293ff.). The terms 'intra-mural' and 'extra-mural' are therefore meaningless, and we can say only that Seds lay on the periphery of the city. The link between the early episcopal complex at Saint Sauveur and any wall-circuit is similarly tenuous. The area around the cathedral, the Bourg St Sauveur, was certainly walled by the eleventh century: but there is no proof of the date at which this circuit was built (Février, 1964: 77). It could be a typical reduced enceinte of late antique origin, in which case its existence could have been a factor in the establishment of the episcopal group on the site of the forum complex; conversely, the wall-circuit could have developed at some point consequent upon the siting of the cathedral. Bishops could build walls too, like Desiderius of Cahors in the seventh century (*V. Desiderii* 16–7, 31, 54), and I think we have to get away from the preconception that cities throughout Gaul had received reduced enceintes in the immediate aftermath of the third-century invasions. In the south-east especially, where the threat had been less immediate, and there were no military detachments on hand to carry out what was a technically skilled operation (Johnson, 1983), we should accept that the shift from the open Roman town to its walled Medieval successor was more of an *ad hoc* development.

In most cities in southern Gaul it is therefore preferable to think of sites not as intra-mural or extra-mural, but as central or peripheral within the urban area. But, whatever terminology we employ, the factors underlying the siting of cathedrals remain the same. Bishops wanted to establish their cathedrals at the heart of the urban area for reasons of security and status. The early Church was dependent on patronage to secure such premium sites. This patronage could come from private individuals or from the state. As Christianity became established as the state religion, it seems likely that in some cities formal provision for the Church was made by the handing over of land in public ownership; but until such space was secured bishops must have carried out their pastoral duties in buildings on the periphery, where a fixed seat could develop for a time. This was less likely to happen where patronage was soon forthcoming. While the Church generally maintained the urban network, and provided a context for its continuing evolution, the siting of cathedrals was therefore the diverse product of particular circumstances within each city.

CHAPTER 14

The fifth-century villa: new life or death postponed?

J. Percival

The suggestion of Roger Agache (Agache, 1978: 436ff.), that in the area of the Somme basin covered by his aerial surveys a number of present-day villages must be supposed to overlie Roman villas, has given a new focus to the debate about the survival or non-survival of the villa into the fifth century and beyond. Agache's proposal can be simply stated: the troubles of the third century were in this region little short of disastrous, and led to the destruction or abandonment of all or most of the villas. The majority of them became isolated ruins, appearing away from later settlement in the air photographs. Some, however, revived, became the centres of settlement themselves and evolved into the villages of the Medieval and later periods. The proposal, as stated, does not imply the *survival* of villas, merely their *re*vival after abandonment or destruction. Nor does it imply their revival as villas, merely that they were re-used and re-adopted as the focal points for settlement. For Agache the answer to the question posed in my title is that there was indeed new life in the fifth century, though whether this was represented by a fifth-century villa is not clear.

Some years ago I myself drew attention (Percival, 1976: 31ff., 172ff.) to a number of areas in northern France where the distribution of villas as indicated by excavated sites seemed to me to be systematically incomplete. I argued that it made no sense in relation to urban centres or to road and river networks, and that we should regard it as part only of the true distribution, the other part of which was hidden from us. I suggested that this other part consisted of villas underlying modern villages, and that a clue to their existence might be the occurrence of place-names with the suffix *-acum*, the form of which goes back to the Roman period. Very simply, the excavated sites were the villas which died; the ones which did not die, or which came to life later, collected settlement around them and were eventually buried beneath it.

One needs, of course, to be discriminating. Villas have to appear *somewhere* on the map, and the chances of their appearing by accident under later buildings can hardly be negligible. The cases to which I am referring are ones in which structural or residential material (bricks, *tegulae*, architectural features, mosaics, pottery and the like) is found at the very heart of a village, usually underneath or alongside the parish church, and this triple coincidence of Roman building / church / place-name in -*acum* could be documented at several dozen sites without difficulty. The coincidence of Roman building / church (without the name in -*acum*) is more common still, with known examples in excess of a hundred. In other words, the occurrence of villas under villages is too frequent to be accidental, and has somehow to be explained.

What emerges from the evidence across France is that the scenario suggested by Agache in respect of the villas of the Somme basin (of revival in the late third century) is only one of a number of scenarios that need to be taken into account when considering the development of Gallic villas as a whole from the fourth to the fifth century. First, is *surv*ival a possibility as opposed to (or in addition to) *rev*ival? If a villa survived, at what date did the village grow around it? If it revived, either as a villa or as something else, after how long an interval did this occur? Was the growth of a village the result of cultural preference, of socio-economic patterns, or of something else? Could it simply have been that a desirable location is likely to attract settlement at any period precisely because it is desirable; or that the ready availability of building materials from a derelict site was itself sufficient to dictate the placing of a new one? For the question of what existed in the fifth century the answers to some or all of these preliminary questions are obviously essential. On one scenario there was a fifth-century villa, more or less comparable with its fourth-century predecessor. On another, it had already been transformed into something rather different. And on another still, it had ceased to function but might do so again at some future date.

It used to be thought that a solution was provided by the literary evidence, particularly that of Sidonius and Fortunatus. Both writers describe establishments which are recognizable as villas of the classical type, and for some scholars this has been enough to show a continuous tradition of villa life from the fourth century through to the sixth and beyond. The well-known description by Sidonius (*Ep.* 2.2) of his estate at Avitacum would seem to bear this out: everything is there, from the summer dining-room to the still functioning plumbing; and the lack of painted wall plaster, of which he makes something of a virtue, is the only hint of any decline in standards. It is all very idyllic, very gracious, and comparable with the younger Pliny's description (*Ep.* 2.17) of his Laurentine villa. It is precisely this, however, which makes one pause: the letter in which the description occurs is clearly a set piece, a literary exercise rather than a genuine attempt to provide information. Who, in real life, would invite someone to stay and enclose a detailed description of the property? In the even more overtly literary description of another house, the Burgus of Pontius Leontius at the confluence of the Garonne and Dordogne (Sidonius, *Carm.* 22), other influences and other emphases combine to produce an entirely different picture (cf. Sivan, above p. 138). Here the emphasis is on strength and security, both natural and artificial. Inside, it is true, are all the traditional comforts, including the summer portico (this time with paintings on a lavish scale) and a suite of baths (again with the plumbing in good working order); but the feel of the place is different, and we seem to be in a different world.

So striking, indeed, is the contrast that one wonders, even from so few examples, whether an overall pattern can nevertheless be derived. It would be something as follows: Sidonius' Avitacum represents the survival of the traditional villa, that is, either a physical survival of an actual fourth-century establishment or one built later in the traditional style (see Fortunatus, *Carm.* 1.18, 19, 20). Burgus, on the other hand, represents a new style, retaining the traditional amenities but incorporating them in an entirely different context (cf. Fortunatus, *Carm.* 3.12). In other words, if a villa survived into the fifth century, with its amenities intact or restorable, you might as well persevere with it and let it take its chance; you might, indeed, given the right circumstances, feel able to build a new villa on the Roman pattern and in a 'Roman' location. You might, on the other hand, if conditions at a given point in time or in a given area seemed less secure, prefer to remove the element of chance and go for something capable of offering a measure of protection.

The idea of a change of this kind in the style and siting of villas is supported by a foreshadowing of it in a number of sites of the fourth century. I have referred elsewhere (Percival, 1976: 175f.) to the late, very military-looking villa of Pfalzel near Trier, and to the remarkable fortified site of Keszthely-Fenékpuszta near Lake Balaton in Pannonia. What such sites suggest is that the kind of considerations which led to the building of Burgus in the fifth century were already being felt in the fourth. To secure oneself from brigandage or intermittent harassment would be within the capabilities of many landlords. This, I take it, is the motivation behind an establishment like Burgus, the siting of which should be seen as a sensible precaution, and perhaps something of a status symbol, rather than anything more grandiose. Interesting in this connection is the rather puzzling site known as the Camp de Larina near Lyon, which Samson argues (rightly, I think) would have been termed a *villa* or *domus* by Gregory of Tours (Samson, 1987: 299ff.). Here, within an area of roughly 21 hectares, is a building which, apart from its apparently Merovingian date, would most appropriately be interpreted as a Roman villa, together with two cemeteries and what appears to be a small hamlet. Samson includes the site in an argument against a general fortification of private properties in the late antique period, pointing out that 'the central residential building...can in no way be deemed to have been fortified'. Yet, as is clear from the published plans, the site as a whole is on a plateau bounded on two sides by steep cliffs, and lies within an Iron Age rampart which was refurbished in the Merovingian period. Ultimately, it seems, it is a matter of what one understands by fortification: this is not a castle, clearly, and not a place where one would feel secure for very long from a determined enemy; but it is a very good candidate for being a Burgus.

If we can take this site as an example of the new style of villa building for which I claimed Burgus as a sort of prototype, what evidence do we have for the old style, that is, the villa which struggled through and was allowed to take its chance? Did such sites exist in any significant numbers, and did they continue in something like their original form, or were they changed out of all recognition? An answer to these questions has to be provided in terms of positive archaeological evidence. Although the survival of a site is likely in principle to have led to its transformation into, or absorption by, something different and therefore largely to its disappearance in archaeological terms, we cannot simply assert survival and regard ourselves as excused the responsibility of proving it. The fact is that survival, if it occurred, would be not an event but a process; this process would involve a villa evolving and changing, declining and recovering, perhaps stopping and starting again, over a period of several generations. We have to assume that not all villas would reach the end of the process, but that many would cease to function at one stage or other in the course of it. In fact, of course, we do not have to assume; there are now quite a few sites of this kind, so that we have the opportunity, if not of seeing their ultimate destination, at least of seeing the direction in which they were going. It is to these sites, and with this aim, that I now turn.

There are, in Gaul as in Britain and elsewhere, villa sites which have yielded late occupation material of one kind or another together with evidence either of refurbishment or of new building. In the great majority of cases the material is very scanty and the structures primitive and temporary: villa ruins are used to provide makeshift shelters for small groups of people, of whose occupation and reason for being there we are entirely ignorant. It may be that these groups were busily farming the land and, given better luck, would in due course have built themselves houses beside the villa and so begun the kind of villages we see in Agache's survey. But we need more evidence than this to convince ourselves that this is the beginning of a new process rather than the last pathetic phases of an old one. We need also to rely on something more than the acknowledged uncertainties regarding the dating of fifth-century material.

We do, however, have a limited number of cases where occupation into the fifth century seems to be rather more than squatting, either because it seems to have lasted longer or because the structures involved are more substantial looking than mere shelters (cf. *Gallia* 42, 1984: 315f.; Coulon *et al.*, 1985). At Plassac (Gironde) there seems to have been extensive rebuilding in the fifth century, and on the basis of pottery and other finds the excavators argue for continued occupation into at least the sixth (*Gallia* 31, 1973: 456; 35, 1977: 452, etc.; cf. Sivan, above p. 140). If this is indeed the villa Blacciacum mentioned in the will of Bertchamnus, bishop of le Mans, of AD 615 we have not only documentary evidence for its survival but a possible explanation of why the site is now occupied by the parish church. The villa of Séviac at Montréal (Gers) has late mosaics which the excavators take to be Merovingian and which they associate with what seems to be a continuation of the site into at least the seventh century; only parts of the buildings appear to have been properly maintained during this period, and the fourth-century baths served as a grain silo (*Gallia* 34, 1976: 487f.; 36, 1978: 415ff.; 38, 1940: 491f.; Balmelle, 1987: 151ff.). Here again, the site is under the parish church. Late mosaics appear also at the villas of Lalonquette (Pyrénées Atlantiques) (Lauffray, Schreyeck and Dupré, 1973; Balmelle, 1980: 121ff.) and Mienne-Marboué (Eure-et-Loir) (Blanchard-Lemée, 1981), both of these in association with the reconstruction of some of the rooms.

To this rather short list we could add, perhaps, another half dozen at which the evidence for occupation into and beyond the fifth century would seem to imply something more than the mere squatting to which I referred earlier. How far it takes us is not at all easy to determine. On the one hand, any one of these sites could, if correctly interpreted, be claimed as an Avitacum, that is, as a site which retained enough of its character as a Roman villa to be describable as such, in a literary context if not in an estate agent's handout. On the other hand, it does not require a very high level of scepticism to see these sites merely as the exceptions which prove the rule. Those at Lalonquette and Mienne, at which the most extensive and unequivocal evidence occurs, are clearly exceptional, both in the size of the villas themselves (they are both enormous) and in the nature of what was being done to them. At Lalonquette the most obvious fifth-century building is monumental rather than residential, and the columns and capitals at Mienne suggest a similar function. More important, the embellishments at Mienne have been interpreted as religious in character, connected perhaps with the establishment of an *oecus*; while those at Lalonquette were succeeded, probably in the sixth century, by a chapel and the beginnings of a cemetery.

As it stands, then, this is not an impressive body of evidence on which to base a theory of widespread survival. It includes no clear example of a villa surviving intact, or even fairly intact, more than a few years into the fifth century, and on those sites where occupation seems to have continued in a significant way it appears to be the survival of the site rather than of the villa as such that we are witnessing. Given that the onus of proof is on those who wish to believe the survival theory, it has to be said that the proof is not here; and, as the examples accumulate of sites which make the first faltering steps and then come to a halt, the possibility may have to be faced that there is not only no proof but no case to prove.

At the moment, perhaps, we are not quite at this point, and it would be better to say that the question remains an open one; this is not because of a reluctance to give a negative answer, but simply because there must be a genuine doubt as to what the available evidence means. The cases of Séviac and Mienne-Marboué, as we have seen, depend to a great extent on the dating of what appear to be late mosaics, and there are, particularly in Aquitaine, quite a number of sites whose mosaics may, on stylistic grounds, have to be assigned to the fifth century or even later, rather than to the fourth century as has hitherto been supposed (Balmelle, 1980; 1987). If this turns out to be so, and if (as now seems likely) a contemporary phase of prosperity can be identified in Bordeaux and elsewhere, a measure of survival in this region at least would seem to be indicated. The case would of course be further strengthened if the various kinds of 'late' pottery associated with Bordeaux could be more reliably and more precisely dated (cf. Sivan, above p. 137).

How far a similar pattern existed in other regions would still be a matter for debate, though a re-examination of the material in earlier volumes of the *Recueil des mosaïques de la Gaule* could well be revealing. It would still be necessary, however, to determine if possible the precise *nature* of the survival, in particular whether the fifth-century or later use of such sites is indicative of a religious rather than a residential / agricultural function. I have referred elsewhere (Percival, 1976: ch.9) to villas which, though destroyed or abandoned at the end of the Roman period or earlier, nevertheless continued to exist as religious sites and therefore as potential focal points for settlement. If, as I have suggested, religion was a factor in some of the sites we have been considering, the possibility has to be faced that a religious development, rather than the survival of villas as such, is the norm.

This can be seen at Chassey-lès-Montbozon (Haute-Saône) (*Gallia* 30, 1972: 424ff.; 32, 1974: 417). What we have here is the very common situation in which the ruins of a villa have been used as a cemetery. The burials respect the building, in the sense that they are aligned with it and are arranged for the most part within its rooms, only a few of them overlying wall foundations and even these following the overall alignment. The number and variety of the burials suggests that the building was used in this way over a considerable period of time, and it was this no doubt which, in the seventh century, led to a reconstruction of this part of the villa, in particular the large central room with its apsidal annexe. The effect of this was to establish a church, the idea for which will have come not only from the presence of the burials, but also (one assumes) from the appropriate layout of this main room and from its convenient east–west orientation (cf. Monségur (Gironde): *Gallia* 31, 1973: 458).

Here, clearly, is a pattern of development which is coherent and conscious rather than accidental. What we have at sites like this is not unlike the emergence of what are commonly called cemetery churches, for which there is a good deal of evidence from the late Empire onwards (Thomas, 1981: 156ff.). A cemetery is established outside the walls of a town in accordance with Roman law; in due course, the cemetery acquires a memorial shrine or chapel, and this eventually gets enlarged into a full-scale congregational church. This happens around such centres as Trier, Bordeaux and Mainz, and in Britain at Canterbury, St Albans and elsewhere. To continue our earlier metaphor, sites such as Chassey and Monségur, though arrested for reasons unknown to us, have gone sufficiently far in a particular direction for us to see where they are going. The next stage, it is not too fanciful to suppose, is for settlement to accumulate around the church and for the village so constituted to remove the original villa from archaeological examination, except for the debris in the graveyard, with which we are familiar from so many other examples.

The sequence of villa ruin / burials / church / village, applicable as it may be to this and other sites, is a schematic one and almost certainly needs modification to accommodate more than a minority of the sites which seem to fall within the overall pattern. It is likely, for example, that in some cases there is a direct development from villa to church, without a burial stage and perhaps even without an intervening ruin. But that the overall pattern exists is now, I think, beyond dispute: to the growing number of sites which exhibit all or most of it we can add an almost embarrassing number which illustrate one or more stages within it. Villa sites used as cemeteries we have in abundance, from all parts of Gaul; cemeteries as forerunners of churches are also common; and we have, most notably from Agache's survey but from other areas as well, examples of villas underlying deserted villages with churches as the only present indicator above ground.

The proposition may have to be faced that for much (perhaps the greater part) of Gaul this is the fifth-century villa: that is, not a villa at all but something entirely different, something indeed that may not have been anything in particular until after the fifth century itself had ceased. Survival of this kind, if survival is the right word to apply, would still be very significant, in that villas had a direct influence on settlement. This is not an argument for continuity in anything like the sense that it is normally understood, but it is an argument for a much less clear and much less uniform break than has often been assumed between Roman and post-Roman settlement patterns. The posthumous influence of villas may indeed have been even greater than this, in that they may have had an effect, if not on rural society at large, perhaps on social groupings. What I mean by this is that there is at least a possibility that the people who lived on a villa estate, the people who buried their dead in the villa ruins, and the people who ultimately came together in a village, were the same people. There is no way of proving this, of course, though I suspect that the survival of the names in -*acum*, to which I referred earlier, may point in this direction. Place-names, as we all know, are a minefield (even if many of the mines are laid by the place-name experts to keep the historians out); but there is at least a *prima facie* case that their survival implies, first, the survival of something to which they could be applied, and second, the survival of groups of people who carried the memory of them. If those groups of people were the former estate workers, the precise nature of what they were doing can only be guessed at. Were they gallantly keeping the system going after the villa owners had withdrawn? Were the villa owners still around and organizing them, though living elsewhere? Were the workers, on the contrary, simply using for their own purposes the material remains of a system which had effectively disappeared? How realistic, for the fifth century, is the concept of a 'villa-owning' class, that is, of a class occupying the middle ground between the aristocracy on the one hand and the peasantry on the other? My own guess is that different answers may be appropriate to different areas, though in the absence of positive archaeological or other evidence it is probably best to adopt a minimalist position. Even on this basis, however, we have a kind of answer to the question with which this chapter began: if I am right in my view that the most frequent and most positive development of a villa into the fifth century was, in the first instance at least, as a religious site, both death and new life are meaningful and appropriate terms to apply to it.

V

Recovery: political and military

Social and economic recovery is not the same as political recovery. The centripetal tendencies of important Gallo-Roman aristocrats, especially those living in the south, and the effective marginalization of Visigothic power, have been already been remarked upon by Heather. 'Roman Gaul' remained in existence during the first half of the fifth century because a significant portion of its population suffered no conscious 'crisis of identity', continued to look to the western emperors for administration and defence, and was not frustrated in its expectations. What was the foundation of the continued success of the imperial system?

Much depends on one's assessment of Roman military capability, and here *Elton* offers a very positive view. According to him, in this period the Roman army continued to enjoy the operational superiority over its enemies which it had demonstrated in the course of the Rhine campaigns of the late fourth century. The barbarian victories of 406–7 and the years immediately following were the result of surprise, overwhelming numbers and unusually competent leadership. However, once inside Gaul the amateurish Germans found themselves confronted by professional Roman armies that were easily able to contain, and even annihilate, their foes. That they did not destroy them was because it was deemed more prudent to attempt to absorb their strength – a strategy that, given time, may well have succeeded (cf. Nixon, Sivan). The most outstanding Roman general was Aëtius (cf. Burgess), whose prolonged but successful campaigning in the 420s and 430s suggests that he was able to deploy a highly mobile and superbly supplied army (though he did not mint his own coin: cf. King). Elton further argues that Aëtius' campaigns show him initiating, not simply responding to, military developments in Gaul. Though fighting took place to the west, rather than to the east, of the

Rhine, and against rebels as well as troublesome German federates and new invaders, Aëtius consistently overcame his enemies, and Gaul was in no sense lost to the Empire.

But, without money. Roman military supremacy, and hence Roman political control, could not be maintained. Elton notes the disastrous consequences for the continued existence of a professional army of the shrinking of the imperial tax-base caused by barbarian settlement (and, one might add, civil discord: cf. Halsall, Drinkwater) in Gaul and Spain; and in this respect he, like Heather, draws particular attention to the loss of Africa. However, unlike Heather, he would put the beginning of the end in the 460s, rather than the 450s, in the context of the turmoil precipitated by the murder of Majorian in 461, and the refusal of Aegidius to recognize his successor, Libius Severus. In Elton's view, Aegidius' withdrawal to the north of Gaul with most of the Gallic army damaged the regular defence of the country beyond repair, and compelled the new emperor to treat directly with the Burgundians and Visigoths in order to obtain the power to oppose him. Aegidius was successfully isolated, but at a price, for it was now that Italy finally threw off the onerous and, above all, crushingly expensive responsibility for the defence of Gaul. Thus it was Roman weakness, not barbarian strength, which created the power-vacuum that allowed the still undistinguished and, despite their stiffening of Roman generals, still basically inefficient forces of Euric to move out of Aquitania. On this argument, the later vulnerability of the Visigothic army to Frankish expansion becomes more understandable, though the Franks themselves were not much better as soldiers, and owed much of their success to Clovis' leadership.

CHAPTER 15

Defence in fifth-century Gaul

H. Elton

At the start of the fifth century the Rhine marked the boundary of the Roman empire and barbarians were to be kept beyond it by any means necessary. On one side were the Romans, on the other the barbarians. But such definitions were never as clear in reality as they seem on paper. Though the political distinctions between one side of the Rhine and the other were clear, the differences socially, culturally or linguistically were less marked. But, while the Rhine was the border, everybody knew that one side was Roman, the other barbarian, and that barbarians should be kept on their own side.

At this point Gaul was under threat from three barbarian groups: the Saxons, the Franks and the Alamanni. The Saxons raided along the Channel coast. The Franks lived across the Rhine north of Mainz and frequently tried to cross the river, both to raid and to settle in the Empire. This settlement could be carried out peacefully; there was no shortage of abandoned farmland, and many farms may have employed these 'illegal immigrants' at low wages. To the south-east of the Franks lived the Alamanni, whose activity was confined to raiding. Their attacks were limited by the Vosges, whereas the Franks were able to move easily into the heart of Gaul through the Belgian plain.

How effectively did the Roman army defend the area? One Roman expedition in 391 is described by Sulpicius Alexander (GT *HF* 2.9):

Arbogast, following the *subreguli* of the Franks, Sunno and Marcomere, out of tribal hatred, arrived at Cologne in the depths of winter, in the knowledge that all the refuges of the Franks could be reached and burnt, since the leaves had fallen and the bare dry woods could not conceal ambushers. So he collected an army, crossed the Rhine and ravaged the Bructeri closest to the bank, and the *pagus* which the Chamavi inhabit.

The motivation, apart from 'tribal hatred', was retaliation for an earlier Frankish raid. The Romans would expect to be successful on this expedition, and not unreasonably. The expedition was well organized (note a river-crossing, a winter campaign and good scouting) and well led. The Romans knew whom they were fighting and how to defeat them. They were careful to nullify a known strength of the enemy, its skill at ambushes. According to Claudian, 396 shows the same picture: Franks and Suevi crawling to make peace, the Rhine quieted by a word from Stilicho. This may be a rhetorical description in a panegyric, but we do not know of any disturbances on the Rhine between 396 and 406.

So, at the start of the fifth century, the Roman army in Gaul was in good condition. It was a standing army, composed of professionals: soldiers and officers still signed up for twenty years' service. Most Romans wore body armour and helmets, inevitably reducing the casualties suffered in combat. The Romans were also masters of siege warfare; they knew how to attack or defend fortified sites. So, when the army fought, it would usually win its battles. Apart from Adrianople, the Romans did not lose a major battle against barbarians between 350 and 500. At the start of the century, the Romans engaged barbarians as often outside the Empire as inside it. Consequently, the army was stationed mostly on the borders of the Empire, and to see numbers of soldiers away from the Rhine must have been a rare event.

The efficiency of the Roman army must, however, be compared with that of its German enemies. How efficient were the armies of the Franks beyond the frontier, or, from the early decades of the fifth century, the Visigoths and Burgundians within it? The overriding impression received of German armies is their amateurism. Though all able-bodied men could fight, they also had to earn a living by farming. Consequently, armies were levied to meet emergencies; they were not standing institutions. With no standing army there could be few professionals, so discipline was weak. The bodyguards in royal retinues would number no more than a few hundred, not enough to make a significant difference in an army of thousands. Individual weapon skills may have been good, but equipment was minimal, and armour was rare, only being worn by kings and nobles, and not always then. The Romans were at their best in open battles and sieges, where the Germans were at their worst. Consequently, German strategy tended to concentrate on ambushes and wearing down the enemy in running fights and raids. The barbarians could take towns, but they usually fell by surprise or to treachery, not because of any skill at siege warfare. Lastly, their intelligence system was weak, often allowing armies to be out-manoeuvred or surprised.

This is a sorry picture. But it does not mean that all barbarian military activities were doomed to failure. The Romans were vulnerable if caught by surprise or if outnumbered, and even the Roman army could not be everywhere at once. Barbarian shortcomings could also be nullified by skilful leadership. Stilicho was never able to defeat Alaric, for example, despite battles in 395, 397 and 402, whereas after Alaric's death a basically unchanged Roman army under Constantius was able to dominate the same Visigoths when they were led by Athaulf, though without defeating them in battle. The skills of the generals made all the difference.

How did the barbarian military react once settled in Gaul? The Visigoths were sufficiently aware of Roman strength not to attack Roman territory unless the Romans were distracted by military action elsewhere. But even this did not help, and Visigothic military history from 418 to 439 was one of unmitigated disaster. The Visigoths tried to capture various towns from the Romans, Narbonne and Arles especially, but were beaten back on every occasion. They could besiege the towns, but could not capture them before their relief by a Roman field army. But these struggles did not destroy the client relationship the Visigoths had with the Romans. When required, for example in 422 or 433, the Visigoths still provided allied contingents for the Romans. Nor did the struggles induce the Romans to eradicate the Visigothic settlement. Though the Romans could have done so, they decided not to. Given time, and contemporaries expected that there would be enough time, the Visigoths would have faded into the background, their kings becoming Roman nobles, as did the client kings of the early Empire. For the moment it was enough for the Romans to contain Visigothic energies and encourage their assimilation.

The case of the Burgundians was similar. They were settled on the Rhine in 413 and by their presence would stop barbarian attacks on the area where they lived. When the Burgundians did attack the Empire in 436, the Romans defeated them quickly, even though the Burgundians had not attacked until there was a distraction in the form of a revolt in Aremorica. When it came to the crunch, the Burgundians were as inferior to the Roman army as was the Visigothic army.

What were Roman armies of this later date like? This is the era of Aëtius, when we know what happened, but not why, and we have very little information about his army. One thing we do know about is its mobility. It was constantly on the move, fighting in Aquitaine, on the upper and lower Rhine, and in Raetia. And wherever it went, it won its battles. To do this, it had to be efficient and it had to be supplied. The mobility shown suggests that the supply network was still functioning effectively. Though it has to be admitted that this is only supposition, it should be noted that, when Litorius relieved the siege of Narbonne in 437, his cavalry rode in with two bushels of grain on their horses; the Roman commissariat was still in working order.

Another striking feature is the continued campaigning. Year in, year out, Aëtius and his men were at war, and eleven campaigns are recorded between 425 and 439. This sort of activity puts a strain on armies, and results in a constant wastage of men and material. For an army to perform effectively under such conditions it needs a good system of replacement of both equipment and manpower.

This, however, is giving the Romans the benefit of the doubt. It assumes that they were managing the defence of Gaul in an orderly fashion. The alternative view is that they were rushing to react to every barbarian attack, shoring up one sector temporarily, before being compelled to dash to another. Is this a valid interpretation? Maybe, but if the Empire was being overwhelmed by a flood of attacks, who were these people, and why did they stop attacking after 439? After 437 the Burgundians caused no more trouble, Noricum was quiet from 431, after 439 the Visigoths did as they were told, and there was only occasional trouble on the northern frontier.

I would therefore continue to argue that the Romans were well in control of the military situation at this time, and that from 440 to 450 Gaul, with the exception of parts of the north, was at peace. The army seems to have been no worse than it was at the beginning of the century. It was still winning its battles, one of the major criteria for measuring the effectiveness of an army. More important politically, it was also winning wars.

Although the reasons for fighting are not as clear-cut as at the beginning of the century, motives are still easily identifiable. The Romans acted against the rejection of their authority (in the case of the revolts in Noricum (431) and Aremorica (435)), outside attacks (the Franks (428)) or attacks from inside (the Burgundians (436) and Visigoths (430, 436)). The settlement of barbarians inside the Empire had altered the area in which the Roman army might fight, but only in the short term. Had things gone as planned, within perhaps a century the Burgundian and Visigothic settlements would have been totally absorbed.

But there were some changes. In the fifth century the Roman army fought exclusively within Gaul. Given its obvious military power, there seems to be no reason why it should not have crossed the Rhine (it did not lose Cologne until 457), so perhaps there was a change in policy, a realization that the destructive strikes of the fourth century into the *barbaricum* were not effective. More importantly, the settlements in Gaul and Spain, and from 455 the loss of Africa, reduced the financial base of the Empire without significantly reducing its costs (cf. Drinkwater, below pp. 212, 216). In this situation the Roman army suffered, and the situation was exacerbated by the hiring of allies, effective in the short term, but resulting in long-term weakness as money invested in the regular army decreased.

But as late as 451 the military situation was still similar to 418. The Burgundians were on or near the Rhine, the Visigoths were in Aquitaine, but there had been no other significant changes. The settlements of various groups of Alans had had a minimal military or political impact, similar to the settlement and infiltration of Franks on the north-eastern frontier. Gaul was still Roman, and, though life may have been a little different in the settled areas, the changes were not serious.

Nothing changed with the Hun attack of 451. It was a barbarian attack from beyond the frontiers, and was met by a Roman army in Gaul. The Romans provided the majority of the troops involved to oppose the Huns, while some Franks, Visigoths and Burgundians fought as allies of the Romans. When led by the Romans, some barbarian military deficiencies (in military intelligence, planning and supply) could be nullified. Why did the settlers fight for the Romans? Self-preservation seems to be the most likely reason. The allied army was only just able to hold off the Huns. Without the allies, the Romans would probably have lost the battle, and then the Visigoths and other allies could have been mopped up separately. The Visigoths would have known this, and, even if they had not, the Romans would have explained it to them. 'United we stand, divided we fall' would have been Avitus' theme as he persuaded Theoderic to fight. But how much choice did Theoderic actually have? Attila had declared that he would march on the Visigoths, and one can envisage Avitus having a second message for Theoderic, that if he would not fight with the Romans, then the Romans would leave the Visigoths to their fate. Theoderic probably had no choice but to fight the Huns, and to do this when and where the Romans wanted.

But, within a decade of the defeat of the Huns, Gaul had changed almost beyond recognition. Majorian's death in 461 marked the end of imperial Roman control of Gaul as a region. The *magister militum per Gallias*, Aegidius, refused to accept the authority of the new emperor, Libius Severus. Aegidius had campaigned with Majorian under Aëtius, and not surprisingly was upset by his murder. What is curious is that he did not declare himself or someone else as emperor, the response usually taken by generals rebelling against the established order (cf. Fanning, below p. 289). With this revolt, Roman imperial control was confined to south Gaul, while north Gaul, and with it most of the Gallic army, remained under the control of Aegidius.

Severus now had the authority, but not the military strength, to dominate the Visigoths or the Burgundians. Aegidius, on the other hand, had the troops (so long as he could pay them), but no authority. Severus could attempt to regain control in Gaul only through the barbarian kingdoms, using the Burgundians and the Visigoths against Aegidius. This led to the Burgundian king Gundioc being created *magister militum per Gallias* in 463. A barbarian king who was simultaneously a Roman *magister militum* illustrates the assimilation achieved by the Burgundians (the Visigoths and Franks did not manage this), but, more importantly, imperial Roman inability to influence Gaul directly.

In the north, Aegidius was quickly drawn into a war with the Visigoths, whom Severus had probably induced to fight by the gift of Narbonne. Aegidius used some Franks as allies or mercenaries in these campaigns. He needed the extra troops, the Franks probably appreciated the work. Yet after his victory at the battle of Orleans in 463, Aegidius made no attempt to conquer the Visigothic kingdom, nor to return Gaul to the Empire. This lack of aggression may have been connected to increasing conflict with various Frankish groups on the north-eastern frontier or to lack of resources. Although what we know of Aegidius' policy seems to have been defensive, he may have had more offensive intentions. In 465 he sent ambassadors to the Vandals, perhaps in the hope of co-operating against the Visigoths. He probably needed such help as, despite the recent victory at Orleans, the authority he had in north Gaul was fragmentary. As well as the Franks, there were Saxons in the Loire valley. The Bretons under Riothamus also fought the Visigoths, sometimes in co-operation with the Italian imperial Romans. We also know of other Roman factions, who could have been subordinate to Aegidius, allied, non-aligned or even hostile. As well as the Roman factions led by the *comites* Paul and Arbogast, others may have existed. Lastly, the north was also threatened by the Alamanni and the Burgundians. Though often portrayed as an independent Roman state in north Gaul, Aegidius and Syagrius' 'kingdom' was probably not much bigger than a day's march from their army.

From the point of view of the Romans in Italy, things were just as bad. Imperial revenue was reduced to a minimum, crippling military capability. Though the imperial Romans retained control of a coastal strip of south Gaul, this was extremely tenuous. Force could be projected into Gaul, the last occasion being in 469, but it was ineffective. With not enough troops, not enough money, faced by capable Burgundians and Visigoths, and, most importantly, fighting for a lost cause, the Romans gave up. One either held all of Gaul, or none of it. There was nothing significant to be gained by trying to hang on to bits of Gaul and, as far as the emperor in Italy was concerned, Gaul had been lost in 461. By 475 the situation was accepted in legal terms, when Julius Nepos granted the Auvergne to Euric, legitimizing its conquest. Despite the howls of protest from Sidonius, Nepos had finished with Gaul. He held Provence, but nothing more, and, after his deposition, Provence too fell to the Visigoths.

Under Euric, the Visigoths had some success and, though they won few battles, they were able to increase their area of control. But this does not seem to be the result of any changes in the army; indeed, they seem hardly to have developed their armed forces after the defeats of the 430s. The only area of change was the establishment of some standing troops, with expeditions wintering in Spain. But their armies were still the same. Sidonius' account of the blockade of Clermont records that Ecdicius, with eighteen cavalry, routed several thousand Visigoths deployed to assault the town. Ecdicius' attack came as a surprise to the Visigoths, catching them in the rear. Even so, it seems hardly likely that he could have defeated even a few hundred Visigoths, unless they were mostly infantry, and untrained and badly led infantry at that. Only this sort of situation would have led to panic among the Visigoths and Ecdicius' victory.

Visigothic military ability was now supplemented by the employment of Romans, for example, Namatius, who fought Saxon pirates at sea. With the weakening of the Roman position in the north, Saxons and other barbarians were raiding all along the Atlantic coast, reaching as far as Spain. Roman nobles also fought in the Visigothic army, some through compulsion, and Sidonius wrote to one friend, Calminius, forgiving him for taking part in the blockade of Clermont.

But these men had little effect. In the north the Visigoths were defeated in 463 at Orleans by Aegidius, in what appears to have been a major battle. Frankish raids on Saintes in 496 and Bordeaux in 498 penetrated surprisingly deep into Visigothic territory. And when the crunch came in 507, at Vouillé, again in Gothia, the Visigoths lost. Their army seems not to have improved since the 430s.

Such a depressing picture may not be totally fair to the Visigoths. They did win some battles, defeating Anthemiolus' expedition against them in 469 and in the same year capturing Bourges from the Bretons, northern allies of the Italian Romans. They were also able to attack the Burgundian territory of the Rhône valley. But these victories were rare and, in general, when the Visigoths fought battles, they lost.

So why did this fighting take place, given that the Visigoths were prone to lose battles? The attack on Clermont was the result of Euric's ambition, encouraged perhaps by Gallic nobles such as Arvandus (cf. Harries, below pp. 306f.; Teitler, below). Fighting tended to take place around cities, since these were the centres of political units; it was just the barbarians' bad luck that they were no good at sieges. Fighting pirates was self-defence. The battle of Orleans was the culmination of two years' skirmishing brought about by Severus' diplomacy. Lastly, the conflicts against the Franks were defensive, that is, they were Visigothic reactions to Frankish offensives. As far as we know, fighting was confined to Visigothic territory.

Although the army is still described as Visigothic, it should no longer be seen as a supplementary layer, on top of the Roman state. We have already seen that Romans of Sidonius' circle could belong to the army. The Romans now had little or no political independence, unless they were part of the Visigothic power structure. Clermont was an exception, but it was not a typical Arvernian town and, though the Romans maintained a separate existence, they had little political power. 'Visigoths' now meant those people who lived in cities ruled by the Visigothic king. The Visigothic army fought for them, Romans and Visigoths alike.

Like the Visigothic armed forces, the Frankish army changed little in the fifth century, despite the transition of the Franks from barbarians living across the Rhine to semi-Roman settlers. In the mid fifth century Sidonius describes them as brave, undisciplined warriors, unarmoured and fond of thrown weapons and both Procopius and Agathias in the sixth century describe them in similar terms. Frankish armies consisted of badly trained, under-armed but brave infantry, similar to the Visigoths and other barbarian armies. So how did they defeat the Romans? Roman campaigns against the Franks almost always ended in Frankish defeats. Even at Soissons where Clovis defeated Syagrius in 486, Syagrius willingly gave battle, so he obviously thought he could win. So did another Frankish king, Chararic, who refused to obey Clovis' summons, and waited for the battle to be decided before committing himself. But with Clovis' victory over Syagrius, there were no Roman armies left in Gaul. The Frankish victory over the Romans was one of default. Yet wars continued to be fought. The Franks fought the Burgundians and the Visigoths, but, even before these wars, they were busy fighting each other. Gregory describes a number of Frankish kings who fought against Clovis, both before and after the battle of Vouillé.

Why did these battles take place? Like Euric, Clovis was an aggressive king. His ambition, supported by his ability, created and won conflicts, and turned scattered communities of Franks into a kingdom.

The Burgundians differed from the Franks and Visigoths only in the degree of assimilation. Though we do not know why, Burgundians and Romans came together very quickly in the second half of the century. From the 460s this may have been the result of Burgundian kings holding Roman offices. Gundioc was *magister militum per Gallias* from 463, and his sons Gundobaudes and Chilperic both held Roman military offices. They had a place in the Roman order, and thus their court became a part of the governing system as far as the indigenous population was concerned. Yet, for all this assimilation, their army was little different from those of the Visigoths and the Franks, though its weaknesses were not as apparent since they only fought the Romans once in the second half of the century, at Lyons in 458.

In conclusion, what does this brief sketch of military history tell us about Gaul? First, that Gallic unity was only a result of having a place within the Empire; 'Gaul' as a concept was a product of higher authority (cf. Drinkwater, below pp. 216f.). Once this was removed, the region fragmented into a number of separate states. Secondly, the Roman army had a distinct superiority over its enemies, whose armies benefited little from their period of settlement in Gaul; cultural assimilation did not include assimilation of military techniques. Thirdly, the history of the growth of states is not just about battles: it can occur without fighting. Gaul was lost to the Empire when the Romans no longer defended the Rhine, and this occurred when they could no longer fund an army in Gaul.

VI

A crisis of identity?

The first half of the fifth century did not, therefore, witness the collapse of Roman Gaul: there was a form of recovery after the crisis of 406–18. However, this recovery was by no means complete; or, perhaps better expressed, in no way did it amount to the re-establishment of the political and military certainties of the late fourth century. As touched upon by a number of contributors in this volume, western emperors no longer resided in Gaul as a matter of course; indeed, they were rarely seen there except in emergencies. Moreover, the transfer of the seat of the Gallic prefecture from Trier to Arles, and the establishment in the same city of the Gallic Council, displaced the administrative centre of gravity of the country from the north to the south. Yet even those living in the relatively secure southern 'Diocese of the Seven Provinces' had to recognize and come to terms with changed circumstances. As we have seen, Roberts has identified the alternative strategies that they might adopt in the wake of the invasions of 406–7 and their immediate aftermath: increased self-help or withdrawal. Elsewhere, at the edge of and beyond the zone of recovery, the adoption of one or the other of these courses of action will have been an even more pressing necessity: as will be seen below, it is likely that large parts of northern Gaul (none of whose communities was, significantly, represented in the Gallic Council) drifted out of the effective control of the imperial administration. Those who chose, or were compelled, to remain in such places had to make shift for themselves; those who chose, or were compelled, to leave them appeared in the south of the country, and beyond, as refugees. Either course of action would have involved some re-assessment by those concerned of the effectiveness of the Roman imperial system and their position within it.

King draws attention to the appearance of gold and silver coinages, imitative of imperial issues but clearly 'unofficial' in origin, in northern Gaul from the middle decades of the fifth century. Although, being very mindful of the grave problems involved in interpreting the numismatic evidence, she is quite properly reluctant to attribute even those groups of coins which can with a reasonable degree of certainty be distinguished one from another to either residual 'Roman' or 'barbarian' mints, she proposes that the earliest silver pieces may have been produced by local remnants of the imperial administration for their own needs: i.e. self-help. One is bound to add that, *pace* Elton, the very existence of 'unofficial' coin production suggests that, despite the efforts of Aëtius, in the north the framework of imperial government continued to suffer disruption and decay.

Halsall and *Drinkwater* emphasize that in all the outlying areas the adoption of measures of self-help entailed *de facto* rejection of Roman authority: like it or not, the people involved were regarded as rebels. Thus Halsall, in his study of a series of rich burials, previously regarded as Germanic but which are better interpreted as Gallo-Roman, proposes that the vacuum created north of the Loire by the expulsion or withdrawal of imperial power (anticipating Mathisen and Heinzelmann, he suggests a weakening of such power even before the troubles of 406–7) may have been filled by local aristocrats, who established themselves as emergency leaders of their communities. Unrecognized by the Roman authorities, they were dismissed and condemned as brigands – 'Bacaudae'. Drinkwater, following a more general examination of the likely effects of the troubles of the first part of the fifth century upon the population and the economy of the south (in which he suggests that a more understanding view might be taken of the 'selfish' behaviour of the great landowners of the region), argues for the possibility of flight away from this area and so comes to a somewhat different, though far from irreconcilable, explanation for the development of the fifth-century Bacaudae. He associates their appearance with resistance to Aëtius' efforts to re-assert imperial control in a north lost to the Roman empire since 406–7.

Flight, associated with resistance to and the breakdown of the social order, in the context of weakening imperial control, is also taken up by *Samson* in an examination of the institution of slavery in the late antique period. Slave participation in the Bagaudic disturbances is attested by our sources: Drinkwater proposes one way of accommodating these references; Samson suggests an alternative.

The prevailing orthodoxy is that large-scale agricultural slavery was never a feature of Gallic society under Roman rule, and that during the late Empire such rural slaves as there were found themselves subsumed within a traditionally subservient peasantry that was rapidly losing what independence it had gained under the high Empire. Samson disputes this, arguing that there is clear evidence for the substantial exploitation of slave labour from the first to the sixth centuries, in the performance of which the slave suffered demeaning and harmful infringements of his personal liberty still not endured by the freeman. Though slave numbers began to decline in the fifth century, this was neither because new victims were not available for enslavement nor because slave labour came to be regarded as uneconomical, but rather because, unsupported by the machinery of the Roman state, owners found it ever more difficult to prevent members of their degraded and resentful work-force from seeking freedom in areas beyond their reach.

Halsall, Drinkwater and Samson together envisage significant areas in the north which, while they might have been in 'Roman Gaul', could be said to be no longer entirely of it: here, surely, may be discerned some 'crisis of identity'. These regions, taken together with those of direct barbarian settlement and control, reflect a major shift in the political geography of the land which, for the first time since Julius Caesar, had important *internal* frontiers. Both Halsall and Drinkwater, however, concede that the campaigns of Aëtius demonstrate that even as late as the mid fifth century the Roman empire was still capable of re-uniting at least some of the lost areas of Gaul with its western rump: as long as Roman military power was sustainable, the northern crisis might be met and even overcome. On the other hand, there are boundaries and barriers other than those that may be drawn on a map; and before the fall of Aëtius there are clear signs that a barrier was being raised even between Gauls who continued to think of themselves and be recognized as Roman citizens and the Empire which for so long had governed their lives and aspirations.

Mathisen illustrates the raising of these barriers by examining those Gallic refugees, in particular those from the north and south-west, who fled Gaul completely in the uncertain years just before (consequent upon a marginalization of Gaul in imperial affairs that began as early as the late fourth century) and, especially, after 407. Having concluded that, for these at least, Gaul was no longer a viable part of the Empire, he also discovers a matching disquiet on the part of those leading Gauls who remained in the country, as they came to sense, even if they were not able to articulate their suspicion, that the Empire no longer gave any thought to their concerns. Though they were still prepared to contend enthusiastically for distinctions and positions within the imperial administration, they usually found their loftiest ambitions thwarted by their counterparts in Italy, and the best they could hope for was high office in Gaul itself. Significantly, at the same time their social links with the Italian aristocracy – whether direct or, through correspondence, indirect – began to wither. The implication is that, while such people continued to feel themselves part of 'a' Roman empire, increasingly they did not necessarily identify the interests of this Empire with those of the Ravenna court (on this 'Gallic alienation from Italian-based emperors' see also Harries). A tension developed between Gaul and Italy which became so marked that we can see some emperors deliberately favouring Gallic notables in order to relieve it.

Mathisen does not neglect the ecclesiastical dimension of this tension. The accepted supremacy of the bishop of Rome was bound to ensure continuing and important contact between the churchmen of Gaul and Italy; but even here we can detect strain. The theme of Gallo-Italian enmity as reflected in church politics is developed in much greater detail by *Heinzelmann* in his analysis of the dispute between the bishops Hilary of Arles and Chelidonius of Besançon, which both parties took before pope Leo I in Rome and in which Hilary was worsted. According to Heinzelmann, after the uncertainty of the late fourth and early fifth centuries and, in particular, after the egregious failure of the Gaul-based usurpers Constantine III and Jovinus – who may have been expected to redress the growing imbalance between Gaul and Italy in imperial priorities, a significant element of the Gallo-Roman aristocracy, both lay and clerical, attempted to create a new force to secure, within the imperial structure, their interests against those of their Italian peers. Their instrument was the Gallic episcopate – now dominated by local nobles, possibly to compensate for their loss of imperial office. The establishment and direction of such an episcopate fell to the redoubtable and ingenious Hilary of Arles, who was able to build on the extraordinary powers enjoyed by the metropolitan of Arles (which, ironically, seem to have been acquired as a result of imperial favour following the defeat of Constantine III, and which may be related to the subsequent privileging of Arles as a focus for Gallic imperial loyalty through the establishment there of the Gallic Council). Support for this venture, including military help, was forthcoming from no less a person than Aëtius. Hilary's eventual downfall, after he had initially enjoyed a degree of success, may indeed be explained by the diversion of Aëtius' attention from Gaul to Italy, which allowed Leo, fully supported by the imperial government, to act to remove this ultramontane challenge.

The psychological distancing of the Gallic aristocracy from the interests of the Empire and the development of the Gallic episcopate are examined further by *Wes*. He argues that the flight of noble Christian converts from the social and political responsibilities of their birth and education, already noted above, involved not so much the rejection of aristocratic values as the ingenious turning of these values against themselves. Thus, for example, according to Eucherius, Hilary and Salvian, the Gallic aristocrat ought to seek *dignitas* in spiritual devotion rather than in the pursuit of a traditional secular lifestyle. For the servant – the body – should respect the master – the soul; and, still more, sons and daughters ought to obey the dictates of their true father, God, by attending to their souls, even if this causes them to go against the wishes of their earthly parents. Instead of being a *dominus* exercising authority over his own *servi*, a man should become the *servus* of the supreme *Dominus*; but in doing so – by perceiving the vanity of human ambition and recognising the true power in the world – he will gain freedom. Curiously, however, the traditional aristocratic values and modes of social intercourse were re-activated when a renowned holy man was elected to a see. As bishop, he enjoyed once again the status and power of an aristocrat; he was expected to receive, and give, the usual courtesies appropriate to his rank; and he could even establish an episcopal dynasty. Wes connects this curious reversal of roles, which caused Salvian much dismay, with the growing aristocratic monopoly of episcopal politics already commented upon by Heinzelmann; but in this respect he makes more of Gaul's need for able and well-connected intercessors between local communities and either emperors or barbarian kings than of outright aristocratic ambition.

The place of religious matters in the context of Gaul's loosening ties with the Empire are also given attention by *Hunt*. Having described the remarkable sense of proximity between Gaul and the Holy Land, created by the movement of pilgrims, their letters, alms and sacred relics, that obtained during the fourth century, and having demonstrated how this proximity was confirmed by the arrival in Palestine of Gauls fleeing the repercussions of the events of 406–7, he argues for a growing sense of distance between the two regions in the years immediately following, and the ensuing need for the Gallic faithful to depend much more upon their own spiritual resources.

The importance of the strain between southern Gaul and the Empire must not, however, be exaggerated, and it should certainly not be thought of as leading to any form of overt separatism. Mathisen points out that Gallic disappointment with the 'Italian' empire arose out of frustration at not having achieved imperial office commensurate with status and ability: unlike their predecessors of the early Empire but like their fourth-century ancestors, fifth-century Gallic aristocrats did not hold back from such competition; and when the opportunity offered itself, as under Constantine III, Jovinus, Attalus and Avitus, they were eager to claim the rewards of imperial patronage, even if this involved supporting a usurper. In short, there may have been resentment, but this was directed against the operation of the imperial system in which they found themselves, not against the system itself. Self-help must always be sought within this system, an idea which, as Muhlberger has shown, lay behind the thinking of the Chronicler of 452 and which remains the most plausible explanation for Avitus' successful claim to imperial power in 456 (sadly, not dealt with directly in this volume, though see Harries, Van Dam). And even such circumscribed self-help was not to everyone's liking. Heinzelmann notes that in the case of Hilary of Arles, as in those of Constantine III and Jovinus, not all the Gallic secular and ecclesiastical establishment was prepared to rock the imperial boat, and that a particular faction within it may have been directly instrumental in bringing him down; and Muhlberger has already pointed out Prosper of Aquitaine's earlier commitment to the centrality of the imperial system.

Against such a background it is hardly surprising that, as Harries and Teitler show us, almost a generation after the 'Chelidonius affair' we find Gallic 'traitors' – men who dared to step outside the imperial framework, and whom we might therefore more charitably characterize as 'realists' – being denounced by their fellow-countrymen; and it becomes understandable why even the 'traitors' remained obedient to the authority of the imperial courts.

Thus, in those areas which the Empire continued to administer and defend on a regular basis, increasing strain between Gaul and Italy may have become apparent. Despite this, as late as the middle years of the fifth century nothing had been done in Gaul or Italy to recognize, still less to resolve, the developing crisis. The Gauls of these regions will have had no conscious coherent awareness of the inherent contradiction between their continuing loyalty to the Empire and the need permanently to secure their particular Gallic interests; rather, they will have sought, as far as possible, to re-establish life in its old routines, based on the restoration of their country to its proper place within the Empire. As Hunt observes, though disrupted, Gallic ties with the Holy Land survived 406–7, and recovered remarkably promptly.

Indeed, it is arguable that, even if the crisis had been recognized, down to the middle years of the fifth century the leaders of what remained of 'Roman' Gaul lacked both the moral courage and the intellectual originality to break with their past. A solution to the country's problems that lay outside the imperial dimension and depended entirely on local resources would have required not only the discarding of hopes of Roman office but also political assimilation with the new Germanic powers in the land. Given the political, fiscal and military debilitation of the western empire, by the middle years of the fifth century such a solution was almost inevitable, but it was desired by few. As *Maas* shows, principally through a provocative application to fifth-century Gaul of a methodology previously used for sixteenth-century Spanish America, though Salvian, by questioning the automatic superiority of (Roman) ethnicity and (catholic) religious orthodoxy, may have begun to move towards a genuinely positive appreciation of the virtues of *Germanismus*, by *c.* 450 such appreciation had still a long way to develop, and indeed would not appear fully until the time of Gregory the Great.

CHAPTER 16

Roman, local, and barbarian coinages in fifth-century Gaul

C. E King

INTRODUCTION

The fundamental problems of coinage in fifth-century Gaul are to
define the extent to which non-imperial coin circulated and to
attribute it to a specific group or groups of people. The chief
difficulty arises in deciding whether 'unofficial' coin was produced by
local leaders who still felt themselves part of the Empire or whether it
was minted by barbarians newly established on Gallic territory.

Attribution is complicated by the fact that the 'unofficial' coinage
was modelled on that already in circulation, i.e. types, legends, and
mint-marks were taken directly from coins with which the population
was familiar. Thus the means of determining which coins are not
official rests on style and the degree of barbarousness, both of which
are subjective criteria. Even when coins can be shown to be
'unofficial' and divided into groups, it is difficult to assign them to a
given group of people when they bear no obvious indication of who
their real minting authority was.

In such circumstances the normal procedure is to examine where
the coins have been found on the assumption that more coins will be
found closer to their mint of origin than further away. This process
works reasonably well as long as there is a relatively large amount of
material and find spots are reasonably well attested. However, only a
small number of specimens are known for many of the coinages
which will be discussed here and they have an even smaller number of

184

provenances. Thus it is difficult to draw definitive conclusions on the basis of the available evidence.

Despite the difficulties outlined above, a number of groups of coins have been isolated and assigned either to barbarian peoples and/or local leaders. The purpose of this chapter is to re-examine the evidence in order to determine the extent to which these attributions can be supported.

The 'official' coinage of the early fifth century in Gaul was a direct descendant of the fourth century, although bronze had virtually disappeared as a coinage metal. After the usurpations of Constantine III (407–11) and Jovinus (411–13), under whom the last abundant issues of silver were produced, the emphasis was on the production of gold, as it was for the Empire as a whole. The unofficial coinages seem to have been minted in either gold or silver, rarely both, and output was sporadic.

EARLY VISIGOTHIC COINAGE

What seems to be the earliest systematic issue of coins attributable to the barbarians is a group of gold and silver pieces minted in the names of Honorius, Theodosius II, and Valentinian III which have been assigned to the Visigoths (Reinhart, 1938; Kent, 1974). In style these pieces are clearly distinguishable from official Roman issues by the long-nosed portrait, small neat lettering, and the elongation of the human figures represented on the reverse.

The gold coins (*solidi* and *tremisses*) are in Kent's view more-or-less contemporary with the pieces they copy, which appeared *c.* 418–25. The solidi had the reverse legend *VICTORIA AAVGGG* (emperor resting left foot on seated captive), the tremisses *VICTORIA AVGVSTORVM* (Victory right, holding wreath and cross on globe). The mint-mark is that of Ravenna. Silver coins were minted also with a Ravenna mint-mark with two reverse legends: *GLORIA ROMANORVM* and the much rarer *VICTORIA AVGGG*. Both have the same type: Roma seated facing on a throne. Unlike the gold, the reverse type of the silver coins is not copied from contemporary official coins from Ravenna (King, 1988).

The issue of these coins seems to have been limited to a brief period of time (Kent, 1974) although the silver can be divided into two groups on the basis of style and weight. The lighter-weight pieces are of an inferior and very linear style, and may represent a later immobilization of the type. Two questions arise from this suggestion: (1) how much later were the immobilized pieces than the originals; (2) why were they restricted to silver? There is no obvious answer to either question, although it should be noted that stylistic deterioration need not imply a long period during which coins were being produced.

There is no particular reason, on the basis of their appearance alone, to assign these coins to the Visigoths. Nor, in the absence of provenanced pieces (with the exception of one specimen in the British Museum found at Richborough in 1913), can a distribution pattern of finds be used to support such an attribution. On what grounds then does it rest? The well-organized and systematic nature of the coinage, i.e. its production in gold and silver and in more than one denomination, suggests it was minted by an authority which had the security, stability and capacity to produce an imitative coinage (i.e. non-Roman) this early (*c.* 418–25). The only non-Roman people settled in Gaul by 418 who possessed these characteristics were the Visigoths. Thus the attribution is plausible but by no means absolutely established, and if this group of coins is Visigothic in origin one could reasonably expect specimens to be found eventually in territory controlled by the Visigoths.

'GALLIC SOLIDI' AND LATER VISIGOTHIC COINAGE

On the basis of their similarity of style Reinhart (1938) also attributed other gold coins minted in the names of Valentinian III, Avitus, Majorian, Libius Severus, Anthemius, Julius Nepos, Leo, Zeno and Anastasius to the Visigoths. Of particular interest here are those of Valentinian III, Majorian, and Libius Severus. These coins have been subdivided by Depeyrot (1986b) on stylistic and typological criteria into a number of groups. He argues that the origin of four of his groups cannot be Visigothic since they are not found in territory controlled by them. The obverse legend is the same as that of official pieces (*DN PLA VALENTINIANVS PF AVG*), as is the reverse (*VICTORIA AAVGGG*) and the reverse type (the emperor holding a long cross in his right hand, a Victory on a globe in his left hand, and resting his right foot on a human-headed serpent). Three of the imitative groups copy the Ravenna mint-mark and the fourth that of Rome. The prototype for the reverse type was first produced *c.* 426 at Rome and then Ravenna. Unlike the solidi discussed in the preceding section, all four of these groups have a particular mark or characteristic which allows them to be readily distinguished from the official coins they copy. This may well have been a deliberate practice and would certainly have made it easy for users of these coins to recognize whether coins were official or unofficial.

Group 1 solidi (17 specimens recorded by Depeyrot) have the letter Z at the end of the reverse legend (Fig. 16.1). This practice is characteristic of eastern gold issues, not western, and it is odd to find it on coins which are in all other respects western. They have a Rome mint-mark. Two find-spots are known: Montay in northern France and Vedrin in Belgium (Lallemand, 1965; Delmaire, 1984). Depeyrot has suggested that these coins may have originated in northern Gaul or Scandinavia, but until there are more provenanced pieces such an attribution must remain conjectural.

Group 2 solidi (25 specimens recorded by Depeyrot) have a large dot on the obverse, usually placed behind the head of the emperor but occasionally in front of the neck. Finds have been documented in Sweden, Poland, and Germany, and this distribution makes it unlikely that the coins were minted by the Visigoths, although more provenanced finds would strengthen this argument considerably.

Group 3 solidi (13 specimens recorded by Depeyrot) have an unbroken reverse legend. Given their diversity of style, it is questionable whether they form a distinct group. Some are quite similar in appearance to the group of solidi with the circle above the emperor's head (Group 4). Two find spots have been recorded: Bury St Edmunds in Britain and Aalborg in Sweden. Again, there is not enough evidence to attribute the coins with certainty.

Group 4 solidi (95 coins recorded by Depeyrot) is by far the commonest, and features a small circle (crown) over the head of the emperor, sometimes with an indication of a hand holding it (Fig. 16.1). Finds have been recorded in Scandinavia, Czechoslovakia, Belgium, and France along the Loire at Nantes and Arçay (Cothenet and Lafaurie, 1969), at Châtelaillon (Lafaurie, 1980) south of La Rochelle, and in the Département de l'Ain in eastern France. Both Lafaurie (1980) and Depeyrot (1986b) argue on the basis of their

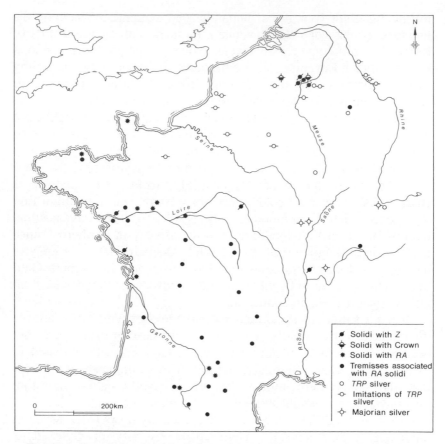

Fig. 16.1 Roman, local and barbarian coinages: fifth-century coin finds in Gaul

distribution outside Visigothic territory that they cannot have been minted by the Visigoths.

Depeyrot dates Group 4 (his Group 1) to *c.* 430–40, primarily on the basis of the date when the hand holding the crown over the head of the emperor, and later the empress, appeared on the official coinage (425 and 430) and the date when the reverse type with the emperor resting his foot on the head of a human-headed serpent was produced (426). Certainly the coins cannot have been minted before the pieces they imitate, but how soon thereafter they began and how long they continued are much more difficult to establish. If Depeyrot's date is accepted or even extended into the 450s, his suggestion that they cannot have been produced by the Visigoths seems reasonable since all of the provenanced finds except one (Châtelaillon) occur outside territory held by the Visigoths at this time.

Lafaurie (1980) has argued that the Group 4 coins may have been minted by Aëtius. He also assigns to Aëtius a group of silver coins in the names of Valentinian III and Theodosius II with a Trier mint-mark (Lafaurie, 1964a; 1987). His attribution of both series to the same source can be seriously questioned. There are no obvious stylistic similarities between the silver and the gold solidi. What Lafaurie has interpreted as a shared characteristic of the two, namely the hand of god holding a crown over the head of the emperor, seems to be no more than a deformation of the diadem ornament in the silver series (King, 1988). The Trier silver coins differ significantly from the gold since they have a Gallic mint-mark (while the solidi copy that of Ravenna) and reproduce types and legends which are not copied from contemporary official silver coins (which the solidi do). Nor can the attribution of the solidi with the crown be reasonably attributed to Aëtius as Depeyrot (1986b) has shown, either on the basis of the distribution pattern or in the context of a delegation of the right to coin, especially as the production of gold and silver coins in the fifth century was normally restricted to the emperor and his *comitatus* (Kent, 1956).

If Depeyrot's interpretation of these solidi is correct, there seem to be four groups, presumably, but not necessarily, produced by different groups of people, possibly in northern Gaul, not earlier than the 430s. If this theory seems unlikely or unpalatable, another hypothesis must be formulated to explain their production, e.g. discontinuous production of an immobilized type by one or two groups. But this suggestion is equally difficult to establish on the basis of the available evidence, which rests on style and the geographical distribution of the finds. Even if it is accepted that some of these groups of solidi were minted in northern Gaul, the question arises regarding who produced them, the Romans or the barbarians.

The next group of solidi relevant to the evolution of gold coinage in fifth-century Gaul are those with the *RA* mark, some of which have stylistic affinities with Group 4 solidi of Valentinian III with the Ravenna mint-mark, and may have been influenced by them (Depeyrot, 1986a; 1986b). The authority by which the *RA* solidi were minted, the mint's location, the significance of their mint-mark and their relationship to the 'Gallic solidi' mentioned in a novella of Majorian (*Nov. Maj.* 7.14) have all been the subject of considerable discussion. These solidi were minted in the names of Valentinian III, Majorian, and Libius Severus and copy the same reverse type as the four groups of solidi discussed above, e.g. the emperor standing holding a long cross in his right hand, a Victory on a globe in his left hand, and resting his right foot on a human-headed serpent. A group of tremisses is associated with these solidi which feature a Victory standing left holding a long cross. The tremisses were minted in the names of Valentinian III, Libius Severus, Zeno, and Basiliscus.

These coins and only these coins are attributed by Depeyrot to the Visigoths, but in defining the limits of this group so narrowly he may have excluded some solidi minted in the name of Majorian which could also be Visigothic but do not have the *RA* mint-mark but *AR* or *RV* instead. These coins can be easily distinguished from genuine Arles and Ravenna pieces by the manner in which the Victory on the globe is represented, which is a sort of figure 8 with a vertical line running through it. This representation is also similar to that of the Victory on the solidi with the crown, where the skirt of the Victory is often a single circle or a series of concentric circles with a vertical line conveying the impression of the body. It is possible that the *RV* and *AR* imitations preceded the *RA* pieces, and if they were not produced by the same die-cutters (which seems unlikely) they were at least undeniably influenced by the style of the *AR* pieces.

The distribution pattern of the *RA* solidi and Victory tremisses (Fig. 16.1) has been used by Depeyrot (1986a) and Callu and Barrandon (1987) to support their attribution of these coins to the Visigoths, and by Lafaurie (1982; 1983; 1984) as evidence for their having been produced outside Visigothic territory by Aëtius under Valentinian III and Aegidius under Majorian and Libius Severus. The difference in interpretation of this evidence rests to a large extent on the date when these coins are supposed to have been minted, since the distribution of the finds themselves is not in dispute. According to Lafaurie (1982; 1984), the *RA* mint produced coins for Valentinian III, Majorian and Libius Severus at the same time as the mint at Arles was producing official coin (*c.* 454–65) under the control of the *magister militum per Gallias*. The *RA* solidi are thus contemporary with coins of the emperors whose type and legends they copy. By implication, their find spots, many of which are in Aquitania Prima, were outside Visigothic territory because the Visigoths did not gain control of this area until 472. Depeyrot (1986a) believes the *RA* coins continued for a longer period than Lafaurie postulates, and argues that solidi minted in the name of Libius Severus became immobilized and were produced after his death in 465 throughout the reigns of Anthemius, Olybrius and Glycerius (467–74). Although no solidi were minted in the names of emperors after Libius Severus, Depeyrot argues tremisses were produced for Zeno and Basiliscus which can be linked stylistically to the immobilized solidi of Severus. This explanation permits the production of solidi and tremisses in Visigothic territory after 472 and is therefore consistent with the distribution pattern of the finds.

Lafaurie (1982), on the other hand, attributes the Victory tremisses to the official mint at Arles, a view contested by Depeyrot (1986a) as being wholly incompatible with the distribution pattern. While Depeyrot's attribution is the more plausible of the two, a map of the distribution of the finds of official issues of Arles in this period might clarify the picture since, if Depeyrot is correct, it should show a different pattern from that of the Victory tremisses.

This group of solidi and tremisses highlights the difficulties of attributing unofficial fifth-century coins. It is clear that, even with a reasonable number of provenanced pieces, very real differences in interpretation can arise using the same evidence. The weakness of Lafaurie's argument in regard to the *RA* coins lies in the ambiguity in much of the coin evidence, his handling of the chronology of various issues, and a certain lack of sensitivity to the functioning of the bureaucracy of the later Roman empire, implicit for example in his contention that the emperor would have established a branch mint, not under his direct control, whose function it was to mint gold. Depeyrot's argument, while more plausible, none the less rests on a relationship between the date of production of these pieces and their distribution pattern, which he has not yet established with absolute certainty because the nature of the evidence will not allow him to do so.

Where were the *RA* solidi minted and what is the significance of the mint-mark? In regard to the latter, Lafaurie (1983) has suggested that it is either a deformation of the marks *RV* and *AR* or conceivably a place-name such as Ratiatum (modern Rezé) on the banks of the Loire near Nantes, a suggestion adopted by Callu and Barrandon (1987), who argue that it was established when the Visigoths found it necessary to deal with the encroachments of the Bretons and Saxons. Depeyrot (1986a) reasonably contends that it is extremely unlikely that Rezé was a Visigothic mint, since the distribution pattern of the finds is not really compatible with its location there and Rezé was too small and insecure to have been the site of a major gold mint. It also seems highly unlikely that the Visigoths would have had a mint on the frontier, barely within their territory. Depeyrot suggests an alternative interpretation of *RA*, in which the letters might have stood for the source of the gold, e.g. *Rivum Argentdublum* (modern Argentdouble, Aude) which, in view of the very different alloy content of *RA* solidi from that of official issues (see below), is possible but far from established. The intended significance of the *RA* mark must remain doubtful in the absence of better evidence. In practical terms, however, it may have been a quick and convenient means of distinguishing these solidi from official issues. Unfortunately, no such simple device exists for separating official from unofficial tremisses since they did not carry an indication of their mint of origin.

Callu and Barrandon (1987) argue on the basis of their gold contents that it is the *RA* coins which are referred to in the novella of Majorian as Gallic solidi of inferior worth. Analyses of three of these solidi, six contemporary official coins and two pieces of Valentinian III with the crown over the emperor's head gave the following results: the *RA* coins had *c*. 23 per cent to 27 per cent silver in the alloy; the official coins had between 1.1 per cent and 2.6 per cent silver; and the solidi with the crown had between 1.09 per cent and 4.66 per cent silver. As Callu rightly notes, there is no doubt that the *RA* pieces form a separate group in terms of their alloy content, but can they be identified as Gallic solidi on this basis? Since the law was enacted under Majorian, it must refer to coins minted before it was in force. But the majority of the *RA* coins were minted after the law came into being (since even some of the solidi minted in the name of Valentinian III were minted posthumously), which makes it unlikely that they can be the 'Gallic solidi' referred to in the law. One must look elsewhere to identify the Gallic solidi.

It is at this point that the discussion of gold coinage in fifth-century Gaul will cease. Although there are imitative solidi of Anthemius and Nepos which may have had a Gallic origin (Casey, 1987), the evidence is far from clear, and until the later coins are subjected to geographical distribution and stylistic analysis it is fruitless to speculate on who minted them and where.

LATER SILVER COINAGES IN GAUL

In preceding sections reference was made to silver coinages. The first, which is definitely linked to issues of gold solidi and tremisses and minted *c*. 418–25, has been tentatively assigned to the Visigoths and needs no further discussion. The second, minted on a weight standard of *c*. 1 g in the names of Valentinian III and Theodosius II, with the reverse legends *VIRTVS* (or *VRTVS*) *ROMANORVM* and three reverse types (emperor standing, Roma seated left on throne, and Roma seated facing on throne) with a Trier mint-mark (*TRPS*), merits further comment. There is no doubt, on the basis of the distribution pattern of finds of these coins (Lafaurie, 1987; King, 1988), that they were minted in northern Gaul (Fig. 16.1). The blundering of obverse and reverse legends, the deformation of the diadem and rather rough workmanship suggest that they may not be the product of an official mint despite the mint-mark (King, 1988). Nor does Trier seem the most likely mint to have produced them, given the number of times it was overrun in the fifth century and its decline as a centre of government after the removal of the imperial administration to Arles in 407 (Chastagnol, 1973; Ewig, 1973; Demougeot, 1980), although Lafaurie (1987) believes it was. Lafaurie has argued (1964a; 1980) that these silver coins were minted by Aëtius, a theory rejected by King (1988), who suggests that they may have been produced by local remnants of the Roman establishment, perhaps to pay locally hired troops or to meet other forms of local expenditure (cf. Halsall, below p. 206).

These coins were extensively copied and the copies are on a much reduced weight standard (or standards) at *c*. 0.5 g and 0.3 g. The legends become progressively more blundered and incomprehensible, while the seated Victory reverse is depicted holding a cross rather than being a Victory on a globe. The geographical distribution of the copies is similar to that of the pieces they imitate, although the copies are found in a heavier concentration on the Rhine (Fig. 16.1). It is reasonable to assume that the copies were not minted by the same authority that produced the 'originals', and that the type may have become immobilized and continued in use after the deaths of the emperors they were intended to represent. The most likely group to have minted these copies are the Franks, although the period of time during which these copies were minted has yet to be firmly established. Lafaurie (1988) believes some at least belong to the last quarter of the fifth century and may authentically refer to Trier as their mint of origin. Neither the 'original' Trier pieces nor the copies can be definitely associated with any of the issues of gold discussed above.

Other issues of silver in fifth-century Gaul are much more ephemeral and it is difficult given the small number of specimens with known find spots to determine who minted them and where. Four of a group of seven silver coins minted in the name of Majorian (with a reverse type representing Victory standing left holding a long cross) have been found near Lyon, Dijon, and Basel (Fig. 16.1), which suggests a different mint and minting authority from the Roma group, but more evidence is needed before a definite attribution can be made. Other pieces minted in the names of Avitus, Anthemius, and Julius Nepos are known (Lafaurie 1964a; 1964b) but they are few in number and no serious attempt has yet been made to classify them or fit them into the context of events in late fifth-century Gaul.

CONCLUSIONS

The problems inherent in attributing imitative gold and silver coins of the fifth century found in Gaul should be clear from the preceding discussion. It is not easy to interpret the coin evidence even when there are reasonable numbers of well-documented find spots for specific groups of them. Distinguishing copies from an 'original' imitative series is also difficult. Most difficult of all, perhaps, is to see how the coin issues fit into the context of historical events and the extent to which they can be viewed as Roman or barbarian.

Lafaurie's contribution to the study of the coinage of the fifth century is important, and he has done much to stimulate interest in this difficult subject. Implicit in his work on both the gold and silver is the belief that the coins are somehow 'Roman', produced locally in Gaul by leaders appointed by the Romans and usually loyal to them. This view allows him to postulate a sort of continuity of Roman tradition and behaviour throughout most of the fifth century, while denying to the barbarians the sophistication or interest to produce coins. This is an important synthesis and an attractive one but, unfortunately, not one supported either by the coin evidence, as I have tried to demonstrate above, or the historical evidence, at least in the case of Aegidius, as I have argued earlier (King, 1988). Depeyrot's approach implies that the various gold issues he analyses may have had different origins and may have been produced by barbarians, although he is prepared to attribute only the *RA* coins to a specific group (the Visigoths). It is virtually impossible to assign the coins he discusses, as he has realized, to either locals or barbarians given the nature of the evidence.

Perhaps the answer lies in a more flexible approach to the definition of Roman and non-Roman in this period, and a closer examination of their interrelationships. But it should be obvious that there will continue to be problems in interpreting the coin evidence which are inherent in its very nature and these make definitive attributions of much of the imitative coinage in fifth-century Gaul extremely difficult to establish.

CHAPTER 17

The origins of the Reihengräberzivilisation: forty years on[1]

G. Halsall

Almost forty years have passed since the publication of Joachim Werner's seminal paper 'Zur Entstehung der Reihengräberzivilisation' (Werner, 1950). Here, Werner argued that we should seek the origins of Merovingian burial customs – i.e. interments in cemeteries in more or less neatly arranged rows (hence *Reihengräber* – row-graves), accompanied by numerous grave-goods, above all weaponry for males and jewellery for females – in a style of burial which appeared in northern Gaul late in the fourth century and which persisted to the mid fifth century. This funerary custom differed from the prevalent rite of the period – interment with a decreasing number of grave-goods, usually vessels – in that the dead were accompanied by more lavish and more varied goods, again typically comprising weapons for men and items of jewellery for women. These burials had long been identified with Germanic newcomers into Gaul, and Werner repeated the then current idea that they were to be specifically identified with *laeti*. To support his claim, there was indeed a general correspondence between the areas in which 'early Germanic' burials were found and those where documentary sources mentioned *laeti* settlements (see Böhme, 1974: 192f. Abb. 66–8, 196 Abb. 69). Werner thus identified some of the more lavish graves of the series (such as Vermand (Aisne) III, grave B) as those of *praefecti laetorum*

---

[1] I must express my debt to the works of H.-W. Böhme, upon which all studies of these graves must be based. I would also like to thank Dr Edward James and Dr Tania Dickinson both for reading the drafts of this paper and for discussing the subject with me over the last two years, thus helping perpetuate what I am sure they felt at times was something of a heresy! Finally I would like to thank Will Coster, who also read the draft of this paper.

(Werner, 1950: 25). He argued that these *laeti* remained in their Gallic settlements until Clovis' conquests, when they joined the incoming Franks and reinforced their settlement of northern Gaul. Unfortunately for this idea, there was a noticeable chronological discrepancy between the written and the archaeological evidence. The historical sources placed the first *laeti* settlements in the period around AD 300, whereas 'early Germanic' graves began to appear only in the late fourth century. Furthermore, the lowly status of the *laeti* hardly tallied with the lavish nature of many of the graves, and the presence of numerous items of weaponry in the burials seemed to contradict the fact that *laeti*, like Roman regular troops, did not own their weapons but were issued them from Roman depots.

In his monumental work on Germanic grave finds between the Loire and the Elbe, H.-W. Böhme (1974) argued instead that these graves were those of *foederati*. In many ways this theory tallies far better with the archaeological evidence, and it is generally followed today. There are, however, problems. The distribution of so-called 'early Germanic' weapon-graves covers practically all of Gaul north of the Loire, and the cemeteries which furnish these graves come from all kinds of contexts – forts, urban cemeteries, rural cemeteries, those associated with villas and so on. If these graves are archaeological traces of *foederati*, we must assume that there was a general policy of signing treaties with innumerable small groups of Germans, who then undertook a massive settlement of northern Gaul – yet these processes excited no contemporary written notice. Moreover, no such graves have been found in the areas where *foederati* were definitely settled, such as Aquitaine. Even the heart of Toxandria, ceded to the Franks in this period, remains strangely and consistently blank on Böhme's distribution maps.

In 1980, Bailey Young drew on the long-known fact that this burial custom was not the product of Free Germany but of northern Gaul, and, to use Böhme's phrase, the 'German-Roman mixed civilisation' (Böhme, 1976: 207) which existed there, to ask whether there was any reason why the change in burial custom had to be linked with ethnicity. Despite presenting a number of examples where very similar changes in rite were linked with social rather than ethnic changes, Young, inexplicably, still fell back on an ethnic explanation: although perhaps not all of these burials were those of German immigrants, they could still be called 'Germanic' in style (Young, 1980). A third German group, the 'Gentiles' were introduced into the question (cf. Wightman, 1985: 253). Still, despite Young's evident unease, the debate upon this group of burials has hinged upon their Germanic ethnicity (cf. the two most recent general works on late antique/early Medieval Gaulish archaeology, Périn and Feffer, 1987, and James, 1988a).

If only for the good health of the discipline, the time has surely come to question this assumption more rigorously. Like so many aspects of Gaulish archaeology of this period, the study of the 'early Germanic' burials has suffered from an inability to ask sufficiently detailed preliminary questions of the evidence, from a willingness to correlate too readily, too simplistically, the excavated data with the documentary sources, and from a desire to apply one hard-and-fast interpretation to what is evidently a very complex problem. Archaeologists have not, in this connection, seriously addressed themselves to the question of why people should wish to place objects in their graves in the first place, and only Young has asked whether these changes in burial rite need relate to ethnicity.

Regrettably, the first of these questions cannot be satisfactorily dealt with here; suffice it to say that the purpose of placing grave-goods with a burial was not primarily religious or ethnic (see James, 1979, for example). The large body of work carried out on Anglo-Saxon cemeteries has revealed that the funeral practice was directly linked to the maintenance of the standing of the deceased's family within the local community (see above all Pader, 1980; 1982), and this is now being demonstrated in Merovingian Gaul (Halsall, 1988, and forthcoming).

The question of how we may decide whether a burial rite is the product of the migration of an ethnic group into another region requires more detailed examination. Gerald Dunning (Dunning, 1968) proposed a series of three questions for determining whether a pottery form could be accepted as having been imported. This can be adapted as follows to the question of whether a burial rite is intrusive:

i. Is it significantly different from the rites of the 'host country'?
ii. Are the rite's geographical origins known with precision and do they lie outside the 'host country'?
iii. If ii. is satisfied, docs the rite appear earlier than, and then overlapping chronologically with, its appearance in the 'host country'?

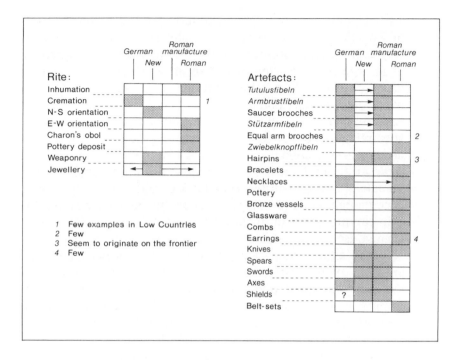

Fig. 17.1 The origins of the *Reihengräberzivilisation*: analysis of the origin of the
'early Germanic' burial customs

The application of this test to the 'early Germanic' graves casts severe doubts upon the interpretation of these burials as the result of a Germanic immigration into northern Gaul (cf. Fig. 17.1).

First, does the rite really differ significantly from that of fourth-century Gaul? We can take the individual aspects of the burial custom separately:

(a) The choice of inhumation is of course no different from the usual Gallo-Roman rite of the period. Although the common north–south orientation of 'Germanic' burials has frequently been cited as a crucial difference, and the general orientation of late Roman graves is indeed often east–west, the latter are not governed by any distinct rule of orientation. The fourth-century burials at Frénouville (Pilet, 1980) are oriented north–south, and the cemetery at Scarponne (Meurthe-et-Moselle; Billoret, 1968) shows the typical late Roman disarray as regards orientation, with north–south and east–west burials occurring together. The 'early Germanic' graves contain pottery, glass and bronze vessels of Roman type, and these are usually positioned in the same way as in typically Roman burials. Another common ingredient of the rite is the placing of a coin in the deceased's mouth or hand – again a Roman tradition and hence no different from other fourth-century burials.

(b) Examination of the choice of grave-goods is another way of attempting to identify an intrusive rite. Again this requires more detailed examination than is possible here but a brief résumé will serve to illustrate the essential points. The most common finds in male graves are belt fittings – buckles and so on. These were once thought to be the badges of Germanic mercenaries, but the chip-carving style of metalwork found on these buckles is Roman (see Haseloff, 1981), and the belt was a symbol of authority used in many areas of Roman life, military and civil (Tomlin, 1976). The distribution of these buckle types shows that they were found primarily along the frontiers of the western empire, with isolated finds elsewhere, including some taken back to Free Germany, probably resulting from service in the Roman army (Böhme, 1976; Haseloff, 1981).

(c) Another major support for the argument that these are Germanic graves is the presence of weapons in them. Whilst it is true that weapon-graves are not usual in the early Roman period, they are more common than has often been supposed (Lintz and Vuaillat, 1987–8), and the weapons in 'early Germanic' graves are almost certainly of Roman manufacture. The axe is a possible exception, being accepted as a Germanic weapon, but even this is not certain. Axes are indeed found in Free Germany but one at least of Böhme's axe types (type B) seems to originate in northern Gaul, and not Free Germany. Our knowledge of the weaponry of later Roman troops is extremely uncertain, and we know even less about what weapons were being made by Romano-Gaulish civilians for their own use.

(d) This leads us to the final argument for the Germanic nature of these weapon-graves: Roman civilians were not legally allowed to carry weapons. The drawback of this reasoning is obvious – legislation does not always reflect actuality. The distribution of late fourth- and early fifth-century weapon-graves is extremely widespread, as mentioned above, and very many of these graves contain no Germanic features at all (as for example at Dieue-sur-

Meuse, grave 101; Guillaume, 1974–5). In late Roman Britain, graves appear on the Lankhills cemetery site (Clarke, 1979) and at Gloucester (Brown, 1975) which are similarly accompanied by belt buckles and knives. The conclusion can be drawn from these male graves that burial with weapons and symbols of authority such as ornate belt-sets was becoming an increasingly popular rite throughout the frontier regions of Roman Gaul in the late fourth and early fifth centuries. Had we no documentary evidence to confuse the issue, it is highly unlikely that anyone nowadays would link the appearance of this rite to a migration of people.

That archaeologists have done so in the past has mainly been due to the female burials. Some of these, in north-west Gaul, contain brooch types of known German origin – *tutulus* (or trumpet) brooches, *Stützarmfibeln* (supporting-arm brooches), saucer brooches and *Armbrustfibeln* (the analogy, with a particular form of crossbow, is, as with the *Tutulusfibeln*, so arcane as to defy translation). That some of the 'early Germanic' weapon-burials have been found in close connection with female burials with these brooches has been sufficient in the past to convince most archaeologists of the Germanic ethnicity of all graves of this type. However, the decoration on (and ultimately the inspiration for) these brooch types is Roman – many bear the same chip-carving motifs as are found on the belt-sets. Examination of Böhme's distribution maps also suggests that certain distinct forms of these brooches were being manufactured on Roman soil (Fig. 17.2). Who is to say that, despite Germanic inspiration, and, perhaps, initial demand, these types were not being made by Romans for Romans? As with the male burials, the other artefacts found in these graves are of Roman manufacture. Claude Seillier's map of 'early Germanic' burials in Picardy – the heartland of this form of burial – reveals furthermore that only about half of cemeteries yielding 'early Germanic' evidence produced female graves with these brooches (Seillier, 1986).

These female burials are, moreover, not as significantly different from other late Roman burials as was hitherto supposed. In other parts of late Roman northern Gaul we can find burials of women with lavish jewellery, as at Sion (Meurthe-et-Moselle) (grave 38: Salin, 1939), the urban cemeteries at Strasbourg (Forrer, 1927) and so on. As Werner noted, the only real difference between these graves and those of the north-west is the absence of brooches (Werner, 1950: 25) and therefore a difference in the way in which women were dressed for their funeral. Is a variation in dress-style between two regions really a strong enough archaeological foundation upon which to build a migration hypothesis?

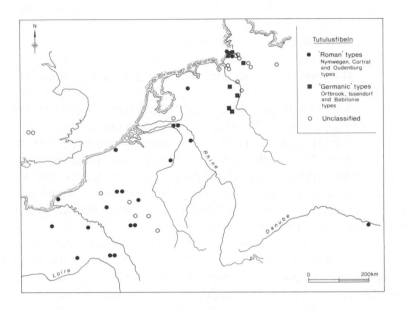

Fig. 17.2 The origins of the *Reihengräberzivilisation*: *Tutulusfibeln* (after Böhme, 1974: map 7)

When we turn to our second preliminary question we find that this, too, cannot be answered in the affirmative. The geographical origins of the new burial custom are, as has long been known, located in northern Gaul (Fig. 17.3). Looking at the rite in general terms – the standard Roman form of burial but with the addition of more numerous grave-goods, including weaponry and belt-sets for the men and jewellery for the women – we can see that it was common across Gaul north of the Loire, west of the Rhine and east of Brittany. What is more, the rite is significantly different from those of Free Germany, where the funerary custom was either cremation, as in Saxony, or an archaeologically invisible rite, as in the Frankish homelands (either cremation or inhumation without grave-goods or a container for the dead, or another form of body-disposal such as exposure on platforms or deposition in rivers). The only analogous graves in Free Germany, the Hassleben-Leuna group of central Germany (*c.* AD 300), are chronologically and geographically too far removed from the north Gallic 'early Germanic' graves to be linked with them. These graves, incidentally, differ far more from the customary burials of the region (cremations) and show certain Roman features, yet no one has argued that they represent an immigration of Romans into the area. They are

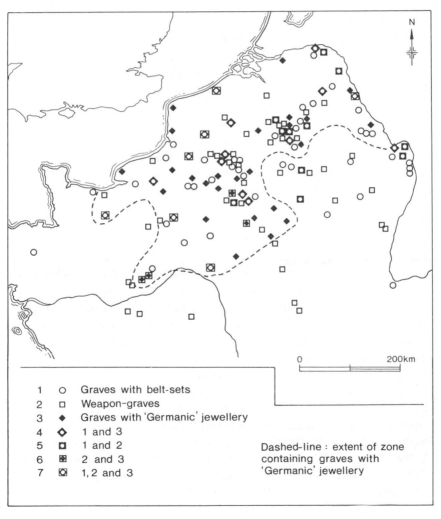

1	○	Graves with belt-sets
2	□	Weapon-graves
3	◆	Graves with 'Germanic' jewellery
4	◇	1 and 3
5	◨	1 and 2
6	⊞	2 and 3
7	◉	1, 2 and 3

Dashed-line : extent of zone containing graves with 'Germanic' jewellery

Fig. 17.3   The origins of the *Reihengräberzivilisation*: Germanic settlement? (after Böhme, 1974: 192–3)

instead explained as 'the momentary pride of an élite' (Young, 1980: 12). Why this interpretation has been applied here but not to the 'early Germanic' graves of northern Gaul is sadly all too easily explained – there are no historical sources for central Germany at the turn of the third century.

The negative answer to the second question removes the necessity to ask the third. The fact, already mentioned, that analogous burials in Free Germany had died out before the appearance of the Gallic 'early Germanic' graves further argues against a Germanic origin for the latter group of burials.

The 'Germanic' identification of these burials can thus be seriously questioned on the basis of the evidence of the graves themselves. The difference between the relatively restricted distribution of the Germanic brooch-burials and the wider spread of 'weaponry and belt-set-graves' and, generally, of jewellery-burials has not been taken into account. Neither has the astonishing lack of archaeological evidence for significant difference from Roman rites, let alone for a German origin. If further arguments are needed, we can turn to look at the archaeology of areas where migrations of Germans are known to have occurred. First, the Visigothic *foederati* in Aquitaine, as mentioned, left no graves of this type. If these burials were a particular trait adopted by German *foederati* on Roman soil, we should expect to find some south of the Loire. Secondly, in their migration into Britain, the East Angles brought their native burial rite – cremation – with them, as is well known. 'Germanic' cremations on Gallic soil are very few, and most are found on the border with Free Germany. If the usual practice was followed in Gaul, we can turn the traditional argument on its head and argue that it is not the richly furnished graves at, for example, Vermand which are those of Germanic immigrants, but the larger number of unaccompanied inhumations. These are, after all, likely to be far more like the burials of the Frankish homelands. Finally, it can be argued that an ethnic minority in the midst of a larger 'host' population is likely to adopt distinctive or exaggerated cultural traits as a means of preserving its identity – these are often more fictive than realistic representations of their original culture (cf. Liebeschuetz, above pp. 81f.). But this argument cannot explain the 'early Germanic' graves. Why should a Germanic minority choose to accentuate its cultural identity by adopting a rite which, as outlined above, was essentially Roman, accompanied by Roman material culture?

If, then, these graves are not those of Germans, whose are they? The archaeological evidence allows us to say, first of all, simply that a new burial rite was adopted across northern Gaul from the late fourth century onwards, and that this fashion peaked around 400. This was basically the traditional late Roman funeral custom but with the addition of more lavish grave-goods. From other sources we can argue that certain common items, such as elaborate belt-sets and cruciform brooches with onion-shaped terminals (*Zwiebelknopffibeln*; Zabehlicky, 1980), were symbols of authority – frequently, though not exclusively, of military authority (Böhme, 1986, renews the argument that the belt-sets are directly connected with the military). In addition, males are also frequently buried with weaponry – a further military symbol of authority.

To explain this we need to consider the social role of the late antique funeral. That this was an important social mechanism – largely because it was one of the few occasions when a large proportion of the community was gathered together – is clear from various sources. It was used by wealthy families to re-assert their standing. We know of a Roman magnate distributing largesse to the poor in a cemetery, on the occasion of his wife's death (Février, 1974: 132). Funeral feasts and the distribution of food, which are suggested by the presence of food offerings in graves, and the discovery on Merovingian cemetery sites of rubbish pits containing animal bones (Halsall, 1988: 51), were further means of re-establishing the ties of dependence between a family and its followers. The sermons of Caesarius of Arles make it clear that to receive food from someone was to enter into a dependent relationship with him (*Sermons* 54.6; cf. also the juxtaposition of scriptural quotations in *Sermons* 54.5: Mueller (tr.), 1956: 269ff.). We should expect the use of the funeral as an occasion for a lavish display of the bereaved family's status in the community and for accentuating the deceased's place in society in times of instability or stress, when a family's position was likely to be threatened by the death of a member. Thus the explanation for the appearance of these lavishly furnished burials in northern Gaul is to be sought in terms of social stress and competition for community leadership. This is underlined by the presence, already mentioned, of symbols of authority in these graves.

If we seek a historical context for this, it can indeed be found in late antique northern Gaul. Van Dam (1985) argues convincingly that the Bacaudae of Roman Gaul were local community leaders who asserted their power as and when the imperial authority could not make itself felt in their region, either through the difficulty of the terrain or through political instability – hence the appearance of Bacaudae in the third and the early fifth centuries, during periods of civil war and separatism, and throughout the Roman period in the Alps, where the inaccessible terrain hindered Roman efforts at control (cf. Drinkwater, below p. 215). This rejection of imperial authority led to the use, by the central government, of the terms Bacauda (in its pejorative sense) and *latro* (bandit) for these leaders.

These provincial elites were taking over the accepted imperial idioms of authority. The distribution map of silver imitation imperial coinage provided by King (above, Fig. 16.1) shows that in precisely the region which yields 'early Germanic' graves, local leaders had adopted the imperial right to mint coins. We know of the fortification of villas. Burgus of Pontius Leontius is the best known from the literary sources, but there are archaeological instances too (Percival, 1976: 174 ff.; above, esp. pp. 158f.; cf. Sivan, above p. 138). Bands of armed retainers or *buccelarii* are also known. While Pontius Leontius was living in Burgus, the Auvergnat noble Ecdicius was defending his region with a private army, and the Byzantine *Life of Daniel the Stylite* (60) similarly describes a Gaulish aristocrat with an armed retinue. Significantly, the word Bacauda seems to mean warrior (Van Dam, 1985: 25 n1).

It is surely no coincidence that the high-point of the so-called 'early Germanic' graves occurs at the same time as the high-point of the activities of the Bacaudae – around 400. When a strong central authority was temporarily restored by Aëtius in the mid century (cf. Elton, above p. 170), the furnished burial rite underwent something of a decline, though perhaps not as marked as was once thought (see James, 1988b), before bursting back into popularity in the confusion of the later fifth century, when the Frankish kings popularized the rite as a means of cementing their authority.

Further archaeological support can be found for the idea that lavishly furnished graves, especially those containing weapons and thus symbols of military power, occurred when the Roman central authority could not make itself felt. The best instance of this is the 'civilisation des sommets vosgiens' of the early Roman period (Welter, 1906; Lutz, 1964). Here, high in the forested mountains of the Vosges, the local population continued to cremate its leaders and place items of weaponry – spears, daggers and axes – in their graves until the early third century (Welter, 1906: 393; Lutz, 1964: 34f.; Babault and Lutz, 1973). Only when the settlements in the high Vosges died out and the population moved to the plain, where Roman authority was more easily felt (the Sarre valley was heavily Romanized; see Lutz, 1978), did these weapon-burials cease to occur.

A more critical consideration of the archaeological evidence suggests therefore that the people of northern Gaul in the late fourth and early fifth centuries took to displaying their power in the community more overtly in their funerals than had hitherto been usual. The removal of effective imperial authority from what had always been a strongly Romanized area created a vacuum in which the local elites competed for the direction of their communities. The presence of Germanic newcomers in these regions added a further element of confusion and competition. This process provides the context for the appearance of these lavishly furnished graves, the terminology for which must be changed, from 'Germanic' or 'federate' to 'high-status'. It must also be stressed that no specific identification is made here. The subjects of these graves might be Roman or German, civilian or military.

The lack of such graves south of the Loire is explained by the greater continuity from Roman to post-Roman which existed there. Not only was the power of the long-established Roman aristocratic families less seriously challenged there but there was generally less of a power-vacuum to be filled. The replacement of the effective power of the Roman central government by that of the barbarian kings was achieved there much more smoothly than in the north.

There are of course problems with the theory expressed here, but they are less important than those raised by the traditional explanations, which have tried to impose too much of an interpretative 'straitjacket' upon the evidence. Any defence of the traditional 'Germanic' explanation must now be based upon a more critical examination of the archaeological evidence. A successful defence of the traditional ideas would also make the archaeology of the Frankish settlement far simpler – since we could trace the movement of Germanic influence more easily. In many ways the most worrying aspect of the thesis presented here is that it may well be right!

CHAPTER 18

The Bacaudae of fifth-century Gaul

J. F. Drinkwater

In two previous articles I argued that the Gallic Bacaudae were neither warriors in a long-standing *Klassenkampf* nor the followers of great aristocrats asserting age-old traditions of local patronage in times of stress (Drinkwater, 1984 [*contra* Thompson, 1952]; Drinkwater, 1989a [*contra* MacMullen, 1966; Van Dam, 1985]). In the first, I expressed the view that the original, late third-century, Bacaudae were essentially a product of their age. They emerged as a result of the collapse of Gallic aristocratic society during the third-century 'Crisis', and should be seen as dislocated peasants who sought security in the leadership of second-order figures of authority: 'lesser aristocrats, yeomen or even visionaries or bandits' (Drinkwater, 1984: 368). They came into direct conflict with imperial authority only when, from the reign of Carinus, it attempted to re-impose its control over the west (cf. Dockès, 1980: 156). In the second, I suggested that the second wave of Bacaudic activity in Gaul, in the first half of the fifth century, was caused by a similar disintegration of local systems of order, but warned that by this time our picture of them may have suffered distortion as a consequence of the intervening debasement of their name, which had become 'a general label for anyone involved in illegal and violent activity in Gaul' (Drinkwater, 1989a: 201). My point here was that there was no continuing Bacaudic movement from the third to the fifth centuries: the pejorative re-application of the term 'Bacaudae', now virtually synonymous with 'bandits', to people whose activities genuinely resembled those of their third-century predecessors was purely fortuitous. However, the scope of my earlier studies prevented me from engaging in detail with the fifth-century Gallic Bacaudae, and my thinking in their respect was correspondingly very speculative. It is my purpose in this chapter finally to give them the close attention that they deserve.

208

The sources for the Bacaudic revolts of the early fifth century are now well enough known (Czúth, 1965; with: Thompson, 1952; 1982: 221ff.; Van Dam, 1985; Drinkwater, 1989a). They may be categorized as: (i) those that mention the Bacaudae specifically by name, and show them causing trouble in many areas of Gaul and Spain from 408 to *c*. 448 (Zosimus, the *Chron. Gall. 452*, Hydatius, Salvian); and (ii) those that scholars consider as referring indirectly to Bacaudic activity, and which seem to indicate particular unrest in the region of Aremorica, in the period *c*. 410–*c*. 449 (Zosimus, Rutilius Namatianus, the *Querolus*, Sidonius Apollinaris, Constantius' *Vita Germani*, Merobaudes).

With the exception of Salvian, the sources that treat of the Bacaudae directly do so disappointingly briefly, and so afford us very little opportunity to probe deeply into the identity and aims of such people. It is not surprising, therefore, that modern historians of the Bacaudic phenomenon have tended to place most weight on their interpretation of the indirect references, and in particular on passages in Rutilius Namatianus and the *Querolus* (e.g. Thompson, 1952: 18f.). Writing *c*. 417, Rutilius Namatianus appears to praise the Gallic nobleman, and Roman official, Exuperantius, for 'teaching the regions of Aremorica to love the return of peace' and, having restored them to liberty and the rule of law, for ensuring that their people were no longer 'the servants of their own slaves' (*De Reditu Suo* 1.213–16). At around the same time, the unknown author of the *Querolus* offered a strange description of life on the Loire:

Men live there under the natural law. There's no trickery there. Capital sentences are recorded on bones. There even rustics perorate, and private individuals pronounce judgement. You can do anything you like there.

(ed. Ranstrand, 17; tr. Thompson, 1952: 18)

These two passages are commonly adduced by those who wish to interpret the Bacaudae as participants in a peasant revolution centred on Aremorica (e.g. Thompson, 1952; Dockès, 1980: 216f., 220); and they indeed cause grave difficulties for those who favour the view that the Bacaudae are better seen as the product of long-established traditions of aristocratic patronage (cf. Van Dam, 1985: 41f., 46ff.).

However, I would argue that the situation is at once more simple, and more desperate. It is simpler because the evidence of Rutilius Namatianus and the *Querolus* must be ruled out as inadmissible. As

Bartholomew has convincingly demonstrated (1982: 266ff.), any mention by the former of social, supposedly Bacaudic, revolution in Aremorica has to be wrung from a hopelessly corrupt text: it is best ignored. With regard to the latter, if the passage concerned is read in its dramatic context, it becomes plain that this life of silvan freedom, whatever else it may have been, was not considered to be illegal: in particular, it could not be classed as *latrocinium*, and so could scarcely have been that of peasant revolutionaries, or even local 'big men' working outside the law (cf. Van Dam, 1985: 46f.). (As to exactly what is at issue here, I remain unsure, but would hazard the guess that we may be in the presence of a slighting, southern Gallic, more precisely Massiliot (Golvers, 1984), reference to Marmoutier-style monasticism.) Without Rutilius Namatianus and the *Querolus* to appeal to, however, our situation becomes more desperate, because to achieve any reliable understanding of the fifth-century Gallic Bacaudae we now have recourse only to Salvian.

Salvian has a great deal to say about the Bacaudae, but he is hardly a disinterested social commentator, or even an historian of acute insight (cf. Jones, 1964: 1060; Gagé, 1971: 436f.; Salvian, ed. Lagarrigue, 1975: 21ff., 29). We must always remember, though we perhaps too often conveniently forget, that the Salvian who identifies as a mortal weakness of the Roman empire the harshness and corruptibility of its taxation system – and so is moved to draw attention to the Bacaudae (*De Gub. Dei* 5) – is the same Salvian who proceeds to argue, and at much greater length, that the Empire was also being ruined by its citizens' love of public entertainments (6) and sexual debauchery (7; cf. Maas, below, p. 277). Furthermore, as is well enough known, his particular account of the sufferings of the weak and their consequences is very confused. He begins (5.21) by giving the strong impression that 'the poor ... the widows ... the orphans' he has in mind as suffering the oppression of the rich and powerful come not from the peasantry, but from the lesser aristocracy or gentry (cf. Salvian, ed. Lagarrigue, 1975: 38f.; Van Dam, 1985: 43; cf. Maas, below p. 281). Next (5.22), when he mentions the Bacaudae for the first time, as people to whom the oppressed flee, he makes no distinction between them and the barbarians, and indeed appears to categorize them *as* barbarians. It is only in the following chapters that he makes clear that what he means is that the Bacaudae are people who live *like* barbarians (5.23), because they are forced to do so (5.26). By then, however, he is declaring (5.26) that the

Bacaudae are no longer a contemporary problem. Finally, it should be noted that it is only after an interval of some twelve chapters (5.26–37) that Salvian moves to examine the miserable plight of the peasant freeholder whom, on current thinking, it is tempting to identify as the most likely recruit for the Bacaudae.

Our sources for the fifth-century Bacaudae are, therefore, meagre and intractable. In dealing with them, it is tempting to proceed along the usual lines, that is to say, by identifying such scraps as seem reliable, and forcing them to fit some pre-conceived pattern; but this would be difficult and unsatisfying. I propose instead to take a different approach, by suggesting various models of economic development and social behaviour, and testing each in turn against the information offered by our sources, in particular Salvian, who, for all his faults, relates much of significance concerning the conditions of his day. This more flexible line of enquiry will lead to some revision of my own previous views on the Bacaudae, and, I hope, raise interesting questions about fifth-century conditions as a whole.

I begin by advancing a hypothesis related to a fundamental but, it seems to me, still very neglected issue, that of the vital statistics of early fifth-century Gaul. If the experience of the Gallic population was in any way as grim as our authorities suggest, as a result of barbarian invasion, civil war, and ensuing disease and starvation (cf. Roberts, above), there ought to have been a significant decline in its numbers, exacerbating a manpower shortage already evident in the countryside from the end of the third century. On this argument, the generation of peasants that was born *c*. 410, and had reached maturity by the time of Salvian's composition of the *De Gubernatione Dei*, must have endured the very worst of the crisis, but should already have begun to benefit from its demographic consequences. Under normal circumstances, in a pre-industrial society a reduced agricultural work-force might expect to enjoy both more freely available land, at lower prices and lower and longer rents, for its own cultivation, and higher wages and a generally more mobile employment market in respect of work done for others (Le Roy Ladurie, 1987: ch. 1). In brief, these people should have begun to experience a rising standard of living, and the more enterprising among them ought to have been well placed to continue the line of prosperous yeomen that seems to have been a traditional feature of Gallic rural society under the Roman empire (Drinkwater, 1983: 173ff.; cf. Herring, 1987: 436ff.). However, of course, circumstances were by now far from normal. In the first half of the fifth century the western empire was burdened by continuing heavy expenditure, principally upon warfare, that had to be funded from a taxation-base that was damaged and shrinking (cf. Bury, 1923: I, 253; cf. Elton, above p. 171); as a result, those who were still available to be taxed were bound to be asked to pay more. In theory, the burden of this extra taxation should have fallen on the shoulders of those who owned the most wealth, the great landowners (so Salvian, *De Gub. Dei* 5.30); however, as I have suggested, these may have already been facing a significant diminution in their incomes as a result of lower agricultural rents, higher wages and, we are entitled to suppose, a depressed market caused by a general contraction of the economy. In other words, such people may well have faced very real difficulties: in considering their actions at this time we should be wary of Salvian's endless moralizing (e.g. 5.17) and so hesitate to condemn these as the outcome of selfish greed. The large landowners had two basic choices. On the one hand, they could accept the situation as it had developed, and seek to enhance their incomes as best they could, through greater efficiency and the introduction of new techniques and new crops (cf. Le Roy Ladurie, 1987: 40, 47, 78f.). (Though this may sound anachronistic, we might bear in mind the, admittedly somewhat earlier, successes of Paulinus of Pella as an improving landlord: *Eucharisticus* 194f.; cf. Drinkwater, 1989b: 148.) On the other hand, they could reject the situation and, through selective application of the power allowed them by the moribund central administration, both escape tax liability and neutralize the advantages that a reduced population threatened to give to the peasantry (cf. Le Roy Ladurie, 1987: 65). It is, of course, the latter ploy that most interests us here. Such neutralization would have involved simply the manipulation of the privileges that had accrued to landlords through the operation of the late Roman taxation system and, above all, through the institution of the colonate (Jones, 1958; 1964: 795ff.). Now, perhaps for the first time in Gaul, landlords: (i) insisted on their rights over the tied tenants that they had on their land, making it difficult for such people to seek better conditions elsewhere; and (ii) used their control over the taxation system to terrorize free peasants to flee to their protection to escape its rigours, i.e. to work a protection racket, *latrocinium*, which is a major theme in the *De Gubernatione Dei* (e.g. 5.58).

This model appears to offer us a completely different explanation for the fifth-century Bacaudae: they arose not out of peasant revolution, nor the operation of aristocratic patronage, nor even a severe disruption of rural society, but rather as a result of the cruel frustration of legitimately rising economic expectations – the classic cause of the *jacquerie* (cf. Le Roy Ladurie, 1987: 65).

The problem is that, set against the evidence of Salvian, this explanation proves to be not wholly satisfactory. First, as Fustel de Coulanges observed over a century ago (1885: 141ff.), if we again discount Salvian's gloomy moralizing, the lot of his poor agricultural workers does not seem to have been especially hard. We should note in particular those, wiser or more experienced than their fellows (5.43), who were able to discriminate between the terms of employment offered by landlords to obtain the best available – even if this meant abandoning their ancestral plots. (I would further suggest that Salvian's blanket-description of the subsequent decline of these people from *coloni* (landed tenants) to *inquilini* (landless cottars) must also be taken with a pinch of salt (*contra* Whittaker, 1987; cf. Samson, below p. 223); it perhaps reflects the comparative failure of some local migrants and, by implication, the comparative success of others, in the years following their move.) On the basis of the demographic model proposed, it would seem that some people, at least, were able to derive advantage from the current demand for labour (market forces always prove stronger than artificial restraints: see Le Roy Ladurie, 1987: 161), so easing social tension. Even more important, however, is the fact that, as we have already seen, according to Salvian it was not the tied peasantry of his acquaintance who joined the Bacaudae, but rather 'the better born and well educated' (5.21).

I would like, therefore, to advance a second hypothesis, based on a development that has received some very useful attention in recent years (in particular, Mathisen, 1984), but whose full implications have yet to be closely considered: that of the long-distance migration of people from parts of Gaul damaged or threatened by barbarian invasion or civil war. Such movement is exemplified by the personal histories of Paulinus of Pella and Salvian himself, both of whom took up residence in the south of the country. Many such refugees will have been poor or, as in the case of Paulinus, at least considerably impoverished. Others, however, as Orosius reports was the case in Spain (7.41.4f.), must have been able to escape with a significant proportion of their wealth. I propose that those who decided to remain permanently in Gaul (i.e. those who did not eventually move on to, say, Italy: Mathisen, 1984: 161ff.; below, pp. 228ff.) are likely to have sought to acquire estates in the region, or to extend those they already held there. I would further suggest that, again perhaps for the first time in the history of Romano-Gallic agriculture, both newcomers and existing landowners may also have striven to consolidate their holdings, both for protection and efficiency of management: the 'great estate' as a common feature of the Gallic landscape was perhaps a development of the early fifth century (cf. Drinkwater, 1983: 174ff.; 1989b: 146f.; Wickham, 1984: 23f.). In such circumstances, contrary to what should have occurred at a time of rural depopulation, increasing competition for labour would have been accompanied by a rising demand for land, posing a further problem for landlords. I would suggest that this might be the explanation for the plight of both Salvian's freeholders – forced to give up their plots – and his gentry – his 'widows' and 'orphans' representing the more vulnerable members of a curial class already burdened by the fiscal responsibilities imposed upon it by the imperial government (Gagé, 1971: 402), whose estates now fell victim to the expropriating activities, the *latrocinium*, of the very wealthy (cf. *Querolus* p. 17, ll. 6–10, ed. Ranstrand). On this argument, we can well understand population movement in the opposite direction to the one already discussed, away from such pressure. Such migration would have required initiative, planning and some degree of transportable property. It was not, therefore, an option freely available to simple peasants, who, both psychologically and economically, will have been bound to the land they farmed (Fustel de Coulanges, 1885: 41; Le Roy Ladurie, 1987: 9), and who, as *coloni*, were anyway in high demand. It was, however, a choice open to lesser aristocrats and gentry. These could flee either to the barbarians, where their property and education might secure them a place in society, or to the Bacaudae: we should note that the only fifth-century Bacaud of whom we know anything in detail was Eudoxius, a doctor of medicine (*Chron. Gall. 452*, 133). At this point, however, this second model runs into difficulties, since it does not explain who the 'Bacaudae' actually were and, in particular, how they might be conceived as offering a comfortable haven for refugee gentry.

What is clear from Salvian is that the Bacaudae were to be found in areas that were under neither barbarian nor Roman control. On the other hand, since he claims that the Bacaudae lived 'like barbarians', we may assume, as a number of scholars have proposed (e.g. Gagé,

1971: 407), that the Bacaudae had set up their own ordered communities. On this basis, it seems to me that there are three possible ways in which such communities came into existence:

(i) The refugees themselves, together with their free and servile dependants (cf. Samson, below p. 224), created their own salvation by moving to good deserted land now beyond the effective limits of the Roman administration. In doing so, they may have provided leadership for indigenous rural populations abandoned by agents of the imperial local and central administrations. Once settled, they could have been joined later by others of their kind.

This model clearly resembles my explanation of the third-century Bacaudae.

(ii) The refugees, with or without their dependants, fled to areas that were outside direct Roman control, but remained under the authority of great aristocrats who had decided not to move south with their fellows.

This model is not very different from Van Dam's conception of the revival of local ties of patronage (cf. Halsall, above pp. 205f.), and may even be seen as corroborating his interpretation of the passage in the *Querolus* discussed above, though to my mind we still need an explanation as to why such activity was not considered illegal. In any event, we should certainly pay more attention to the rise of the late Gallo-Roman warlord, and consider in particular why it is so late in the day before we actually hear of such individuals by name.

(iii) The refugees moved to a specific area which, though still nominally 'Roman', had something of the look of a barbarian state in the eyes of those of in the south.

This last model must make us think once again of Aremorica. Even if we discount the evidence of Rutilius Namatianus and the *Querolus*, and ignore for the moment the remarks of Salvian, the strong impression given by the remaining sources that deal with the Bacaudae, either directly or indirectly, is one of continuing disobedience to Roman rule, and a strong inclination to act on their own, or in their own interests, on the part of the inhabitants of Aremorica virtually throughout the fifth century (Dockès, 1980: 205). This attitude is all the more interesting because similar resistance to central control is detectable in this region in the Medieval and early modern periods, an intractability that has been traced back to local conditions that militated against the rise of a great aristocracy and so promoted a certain degree of social equality (Le Roy Ladurie, 1987: 148f., 153; cf. Halsall, above Fig. 17.3). It is easy to imagine how similar conditions, coupled with a resistance to the imperial tax-collector, might have attracted refugees from the curial class in the early part of the fifth century; and here, of course, we approach once more the thinking of E. A. Thompson.

So far, so good: none of the three models of external communities proposed above should be taken as exclusive; all three may well have operated in Gaul in the first half of the fifth century. However, the problem remains as to how and why these came to be called 'Bacaudic' since, as I have already remarked, there are strong grounds for believing that by this time the term 'Bacaudae' had come to be applied to common outlaws (Drinkwater, 1989a: 201; cf. Van Dam, 1985: 48f.). In attempting to answer this question, I would first like to widen the scope of this discussion.

Whatever we choose to make of the Bacaudae in detail, the very fact of their existence is deeply instructive, and very relevant to our general theme, 'Fifth-century Gaul: a crisis of identity?'. As one whose main interest to date has been the history of Roman Gaul down to the fourth century, I have been particularly struck in coming to grips with its fifth-century successor by the strong impression of dislocation and, above all, space (Drinkwater, 1989a: 201; cf. Shaw, 1984: 50; Samson, below p. 227). In brief, even if educated contemporaries thought that 'Roman Gaul' continued to exist after *c.* 407, I do not (Drinkwater, 1987: 255; 1989b: 152).

'Roman Gaul' resulted from the Roman military presence on the Rhine: the Rhine frontier gave 'Gaul' its shape and meaning (cf. Elton, above pp. 175f.). In the fifth century, although there may have been some general policy of continuing to hold the Rhine (cf. Elton, above), the position was clearly not as before. Specifically, west of the river there developed internal frontiers beyond which the imperial writ did not run, and over which refugees from imperial rule could seek asylum. The political geography of the country had changed, and now more closely resembled that which had existed on the eve of the Caesarian conquest. Such considerations are, I would argue, of prime importance in any study of imperial political and military policy of the period. To maintain itself, i.e. to protect itself and fill its treasury (cf. Elton, above p. 171), the Roman state needed to recover as many as possible of the lost territories. It was too weak to wage indiscriminate war against the barbarians who had settled, or were settling, on Roman soil, therefore its obvious strategy was, while attempting to limit further barbarian expansion, to concentrate on the gaining of those areas that had drifted out of Roman control but which, as yet, had not been claimed by Germans. In brief, in the north at least, imperial generals operated a policy not of 'defence', or even 'policing', but of considered *reconquest*.

I feel that such a motivation indeed explains the campaigns of Aëtius and his lieutenants in the second quarter of the fifth century, when again, albeit for the last time, the Roman state was able to re-exert its power north of the Province (so Wood, 1987: 252f., 257); and I would propose that such considerations also help towards a closer understanding of the 'Bacaudae'. Up to this period the members of the 'external' communities suggested above may well have considered themselves to be involved in no direct rebellion against Rome. They probably thought of themselves as 'Roman'; they may even have continued to recognize the authority of the western emperor, if on their own terms; they will certainly not have called themselves 'Bacaudae'. However, when the attempt was made to re-integrate them fully within the Roman empire, they resisted, if necessary by force, with the help of their dependants, free and slave. In short, it was these people who acted to forestall the frustration of their hopes, not the peasants of the south. This is the way I would interpret the revolt of Tibatto; and I would suggest that he may have been aided in his enterprise by the Aremoricans, fearful of the renaissance of imperial power. The *Roman* authorities called those involved in such resistance *rebelles ... perditi* (Salvian, *De Gub. Dei* 5.24); or, more colloquially, 'bandits' – *Bacaudae*.

CHAPTER 19

Slavery, the Roman legacy

R. Samson

Sidonius to the Lord Bishop Lupus, greeting ... I commend to you ... the suppliant bearers of this letter ... They discovered that a kinswoman, who had been abducted in a raid of Vargi ... had been brought here a number of years ago and sold; and so they have been searching for her ... Meanwhile this same woman died in the house and in the ownership of my agent. She had indeed been sold quite openly: the transaction (the parties to which are strangers to me) was recommended by a certain Prudens ... now living at Troyes; his signature in the capacity of a good and sufficient co-promiser appears in the register of the market.

(*Ep.* 6.4)

In late fifth-century Clermont, we see the buying and selling of slaves, the written record of such transactions, and even their official registration at the municipal market. A century later, in 583, the church Council at Lyons (c. 2) insisted that bishops kept the bill of sale, with price and date of purchase, of any captives they bought. The power of sale of another human being and the recording of such an exchange in writing in fifth- and sixth-century Gaul are testimony to the continuity of one of the most inhuman of Rome's legacies.

Our evidence is anecdotal, and contemporary eye-witnesses who moan about decay and collapse cannot realistically be accredited with the analytical tools or the long-term perspective necessary for a study of change and developments in social organization. This poses problems for historians concerned with wider questions about slavery and its importance. 'We have no statistics of the absolute number of slaves or of their relative number to the free population' (Jones, 1966: 295f.), nor even a form of evidence to allow some quantitative estimate of the proportions of slaves, serfs, and free peasants in fifth-century Gaul. Fifth-century Gaul, like sixth- to ninth-century Gaul, also lacks good archaeological evidence of settlements (cf. Percival, above), unlike high Roman Gaul. Not that Roman settlement evidence has been much exploited to analyse social relations. The emphasis is on villa owners, not their dependent labour force (Smith, 1978; 1982).

Fifth-century Gaul is, of course, well served with legal codes: scholars make use of the codices of Theodosius and Justinian for late Roman law, and also the law-codes of the barbarian successor states, Visigothic, Burgundian, and Frankish. Here all social ranks, both sexes, and even children figure. However, legal matter is intractable in questions of quantification. Numerous references to particular social groups imply legal difficulties rather than a preponderance of the group in society, otherwise we should imagine a superabundance of fifth-century slaves. The Salic law for northern Gaul deals with slaves in 13 per cent of its clauses, while slaves figure in 46 per cent of the Visigothic legal chapters (Bonnassie, 1985).

The epigraphic evidence for slavery in Roman Gaul and other provinces is small. MacMullen (1987) cites this as indicating their absence in the fields, concluding that agricultural labour must have been predominantly performed by *coloni*. Yet a corpus of epigraphic references to *coloni* reveals them to be even less commonly recorded in stone than slaves (Johne, Köhn and Weber, 1983). Without some theory as to who could afford the erection of tombstones and above all why – and the sociological context is all-important for explaining why freedmen were probably fifty times more likely to have a stone set up to them than slaves (Bradley, 1984; Samson, 1989) – the attempt to use it quantitatively was doomed to failure.

Although MacMullen argued from the epigraphic evidence that slavery was not prominent in agricultural production, without suggesting why it was not, he followed the broader overview of late Roman society current among many historians. Alföldy (1985: 187, 203, 186) is orthodox for non-Marxist historians:

In late Roman society ... the owners of *latifundia* were ... the dominant elite in the economy, while the unpropertied masses of the lower population were increasingly dependent upon the large land owners.

Slavery had already lost its importance as a social and economic institution. But the result was not that slavery gave room to free labour; rather, free labour and slavery declined together.

New forces in society first came about from the fifth century ... But they could not change the foundations of the late Roman social system in that century. The social system of late antiquity was not even replaced by a totally new social structure in the sixth century.

Without the widely held belief that slavery was unimportant in late Roman society, MacMullen would not have used such a premise to explain the lack of epigraphic references to slaves. This general belief is itself the product of general theories about historical changes, but before turning to them we should be clear about our own analytical conceptions of slavery.

Alföldy (1985: 191) offers us the odd perspective that 'the distinction between free and slave now had only a theoretical importance, for the system of compulsion relating to taxes, services, and the inheritance of occupations constituted a new form of unfreedom'. But neither the payment of tax nor the forced inheritance of parental occupation constitutes slavery. Others cloud the issue, insisting that there is the problem that the semantic meanings of *servus* and *ancilla* change through time. Many stress legal rights or status as the crucial distinction between slaves and the 'free'. Being owned as chattels, sold and separated from their family or suffering the threat thereof, having to work at the task set by their master, owning nothing outright as personal possessions, being beaten for displeasing their master, these things together distinguish slaves, not the right to bring a lawsuit to court. The definition of slavery must be complex, involving not only legal and social disabilities, but also labour, its control, and ownership of its produce (see Müller-Mertens, 1985 for conflicts of definition and analysis).

As far as these latter categories are concerned, fifth- and sixth-century sources reveal those termed *ancillae*, *servi*, and the genderless *mancipia* performing every imaginable task, as bakers, millers, physicians, cooks, spinners, swineherds, or porters carrying Sidonius' tent (*Ep.* 4.8.2), and above all as agricultural workers; but were they indeed slaves? I argue that most were. Many were bought and sold as we have already seen. St Germanus bought Irish slaves in Gaul to free them. 'One gets the impression that hagiographers considered the virtues of their saint incomplete if they were unable to furnish proof of their merits in the [redemption of captives]', suggests Verlinden (1955: 665f.). The transfer of ownership kept slaves on the move. Andarchius belonged first to senator Felix, then duke Lupus, later king Sigibert, starting in Marseilles and ending in Clermont (GT *HF* 4.46). Movement broke up families, 'sons were torn from fathers and mothers separated from daughters', to the great distress of the *servi*, leading not only to wailing and attempted flight, but even suicide (GT *HF* 6.45).

A law of Constantine (319) threatened masters with the charge of murder if they killed their slaves intentionally. And yet, 'If a master beat a slave with a rod or whip and put him in chains to guard him, and the slave dies, the master need have no fear of prosecution' (*CTh* 9.12.1). As Watson (1987) notes, the real difficulty was in finding a free man who would prosecute another for having beaten his slave to death. Early Medieval laws neglected even this feeble protection. It remained for the Church, at the Council of Yenne (c. 34) in 517, to threaten masters only with excommunication for killing a *servus* without a judicial pronouncement. Control and punishment of slaves was frequently achieved through mutilation; cutting ears and slitting noses appears in a wide range of documents (e.g. GT *HF* 5.48). References to branding probably represent direct continuity of the Roman practice of branding F H E (*fugitivus hic est*) plus the owner's initials on the runaway slave's forehead, not an uncommon practice in the late Empire (Bradley, 1984: 119).

In Roman law, slaves owned nothing as personal possessions. Slaves could hold their *peculium* but not own it; it belonged to their master, who could withdraw it from the slave, even when freed (e.g. *Dig.* 41.2.49.1; 20.3.1.1; *CJ* 11.50.2.3). Pope Gelasius (492–6) quashed a church slave's will on the grounds that the slave's *peculium* was legally church property.

The more complex definition therefore allows us to recognize that slavery existed in late antique Gaul, but lack of empirical data makes it difficult to estimate how common it was. We rely on general historical pictures. One that leads to the conclusion that rural slavery never played an important role in Roman Gaul observes the long-term changes from the Iron Age to the fifth century. Edith Wightman (1978) saw in great late Roman landowners reminiscences of past Celtic chieftains with innumerable dependants or clients. A 'thin veneer of Romanization' is seen to be stripped with a return to 'traditional' social relations. Drinkwater (1983: 170f.) sums up:

We have signs of some form of large-scale landowning among Caesar's Gallic nobility of the late Iron Age; and we have firm evidence for this practice in fourth- and fifth-century Roman Gaul. It is generally agreed that the landlords of both periods exploited the labour of a, at least nominally, free population, not that of slaves. It has therefore reasonably been claimed that between these chronological extremes we are entitled to expect a degree of continuity ...

Is it useful to telescope Celtic chieftains with warrior bands and dependent clients, Gallo-Roman landowners with *coloni*, and fifth-century aristocrats with serfs into an analytical relationship of elites and dependants, or, as Van Dam (1985) calls it, 'leadership and community'? Surely the *nature* of exploitation, not its existence as the source of elite power, is of interest in our study of late antique and early Medieval society?

Who worked the fields and tended the livestock on the villas of the high Roman period is the central question. Were the farmhands slaves or free? 'Even Agache, who earlier strongly championed the notion that his Picardy villas were slave-worked now seems to have changed his mind', writes Drinkwater (1983: 184, quoting Agache, 1973: 38, 48, and 1978: 361). Such scholarly vacillation is symptomatic of the ambiguities of the evidence. In recent papers dealing with economic aspects of Romano-British villas (Branigan and Miles, 1988) there is no discussion of the nature of the dependent relations of 'labourers', as they are denoted in the book's only villa plan to postulate their possible living-quarters; the word 'slave' appears twice. I have argued that the nature of the social dependency of these 'farmhands' has been systematically ignored; I also believe many of the 'farmhands' to be slaves (Samson, 1989; forthcoming). In any case, the general consensus must underestimate rural slaves' numbers, for general discussions treat them as non-existent. Orosius (7.40.8) spoke of Didymus and Verinianus raising a private army from their agricultural slaves; later a Visigothic king despaired of 'slave-owners who, intent only on working their fields, thrashed their multitude of slaves', and were now uninterested in war (*Leges Visig.* 9.2.9). Even in the fifth century, I believe, rural slaves were important, but their number was certainly declining. Why?

Some assume there is an in-built tendency for slavery to dwindle away if new sources of slaves are not continually found, either because slaves will not reproduce quickly given poor nutrition, living conditions, and health care, or because a small proportion of slaves will always be awarded their freedom as thanks for devoted service. Attempts to credit the Church with an ameliorating role are thankfully becoming rarer. It did not oppose slavery on theological or humanitarian grounds. If manumission was a salutary act for the soul, as was any sacrifice, divine sanction no more altered the keeping of slaves than it ended fornication, theft, and murder. Moreover, the Church was a major holder of slaves. In 517 the Council of Yenne (c. 8) forbade abbots to free slaves, 'for it is not just that slaves should be free while monks are constrained daily by the *opus rurale*'. Note that monastic slaves are conceived of as doing rural work.

The question of self-perpetuation notwithstanding, the fifth century saw more warfare in Gaul than the previous four centuries; opportunities abounded for the capture of new slaves. Bloch (1947) saw the fifth-century wars as marking a highwater point in Gallic slavery. Moreover, new slaves frequently came from among the free, either 'voluntarily' or illegally. The poor submitted themselves to the patronage (*patrocinia*) of the rich but by pledging them their land; those that had lost all fled only to become slaves on new estates, at least according to Salvian (*De Gub. Dei* 5.58–9; cf. Drinkwater, above p. 213). The seventh-century *Angers Formulary* gives models of documents to be produced for three types of self-sale, including one, the result of poverty. *Lex Salica* (39.3–5) had to deal with the illegal sale of the free abroad, as happened to the kinswoman stolen by the Vargi and sold to Sidonius' agent. The 'natural' demographic explanation for the extinction of slavery is fraught with problems; it relies on the quantification of innumerable unquantifiable phenomena which make up the increases and the decreases in the total slave population, phenomena which are largely social and not 'natural'.

In contrast, the traditional Marxist version makes the fifth century crucial for the disappearance of slavery. In part the argument sounds bourgeois: the landowners and slave-masters recognized the unprofitability of slaves who lacked incentives and thus turned them into serfs. This was Bloch's (1947) argument. But was slavery unprofitable? 'Owners could afford to pay high prices for slaves, precisely because of the high productivity which could be forced out of them on larger farms' (Hopkins, 1978: 111); not everyone thinks so. Even if this vision of increased productivity through entrepreneurial incentives held good, it seems highly unlikely that Roman or German masters would have recognized the economic sense of liberating the pent-up productive potential of their slaves. 'There was no clear conception of the distinction between capital costs and labour costs, no planned ploughing back of profits, no long-term loans for productive purposes' (Finley, 1973: 117). Even if they had been aware of it, they would not have been motivated to lose the social status that slave-owning conferred.

The Marxist argument, on the other hand, also stresses the active struggle by slaves to escape their condition. Intensely disliked by non-Marxist historians, it has much to recommend itself. If we understand struggle not as armed revolution (thus setting aside the vexed question of Bacaudic unrest, in which slaves undeniably participated; cf. Drinkwater, above p. 215), but as the attempt to kill masters (and get away with it), sabotage work, escape by flight to somewhere less intolerable, gain emancipation by any means, even simply by toadying, then we shall have a key to understanding why the fifth century was crucial.

Yet a conflict-of-interests approach is widely accepted by non-Marxists in the sphere of individuals against the state. The changes in late Roman social organization are 'best encapsulated in the concept of alienation, alienation of Roman society from its state system' (Alföldy, 1985: 187). Wickham (1984) has tax-evading aristocrats turning their backs on the state machinery, starving it of necessary funds, preferring to keep the surplus themselves in the form of rents, while peasants are also seen as seeking to avoid taxation, ending up 'in the hands of the aristocracy' by submitting themselves to private patronage: the modern scholar's version of Salvian. Are landowner–peasant relations portrayed realistically? Wickham himself suggests 'that the chief beneficiaries of the fall of the Roman state and the transition to feudal society were the peasantry' (Wickham, 1984: 30), so what of his claim that peasants 'ended up in the hands of the aristocracy'? If landlords were to prove the greater of the two evils, why did the peasants not comprehend this, especially as the landlords were ever present, unlike the tax-collector, whose visits were infrequent? Indeed the *coloni's* tax-collector under Valens (364–78) was the local landowner's agent. Landowners are seen as calculating self-interest against the state, with which they had much in common, and to some extent *were*, while the peasants are seen, foolishly and to their cost, as sympathizing with nobles, against whom they shared natural animosity.

Van Dam (1985: 26) opposes a 'conflict model' which implies 'animosity between peasants and lords, as if from the peasants' point of view aristocratic lords were always an unfortunate and unnecessary imposition upon them'. Undeniably there were happy slaves. The stereotypical positive characteristic of slaves was their loyalty. Bradley (1984: 36f.) suggests that, 'It is significant that despite their conventionality such stories could still circulate at the turn of the fifth century with their collective emphasis on loyalty and obedience.' The slaves who were the most trusted, and given the most power over other slaves, were largely domestic. Those far from the master's household, those in Columella's prison-like slave-quarters, and those raped (certainly it must have been commonplace for *ancillae* to bear their master's children, given the amount of legislation concerned with the phenomenon; one may assume many such liaisons were not fully voluntary), or beaten near to death were probably less than enamoured of their tormenter and exploiter. It is hard to imagine that many slaves saw their relationship to their masters as fortunate, if only because masters tended to denigrate or hate their 'speaking tools'. Pope Leo I (440–61) wrote, 'those who have not been able to obtain their freedom from their owners are raised to the dignity of the priesthood, as if servile vileness could receive this honour ... the sacred ministry is polluted by such vile company' (*Ep.* 4.1; Jones, 1966: 289). The supposed conscience of fifth-century Gaul, Salvian (*De Gub. Dei* 4.3-6, 4.26), called slaves bad, abominable, and obscene; Jerome was contemptuous of them (*Ep.* 54.5); the late Roman stereotype had them interested only in their bellies and theft. Some slaves did not love their masters, as the slaves of the *negotiator* Christopher did not love him for the merciless flogging he gave them. They killed him (GT *HF* 7.46).

Murder was an extreme form of struggle, also unwise, bringing the full force of the kin and state's wrath upon the unfortunate. One of Christopher's murderers was caught, tortured, mutilated, killed, and hung from a gibbet in Tours. Subterfuge was safer. In Spain masters had to be protected in law from slaves who sought refuge in a church, complained of oppression, and were then compulsorily sold to a new master through the priest's intercession (*Leges Visigoth.* 5.4.17). Slaves might simply lie, claiming they had been freed, or that one of their parents had been free and their master, while alive, had illegally kept them in servitude. Marriage between a slave and *colonus* or *colona*, involving a change of residence, might encourage slaves to improve their status surreptitiously. Pope Leo complained of slaves becoming priests; it was canonically forbidden. The Council of Orleans (c. 8) in 511 dealt with the problem of bishops ordaining slaves, unaware of their slave status, implying the slaves kept quiet about it. Some moves did not change a slave's lord, but improved her or his social position. Most commonly, when freed, ex-slaves remained the dependants of their former masters. The Burgundian laws reveal a freedman remaining in the lord's household unless 12 *solidi* were paid, while a slave sold into another land who returned (and one wonders how and why) was to remain free but in the former master's *patrocinium* (*Lex Burg*. 57 and *Const. Extr.* 21.3.). This is precisely what Bradley (1984: 91) notes of Roman manumission: 'when slaves were set free they did not in consequence find themselves absolved of all responsibilities towards their former owners, now patrons'.

Such improvements of the slave's lot seldom involved the blatant loss of a master's rights. These transformations of slave into serf were not traumatic and occasioned little comment. The flight of slaves was otherwise. And flight was not insignificant in the Roman empire (Bellen, 1971). If anything, it became more common in the fifth century. 'The military situation at the beginning of the fifth century sometimes forced the state to enlist slaves into the army, promising them freedom' (Maass, 1985: 546; *CTh* 7.13.16). 'Around the middle of the fourth century began a religiously motivated slave-flight' either into monasteries or wandering in radical imitation of Jesus, as in the case of the *circumcelliones* in North Africa (Laub, 1982: 107). The Visigothic law-codes treated it as the single greatest social ill of their society. Slaves in flight would pretend to be free (*CJ* 6.1.1). In fifth-century Burgundian Gaul there were laws to prevent fugitive slaves being supplied with letters to aid escape (forged documents, perhaps manumission charters?) or with false hair (as disguise, or was slave hair short-cropped?) (*Lex Burg.* 6.10; 6.4.). The *Lex Salica* (26.1–2) prohibited people from illegally manumitting other people's slaves. Who was it that helped slaves? Perhaps rival lords sought to gain new dependants, but landlords also pressured the government to extend and enforce laws preventing tenants and *coloni* from moving elsewhere (Jones, 1966: 292f.). *Coloni* or *actores* (probably slaves) also concealed fugitives (*Lex Burg.* 39.3).

The legal sanctions against aiding slaves were severe. The Burgundian law demanded that strangers, lest they be fugitive slaves, be brought to the local judge, while rewards for the return of slaves to their masters were made compulsory: 1 *solidus* for the slave, 1 *solidus* for every hundred miles travelled (*Lex Burg.* 39.1–2; 20.3). Yet flight proved effective, demonstrated by the varying time limits successive kings placed on slaves' successful 'free' life elsewhere after which they could not be returned to their former masters.

Flight became more common and more successful for the same reason that laws threw more responsibility on individuals to report the presence of strangers and threatened harsher penalties for conspiracy: the state apparatus was weakening; the police force and the local administration were less well organized; the limits of legal jurisdiction were contracting (cf. Drinkwater, above p. 216). An aggrieved party approached the bishop in Clermont, who used his influence to achieve justice in Troyes through its bishop. Where were the former Roman secular provincial authorities? The Burgundian laws treated other kingdoms as beyond their jurisprudence. Slaves taken to another land might become free, the free taken there might become slaves; the purchase of a slave from a Frank in the Burgundian kingdom was suspect and required a witness (*Const. Ext.* 21.3; *Lex Burg.* 56.1–2). An Auvergnat senatorial family could not get back its relative, Attalus, seized and enslaved by a Frank in northern Gaul (GT *HF* 3.15): if sufficient distance was traversed across Gaul, public authorities could prevent neither the well-to-do from being enslaved, nor slaves from fleeing.

The wars of the fifth century meant more opportunities for enslaving others, yet, far from increasing the number of slaves, they dealt the state machinery – necessary to protect slave-owners' right to possess, exploit and torment fellow human beings – a severe blow. It was never the case that slaves had nothing to lose but their chains: there was always the threat of losing life and family too. The transformation of antique to feudal society occurred when masters lost the certainty of that threat.

CHAPTER 20

Fifth-century visitors to Italy: business or pleasure?

R. W. Mathisen

One way of approaching the question of the degree to which Gaul remained a part of the Roman empire during the fifth century is to ask whether Gauls showed by their actions that they considered themselves to be a part of a world which extended beyond Gaul. This study will investigate one kind of action in particular: Gallic contacts with Italy (for contacts with the Holy Land, see Hunt, below). By looking at the frequency of, and the reasons for, such contacts, it may be possible to ascertain the Gauls' conceptions of their own role within the Roman empire.

One might begin by identifying three main categories of Gauls who undertook foreign travel: (1) 'refugees', that is, those who left Gaul and never returned; (2) those who were compelled to go abroad as a result of official responsibilities, both secular and ecclesiastical; and (3) those who traveled purely of their own volition, for personal reasons.

The case of Gallic refugees might be considered first. In the early years of the fifth century, some Gauls responded to administrative re-structuring, political unrest, and barbarian invasions by traveling to Italy – and remaining there on a permanent basis (Mathisen, 1984; cf. Drinkwater, above pp. 213f.). These refugees, by abandoning their Gallic affiliations, would seem to be indicating by their actions that they believed that Gaul was no longer a viable part of the Empire.

It generally is assumed that there was an accelerated aristocratic abandonment of northern Gaul after the transfer of the Gallic prefect from Trier to Arles c. 395 (Stroheker, 1948: 19f.; Prinz, 1965: 48; Wightman, 1970: 250; 1985: 254f., 302, 308; cf. Heinzelmann, below pp. 243f.). A growing disinclination on the part of aristocratic Italians to visit northern Gaul is attested by Symmachus in a letter written *c*. 402 to his Gallic friend Protadius: 'if you consider that now the best prince and the chief magistrate are absent, no one of our order travels to and from the neighborhood of the Rhine – which is not to say that it never happens, or that someone unknown to me might undertake so great a trip on private business' (*Ep.* 4.28). The appearance of several aristocratic Gauls in Italy at this time probably also was related to this official withdrawal. As will be detailed below, the brothers Minervius, Protadius and Florentinus, who had connections in both Trier and Aquitania, held office at Rome in the late fourth century (Stroheker, 1948: 19; *PLRE* I, s.v.; Matthews, 1971: 1096; 1975: 261f.). And at about this time, the body of Valeria Vincentia, the wife of Fabius Maianus, who probably accompanied her, was transported from Trier to Pavia for burial (Gabba and Tibiletti, 1960).

Soon thereafter the reasons to leave became even more persuasive for some Gauls. After the revolt of Constantine III in 407, several imperial officials decided that their interests could be served better in Italy. These included the *consularis Viennensis* Eventius, who, accompanied by his wife Faustina, departed for Rome (*AE* 1953: no. 200; *PLRE* II, 413; Marrou, 1952; Matthews, 1975: 275 n3), as well as the prefect Limenius and the master of soldiers Chariobaudus (*PLRE* II, s.v.).

Many other departures for Italy by *saeculares* in the early fifth century were caused, or perhaps influenced, by the barbarian invasions (Zosimus 6.3.1–3; Stevens, 1957). In 442, the young Gauls Remus and Arcontia were buried in Rome; they may have come from north-western Gaul (*ILCV* no. 266; cf. *PL* 58.66–8). The mid fifth-century patrician Merobaudes, who apparently possessed estates near Troyes, was active in Spain and Italy, but not in Gaul (Clover, 1971: 7, 34ff.; Barnes, 1975: 159ff.; Mathisen, 1986: 47f.; *PLRE* II, 756ff.). The Visigothic arrival and settlement in Aquitania in the years after 412 in particular caused many Gauls to depart. Several were visited in 417 by Rutilius Claudius Namatianus. He mentioned his young Gallic relative Palladius of Poitiers, whom he had left behind at Rome (*De Reditu Suo* 1.208–13; *PLRE* II, 448, 819). Palladius has been identified with the *vir inlustris* Palladius Rutilius Taurus Aemilianus, who in his *De Re Rustica* mentioned estates in Italy and Sardinia, but not in Gaul, perhaps because they had been abandoned (Stroheker, 1948: 197f.; Matthews, 1975: 328 n3; Wightman, 1978: 113). There is no evidence that Palladius ever returned. Even better evidence for emigration is provided by Victorinus, a former vicar of Britain, whom Rutilius referred to as 'a wanderer, whom the capture of Toulouse compelled to settle in the Tuscan lands and worship foreign gods' (*De Reditu Suo* 1.495–6; Courcelle, 1964: 68). Further up the coast, Rutilius visited the aforementioned Protadius, of whom he said, 'he exchanged his paternal inheritance for middling estates in Umbria' (*De Reditu Suo* 1.551–3). Protadius, therefore, had decided to remain in Italy, on a lowered standard of living. His brothers may have done the same.

Shortly thereafter, a number of Gallic clerics began to surface in Italy. In the 430s, Justinianus, an exiled bishop of Tours, died at Vercelli (GT *HF* 2.1, 10.31). A Gallic deacon Aper, buried at Vercelli, also may have moved around this time (*CIL* V, 6727). *Circa* 440, Prosper of Aquitania settled for good into a position in the Roman curia (Markus, 1986: 31ff.; cf. Muhlberger, above pp. 29ff.). And in the late 460s, the *calculator* Victorius of Aquitania composed a paschal *cursus* for pope Hilarus at Rome (Gennadius, *Vir. Inl.* 88). Some noble Gauls eventually became Italian clerics (Matthews, 1975: 152; Mathisen, 1979c). *Circa* 395, Meropius Pontius Paulinus settled at Nola in Campania, where his family had property; he eventually became bishop (*PLRE* I, 681ff.). In the 460s, the noble Gaul Bonosus was a priest at Pavia (*V. Epiphanii* 35). And in the 470s, Magnus Felix Ennodius, some of whose family came from the area of Arles, departed for Italy, where he took up the religious life and *c.* 514 became a bishop, also at Pavia (*PLRE* II, 393f.; cf. Mommaerts and Kelley, above pp. 114ff.).

The aforementioned individuals left Gaul and settled permanently in Italy at a time when Gaul was facing difficulties but Italy was still relatively secure. They essentially renounced their Gallic ties and affiliations. There is no evidence that any of them ever returned, even to visit. At the same time, other Gauls also relocated to other areas of the Empire (Mathisen, 1984).

Some Gauls, however, did return home after their visits to Italy. Visits in the 'official' category could involve either religious or secular business. Most religious visits involved appeals by disaffected Gallic clerics to the bishop of Rome. In the early fifth century, for example, Victricius of Rouen, who had been accused of heresy, appealed to pope Innocent in Rome. He was accompanied by a train of dependents (Paulinus of Nola, *Ep.* 17–18). In 417, Patroclus of Arles met with pope Zosimus (*MGH*, *Ep.* 3.10–12); and *c.* 430, the Gauls

Prosper and Hilarius brought their theological complaints to pope Celestine (*PL* 50.528–37).

Other appeals were made by deposed bishops. *Circa* 430, Brictius of Tours was expelled on charges of adultery and practising magic arts, so, 'coming to Rome, he reported to the pope everything which he had suffered' (GT *HF* 2.1, 10.31). In the mid 440s, bishop Chelidonius of Besançon, who had been deposed for marrying a widow and passing the death sentence, appealed to pope Leo. In this case, Hilary of Arles also traveled to Rome to prosecute Chelidonius, albeit unsuccessfully (Leo, *Ep.* 10.3–4; *V. Hilarii* 17–21 [22–7]; *Nov. Val.* 17; *V. Romani* 18; Mathisen, 1979a; cf. Heinzelmann, below). Shortly thereafter, Hilary sent two delegations to Rome in attempts to patch up his quarrel with Leo. The first was led by his presbyter Ravennius, and the second consisted of the bishops Nectarius of Avignon and Constantius of Uzès (*V. Hilarii* 17 [22]). Other complaints to Rome dealt with supposedly irregular ordinations, and were made against Maximus of Valence in 419, an unnamed bishop of Lodève in 422, Fonteius of Vaison *c.* 449, Hermes of Narbonne in 461, Marcellus of Die in 463, and some unnamed bishops of Nice in the 450s and 460s (*MGH, Ep.* 3.18–32; *Conc. Gall.* 314–506, 107–10; *PL* 20.756, 772–3, 54.945–50, 984, 58.12–17). These cases involved a good deal of going to and fro between Rome and Gaul. Gallic bishops also forwarded theological inquiries, as in the mid 450s, when Rusticus of Narbonne sent his priest Hermes to Leo (*PL* 54.1199ff.), and *c.* 453, when Theodorus of Fréjus sent a similar letter (*PL* 54.1011–14).

Gallic ecclesiastics, therefore, often traveled to Rome on official business. In some cases, the principals themselves went. In others, they merely sent representatives. But, in all such cases, the appellants believed that they had something to gain by communicating with the pope in Rome.

On other occasions, Gauls visited Italy on secular official business. In the early fifth century, Gauls still held office sporadically in the central administration, such as the aforementioned three brothers: Minervius served as *magister officiorum c.* 395, *comes rei privatae* in 397–8, and *comes sacrarum largitionum* in 398–9; Florentinus was *quaestor sacri palatii c.* 395 and *praefectus urbi* in 395–97; and Protadius was *praefectus urbi* in 400–1 (*PLRE* I, ss.vv.). They, however, as suggested above, may already have moved to Italy by this time. Cl. Postumus Dardanus was *magister libellorum* and *quaestor sacri palatii c.* 400, and his brother Claudius Lepidus was *magister memoriae* and *comes rei privatae* at about the same time (*PLRE* II, s.v.). Rutilius Claudius Namatianus served as *magister officiorum* in 412 and *praefectus urbi* in 414 (*PLRE* II, s.v.); his father Lachanius had been *quaestor sacri palatii* and *praefectus ?urbi* rather earlier (*PLRE* I, s.v.). Curiously, these seven individuals represent only three families.

Subsequently, however, Gauls in the central administration, and especially in high-ranking office, are few and far between (cf. Heather, above p. 91). A policy of preferring Italians in Italian offices, and Gauls in Gallic offices, seems now to have been implemented (Stroheker, 1948: 48ff.; Matthews, 1975: 334f.). Nevertheless, several Gauls still can be found in Italian offices of lower rank. Polemius Silvius served in *palatio*, presumably in Italy, at some time before 438 (*PLRE* II, 1012f.); Consentius of Narbonne served as a *tribunus et notarius* in the consistory of Valentinian III (*PLRE* II, 308f.). A number of other Gauls also may have held their offices in Italy: the anonymous fathers of Sidonius Apollinaris and his friend Aquilinus served as *tribuni et notarii* under Honorius (*PLRE* II, 1220, 1227), and a certain Maximus had been a *palatinus* (*PLRE* II, 746).

A special case occurred in 455, when the Arvernian aristocrat Eparchius Avitus was declared emperor in Gaul (cf. Harries, below p. 301). In October, he entered Italy, accompanied by many of his supporters (Mathisen, 1981a). In fact, his son-in-law, Sidonius Apollinaris, encouraged his friends to come along and 'to take up the responsibilities of Palatine service' (*Ep.* 1.6.1). Many Gauls seem to have done so. Avitus' patrician and master of soldiers, the Gaul Messianus, served him in Italy, at Ravenna (*PLRE* II, 761). The aforementioned Consentius of Narbonne returned to Rome as Avitus' *cura palatii* (*PLRE* II, 308f.). Sidonius himself obtained the office of *tribunus et notarius*, as did another likely relative of Avitus, Avitus of Cottion (Mathisen, 1979c). Other Gallic *tribuni* at this time perhaps include Avitus' ambassador to Spain, Hesychius, and Sidonius' friends Eutropius, Gaudentius and Catullinus (*PLRE* II, 554f., 495, 272f.; cf. Harries, below pp. 300f.). One can safely assume, however, that none of these Gauls in Italian office maintained their positions after Avitus' fall in 456 (Mathisen, 1985).

Indeed, after 456, only two Gauls are known to have served in Italy in an imperial administration. In 468, Sidonius Apollinaris was named prefect of Rome by the Greek emperor Anthemius (*PLRE* II, 115ff.). And in 474, Sidonius' brother-in-law Ecdicius was appointed patrician and master of soldiers by another Greek emperor, Julius Nepos (*PLRE* II, 383f.). In 475, Ecdicius was recalled to Rome, but only to be replaced by Orestes (Jordanes, *Getica* 241). Some evidence even suggests that he and his sons may have remained there (Cassiodorus, *Variae* 2.22): he may have felt it unwise to return to Visigothic Clermont. One also might note here the case of Magnus of Narbonne, named by Majorian to be western consul for 460 (*PLRE* II, 700f.). He, however, probably held his office in Gaul.

The office-holding of some Gauls, however, got them into trouble, and they were haled off to Italy after being charged with treason (cf. below, Harries, Teitler). In the late 450s, for example, the Gallic count Agrippinus supposedly was taken under arrest to Rome (*V. Lupicini* 11; Mathisen, 1979b). In 468, the Gallic prefect Arvandus was tried before the senate in Rome (Sidonius, *Ep.* 1.7.5; Cassiodorus, *Chron.* 1287). And in the early 470s, the traitor Seronatus likewise presumably was tried in Rome (Sidonius, *Ep.* 7.7.2, 2.1.1, 5.13.1–4). These visits would suggest that the imperial government, at least, considered Gaul still to be a part of the Empire, even if the Gauls involved may have indicated by their actions that they had their doubts on the matter.

Other Gauls visited Italy as members of delegations concerned with official secular business. In the 440s, bishop Germanus of Auxerre represented the revolting Aremoricans on an unsuccessful mission to the imperial court at Ravenna (*V. Germani* 28ff; Mathisen, 1981b). An equally celebrated case occurred in 468, when a delegation of distinguished Gauls, including the ex-prefect Tonantius Ferreolus and the senators Thaumastus and Petronius, traveled to Rome for the trial of Arvandus. Another Gaul, Auxanius, also was in Rome at the time (Sidonius, *Ep.* 1.7). Similar delegates probably went to Rome for the prosecution of Seronatus.

Gauls seem, therefore, to have traveled regularly to Italy on ecclesiastical or secular official business. When they had something to gain from Italian officialdom, they often would go to Italy. Gauls also were perfectly willing to go to Italy to hold official office. Their failure to do so more often probably resulted not so much from lack of desire, but from lack of authentic opportunity. When valid opportunities did arise, as during the reign of Avitus, many Gauls leapt at the chance. All this would indicate that officially, at least, many Gauls did believe that Gaul still was a part of the Roman empire during most of the fifth century, even if only on their own terms.

One now might ask just what was the extent of the non-official contacts between Gaul and Italy. Early in the fifth century, it was still standard policy for well-bred young Gauls to pursue their education in Rome. *Circa* 400, Germanus of Auxerre, for example, 'after the Gallic schoolrooms, added the knowledge of law in the city of Rome to the fullness of his perfection' (*V. Germani* 2). At the same time, the Gauls Nemesius and his brother also were in Rome to study (Symmachus, *Ep.* 4.54–6, 9.54; *PLRE* II, 775, 895, 1233); so too was Rusticus, a young man of Marseilles, to whom Jerome wrote in the early fifth century (*Ep.* 125.6). And Rutilius Namatianus' young friend Palladius, to whom he bid farewell in 417, also was a student in Rome. Subsequent examples of young Gauls broadening their experiences at Rome, however, are difficult, even impossible, to find – which is not to say, however, that such visits did not remain a theoretical ideal. In 455, Sidonius Apollinaris persuaded his friend Eutropius to accompany him to Rome, saying, 'although you are active at home, your helpless despair makes you afraid to undertake a journey, and you fear to set out' (*Ep.* 1.6.2). Eutropius clearly never had been to Rome before (*Ep.* 3.6.1; Mathisen, 1979b; cf. *Ep.* 9.14.2–3).

Other Gauls at this time found more compelling reasons for going to Italy: they hoped to find personal security there. The possible case of Ecdicius and his sons already has been mentioned. And in 479, the Visigothic-appointed *comes* and *dux* Victorius, supposedly fearing for his life because he was 'excessively carnal in his love of women' at Clermont, fled to Rome accompanied by Sidonius' son Apollinaris (GT *GM* 44; *HF* 2.20). Others, one might imagine, would have gone to Rome on a religious pilgrimage. On the occasion of both his visits to Rome, Sidonius mentioned the reverence that he paid to the saints of the holy city (*Ep.* 1.5.9, 1.6.1). In both instances, however, he had gone there for official, political reasons. There is not, in fact, a single attested case of any Gaul going to Rome for any devotional reasons at this time. In only one known instance did Gallic ecclesiastics travel to any place in Italy for reasons of piety. *Circa* 455, bishop Namatius of Clermont sent priests to Bologna to obtain relics of saints Agricola and Vitalis (GT *HF* 2.16).

One seeks in vain, finally, for any purely social visits by Gauls to Italy in the fifth century. Even in the early part of the century, Gauls declined to do so. Sulpicius Severus, for example, declined repeated invitations from Paulinus of Nola (*Ep.* 17). This is not to say, however, that the Gauls were averse to travel for purely social reasons; but all of this travel was restricted to within Gaul.

The discussion this far indicates that, contrary to some suggestions made in the past (Stroheker, 1948: 62; Jones, 1964: 553f.), Gauls did in fact often travel outside Gaul, and especially to Italy, in the fifth century. Most of these visits were for official reasons. On this basis, then, one might conclude that administratively, at least, many Gauls still considered themselves to be a part of the politico-religious Italian empire even up to *c.* 470. On the other hand, however, the evidence for travel outside Gaul for purely personal reasons is much more skimpy, and mostly limited to the beginning of the century. This could lead one to suggest that the social connections between the Gallic and Italian aristocracies were unravelling, and that the Gallo-Roman aristocracy, as regards its personal relationships, no longer considered itself closely bound to Italy and other parts of the Empire.

But, before accepting this conclusion simply on the basis of a bare enumeration of visits alone, it might be useful to look at some of these visits in more detail, and to ask whether the activities of the visitors, or the refugees for that matter, give any indications of continuing close social or family ties between the Gallic and Italian aristocracies. One question which might be considered is the extent to which the many Gallic expatriates of the late fourth and early fifth centuries maintained their ties to Gaul. In one instance, at least, they did. Paulinus of Nola corresponded regularly with his Gallic friends (Walsh, 1966–7: *passim*). And, even if they did not actually visit each other, at least their couriers made the trip. The constant comings and goings of these messengers presumably demonstrate the kind of regular social intercourse between Gaul and Italy which existed around the turn of the century. Similar epistolary exchanges also occurred between Symmachus, Ambrose and Ausonius, and their Gallic and Italian correspondents. But did this phenomenon continue on into the fifth century?

Over 300 letters written by some forty Gauls survive from the years *c.* 420–500. But, of all these, the only extant letters to Italians are those of Sidonius, which he wrote to Campanianus, Candidianus, and the prefect of Rome Audax (*Ep.* 1.8, 1.10, 8.7). But even the first two of these were written while Sidonius was in Rome in 467–8 on official business. Only the one to Audax shows social intercourse between Gaul and Italy *per se*. One also might note that Ruricius of Limoges, a supposed relative of the Italian family of the Anicii (Fortunatus, *Carm.* 4.5.7–8; cf. Mommaerts and Kelley, above p. 111), did not think enough of his Roman relatives to include a single Italian, or even non-Gallic, correspondent in his voluminous collection of eighty-two letters. For him, apparently, his foreign relatives did not count for much in real life. This failure of Gallic aristocrats to include many Italians (or other foreigners) among their personal correspondents after the early fifth century seems significant. It would appear on this basis that the Gauls had few personal ties in Italy which they deemed worth cultivating.

Finally, to what extent did the Gallic visitors to Italy in the fifth century avail themselves of any social ties that they had there? One notes that in the 440s, Germanus of Auxerre did have social interactions with several high-ranking court officials at Ravenna (*V. Germani* 35–9). There is no indication, however, as to whether he had known these individuals before his arrival. And one cannot but note that he had to lodge in a *diversorium*, or inn, while he was there: apparently, he had no friends with whom to stay. More positive evidence comes from Hilary of Arles' delegation to Rome in the late 440s. His representatives sought aid in particular from Hilary's old friend Auxiliaris, a Roman aristocrat of some standing (*V. Hilarii* 17 [22]; *Nov. Val.* 8.1–2). One might expect to find similar evidence for close Gallo-Italian aristocratic relations, if any existed, in the years 455–6, when the Gaul Avitus actually became emperor in Rome. But one searches in vain for a single Italian appointed to serve in Avitus' administration. Avitus seems to have had no friends or allies in Rome at all (Allard, 1908: 427). In fact, his actions so alienated the senate in Rome that there was rioting in the streets and a conspiracy was formed against him (GT *HF* 2.11; John of Antioch fr.202). Sidonius' experience in Italy was the same. In 467, when he arrived in Rome on an Arvernian delegation, he, like Germanus, had no one with whom to stay, and he too had to take rooms in a *diversorium* (*Ep.* 1.5). Only later was he received into the home of the Roman senator Fl. Synesius Gennadius Paulus (*Ep.* 1.9.1; *PLRE* II, 855). Even the appointments of Sidonius and Ecdicius to high offices of state at this time probably demonstrate not close ties between Gaul and Italy, but the need, in part, of foreign emperors to drum up support outside Italy in order to counterbalance the influence of the Italian aristocracy.

There is little evidence, therefore, for the maintenance of any sort of close ties, through either visits, correspondence, or patronage, between the aristocracies of Gaul and Italy in the fifth century after *c.* 420. Whereas personal visits and communications were relatively common at the very beginning of the century, it would appear that afterwards the social ties between the Gallic and Italian aristocracies had become very remote.

It might be useful to conclude with a few thoughts on why this situation had arisen. It may be that the Gallic reluctance to travel abroad resulted from something more than the difficulties of travel (so Loyen, 1943: 60f.; Jones, 1964: 553): the lack of Gallic interaction with the Italian aristocracy more likely results from Gallic perceptions of Gallic relations with Italy, and foreign parts in general. The increasing concern in Gaul with strictly local interests and affairs at this time is well known (cf. Heinzelmann, below p. 243). In part, this phenomenon would have been a result of a perceived neglect of Gaul by the imperial government ever since the late fourth century. The Gallic panegyricist Latinius Pacatus Drepanius blamed this neglect for the revolt of Magnus Maximus (383–8) (*Pan. Lat.* 2(12).23–4). The *Expositio totius mundi et gentium* (58) noted that Gaul, 'always has need of an emperor, it creates one on its own' (cf. Ammianus 15.5.2; Theophanes, *Chron.* 5931). This sentiment was expressed most eloquently by Sidonius Apollinaris. In his panegyric to Majorian at Lyons in 458, he noted, 'ever since the time of Theodosius ... my Gaul has been ignored by the emperors... Held in contempt for so many years, her nobility has lain prostrate...' (*Carm.* 5.354–62). Given this perception, it should be no surprise that Gauls tended to discount their foreign social, and political, ties. Certainly, Gauls were not averse to holding imperial office if the opportunity arose. But, as already seen, such opportunities arose only rarely, and this merely strengthened the Gauls in their isolationist views. Socially, moreover, the Gauls seem not to have maintained, or pursued, ties with the Italian aristocracy at all.

These conclusions would seem to contradict some recent suggestions about the ties between Gaul and Italy in the fifth century. The idea that there was a strong Gallic family element in the Italian aristocracy which was both cultivated and maintained probably can be put to rest (Oost, 1968: 237; Twyman, 1970), as can the assertion that there was a native Gallic 'faction' which participated enthusiastically in the activities of the senate in Rome in the 430s and later (Moss,

1973). Nor, finally, does it seem likely that the southern part of Gaul should be considered just as an appendage of Italy in the fifth century (Van Dam, 1985: 2).

No, it would appear that after the revolts and barbarian invasions of the beginning of the fifth century, Gaul entered a period of transition. Gauls and the Gallic aristocracy now began to keep pretty much to themselves. Did they consider themselves part of the Roman empire? Administratively, as long as it was possible, they showed by their actions that, when it suited them, they did. But socially, their ties and activities became limited almost exclusively to Gaul. Even if they considered themselves to be 'Roman' in a cultural sense, as they certainly did (Mathisen, 1988), they did not cultivate this *Romanitas* outside of Gaul.

CHAPTER 21

The 'affair' of Hilary of Arles (445) and Gallo-Roman identity in the fifth century[1]

M. Heinzelmann

THE AFFAIR

The main sources for the 'affair' consist of the two legal instruments that brought it to its climax, and its conclusion. These, to be sure, and with great partiality, reproduce the point of view of Hilary's opponents. They comprise: (i) a letter written by Leo I, setting out his papal *sententia* in the matter of the bishop of Arles; and (ii) an imperial edict of 8 July 445, dealing with the same case (*PL* 54: 628–36; *Nov. Val.* 17.101–3). To judge from their contents, both documents appear to have been drafted in response to the overreaching activity of an ambitious metropolitan. Their particular stimulus was Hilary's acting outside the borders of his ecclesiastical province, Viennensis, against Chelidonius of Besançon, metropolitan of Sequanensis. Chelidonius, for his part, had journeyed to Rome to obtain from Leo (pope since 440) the lifting of the sentence (probably deposition) that Hilary, or a church council under his presidency, had passed on him. As soon as Hilary learned what was happening, he himself hastened to the Holy City. He participated in at least part of Chelidonius' retrial, but left Rome as quickly as he had come before the process was complete.

The content and place of issue (Rome) of the imperial edict, which was addressed to the 'episcopi Gallicani et aliarum provinciarum',

---

[1] The author regrets that Mathisen, 1989 (see 1979d) was unavailable to him at the time of writing this chapter.

suggest that both this document and the undated papal letter were virtually contemporary: Leo might even have despatched the two texts together to Gaul (Langgärtner, 1964: 75). Leo justifies his intervention in terms of the *principatus* – the edict has *primatus* – of the Apostolic Prince, and hence of the see of Rome, over the whole Church. On this basis, he declares his desire to follow precedent and collaborate with the Gallic bishops in 'restoring the condition of the Gallic Church' ('statum vestrarum ecclesiarum componere', *PL* 54: 629). He will eschew all novelty; for it is novelty – 'nova usurpatio, nova instituentes, novis praesumptionibus, novitas' (*ibid.* 629, 630, 636) – that Hilary intends and, in doing so, jeopardizes the *status ecclesiarum*. According to Leo, Hilary's disobedience to papal authority was a means whereby he would subject all the Gallic bishops, in whose ordination he was falsely claiming rights of interference, to his power ('suae potestati'); and in aiming for such subjection he was grossly infringing upon the rights of his fellow metropolitans (*ibid.* 630). Contrary to 'Hilary's habitual lies' ('quod potest ... Hilarius pro suo more mentiri', *ibid.* 636), the Holy See desires the control of ordinations in Gaul not for itself, but for the Gallic bishops. To this end, Leo's letter strictly forbids bishops voluntarily to cede their prerogatives 'to others' (understand: 'to Hilary'): if a bishop wishes, as 'desertor honoris', to assign his prerogatives to some other person, to whom he is tied by personal obligation ('gratia personalis'), these should not pass to this person, but rather to the 'longest serving' bishop within his province (*ibid.* 634). Leo's letter also mentions that Hilary came to Rome uninvited, and that in the course of Chelidonius' appeal (*causa*) he was given the opportunity to speak on this matter. On this occasion, Leo says, he disputed the authority of the Holy See 'verbis arrogantioribus', declaring that the whole affair was the concern of none but himself and the bishops of Gaul. Subsequently, the letter relates, the earlier judgement against Chelidonius was reversed, and his office and rank were fully restored to him.

Once this first proceeding was over, Leo's letter continues, there followed the hearing of a complaint by bishop Projectus, according to whom Hilary, exploiting the former's illness, had 'invaded' his see (the identity of which is unknown) and transferred his episcopate to a successor without his approval. In this context, Leo's letter mentions the privileges earlier won by Patroclus, one of Hilary's predecessors, declaring that the prerogative in question, by which the bishop of

Arles was permitted to ordain bishops even beyond the borders of Viennensis, had in the meantime been withdrawn, 'meliore sententia' (*ibid.* 632). When Hilary was finally summoned to speak on this matter ('quaereretur ad causam'), he seems to have fled. His biographer, a former pupil, explains this retreat by saying that Hilary had realized that he was now well on the way to being transformed from witness to accused (*Vitae Sanctorum*, ed. Cavallin, 1952: 99); and that this transformation was being hastened by the enmity of a group of *potentes*. (The attendance of Roman senators at Leo's episcopal court is, it may be noted, attested on other occasions: Ensslin, 1937: 370f.)

Obviously, however, Hilary's flight permitted his enemies to saddle him with still more charges, concerning which, in a manner quite different from the two preceding cases, no specific complaints had been laid. So, the papal letter complains, the bishop of Arles, while celebrating ordinations in the outlying provinces, was accompanied by an armed escort ('militaris manus'); and it was with the help of these troops that he perpetrated the over-hasty ordination of outsiders, while the communities concerned were still in mourning for the death of their former bishop (*PL* 54: 633). Leo reminds the recipients of his letter of the customary procedure for the election of a bishop, which required the endorsement of the clergy, the attestation of the *honorati* and the agreement (*consensus*) of the city council and population (*ibid.* 634). Besides contravening these regulations, Hilary was also accused of having too frequently excommunicated laymen (*ibid.* 635).

Given the accumulation of charges, Leo's judgement appeared entirely fitting: Hilary forfeited his rank as metropolitan, was forbidden to call any more councils, and lost his rights of participation in episcopal courts. He was also barred from attendance at ordinations (*ibid.* 634).

Valentian III's *lex edictalis* generally confirms Leo's decision, while pointing up certain aspects of the charge. It specifies that Leo's sentence *per Gallias* would have been valid, even in the absence of the *sanctio imperialis*; and it gives particular prominence to three points: (i) the confirmation of papal *auctoritas in ecclesias*; (ii) the general outlawing of the use of armed forces in church affairs; and (iii) the instructions to provincial governors to bring recalcitrant bishops before the Holy See. For failure to comply with these ordinances, the officials responsible were threatened with a heavy fine. The ostensible aim of the imperial edict was to bring to an end the disturbances ('abominabilis tumultus') that had resulted in the Gallic provinces from the military occupation of cities. It is clear, however, that rather more was at issue: the author of the novella reckons with an important group of bishops likely to react to the content of his directives with something more than reluctance. One may identify these prelates with those reproached in Leo's letter for having allowed their personal links with Hilary to cause them to give up their prerogatives. In addition, and in similar vein, the edict anticipates the existence of imperial administrators disinclined to support combined papal and imperial intervention in Gallic affairs.

Though the novella lays great stress on the military element in Hilary's activities, further details in respect of the origin, quality and leadership of these troops ('manus armata') are missing. Since it is hardly likely that the bishop of Arles had a body of soldiers permanently at his disposal (Heinzelmann, 1976: 82, with n128), we should identify these men as a detachment from the regular army, under the command of either the *magister militum* of Gaul or the *magister militum* of the western imperial army, both of whom had their headquarters in Arles. In fact it was to the latter, the *patricius* Aëtius, that the imperial edict was addressed; that this involved the bypassing of the praetorian prefect of Gaul (with some probability, Auxiliaris, a friend of Hilary: Heinzelmann, 1982: 566) is perfectly understandable, given the patrician's superior rank and the application of the edict, which extended beyond the sphere of Gaul. Now, the early sixth-century Life of St Romanus of Condate reports that, at the time of his deposition of Chelidonius, Hilary enjoyed the favour of both 'the patrician' and 'the prefect' (Martine, 1968: 260; see 57 for the composition of the *Vita*); and, as far as the former is concerned, the only possible identification is with Aëtius (Heinzelmann, 1982: 546). It is consequently highly likely that the recipient of Valentinian's novella of 445 had afforded military backing to the policies of the bishop of Arles. In these circumstances, Aëtius' consulship of 446 may be regarded as an imperial reward for his acquiescence in the developments of the preceding year (Demougeot, 1983: 16).

THE BACKGROUND TO THE AFFAIR

Let us now turn to the events which led up to the arraignment of Hilary, as described in the papal letter and the edict, in order to reach an understanding of, on the one hand, such combined intervention by the western patriarch and the central Roman government and, on the other hand, Hilary's motives. I have first to set out those points that bear the main weight of my argument in this chapter, beginning with my main thesis. I would argue that after the bloody ruin of the usurpations of 411 and 413, both of which had been supported by the Gallic aristocracy, significant elements of this aristocracy sought, within the Roman imperial framework, to re-establish their own strong Gallic power-base, with which they might successfully counter-balance the particular interests of Italy and the centre (cf. Mathisen, above p. 237; Harries, below pp. 303f.). A main instrument of this 're-armament', which in character was both political and moral, was the significant development of the structures of the Gallic church. Particular stress was laid on the episcopal office which in Gaul, far more than in the other provinces of the Roman empire, came to be almost exclusively the preserve of the aristocracy, and which in the course of the fifth century had consistently gained in importance in the political and economic affairs of the Gallic *civitates* (Heinzelmann, 1988). It was in the context of this church-based enhancement of the Gallic position that Hilary was, with the support of a large section of the Gallo-Roman aristocracy, accorded a leading role. The most important weapons at his disposal were: the systematic placing of his 'own' people in vacant sees; an intensification of episcopal influence through the founding of new sees; and the regular holding of synods, with the aim of creating a more effective co-ordination of bishops' activities, especially with regard to their exercising political and social control over the *civitates* (cf. Loseby, above p. 147). This is to say that, contrary to Leo's polemic, Hilary was certainly no enemy of the established authority of metropolitan bishops in Gaul even though, in imitation of the secular civil administrative structure of the country, he sought to establish a primacy of the see of Arles.

To appreciate the motives of the Gallic aristocracy we must go back still further in time, to the end of the fourth century when, even before the invasions of 406–7 and the usurpations of 411 and 413, the transfer of the imperial residence out of Gaul severely restricted the opportunities of the great Gallic families for social advancement and self-enrichment (cf. Mathisen, above pp. 228f.). In the same period, in the distribution of high imperial posts, increasing consideration was given to the local interests of the aristocracy of each province, with the result that it was only occasionally that Gauls stood a chance of appointment to office outside their own country (Stroheker, 1948: 48f.). One direct consequence of this change of policy may well have been the diversion of many Gallic aristocrats into high office within the Church, not to mention the numerous monastic foundations of the early fifth century (Prinz, 1965: 62ff.). These monasteries served both as nurseries for the new aristocratic-ascetic spirituality (Heinzelmann, 1976: 49ff., 185ff.) and as recruiting agencies for appointments to the higher clergy. This was already the case in respect of Martin of Tours' monastery at Marmoutier, founded towards the end of the fourth century; according to Sulpicius Severus, 'multi nobiles' were to be found among those who dwelt there, 'pluresque ex eis postea episcopos uidimus' (*V. Martini* 10, 8). One of these future bishops was Heros, who, in 407/8, was installed by Constantine III as bishop of Arles, the usurper's new seat of residence, in the teeth of opposition from the clergy and people of the city (Griffe, 1964–6: II, 237). In the same period, Honoratus founded Lérins. Honoratus came of a family ennobled by its gaining of the consulship; other *patres* founded further monasteries in Marseille and its environs – a fact that even finds mention in the *Chronicle of 452* (86). That an increasing number of such people came from central and northern Gaul has led to the characterization of the Lérins monastery as the 'refugee-camp' of the north Gallic aristocracy (Prinz, 1965: 47ff.). On the other hand, in any assessment of this north–south movement one should take into account, besides flight from the barbarian invasions of 406–7, the positive attraction of the Gallic aristocracy to the court of Constantine III, exemplified above by the case of Heros.

Constantine III fell in 411, and took his bishop with him. Heros was replaced by Patroclus, a client of the victorious *magister militum*, Fl. Constantius. Arles had the latter to thank for its basilica Constantia (Benoit, 1951: 54f.). Above all, however, it is Constantius whom we must consider as having been behind pope Zosimus' (417–18) granting of unprecedented privileges to the see of Arles (Langgärtner, 1964: 26ff.; cf. Fuhrmann, 1953: 149ff.). By virtue of these prerogatives, Arles obtained metropolitan power over the provinces of Viennensis, Narbonensis I and Narbonensis II, the right to issue letters of introduction (*litterae formatae*) to Gallic clergy for travel outside Gaul, and a primacy, albeit undefined, over all the Gallic provinces. The substantive administrative monopoly of the Arles church in the issuing of *litterae formatae* is specifically advertised in a civil law promulgated only a year later by the emperors Honorius and Theodosius at the suggestion of the prefect of Gaul (*MGH, Ep.* 3: 13–15; ed. 17 April 418). It is to be noted that this law concerned the re-establishment of the *Concilium septem provinciarum* in Arles, the aim of which was 'to focus the loyalties of the Gallic upper classes upon their new capital in the south' (Matthews, 1975: 334).

The particular papal regard for Arles in these years is probably attributable solely to the all-powerful influence of Patroclus' patron, Fl. Constantius; it speedily evaporated on the death of the latter. Only five months later, pope Boniface called upon the bishop of Narbonne not to tolerate any interference by the Arles church in his province (*Ep.* 12, dated 9 February 422; *PL* 20: 772–4). However, the see continued to enjoy the considerable political influence bestowed upon it by recent events, and by the residual favour of the civil and military administrations. In an edict of 425, again addressed to the Gallic prefect, and concerning the persecution of heretics, Patroclus was instructed to undertake corrective procedures against Gallic bishops suspected of heresy (Ensslin, 1937: 372); and the murder of Patroclus, in the following year – which Prosper (1292) laid at the door of the western *magister militum*, Felix – would likewise underline the political role of the bishop of Arles. In identical vein are the events that, in 427–30, led to the consecutive elections of Patroclus' two successors, the kinsmen Honoratus and Hilary (Heinzelmann, 1976: 76f.; and below).

It is clear that in southern Gaul the episcopal office played a preponderant part in the political and social life of the *civitates*, quite apart from its religious role. The political aspect of the episcopate is fully confirmed in a contemporary letter of pope Celestine (dated 25 July 428: *PL* 50: 429–36). According to this, there was in the territories of those to whom the letter was addressed – the bishops of Viennensis, Narbonensis I and Narbonensis II – a widespread abuse in that, contrary to the will of the local clergy and populace, bishops were being ordained in communities where they were not known (*ibid.* cap. IV–V: 431). Indeed, Celestine complained, a number of bishops had been enthroned who had no record of church service and who had not even previously taken holy orders (*ibid.* cap. III: 430). Such prelates were frequently recruited from members of the laity who were embroiled in the political disputes of the day (*ibid.* 430: 'laicos ... quorum crimina ... per omnes pene sunt nota provincias'); others came so often as outsiders (i.e. from monasteries) that, to all appearances, 'novum quoddam, de quo episcopi fiant, institutum videatur esse collegium' (*ibid.* 431; cf. also cap. I: 430f.).

Honoratus certainly fits this picture: having previously held no clerical position at Arles, he was brought out of his monastery at Lérins and ordained bishop of that city. His first concern was, therefore, to reconcile himself with the populace of Arles, which had been opposed to his election ('prima ei cura concordiae fuit'); according to his biographer, Hilary, this is what he achieved (*Vitae Sanctorum*, ed. Cavallin, 1952: 69). The question as to actually who engineered Honoratus' elevation against the wishes of the local population finds answer in the events that took place at the end of his brief period in office. Then, the dying bishop, in the presence of the serving prefect of Gaul and certain of his predecessors (*praefectorii viri*), nominated Hilary as his successor (Heinzelmann, 1976: 77); and thereupon the Gallic *magister militum*, aided by his troops and a few citizens co-opted for the purpose, organized the 'election' of a man who was designated by his kinsman, Honoratus, and whose selection was obviously in full agreement with the thinking of the leading administrators of Gaul.

HILARY'S ACTIVITIES AND THE REACTION AGAINST THEM

Hilary would later himself intervene in the appointment of suffragan bishops, and in close collaboration with the military and civil authorities represented at Arles. On the other hand, it was the synodal activity of the metropolitan bishop that provided the first opportunity for the full development of an enduring interaction between the ecclesiastical and the secular power-structures, the more so since this activity was undoubtedly in accordance with the principles involved in the reconvening of the *Concilium septem provinciarum*.

If yearly attendance at the latter was required of representatives of individual *civitates* – *honorati* and *curiales* – so, according to a resolution of the synod of Riez, in 439, high-ranking officials (*iudices*), *curiales* and *privati* had a duty (*oportet*) to make an appearance at ecclesiatical provincial councils, alongside the senior clergy (*Conc. Gall.* I, 73, can. 8). (This was still the case in 529, at a council in Orange, held in the presence of the prefect and seven *inlustres*: *MGH, Conc.* 44ff., 54f.) Furthermore, the attendance of laymen at Hilary's synods often followed from the need to deal on the spot with those of them subsequently sentenced to excommunication (*Conc. Gall.* I, 73, Riez, can. 7/8; 81, Orange, can. 10; 98, Vaison, can. 5). As we have already seen, according to Leo's letter of 445, Hilary availed himself all too frequently of excommunication as a weapon against the laity. Among other instances, he inflicted ecclesiastical punishment on those laymen involved in the election to the see of Embrun, on the occasion of the synod at Riez (*Conc. Gall.* I, 65, can. 1); and he generally threatened with such punishment anyone, lay or cleric, who opposed the Church or, especially, his own bishop, or who made common cause with the enemies of the latter (*Conc. Gall.* I, 73, Riez, can. 7; 99, Vaison, can. 6). That, in other respects, bishops were laying claim to an increasingly more influential position within city life (Heinzelmann, 1988: 37ff.) is indicated both by a resolution of the synod of Riez – concerning a bishop whose election was not in accordance with canon law – forbidding them to exercise their authority in the public *loci* of the *curia* and the *civitas* (*Conc. Gall.* I, 67), and by other resolutions of Hilary's councils dealing with the legal position as it related to asylum, manumission and adoption (can. 5–7, Orange; can. 9–10, Vaison).

For sure, the proceedings of Hilary's three councils held at Riez (439), Orange (441) and Vaison (442), and probably those of the second council of Arles (443/4?; *Conc. Gall.* I, 111ff. [442–506]), provide only a partial reflection of his activities in this regard: it is hardly likely that Hilary waited for ten years after his election before summoning his first council. That the known councils differed significantly in character is discernible from their attendance lists. In Riez, fourteen bishops from the area directly within Arles' sphere of influence (southern Viennensis, Narbonensis II and the Maritime Alps) came together to put right an uncanonical episcopal election. Orange, two years later, witnessed not only the presence of a representative of the see of Vienne but also that of the metropolitan bishop of Vienne in person, whose predecessors (and successors) bitterly resisted the claims of Arles. It may be that particular personal obligation – Leo's *personalis gratia* – was at work here as, for example, it is patently demonstrable in the attendance of the second metropolitan, Eucherius of Lyon: a leading figure in the ascetic movement of the Gallic aristocracy, and a former resident of Lérins. The operation of personal ties is also strongly suggested by the fact that Eucherius was accompanied by his two sons, both former pupils of Hilary at Lérins: Salonius, bishop of Geneva, and Veranus, deacon of Lyon (*Conc. Gall.* I, 87). Links can also be established between Hilary's 'home-monastery' of Lérins and at least two other bishops on the Orange list: Maximus of Riez and Theodore of Fréjus (Prinz, 1965: 60). Hilary's personal admonition of absent bishops, proclaimed in canon 29 of the Orange council (*Conc. Gall.* I, 86), seems to have borne fruit in the following year at the council of Vaison, at which twenty-three bishoprics were represented (*Conc. Gall.* I, 102).

Hilary's relationships with the bishops of his episcopal province are retrospectively illuminated by a letter from nineteen prelates to pope Leo, written shortly after the death of the bishop of Arles (*MGH, Ep.* 3: 18–20; those who sent it are named in Leo's reply of 5 May 450: *ibid.* 20f.). In this document which, by reference to the *instituta principum* ('imperial prerogatives'), makes much of Arles' administrative function (mention is made of it as the seat of the prefecture and of other *potestates*), the nineteen bishops plead for the city's pre-eminence on the grounds that they, like their predecessors, were appointed to office by its bishop (*ibid.* 19). In some cases, indeed, and a possibility which up to now has been generally overlooked (though cf. Loseby, above pp. 144f., 147), the very sees themselves may have owed their creation to Hilary. Thus bishops of Thorame and Castellane (Maritime Alps) are attested only at Hilary's councils; and it was under Hilary that for the first time the neighbouring cities of Nice and Cimiez were each simultaneously provided with a bishop. In addition, the sees of Toulon, Antibes, Avignon and Carpentras could be foundations of the bishop of Arles; those of Vence, Apt and Riez, however, probably go back to his predecessors (Duchesne: 1907: I; Griffe, 1964–6: II, 120ff.; Duval, Février and Guyon, 1986; Biarne *et al*, 1986). Very striking is the undoubted novelty of a bishop of Uzès, an *oppidum* that, according to the *Notitia Galliarum*, was at the beginning of the fifth century still classified as a *castrum* (*Not. Gall.* 15.10.609). This bishop, who as a close intimate of Hilary represented his case at Rome, was the sole representative of Narbonensis I both at Hilary's councils and among the signatories of the letter of 450: it seems inexplicable that Hilary's opponents never objected to this. The diocese of Uzès must have been created out of the city-territory of Nîmes; and in this case, as in those of the other episcopal foundations, one must assume close collaboration with the civil authorities. Such a relationship found specific mention at the contemporary council of Chalcedon, as testified by the Latin translation of canon 17: 'Si qua vero potestate imperiali civitas nova constituta est, aut certe constituatur, civilibus et publicis formulis etiam ecclesiasticarum parrociarum ordo celebretur' (Mansi, 1901–27, VII: 397; read XVII instead of XXVI; Hefele and Leclercq, 1908, II: 801, can. 12; *ibid.* 805f., can. 17). As to other aspects of the administrative procedure involved in the foundation of church sees, the sources are silent.

In contrast with his activity in his own province, Hilary's plans with regard to the rest of Gaul remain unclear, given the lack of detail provided by our sources. According to his *Vita*, he often (*saepius*) sought out Germanus of Auxerre in order to discuss with him the personal problems of the senior clergy (*Vitae Sanctorum*, ed. Cavallin, 1952: 98; ch. 21). It was on the occasion of one such visit, we are told, that nobles and *mediocres* brought to his attention the delicts of the metropolitan of Besançon – the marriage of a widow and, in an earlier capacity, probably that of provincial governor, the imposition of death sentences (Mathisen, 1979a: 164). Hilary and Germanus are supposed thereupon to have taken counsel of each other, sat in judgement on Chelidonius, and declared him guilty. The relationship between Germanus and Hilary is incontrovertible (*V. Germani* 23), but the role of the former in the Chelidonius affair has recently been questioned (Thompson, 1984: 57ff.; Wood, 1984: 15). Most recently, it has been very plausibly argued that Germanus' final trip to the empress Galla Placidia in Ravenna, in 445, should be placed in the context of an attempted mediation during the proceedings of Hilary in Rome: Scharf, 1991). On the other hand, it seems plain that this affair on its own would hardly have led to Hilary's downfall. In this respect, further damage – unexpected by Hilary – was done by the taking up of Projectus' complaints which, in Roman eyes, could stand proxy for a whole series of identical goings-on that had not resulted in the wave of protest so much desired by Rome. Projectus' protest provided the long-awaited opportunity to be shut of Hilary and his *monarchia* (*V. Romani* 18).

All of this occurred, without doubt, at a time when Hilary was unable to count on his usual political support: scholars have, with good reason, drawn attention to the diversion of Aëtius' interests towards Italy during the 440s (Zecchini, 1983: 239; Demougeot, 1983: 11ff.). Furthermore, Hilary's links with Gallic prefects could not always be relied on. To be sure, probably during the first half of 445 and *after* his flight from Rome, he received aid in his dealings with Leo from the prefect Auxiliaris (Heinzelmann, 1982: 566); but it seems that two other prefects who held office in Gaul: the Italian Albinus (quarrelling with Aëtius in Gaul in 440: Prosper 1341; cf. Scharf, 1991: cap. ix, indicating that this same Albinus was Italian prefect during the process of Hilary in Rome) and Marcellus (441–3), should be counted as belonging in the enemy camp. The latter is in fact mentioned in an inscription set up by bishop Rusticus of Narbonne in 445 (*CIL* XII, 5336 – see: Chalon, 1973: 223ff.; Atsma, 1976: 10ff.). The inscription celebrates the completion of the reconstruction of the cathedral of Narbonne, begun in 441, and names those persons who had contributed to the work. Amongst these we find, in pride of place, Rusticus himself, who identifies himself as the son and nephew of bishops and who (as in three other inscriptions) employs a system of dating based on his own years in the episcopal office (Heinzelmann, 1976: 197f.; also 108f.). This self-confident metropolitan bishop of Narbonensis I never attended any of Hilary's councils, and, in the building of his cathedral church, was supported by another leading opponent of Hilary's pretensions, bishop Venerius of Arles. According to the evidence of the inscription in question, both came from the same monastery in Marseille, where they both had served together in the clergy (Atsma, 1976: 11f.). The first contributor on the list, Orosius, is probably also to be connected to Marseille, where already in the fourth century we find a bishop bearing this otherwise only rarely attested name. To this group was now attached the prefect Marcellus who, in each of the two years of his period in office – which fell, without doubt, during the first years of the reconstruction: 441–3 – made available from public funds the considerable sum of 1,600 solidi (Heinzelmann, 1988: 34 and n48). His connection with Narbonne, as attested by the inscription of 445, deserves to be regarded as equal in significance to that of the *magister militum* Fl. Constantius – founder of the basilica Constantia and patron of Patroclus – with Arles.

CONCLUSION

One is bound to relate the important group with common anti-Arles interests of the Rusticus inscription to Projectus' appeal to Rome, whenever this occurred, and so to the fall of Hilary in 445. Thus Hilary failed to achieve his political aim of creating a pan-Gallic solidarity. As had already been the case in respect of the support or opposition shown to the usurpations at the beginning of the century, dissension within the Gallic ruling-class was too great for the creation of a common viewpoint. Such disunity may be seen as proof of the continuing influence of a significant group of conservatives within the Gallic aristocracy, who favoured the traditional imperial structure and strong central government, and who were hostile to more recent thinking regarding the likely advantages of increased political independence on the part of the Gallic administration. Without doubt, these opposing conceptions reflect different strands in the conception of Gallo-Roman identity in the fifth century.

CHAPTER 22

Crisis and conversion in fifth-century Gaul: aristocrats and ascetics between 'horizontality' and 'verticality'

M. A. Wes

People associate with each other in essentially two ways: horizontally, i.e. on an equal footing; and vertically, i.e. on an unequal footing. Two models of social organization may be proposed as representing the extremes of these two kinds of human intercourse. In the horizontal model, which may be visualized as a straight line, there is absolute equality and absolute freedom; decisions about the community as a whole are taken by consulting all groups concerned. The vertical model may be represented as a pyramid. The man at the apex of the pyramid can only associate with members of his society vertically. All other members of society occupy positions inside the pyramid and on its side surfaces; all depend on the man at the top. This *domus* is ruled by the *dominus* with absolute power. Subordinates are all more or less in the position of *servi*. Ideally a relationship of mutual *fides* exists between the *dominus* and his *servi*, maintained by *beneficia* from top to base, and *officia* from base to top.

Gallic society in the fifth century can be described as a set of such pyramids (Fig. 22.1). The *domini* – or *patroni* – at the apices of these pyramids are the leaders of the aristocratic families and the various groups of Germans established in Gaul. Together they form a complex network of relationships, partly friendly, partly hostile, and in a state of continual flux. While communication within each separate pyramid is vertical, communication between the apices of all these pyramids is in theory horizontal. Of course there are differences – one *dominus* or *patronus* has more *honor* and *dignitas* than another – but the fact that there are *primi inter pares* does not affect the fundamental equality of the *pares*, including the *primi* (Fig. 22.2): these differences, however, pale into insignificance compared to those

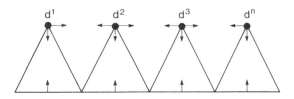

Horizontal communication or 'horizontality': between *domini*,
$d^1 - d^2 - d^3 - d^n$ within a single truncated pyramid.
Vertical communication or 'verticality': from
$d^1 - d^2 - d^3 - d^n$ downwards (and vice versa).

Fig. 22.1   Crisis and conversion in fifth-century Gaul: horizontal communication

between the top layer of *potentiores* and the bottom layer of the *vulgus humile*. A set of pyramids, of which the apices are interrelated in a network, can be described as a truncated pyramid. Instead of one all-powerful leader at the top, there is a group. A relative equality exists between the members of this group: they are not mutually dependent. Together they control and regulate the life of the whole community.

Through the traditional education, a young man who is born and grows up as a member of the Gallo-Roman elite is schooled in the matter of horizontal communication. On reaching manhood he is expected to occupy his position on the top face of the truncated pyramid, where his main task is to promote the interests of the particular pyramid entrusted to his rule and protection. Specific schooling in how to deal with *humiliores* is unnecessary. Knowledge of the correct conventions on the horizontal plane, with its relatively small inequality, implies command of the correct conventions in vertical communication.

For Sidonius it goes without saying that someone who has reached a high position can benefit his friends, harm his enemies, and give glory to his descendants. When his friend Gaudentius has been appointed as *vicarius VII provinciarum*, Sidonius compliments him on being quite free of 'that disdain of public service which is characteristic of the slothful'. Thus he distinguishes himself from those who 'praise the leisured lives of those who hold no office – not

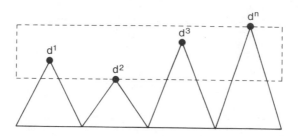

Differences between *domini*, $d^1 - d^2 - d^3 - d^n$, do not affect their fundamental equality, and pale into insignificance compared to those between them and the *vulgus humile*. Along the line $d^1 - d^n$ there is a *primus* but he is *inter pares*.

Fig. 22.2 Crisis and conversion in fifth-century Gaul: *primi inter pares*

from any eagerness for perfection but simply through vicious indolence' (*Ep.* 1.4; cf. Harries, below p. 301). This remark implies that those who voluntarily relinquish worldly *honores* and public service urged 'eagerness for perfection' in defence of their *inertia*, as Sidonius calls it.

'Disdain of public service' (*militandi fastidium*) and 'eagerness for perfection' (*studium perfectionis*) are discussed at length in a letter in which another Gallic aristocrat tries to persuade one of his relatives to renounce the world and public service, and offer himself as *Deo militans*: it is the *Epistola Paraenetica ad Valerianum Cognatum De Contemptu Mundi et Saecularis Philosophiae* written by Eucherius of Lyon in 452. Probably soon after 410, Eucherius, having already made his mark in public service, withdrew from the world to Lérins, together with his wife and his two sons Salonius and Veranius. This kind of adult *conversio* can rightly be called the result of an identity crisis.

The arguments adduced by Eucherius are a mixture of rebellion against established aristocratic values and reasoning on the basis of the same values. 'It is right that the better part asks for more devotion', notes Eucherius, for it yields more *dignitas*, and 'we should consider with all care where the dignity of our substance finds itself most in abundance.' A *dominus* not only merits more attention than a *famulus*; it is also in people's interest to pay more attention to a *dominus* than to a *famulus*. Soul and body, *anima* and *caro*, are to each other as *domina* and *famula*. More attention should therefore be paid to the salvation of the soul than to bodily welfare. So far none of this sounds very rebellious.

The first duty of a well-bred man is 'to perceive one's true father and, having perceived him, to acknowledge him'. This, too, seems hardly rebellious, except that by 'true father', *proprius auctor*, Eucherius does not mean one's biological father, who is only a father in the flesh, but God. Acknowledgement of God is met by directing all our attention to the soul: 'the one can by no means be attended to without the other. Thus whoever has given satisfaction to God, has at the same time taken care of his soul, and, conversely, whoever has taken care of his soul, has at the same time given satisfaction to God.' From the point of view of a father, whose son leaves home one day in search of God, this *is* rebellion; but Eucherius is telling Valerianus that by obeying his father he is harming his soul. Eucherius takes his incitement to rebellion further when he compares a conversion to God to the acceptance of an offer of adoption. He phrases this as a rhetorical question: if an illustrious and wealthy man wished to adopt you as his son, then surely you would embrace that opportunity and no obstacle could be great enough to prevent you from achieving that goal? Well then, God calls you as his adopted son: 'the God of the universe and the Lord of the world summons you into adoption, bestowing upon you (if you want) the alluring title of son, by which he calls our God his only son' (cf. Rom. 8; Gal. 4; Eph. 1). Whoever refuses such an offer can justly be accused of being slothful.

People are fascinated by 'the dignity of honours', Eucherius goes on, but what is this *dignitas* really worth, if *boni* and *mali* alike can gain it? As a true-born aristocrat, he objects to the fact that the wrong people win *honor* and *dignitas*. He therefore has a clear reply to Sidonius' complaint about the 'disdain of public service': 'isn't it a far greater honour to choose rather to remain unhonoured with honours of this kind and to be valued more because of one's own manners than because of promiscuous honours? ... the truly excellent turns the honours of the world into the honours of heaven.'

Eucherius' eldest son, Salonius, was barely ten years old when his father took him to Lérins (cf. Eucherius, *Instr.* 1, praef.). After his father had taken up the life of a recluse, his further education was successively entrusted to Honoratus, the founder of the monastic community of Lérins, Hilary, Vincentius, and Salvian. Salvian also taught Salonius' younger brother, Veranius (cf. Salvian, *Ep.* 8.2). One can hardly say that Salonius and Veranius turned their back on the world as the result of an identity crisis: they were simply taken along by their father. As obedient sons, both followed in his footsteps: Eucherius became bishop of Lyon; Salonius became bishop of Geneva; and Veranius became bishop of Vence.

Honoratus' own case, however, clearly points to an identity crisis, and an identity crisis which, unlike that of Eucherius, manifested itself at an early age. Honoratus, who was born *c.* 365, must have been about twenty years old when he was baptized. Somewhere between 385 and 395 he left home, together with his brother Venantius, whom he had infected with a similar spiritual zeal: 'despising all human intercourse and favor, they both burnt with a love of solitude' (*V. Honorati* 10.3). A third person involved was one Caprasius. The two brothers regarded him as their 'father in Christ', and in fact they called him 'father' (*ibid.* 12.1). The term *abba, pater*, indicating someone's 'spiritual father', is quite common in the monastic milieu. However, when Honoratus and Venantius set out, they were not yet monastics. Not without reason, Hilary strongly emphasizes the element of rebellion against paternal authority in his account of this *conversio*, the *Vita Honorati*. This is so striking that one begins to suspect that such a *conversio* was essentially a form of rebellion against the father.

Conversio not only entails disdain of public service, it is identical with disdain of noble birth, and this is something which never appealed to Sidonius Apollinaris, not even after he became a bishop. When Sidonius' brother-in-law received the title of *patricius* in 474/5, Sidonius wrote a jubilant letter to his wife (*Ep.* 5.16). How very different is Hilary's attitude: 'the height of nobility is to be numbered among the sons of God', the 'glory of the ancestors' is wholly irrelevant, and the only way of adding lustre to one's 'dignity' is by showing contempt for all those 'empty and superfluous honours' (Hilarius, *V. Honorati* 4.1). This is hardly an attitude which Eucherius, Honoratus, Hilary etc. can have expected normal fathers to condone. Radical dedication of one's life to God brought shame upon one's family – 'the common glory of their family was being snatched away' (*V. Honorati* 5.3); this meant a head-on collision with the *pater familias*: 'as a youth [Honoratus] scorned the things that delighted his aged father' (*ibid.* 7.1). But as a son the *conversus* was not without recourse; he could mobilize the will of God against the will of his father: 'let others delight in gold and silver and country estates and slaves and high offices, "the world passeth away, and the lust thereof: but he that doeth the will of God abideth for ever"' (1 John 2.17).

Hilary's formulation of the actual *conversio* of Honoratus is highly interesting: 'he shook off the yoke of liberty, taking up the yoke of slavery to the Lord'. The 'yoke of liberty' is the strait-jacket of a life lived according to the values and rules of the late Roman aristocracy. Instead of this, Honoratus takes upon himself the 'yoke of slavery'. For a slave there is the possibility only of vertical communication with his *dominus*. If he now puts God in the place of his earthly *dominus*, his position as a slave remains unchanged, but he has been freed from his former lord. To exchange *libertas* for *servitus* is the most radical and, in the view of a Roman aristocrat, the most absurd step one can take: 'he was suddenly completely changed into another man from what he had been', Hilary wrote (*V. Honorati* 8.3), and immediately applied this to the relationship between father and son: 'so that his father grieved as a parent would grieve who had been bereft of his son'. And in the next paragraph: 'Then for the first and only time did [Honoratus] refuse to yield to his father, when he was hastening to become the son of God.'

Whoever chooses God as his father rebels against his biological father, and conversely, whoever remains obedient to his biological father rebels against God. When Hilary relates his own dilemma after Honoratus has pressed him to follow his example, he describes his position before his *conversio* as that of one who is *contumax Deo*. Eucherius praises him for having left his *domus* by following Honoratus to Lérins. But he praises him even more for voluntarily returning to Lérins after first having followed Honoratus to Arles when the latter became bishop there (*De Laude Eremi* 1).

What are the implications of *conversio* for the everyday life of a *conversus*, in particular for his conduct to his fellow men? He no longer sleeps more than is necessary; he prays and reads a great deal; he says little and that in a friendly manner; he undergoes injustice with equanimity; he is generous, hospitable, and full of compassion for all; he leaves the world for what it is (*in ore rarior mundus*); but above all he is not presumptuous (*V. Honorati* 9.2–3). In short: horizontal communication. But this is of an entirely different nature from the horizontality enacted on the top surface of our truncated pyramid. The true *conversus* has done with the notion of the world as a set of small pyramids whose apices form a horizontally interrelated network. The true world is the infinitely larger pyramid with God at its apex, and human beings at its base. From the high vantage-point occupied by God the Father all people are equally minute (Fig. 22.3). Horizontal communication between people follows naturally from the awareness of the immeasurable distance – vertical – between God and man.

Conversio is also compared to a liberation from a prison and the emotional state associated with it: 'bitterness, harshness, and fierce anger gave way to freedom' (Hilarius, *V. Honorati* 17.5). Thus *conversio* – 'an amazing and marvellous change' – is as much a change from slavery (*pharaonica servitus*) to freedom (*libertas*) as a change from freedom (*libertas*) to slavery to the Lord (*dominica servitus*): Honoratus is described as 'being truly made the slave of all' (*ibid.* 18.2; cf. 1 Cor. 9.19).

All those who came to Lérins out of desire for this *divina servitus* called *Honoratus* their *dominus*, their *pater*. They regarded him as the alternative for which they had given up their *patria*, their *propinqui*, and their possessions. Among them was Salvian (Hilarius, *V. Honorati* 19.1–2). Salvian himself does not write about his own family, and there is no *Vita Salviani*. Perhaps there is an autobiographical element in a passage in the *De Gubernatione Dei*, where Salvian remarks somewhat bitterly that when a *nobilis* is converted to God he at once loses his status of *nobilis* and is even treated with contempt (4.32–3). For Salvian the conclusion is plain: there is no place in this world for the good. His argument strongly reminds one of Eucherius' complaint that there is no longer any distinction between the good and the evil in the world.

In the case of a married *conversus*, it was not always easy for a woman to follow her husband in his rejection of the world. This can be inferred from the letter that Salvian addressed to his parents-in-law, partly on behalf of his wife, Palladia. From the letter it appears that they had written to her parents before, but these letters remained unanswered. Palladia's parents clearly disapproved of her having followed her husband in his *conversio*, and it seems natural to suspect that Palladia suffered from the severance of relations after what Salvian now lightheartedly calls his *conversiuncula*. In spite of the letter's submissive tone, Salvian makes it quite clear that he is defending a just cause: 'Indeed, I ask pardon because you are angry, but I cannot say that what I have done is bad' (*Ep.* 4.9). At the same time Palladia insists (*via* Salvian) that she never disobeyed or resisted

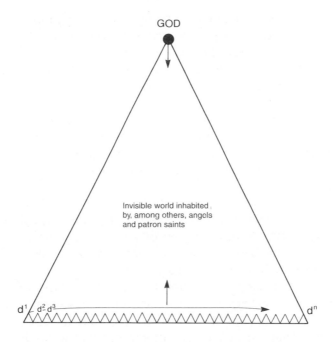

GOD

Invisible world inhabited
by, among others, angels
and patron saints

d^1 d^2 d^3 d^n

God stands at the top of a single gigantic pyramid.
Compared to the vertical distance between God and
man, the distance between individual *domini* and
their dependants is minimal.

Fig. 22.3 Crisis and conversion in fifth-century Gaul: vertical communication

her parents: 'as you know, I have never offended you by
undutifulness or obstinate disobedience. I submitted to your will by
marrying the man of your choice, the man whom you wished I should
obey' (*ibid.* 4.11).

The true *conversus* withdraws completely from the world to a
solitary life. He does not wish to take orders, let alone become a
bishop. He parts with all his possessions. But, in due course,
everyday reality in combination with the ideal of a life lived in charity
and humanity makes concessions necessary. The man who as a
servus Dei takes up the cause of an outcast without carrying much
weight in the world discovers that his efforts are to no avail.
Eucherius was already aware of this; Salvian learned it in practice.
When one day he turned to a wealthy and powerful man and requested

him to forgo his intention of robbing a poor neighbour of all his possessions, he came away empty-handed. Moreover, he felt gravely insulted because the rich man justified himself on the grounds that he had sworn by Christ that he would rob the poor man of his few possessions and that he was bound to his oath. 'What could I do?', Salvian cries in exasperation. 'I left' (*De Gub. Dei* 4.74–5). If the same poor man had appealed to Sidonius Apollinaris in his capacity as bishop, Sidonius could have approached the grasping rich man on the level of the horizontal communication within the 'old boys' network'. What benefit could the faithful draw from a bishop who was ineffective as a *patronus*?

Rejection of the world as a result of a *conversio ad Deum* was to a certain extent cancelled when the *conversus*, often unwillingly, was mitred. Honoratus became bishop of Arles after presiding over the *conversi* of Lérins. His successor in Lérins, Maximus, became bishop of Riez. Maximus' successor, Faustus, also succeeded him as bishop of Riez, just as Hilary had previously succeeded Honoratus at Arles. Lupus was made bishop of Troyes; and Eucherius became bishop of Lyon. Only Lupus' brother Vincentius and Salvian failed to obtain bishoprics. Again, it may be no coincidence that in his *Euchariston ad Faustum Episcopum* (*Carm.* 16) Sidonius mentions only those men from Lérins (apart from the already legendary Caprasius) who became bishops in later life. His letters to Faustus and Lupus show that he considers them as peers on the level of aristocratic horizontality (*Ep.* 6.1.1 and 3;   7.13.1). Indeed, the fact that Lupus apparently complained about being treated with insufficient respect by Sidonius (cf. *Ep.* 9.11.5) hardly chimes with the attitude of someone who has turned his back on the world. Sidonius apologizes profusely and begs him to believe that any possible slight was unintentional (*Ep.* 9.11.8). After fifty years as bishop, Lupus has made a complete return to aristocratic horizontality. According to Sidonius, Faustus seems to have been more successful in resisting the world as a bishop: 'You have not made your new dignity a pretext for relaxing the rigour of the old discipline' (*Ep.* 9.3.4; cf. *Carm.* 16.116–17).

In this connection a letter from Salvian to Eucherius is interesting (*Ep.* 2); it was written shortly after the latter's investiture as bishop of Lyon. It appears that Eucherius has conveyed his regards to Salvian through a pupil but without the additional compliment of a personal letter. Salvian is offended and demands satisfaction: Eucherius has treated him patronizingly. It is the typical arrogance, Salvian remarks, of someone who has recently been appointed to a high office. On at least one occasion Salvian himself was reprimanded on this account, as his fragmentary letter to bishop Agrycius shows (*Ep.* 3). We gather that somebody has pointed out to Salvian that he owes Agrycius apologies for showing a marked lack of respect. Salvian in fact apologizes, but in a somewhat ambiguous manner.

This Agrycius is generally identified with Agroecius, bishop of Sens, who wrote a treatise, *De Orthographia*, dedicated to Eucherius. When Sidonius Apollinaris was invited to Bourges in 470 to adjudicate in the rivalry over the vacant bishop's see, he humbly appealed to Agroecius for his aid (*Ep.* 7.5). At the time, Agroecius was metropolitan of Senonia, and Sidonius had only recently been consecrated. Sidonius accordingly approached Agroecius with due reverence, and assured him that he would be wholly guided by his judgement. In a letter to Perpetuus, bishop of Tours, we are told how Sidonius acquitted himself of his task. The letter (*Ep.* 7.9) contains the complete text of the speech in which Sidonius announced and justified his choice before the congregation of Bourges. The speech is a small masterpiece of rhetorical and diplomatic skill. We assume that he took his decision to appoint a layman, Simplicius, as bishop after consulting with Agroecius, who in fact travelled to Bourges to assist Sidonius.

Sidonius starts: 'If I nominate a monk ... even though he possesses the special claim of having followed the life of an anchorite, my ears will straightway be assailed by the noise of ignoble pygmies raising a confused uproar on every side. "This nominee", they will protest, "discharges the office not of a bishop but rather of an abbot; he is better qualified to intercede with the heavenly Judge for our souls than with an earthly judge for our bodies."' Next he explains why he did not wish to nominate a cleric: 'If I nominate a cleric, his inferiors will be jealous of him and his superiors will disparage him.' Sidonius then goes on to discuss the possibility of nominating an imperial official (*militaris*). In that case, he predicts, 'all will rise to their feet saying: "Because Sidonius was transferred to the ranks of the clergy from a secular profession, he is reluctant to take as colleague a metropolitan from the ranks of the clergy; he is swollen with pride of birth; he is uplifted by the insignia of his dignities; he looks down on the poor of Christ."'

What then is the advantage of Sidonius' candidate Simplicius? Sidonius' answer fits perfectly into the system of values proper to aristocratic horizontality. Simplicius comes from a good family, whose members have distinguished themselves as prefects and bishops: '... we found that he occupies a leading place among the Eminents (*inter spectabiles*)'; 'his wife is descended from the illustrious stock of the Palladii, who have held professorial chairs or episcopal thrones with credit to their order'; his father Eulogius and his father-in-law Palladius had both been bishops in Bourges. 'As I have heard, you rated his claims above those of his father and his father-in-law when you cried out that he ought to be instituted into the priesthood; but on that occasion he came home loaded with praise, since he chose to be honoured by his parents' advancement rather than by his own.' Above all, Simplicius holds his own in the hard world of the *potentiores*: 'Time and again, when the necessity of undertaking an urgent embassy was laid upon him, he stood as spokesman of this city before skin-clad monarchs or purple-clad princes' (cf. Van Dam, below p. 326).

Sidonius also has some consideration for the idea that a bishop should adopt a modest attitude toward his fellow men. But such modesty should not be taken to excess: he must not fraternize with all and sundry: 'If it is a question of human kindness he is at the service of citizen, cleric, and alien, the least as well as the greatest, even giving more than a sufficiency'; 'he is a man wholly incapable of self-advertisement, he seeks the goodwill, not of all men, but only of the best, he does not make himself cheap by indiscriminate familiarity but enhances his value by carefully choosing his associates ... He is simple in dress, genial in converse, an equal among his comrades, pre-eminent as a counsellor.' In short, 'the state is able to find in him something to admire and the church something to love'.

But not everybody in Bourges was pleased with the nomination of Simplicius: 'a few of the presbyters twittered in holes and corners, but they did not make even the slightest murmur in public'. There can be no doubt that Salvian, had he been in Bourges, would have sided with these dissenting priests. For him it was divinely ordained that the true Christian should do away with his possessions and it was a permanent aggravation to him that in practice virtually no one heeded this ordinance. In his *Epistula* 9, written to Eucherius' son Salonius, he bitterly observes that people in their lack of faith bequeath large fortunes to their families, but think it a waste of money to leave anything to the Church, although it would in fact be in their own interest to give all their possessions to God, i.e. the Church, in the hope of receiving eternal life. 'This very malady is common, not to worldly men only, but even in those who arrogate to themselves the name of religious: converts, priests, and – what is much more deadly – even bishops.' This angers Salvian to the very core of his being. All he can do is to take up his pen. The result: his four books *Ad Ecclesiam.*

The tenor of the *Ad Ecclesiam* and the mental attitude underlying it are diametrically opposed to the way in which Sidonius approaches the Church and the world. Salvian refuses to compromise: anyone who wishes to be truly *dignus Domini* must obey the Biblical injunctions of Matt. 19.21 – 'if thou wilt be perfect, go and sell that thou hast'. Salvian also insists that, just as a son should not put his own father before God, so a father should not put his own son or daughter before God: 'he that loveth son or daughter more than me is not worthy of me' (Matt. 10.37). The true believer is characterized by 'the humility of one who pays his debts'. Accordingly, when someone offers his property to God, 'let him offer it not as with the boldness of one who gives a gift. Let him not offer his gift with the confidence of buying redemption, but with the duty of supplication' (*Ad Eccl.* 1.54). Salvian demands the equality of all believers before God. Horizontality in human intercourse is thus a consequence of verticality before God. This horizontality has nothing in common with the horizontality of a democracy: it is theocracy.

CHAPTER 23

Gaul and the Holy Land in the early fifth century

E. D. Hunt

In the history of Christian pilgrimage to the Holy Land, Gaul has just claim to a prime position. From this region of the Roman empire comes our first detailed description of a journey to the holy places, in the account of the Bordeaux pilgrim of 333. For this long-distance traveller the land routes of the Empire linked the Atlantic seaboard of Gaul to the Biblical lands of Palestine: here lay the objective of his journey and focus of the religious world which he inhabited, with Jerusalem at its centre – its new Christian status reflected in the churches of Constantine even then rising at its most sacred sites (Wilkinson, 1981: 153ff.; Hunt, 1982a: 55ff., 83ff.; Constantinian churches: *Itin. Burd.* 594f., 598f.). The traveller from Bordeaux broke his journey, it can be deduced from his account, with a stay in Constantinople – with Jerusalem the twin 'pole' of the new Constantinian empire. His route home took him through Rome; but it was long since that all roads had led there, and the returning pilgrim gives no hint that the city held any special significance for him (*Itin. Burd.* 612, 4; cf. 571). Fifty years later the lady Egeria and her companions arrived in the Holy Land *de extremis terris* (*Itin. Eg.* 19.5): she is usually taken to have originated from the Spanish side of the Pyrenees, but has now been claimed again for Gaul (Sivan, 1988a, cf. 1988b). Whether a Spaniard or a Gaul, Egeria confirms the perspective first sighted in the Bordeaux account: a Christian Mediterranean empire seen from its western edges as revolving around Jerusalem and Constantinople – for it was here in Constantinople that Egeria was based for her travels in the east, and offered thanks for her pilgrimage at its churches and martyr shrines (*Itin. Eg.* 23.8–10).

The Bordeaux pilgrim and Egeria journeyed mainly by land. Yet the harbours of southern Gaul – Marseilles or Narbonne – might have offered them ready and relatively speedy access by sea to the eastern Mediterranean. A fair wind, and only some three weeks or so separated the western provinces from Alexandria or the coast of Palestine (Rougé, 1966: 99ff.; Hunt, 1982a: 72ff.). Such was the experience of Sulpicius Severus' Postumianus and his colleagues, who set sail from Narbonne only to arrive in Alexandria when the purges of bishop Theophilus against 'Origenist' monks were at their height (*c.* 400), then temporarily retreated from this turmoil to the company of Jerome in Bethlehem for six months, before it was politic to return to investigate the true objective of their journey, the monks of the Egyptian desert (Sulpicius, *Dial.* 1.3, 6–9.). Holy men, of course, as much as holy places, lay at the goal of these great journeys which united west and east in the Christian empire. Egeria's enthusiasm had been directed as much at the saintly bishops and monks and their virtuous deeds as at the Biblical sites to which they conducted her: indeed in her eyes the holy men represented a present continuation of the scriptural history which she saw visualized in the landscape of Palestine (*It. Eg.* 20.13). This was a history which her 'sisters' – as she addresses her correspondents in the far-off west – knew from their Bible reading, but which now through the mediation of Egeria's pilgrimage and the description of her journey which she sent them was brought vividly closer to home: 'it may help you, loving sisters, the better to picture what happened in these places when you read the holy books of Moses' (*Itin. Eg.* 5.8; tr. Wilkinson, 1981: 98; cf. Hunt, 1982a: 84ff.). In the same way the Bordeaux pilgrim's account of Biblical history enshrined at the holy places would serve to unite the congregations of south-west Gaul among whom it circulated with the distant origins of their faith in the Holy Land.

The pilgrims, then, with their journeys on record in the descriptions they provided, were important intermediaries in holding together west and east in a Christian empire. Increasingly, too, the union was cemented in the transfer of relics, a natural concomitant of the vogue for pilgrimage, which brought the people and places of Biblical history in the Holy Land actually into the midst of congregations far afield in the west (Hunt, 1982a: 128ff.; Brown, 1981: 88ff.). In, for example, a fragment of the Cross, such as Sulpicius Severus received from Paulinus of Nola for the dedication of his church at Primuliacum, Jerusalem and its holy sites were in a vivid sense transplanted to Gaul: the significance of the Biblical events which the Cross represented was now to be beheld, as Paulinus reminded Sulpicius, in this tiny fragment which they had in their presence (Paulinus of Nola, *Ep.* 31.1; cf. 32.11). In some typically evocative pages on the subject of pilgrimage and the cult of relics, Peter Brown has spoken of late antique Christianity feeding 'on the facts of distance and on the joys of proximity', and of a 'carefully maintained tension between distance and proximity' (1981: 86ff.). To Christians in the south of Gaul the Holy Land was (self-evidently) physically distant, indeed needed to be if it was to be the objective of the pilgrim's *desiderium*; but at the same time the process of pilgrimage – the eye-witness descriptions, the written accounts of journeys, most of all perhaps the travelling parcels of Biblical earth or *lignum crucis* – elided that distance into a pious consciousness of the near presence of the Holy Land and its sacred history.

The initial publicity for the conference from which this book derives suggested as its central question 'the extent to which Gaul may be said to have still been a part of the Roman empire after 31 December 406'. I trust it is not too contrived to claim for what I have been saying so far some degree of relevance to this question. To the extent that the Roman empire evolved into a Christian world in the generations after Constantine, then the pattern which I have been sketching certainly engages Gaul into that community of the faithful which looked to the Holy Land as its focus. In the years on either side of 406 the focus was made all the sharper, at least for an elite circle of 'professional' devotees in the west, by the presence in Bethlehem of Jerome, at the nucleus of a far-flung network of Christianized *amicitia*, through whose channels he dispensed scriptural erudition and ascetic exhortations (Rousseau, 1978: 114ff.). Jerome's location was surely not coincidental to the workings of these communications: settled at the holy places he had ready-made avenues of contact in the visitors and pilgrims he received in his monastery, and his pronouncements carried with them the authority of the Biblical land of their origin. As with the returning pilgrims and their relics, Jerome's correspondents may be said to have been switched into the 'national grid' of the faith which emanated from the holy places.

It is from correspondence of Jerome, of course, that we hear most vividly of the devastation done to Gaul by the Vandals, Suevi and their associates in their advance after 406: everything overrun 'between the Alps and the Pyrenees, between the Ocean and the

Rhine', cities besieged and captured, their populations killed or ravaged by famine (*Ep.* 123.15; cf. Courcelle, 1964: 82ff.; cf. Roberts, above p. 97). That information on these events, doubtless highly coloured, derives from a source thousands of miles separate from them is in itself a classic reflection of Peter Brown's paradox of distance and proximity: geographically distant, yet Jerome in Bethlehem visualized as though at close quarters the destruction of Gaul. It is looking through the pilgrim's lens from, as it were, the wrong end. The raw material for his graphic depiction will have been supplied by refugees from the west who now turned up in ever-increasing numbers, Jerome affirms, at the doors of his Bethlehem monastery, forcing him to turn aside from writing his commentary on the prophet Ezckicl to attend to their needs (*Comment. in Hiez.*, prefaces to books 3, 7, and 8; cf. Mathisen, above pp. 228f.). The barbarian invasions thus contributed another component to the pattern of contacts across the Mediterranean, as the holy places, and the holy men who dwelt in their vicinity, were perceived as a safe haven from the dislocation of life in the western empire. What Peter Brown called the 'therapy' of distance involved in a journey of pilgrimage took on added significance against the disturbed background of the early fifth century.

The introduction of refugees into the traffic-flow between Gaul and the Holy Land brings me to the specific question I am aiming to address: in what measure, if at all, were the kind of connections I have been summarizing, the symbolic proximity of western Christians and the holy places, affected by the succession of barbarian inroads from late 406 onwards? To set the advent of the refugees into perspective, let us return to the comings and goings at Jerome's monastery in Bethlehem. Precisely in the autumn of 406, before the onset of the Vandals, the monk Sisinnius arrived from Gaul. Already known to Jerome from a previous visit, Sisinnius came as an emissary of Exsuperius, the bishop of Toulouse (Jerome, *Comment. in Zach.*, prologue; *Ep.* 119.1; *Comment. in Amos*, III prologue (date); cf. Crouzel, 1972). Besides correspondence from Exsuperius, Sisinnius presented Jerome with numerous requests for points of Biblical exegesis from the *sancti fratres ac sorores* in the neighbourhood of Toulouse, as well as copies of the writings of Vigilantius, the priest whose hostile views on the subject of the cults of saints and their relics were attracting attention in southern Gaul: Jerome had first been alerted two years earlier, when he had asked to be sent copies of

Vigilantius' output in order to compose a riposte (Jerome, *C. Vigil.* 3; *Ep.* 109.4;   Crouzel, 1972: 140ff.;   Kelly, 1975: 286ff.;   Stancliffe, 1983: 301ff.).   In addition to fodder for Jerome's learning, Sisinnius arrived with more material offerings from Exsuperius' congregation in Toulouse for the support of Jerome's fellow monks in the Holy Land and further afield in Egypt.   So eager indeed was Sisinnius to fulfil this second part of his mission in Egypt that he hurried from Bethlehem before the year's end, claiming the pressing needs of the Egyptian monks as a result of drought and famine.   Jerome was obliged to complete the replies he was sending back with him – which included his commentary on the prophet Zechariah, dedicated to bishop Exsuperius – at greater speed than he had expected, and he lamented their unpolished state and the hasty nocturnal copying: the vitriolic pamphlet contesting the views of Vigilantius was the product, he would have us believe, of a single night's work (*C. Vigil.* 17;   cf. *Ep.* 119.1, *Comment. in Zach.* II prolog., III prolog.).

Sisinnius' journey, and the contents of his baggage, provide revealing confirmation, on the very eve of the barbarian advance, of the sense in which Bethlehem, the holy places and the holy men who inhabited them, were perceived as an extension of the Christian brotherhood of southern Gaul.   For the correspondents whose enquiries were delivered by Sisinnius, Jerome's cell in Bethlehem was a fount of authoritative scriptural learning and theology;   not least for bishop Exsuperius himself, characterized by Jerome as 'fervent' in the reading of holy scripture, whom he begs to be present with him in his prayers in the writing of the Zechariah commentary, even though he was physically far distant (*Comment. in Zach.* prolog., II prolog.; Labrousse, 1968: 558ff.;   Crouzel, 1972: 129ff.).   A similar atmosphere of distance dissolved in a community of Biblical study emerges from two other letters, again to correspondents in Gaul, which Jerome wrote shortly after Sisinnius' hurried visit in late 406. Two ladies well versed in their Bibles, Hedybia and Algasia, had sent lists of queries on specific points of exegesis for Jerome to answer. Their letters had been carried from 'the shore of the Ocean and the furthest lands of Gaul' by the aptly named Apodemius, whose travels across the Roman empire had been aimed not at Rome, as Jerome emphasizes, but at the 'bread of heaven' which was Bethlehem (*Ep.* 121 pref.).   Reminiscent of the queen of Sheba visiting the court of Solomon, the pious Algasia through her emissary Apodemius had sought the scriptural knowledge of Jerome in the Holy Land –

although Jerome is at pains to disclaim for himself the wisdom of Solomon. Even so, he avers, Algasia preferred to consult him far away in Bethlehem than submit herself to the learning of a local priest at home (*Ep.* 121 pref.; on his identity, Cavallera, 1922: I, 311; Griffe, 1964–6: III, 150). In Hedybia's case, too, Jerome was preferred to local talent, though here the comparison was rather with the doyens of secular letters in Gaul; in particular with a distinguished ancestor of Hedybia's, the fourth-century Bordeaux rhetor Delphidius. In Jerome's fancy, Hedybia shares with him across the Mediterranean her desire to understand the scriptures and the 'law of God', which she cannot share with luminaries of the world such as Delphidius had been, even though much closer to hand in Gaul (*Ep.* 120 pref.; cf. *PLRE* I, 246). As Egeria's sisters were to be brought to a greater understanding of their Bibles by the record of what the pilgrim had seen at the holy places, so it was to him in the Holy Land that Jerome's fellow devotees looked for the theological elucidation of scripture.

But Sisinnius, we recall, arrived in Bethlehem with more than questions about the meaning of scripture: he was also there to distribute the alms gathered from the Christians of Toulouse to assist the monks at the holy places and in Egypt. In addressing Exsuperius, Jerome hailed him as one 'mindful of all the brethren who serve the Lord in the holy places, through whose refreshment you make for yourself friends of the mammon of unrighteousness' (*Comment. in Zach.* prolog.). Sisinnius was in a hurry to carry this refreshment on to the holy men of Egypt, in order that 'their dry lands might be watered by the generously flowing fountains of Gaul' (*Comment. in Zach.* II prolog.). In other words, for Exsuperius and his congregation, the Holy Land and Egypt, holy places and holy men were sufficient of a conscious reality to be bound to them through organized giving and distribution of charity. Such far-flung generosity was not, of course, unique to the Christians of southern Gaul. Individuals and communities elsewhere in the west sent contributions to the Holy Land, and in the context of a polemic against the bishop of Jerusalem Jerome could accuse him of growing rich on the proceeds of the 'faith of the whole world' (*C. Ioh. Hier.* 14; cf. *Ep.* 75.4, with Hunt, 1982a: 146f.). That it was a regular practice appears also from Jerome's sharp-tongued response to the opinions of Vigilantius, a text which, as we have seen, formed part of Sisinnius' return luggage. Vigilantius had attacked the habit of sending contributions to Jerusalem 'for the benefit of the saints', which Jerome countered by citing the example of St Paul and the injunctions of his Letters (*C. Vigil.* 13). But this was more than a generalized debate. Vigilantius had himself been in the Holy Land in 395, and had visited Jerome in Bethlehem: it was the time when the contention over Origenism was dividing the monks of Bethlehem and Jerusalem, and Vigilantius had made a hasty departure. Yet on that occasion, Jerome alleges, he had not been averse to arriving with charitable contributions for the monks at the holy places (*C. Vigil.* 13; cf. Hunt, 1982a: 191f.; Stancliffe, 1983: 301ff.). Vigilantius, then, had first-hand experience of the Holy Land and of the widespread piety which was centred upon it; and when later, as a priest in tne south of Gaul in the years just after 400, he came to denounce such piety, it was against this background of his own pilgrimage and the continuing flow of the donations of the faithful – carried indeed by Sisinnius in the very same luggage which also brought to Jerome his copy of Vigilantius' hostile opinions.

The Holy Land connection has more relevance to the arguments of Vigilantius than has sometimes been supposed. His strictures against the veneration of martyrs and their relics, against the associated liturgical practices (e.g. nocturnal vigils) and the miracles of healing, and more generally against monasticism and ascetic conduct – have usually been taken as directed against developments local to Gaul and the region of Vigilantius' preaching (e.g. Rousseau, 1978: 120; Stancliffe, 1983: 273ff.; cf. Griffe, 1964–6: III, 226–30). That is obviously true; yet they are also developments which reflect the sense of community, of 'proximity', with the Holy Land which has been my theme. The importance of physical relics in giving substance to this proximity has already been alluded to; and it was the honour accorded to such 'bits of dust enclosed in precious linen' which Vigilantius contested (*C. Vigil.* 4). Jerome responded by citing the recent instance of the transfer, on the orders of the emperor Arcadius, of the bones of Samuel from the Holy Land to Constantinople, when he imagined the congregations of the faithful *en route* from Palestine to the Hellespont receiving the relics 'as if they perceived the prophet alive and present with them', and united in a chorus of praise (*C. Vigil.* 5). Jerome might well have extended the chain of relic receptions as far as the western provinces: for Vigilantius, we may take it, will have observed similar enthusiastic scenes, and the attendant foreshortening of the distances of time and space, surrounding the packages of Holy Land earth or fragments of the Cross which found their way to Gaul.

Sisinnius' mission of charity, and Jerome's rebuttal of Vigilantius, belong in the last months of 406. In the following year Jerome penned a letter, replete with Biblical testimony on the subject of repentance, to a certain Rusticus. He was known to the Hedybia whose scriptural queries Apodemius had brought to Bethelehem from the far west of Gaul, and it seems probable that it was the same Apodemius who also carried back this letter to Rusticus (*Ep.* 122; cf. Cavallera, 1922: II, 52). The ground for Jerome's exhortation to repentance was that Rusticus was reported to have wavered from his commitment to abstain from sexual relations with his wife. He cannot have had much opportunity to lapse, since the wife Artemia was now in the Holy Land, having come on pilgrimage to the holy places to pray for her husband's salvation (cf. Heather, above p. 93): it was she who had alerted Jerome to his backsliding. Rusticus, it appears, had undertaken to follow Artemia on her pilgrimage, but his intentions here too had been unfulfilled, for the couple found themselves separated by the 'rabies barbarorum et imminens captivitas': while she reiterated his name in her prayers 'at the revered places of our Lord Saviour's resurrection, cross and cradle', he was left behind to witness 'the deaths of friends and fellow citizens, the destruction of towns and villas' (*Ep.* 122.4). Even so, Jerome can still regard the beleaguered Rusticus, rather as he had bishop Exsuperius at Toulouse, as 'present in faith' with his wife at the holy places, although 'absent in body', united across the Mediterranean in a common sense of devotion embracing the furthest shores of Gaul and the land of Christ's incarnation. One is tempted to suspect that the evidently weak-willed Rusticus himself may have been somewhat less enthusiastic about making common cause with his wife in pious endeavour, and found in the barbarian raids a provident pretext to remain behind in Gaul and attempt to recover his property.

Many of Rusticus' compatriots, as we have seen, took the opposite course and fled the barbarian disruption for a hoped-for safe haven at the holy places, straining the hospitality resources of monasteries like Jerome's at Bethlehem. The bond of Christian piety which held together opposite ends of the Mediterranean took on new tensions: Jerome's writings from these years are pervaded by the dark cloud of catastrophic events in the west (most notably *Ep.* 127.12ff.; cf. Courcelle, 1964: 49ff.). In one sense, of course, that can only mean that the channels of contact not only remained open, but flowed with fresh urgency in the stream of refugees. Yet there are hints of a change. For some at least, rather than reinforcing its 'proximity', the unsettled times actually distanced the Holy Land. In 412 Jerome wrote to another Rusticus, a young man from the area of Marseilles (usually identified with the future bishop of Narbonne) (*Ep.* 125; cf. Cavallera, 1922: I, 320; Griffe, 1964-6: III, 319ff.; Kelly, 1975: 297). Jerome had heard of Rusticus' intent to become a monk, and now contributed a lengthy letter of advice on a monastic vocation. It is a letter devoid of any emphasis on affinity for the holy places on the part of Rusticus, in contrast (for example) to Jerome's responses to Hedybia and Algasia; and whereas in those letters Jerome had welcomed the references of Biblical questions to himself in Bethlehem rather than to local teachers, he now recommended Rusticus to seek instruction in the monastic life from his own bishop Proculus of Marseilles, who would 'surpass' Jerome's writings with his 'living and present voice' in keeping the young man on the right path (*Ep.* 125.20.2). The holy places, and the teaching which emanated from them, seem to have lost that 'present' force which they possessed in my earlier examples. Rusticus, moreover, is referred to another local Gallic mentor now setting an example of Christian charity in the wretched circumstances of the time: this is none other than Exsuperius, bishop of Toulouse, 'in his fastings tormented by the hunger of others' (*Ep.* 125.20.3). Already in 409, in the letter where he depicts the progress of the barbarian advance through Gaul, Jerome had alluded to the efforts of bishop Exsuperius in saving his city from destruction at the hands of the invaders (*Ep.* 123.15.4; cf. Courcelle, 1964: 83f.; Labrousse, 1968: 574). The bishop whose thoughts in 406 had been directed to the holy places and the support of the monks who inhabited them now had more pressing concerns at home: Bethlehem has receded into the distance, and we may doubt whether Exsuperius and his congregation, amid their domestic emergency, had resources to spare any longer for such remote generosity.

Two years after advising Rusticus on his monastic calling, Jerome wrote to that 'most noble of Christians, most Christian of nobles', Cl. Postumus Dardanus, twice praetorian prefect of Gaul (*Ep.* 129; cf. *PLRE* II, 346f.; with Matthews, 1975: 323f.). Dardanus had an interest in the Holy Land or, more precisely, its relationship, if any, to the 'promised Land' of Biblical prophecy, which the faithful would one day possess. Jerome's response was to reassure Dardanus of what he already believed, that this promised Land was, of course, not literally to be identified with the geographical region which the Jewish people had come to occupy after the exodus from Egypt: it was a matter of spiritual understanding, which could not be confined to the narrows of literalist interpretation. Such understanding, though, left little room or regard for the actual Holy Land and its places of pilgrimage, which thrived precisely on a 'literalist' reading of the Bible (Hunt, 1982a: ch. 4 *passim*). Dardanus signalled his rejection of this kind of Holy Land concern by seeking release from the political turmoil of contemporary Gaul not in flight to the holy places, but in the fortified protection of his family retreat high up in the Alps. If there was to be any question of a terrestrial location for the Promised Land, for Dardanus it would be here, in the estate to which he gave the name 'Theopolis', rather than in far-off Palestine (*ILS* 1279; Marrou, 1954).

With Dardanus we are brought back to the theme of refuge: we are entitled to call him a 'refugee', one seeking to escape the resentment of leading Gauls at his execution of the local usurper Jovinus in 413 (Sidonius, *Ep.* 5.9.1; cf. Rutilius, *De Reditu Suo*, 307–8). With his own properties affording him a suitable refuge, perhaps he had no need to contemplate a more drastic displacement further afield. But for other highly placed victims of civil war – as of the advance through Gaul of the Vandals and their company a few years earlier – it was the holy places of Palestine which continued to offer sanctuary: for that pair of bishops, for example, Heros of Arles and Lazarus of Aix, who fell with the defeat of the regime of Constantine III in 411, and subsequently emerged to denounce Pelagius in the Holy Land (Hunt, 1982a: 206f.). To the same category, perhaps, belongs the famous anonymous Narbonensian and ex-official of Theodosius whom Orosius encountered in conversation with Jerome in Bethlehem (Orosius 7.43.4ff.; cf. Matthews, 1971: 1085ff., with *PLRE* II, 1232; cf. Heather, above p. 89). He has attracted more interest for his revelations about the political philosophy of the Gothic ruler Athaulph than for his own reasons for being in the Holy Land, but these surely are not unconnected with the collapse of Athaulph's ephemeral regime at Narbonne in 413–14; for one described by Orosius as *religiosus*, the holy places beckoned amid the downfall of a Gothic government with which he had evidently been closely involved (Matthews, 1971: 1092f.; Wolfram, 1988: 161ff.).

That we owe our tantalizingly brief glimpse of this man to the recollections of Orosius, himself a refugee from the barbarian inroads into Spain, is confirmation that the Holy Land continued to stand out as a focus of faith and refuge against the backcloth of political disturbance in the west. For it was Orosius, too, who reasserted that 'proximity' of the land of the New Testament by providing the western provinces with some of its most influential and distinguished relics, those of St Stephen (Hunt, 1982a: 211ff.; 1982b: 106f.). I have spoken of 'hints' of change – in the redirection of charity, and the recourse to local teaching and spiritual advice: yet they are not much more than hints, for, by and large, the Holy Land connection (as I have termed it) evidently survived, even prospered from, the disruption of the early fifth century.

CHAPTER 24

Ethnicity, orthodoxy and community in Salvian of Marseilles

M. Maas

The perceived contrast between Roman civilization and barbarian irrationality and ferocity played a role of fundamental importance in the Roman imagination. This opposition underlay an ideological system that accepted the need and possibility of transforming barbarians into Romans (Dauge, 1981: 805ff.). Ladner has described it as an 'ethical contrast between an empire of peace, ever to be renewed, and proud or rebellious people, unwilling to submit' (Ladner, 1976: 12). With the breakdown and eventual collapse of Roman authority in Gaul in the fifth century, however, came renewed challenges to such ideological certainties and traditional categorizations of cultural difference. Though the Germanic peoples had been present in the Roman consciousness for many centuries, they had never been so firmly established on Roman territory in the absence of Roman power itself. Assimilation could no longer be on Roman terms. Under these circumstances, how did the Gallo-Romans and the invaders perceive one another and how were they able to express these differences and give them meaning? This book has set us the problem of exploring a crisis of representation created by the new political and cultural realities.

In addition, our topic suggests some sort of historical development as well, for crises have causes and resolutions. Scholars have devised different labels for the historical changes: *The Formation of Christendom* (Herrin, 1987), or *Des Goths à la nation gothique* (Teillet, 1984), or *Before France and Germany* (Geary, 1988), to sample the titles of some recent books that deal in different ways with our period. This selection indicates that we perceive a transformation of some sort, but we disagree about how to characterize it and write its history. Can we write a narrative history in the conventional sense? I would suggest that what we want as much as a history of politics, institutions or social forms (and we do need them) is a history of changing perceptions and evaluations of cultural difference. Such a study would serve as an introduction to the synthesis of the Germanic and Roman cultures in Gaul. Our sources, however, give us only Roman points of view; out of reach are the ideas of the invaders. We hear only Romans talking in their laws (Bianchini, 1988), letters, and sermons about barbarians as 'others', and they do not speak with unanimity. Though we wish to remain faithful to this disparate evidence, it cannot be adequate to our historical concerns, for, to say the obvious, our categories of explanation and our sense of historical significance vary so dramatically from theirs. How then to begin a history of the changing perceptions of identity that characterize our period?

Salvian of Marseilles, the fifth-century scold and 'master of bishops' (Gennadius, *Vir. Inl.* 67), is a useful starting point both for the problems of definition and cultural change in this period and for our difficulties in approaching them. As a member of the first generation of Gallo-Romans for whom the Roman empire was no longer a meaningful presence, he grappled with the barbarian presence in the terms and categories available to him – as a well-born, well-educated man, who had renounced his upbringing (Salvian, *Ep.* 4) and taken on board much of the monastic world view of the community at Lérins while maintaining a somber interest in worldly society (Paschoud, 1967: 293ff.; Fischer, 1976: 28ff.; Leonardi, 1977: 604). These ascetic values put him on the fringe of his own society and enabled him to criticize both the aristocracy and the Church. Nor was he blind to the depredations caused by the invaders (Favez, 1957: 83; Cleland, 1970). In all of this he was unremarkable and would seem to be a man of his times. In addition, however, Salvian added something to the debate about the Roman-German relationship that we might call a relativistic view of barbarism. He argued that degree of knowledge of moral behavior determined proper action, not ethnicity or orthodoxy. We see this in his original idea that the barbarian is good not because he does not sin but because he is not aware of his sin (e.g. *De Gub. Dei* 4.60ff.; Paschoud, 1967: 301). We must wonder at the significance of this imaginative jump.

Salvian presented this idea in his most influential work, *On the Government of God*. The book sought to answer a question much on the minds of his fellow Romans, shocked by recent events: 'why, if everything in this world is managed by the care, governance and judgment of God, is the condition of the barbarians so much better than ours?' (3.2) – a pressing question indeed and far from academic. Salvian developed an answer in terms of divine providence.

On the Government of God attempted to show that God had not failed to govern humanity, but that in fact the sad state of Roman affairs represented divine judgment and punishment for Roman sins. As Salvian explained: 'As God always governs, so too he always judges, for his government is itself judgment' (4.4). *On the Government of God* (possibly a reworking of sermons) was intended to 'benefit the minds of the sick' (*On the Government of God*, preface), and in his view Roman society badly needed his medicine. The first two books of *On the Government of God* draw examples from the Bible to show God's judgments in history. The third book illustrates a proper Christian life by way of contrast in vivid technicolor of Roman Christian vice and barbarian Christian virtue. Book four develops Salvian's surprising approach to barbarian virtue, as we read: '... what with them is ignorance is in us transgression, since there is less guilt in ignorance of the law than in contempt of it' (4.86f.; 4.60ff. etc.). Book five is much beloved by social historians for its details of the miseries of daily life for the poor and the abuses of the government and the aristocratic elite (cf. Drinkwater, above p. 210). Book six especially condemns circuses and games. Book seven attacks Roman Carthage as a cesspool of vice, and the last book offers a brief recapitulation.

Salvian was not an ethnographer concerned with describing cultural characteristics for their own sake, yet perceived differences between Roman and barbarian are the building blocks of his theory of divine government. Indeed, the presence of the invaders raised the question that *On the Government of God* addressed. The work takes its shape from several oppositions that are stated with different degrees of directness: Roman *versus* barbarian, orthodoxy *versus* heresy (he does not concern himself with pagan barbarians: 3.1ff.), civilization *versus* barbarism. When Salvian explained that God had not forsaken the government of mankind but was punishing the Romans for their sins, he joined a long debate about the causes of the fall of the Empire (Mazzarino, 1959; Paschoud, 1967, 1975). Whether or not Salvian knew Tacitus' *Germania* (Paschoud, 1967: 301), he went somewhat beyond the Roman inclination to glorify the 'noble savage'. When he argued that the Goths and Vandals could be more virtuous than the

Romans despite their imperfect knowledge of the true faith, he undermined the assumption that being Roman and orthodox guaranteed superiority. This suggestion that ethnicity or orthodoxy need not determine morality anticipates a Medieval community in which these distinctions are no longer primary. Rather in the same spirit, Salvian's contemporary Prosper of Aquitaine wrote that 'the grace of Christianity is not content to have the boundaries of Rome as its limits; for it has submitted to the sceptre of Christ's cross many peoples whom Rome could not subject with its arms' (Prosper, *De Vocatione Omnium Gentium* 2.16 – tr. Markus, 1985: 38; Ladner, 1976: 24f.; cf. Muhlberger, above pp. 29ff.).

Salvian did not speak for all of his contemporaries. Victor of Vita, the Carthaginian cleric and chronicler of the Vandal persecutions, objected heatedly to the sort of attitude toward barbarians that Salvian represented. Victor wrote: 'Quite a few of you delight in the barbarians and you praise them in your condemnation [i.e. of Roman society], but take heed of their very name and understand the nature of their behavior. Can they be called by any other than their true name of barbarian, embodying as they do the essence of ferocity, cruelty, and terror? ... They know nothing other than to hate the Romans' (Victor of Vita 3.62; Parsons, forthcoming).

The implication that new forms of 'Medieval' community might be lurking in Salvian's attitude have proved most problematical to modern interpreters. Opinions are strongly worded (Lagarrigue, 1964: 70; Vogt, 1967: 58). Should we understand Salvian as a true Roman patriot or as a defeatist collaborator with the Germans? Is it 'complete nonsense' to see Salvian at the confluence of antiquity, Christianity, and Germanism (Paschoud, 1967: 301) or is he a 'prophet of the mission of the German peoples' (Fischer, 1948: 262)? Does he have any 'real' knowledge about the barbarians at all (Paschoud, 1967: 297)? While it can be amusing to examine the historiography, we need only note here that Salvian still arouses strong feelings of nationalism and political argument. We need a calmer way to approach the question of perception of the other in the fifth century.

I would like to draw attention to a slightly different approach to writing the history of intercultural contact. I refer to the book *The Conquest of America* by Tzvetan Todorov (1984). Though concerned to describe, through close analysis of different texts of the period, the subtle shifts in perception and consequent changes in their respective mental structures of the Spanish and Native American civilizations in the sixteenth century (Marcus and Fischer, 1986: 104ff.), Todorov offers some categories of analysis that can be useful to us as we try to understand the development of a new consciousness in Gaul at the end of antiquity. In his pages devoted to the 'Typology of Relations to the Other' (Todorov, 1984: 185ff.), he suggests three axes on which to locate the 'problematics of alterity'. He considers them independently on the assumption that they cannot be reduced to one another nor do they necessarily originate from the same source.

The first axis that Todorov suggests is axiological, that of value judgment. It concerns the 'other' as good or bad, beloved or hated, equal or inferior in the eyes of the examiner. The second axis is praxeological and has to do with the degree of distance felt toward the other. Todorov suggests two possibilities: 'I embrace the other's values, I identify myself with him, or else I identify the other with myself, I impose my own image on him' (Todorov, 1984: 185). The third axis of interpretation that Todorov suggests falls on an epistemic level: what do I know about the identity of the other? (*ibid.*). This is obviously open-ended but nevertheless important because only by attaining some degree of mutual comprehension can genuine cultural synthesis take place.

Todorov discusses how these three axes found expression in the Spanish treatment of the Americans: ranging from simple objects to be enslaved, perhaps not even worthy of conversion, to victims of colonialist exploitation as producers of valuable goods, to being people who might be accepted to some degree on their own terms (Marcus and Fischer, 1986: 105). Thus he does construct a history, but one of gradual shifts in imaginative categories. He takes into account deeply rooted moral positions as well as differences between the Spaniards and Indians in the ways they communicated and their vocabularies. In this way he describes the role that interpretation plays in shaping cultural change while emphasizing the impossibility of pure description of other peoples and their lives (Marcus and Fischer, 1986: 106).

The circumstances of the end of the Roman empire in fifth-century Gaul were obviously not the same as those of the creation of a Spanish empire in the Americas, but Todorov's typology of 'alterity' can be quite useful to us for several reasons. First, he contrasts writers by criteria not based on issues of patriotism or collaboration, and he avoids questions of the 'objectivity' of writers as a basis for comparison. Todorov's typology also allows us to approach a complex set of interactions, namely the alteration of perceptions of barbarians and Romans, without the frustration of seeking linear developments of ideas between writers divorced from historical context. Description of the barbarians is more than just a *topos* developed by a series of authors. Thus we can transcend the problem of genre, that is to say of trying to compare attitudes expressed in such different categories as sermons or laws, and at the same time seriously consider each of these types of expression as legitimate and appropriate responses to contemporary crises. We can avoid, for example, dismissing Salvian as 'only' treating the barbarians in clichés because he uses them in the service of his theory about divine providence (e.g. 4.65ff.; Vogt, 1967: 59). It is in fact Salvian's very utilization of clichés about barbarians in *On the Government of God*'s scheme of divine providence that must be accepted as a valid statement of the limits of his social imagination. His use of clichés is but one example of the sort of mediation without which cultural transmission cannot occur. Todorov's method of analysis alerts us to issues of ethnographic interpretation. He reminds us that the 'problematics of alterity' have a life in many forms of communication, and he does not privilege any one of them. He makes us recognize that ancient ethnographic observation does not gain more legitimacy when it takes the form of a superficially more 'objective' description in a historical narrative than in a pointedly manipulative sermon. Let us turn then to analyse Salvian on each of the axes that Todorov suggests. This will not produce a brand-new Salvian, but it can give us tighter control of our own approach to him as we develop a putative history of changing perceptions.

On the axiological level, Salvian's value judgments seem at first to be rooted in the traditional opposition between Roman and barbarian and expressed in the usual clichés, but he advanced beyond the use of these commonly held value judgments to a kind of relativism that rendered positive his ultimate evaluation of the barbarians. For Salvian the barbarians were superior to the Romans because of their love for one another (5.15), their piety (even if misguided), their avoidance of the sins of the cities (6.35, 39), and their sexual purity (7.24–45). He understood the circumstances to be the same in Spain and Africa as well as Gaul (7.87–90; Paschoud, 1967: 298). If at times they might be criminal and guilty of sin, it was because they were ignorant of the truth. The Romans' sin was worse because they should have known better. As he wrote, 'we who have the law of

God and spurn it are much more guilty than they who do not have it at all or know it. No one despises what he does not know' (4.64). In Salvian's theory of divine providence, value derives ultimately from conformity to Christian teaching. This was not dependent upon ethnicity. Surprising as such a notion might be, it can be understood simply as an inversion of the traditional distinction between Roman and barbarian and does not reveal any new conceptual categories. Salvian expressed his reversal in this well-known passage: 'Meanwhile the poor are being robbed, widows groan, orphans are trampled, so that many of them, including some from not obscure families with a liberal education, flee to the enemy lest they perish under the affliction of the public persecution. They seek Roman mercy among the barbarians since they cannot endure the barbarous inhumanity among the Romans' (5.21; cf. Drinkwater, above p. 210). This perspective on Roman barbarity implies a possible equality at the expense of ethnic hierarchy, but under no circumstances can it be seen as a call for Romans to start acting like Goths.

Thus we see that his attitude toward Roman society remained somewhat ambivalent. Unlike Caesarius of Arles, who wrote in the next generation and used the Chosen People of the Bible as his point of reference (Daly, 1970: 11), Salvian still found value and virtue in the Romans of antiquity (e.g. 1.10–11; Teillet, 1984: 169f.). His interpretation of contemporary decline would have made little sense without such a contrast with vanished Roman grandeur, clichéd as it may have been; his historical scheme to some degree required the Roman past (Pellegrino, 1940: 218ff.). But Salvian distanced himself from the Romans of his own day in several ways. This is clearly seen in his attacks on Roman vice and corruption in *On the Government of God*. He believed that divine favor had passed to the barbarians and ensured their victory (7.26–8; Paschoud, 1967: 296, 302). He broke with the Eusebian scheme that tied the destiny of the Roman state to the development of Christianity. Yet it was from his experience at Lérins that he derived new categories alternative to Romanness. He placed himself in a special group, that of men in religious orders and religious laymen (4.13; Fischer, 1976: 81ff.). Such individuals he believed to follow divine precepts correctly: 'Deny yourself that you may not be denied by Christ; cast yourself off that you may be received by him.' Despite such admonitions, Salvian never advocated the monastery as the cure for all social ills (Leonardi, 1977: 604f.).

Personal not societal reform remained his objective (Cleland, 1970: 274).

Some truth may be found then in the assertion that Salvian never challenged the fundamental principles of differentiation between Roman and barbarian, but to conclude that he remained a 'true Roman' (Dauge, 1981: 375) perhaps draws the wrong conclusion. His need to explain contemporary events and to justify his explanations led him to value judgments grounded in Christian precepts, even though they found expression in the traditional social categories of Roman and barbarian. Salvian's work clearly implies that one need not be a Roman to be a good Christian, nor even an orthodox Christian to be a good man. He did not, however, express this idea clearly in new social categories.

It is most effective to discuss Todorov's second axis, the praxeological or distancing axis, in terms of his treatment of religious orthodoxy. Christian values truly enacted provided the measure of virtue for Salvian and the basis of identification with the barbarians. In his limited rapprochement with them, Salvian was not constrained by considerations of orthodoxy. He offered a revolutionary evaluation of Germanic Arianism. He reasoned that, although orthodox Romans possessed true doctrine and Arians were in error, the barbarians remained morally superior. They had been converted to Arianism through Roman error and their Bible was incomplete, not false. Because of their ignorance they could not question their own doctrine or interpret it correctly (Paschoud, 1967: 299f.). He expressed no identification with the barbarians *qua* barbarians, but as errant (because falsely educated) Christians they found much favor in his eyes. Their Arian heresy created a distance certainly, but not an unbridgeable one. In consequence, we find in *On the Government of God* an odd disjunction: Salvian was ready to accept the invaders as Christians but not as barbarians, and he accepted them as a Christian, not as a Roman. But even in this he subverted the distinction between orthodoxy and heresy that was so significant in the minds of his contemporaries. This led in turn to an idealization of the barbarians (Paschoud, 1967: 300). Salvian did not see them 'as they really were' but imposed his own image upon them. His assertion that ignorance of sin excused wrongdoing among the barbarians enabled the idealization by freeing the invaders from the burdens of their heresy and their ethnicity.

Previously it was suggested that Salvian moved toward a relativistic notion of barbarism which determined a person's status by his ability to discern the truth. He always remained the determiner of that truth, however, and his 'relativism' did not bring him to a better comprehension of barbarian society. Salvian's appreciation of invaders based itself not on ethnic or social but moral and behavioral grounds. In practical terms he advocated no missionary endeavor to provide the barbarians the education in doctrine that they lacked. He did not put forward any argument for a Christian community indifferent to either ethnic or doctrinal categories.

Finally, on Todorov's epistemic axis we must consider what Salvian actually knew about the barbarians. Again, an odd disjunction appears (Paschoud, 1967: 300). On the one hand, Salvian described the invaders as embodiments of moral ideals. This seems odd to us and certainly outraged men like Victor of Vita. On the other hand, he was far better informed than we about the brutal facts of co-existence. Did he willfully distort the truth? I think we should be wary of such a question. While one scholar has correctly noted the limits of Salvian's interest in the Goths as people (Teillet, 1984: 165), we may ask if Salvian would have appeared to be more interested in them if he had described their dietary laws or kinship structure or recorded their poetry? We must understand the ways of showing interest available to him and not overestimate the value of more formal, ethnographic description. What could have been more 'real' for him than to show them as instruments of God's will? One thing at least is certain: his knowledge of the barbarians did not call into question his own categories.

In his sketch of Roman attitudes toward barbarians in the late antique period, Ladner traced the development of a 'synthesizing conception' culminating in Gregory the Great, 'the first among great Roman leaders who genuinely appreciated barbarians as human beings' and for whom it was no longer necessary to distinguish Roman and barbarian in moral terms (Ladner, 1976: 25f.). Such a synthesis could be a convenient end point for a history of shifting Roman perceptions of the 'other', and surely Salvian represents a stage of this development. As I have attempted to suggest, however, through the application of Todorov's axes of interpretation, Salvian's perception of the barbarians was the sum of several quite different interpretative positions (value judgment, distance, and knowledge), each with a history and realm of association independent of the others.

They enable us to see Salvian's originality as well as the limitations of his imagination. Comparing Salvian with other writers in this way can help us write a nuanced history of cultural definition in the fifth century (cf. Wood, above p. 16). These analytical options can sharpen our perceptions of what the Romans meant, and what we mean, by the opposition of Roman and barbarian.

VII

The resolution of the crisis

As Maas reminds us: 'crises have causes and resolutions'. The recovery of Roman Gaul during the first half of the fifth century was real, but very brittle, and hence inherently insecure; Salvian's complaints regarding the condition of Gaul by the 440s, however tendentious and exaggerated, cannot be ignored. The country could not persist in its current state. Though the precise dates and circumstances are disputed, there is general agreement that discernible change began to occur from the middle of the century. As the western empire weakened, the barbarians grew in strength and confidence, and pressures mounted on leading Gauls to re-assess their political allegiance to the Empire – an allegiance that was not significantly underpinned by economic interests.

It was in the 450s, consequent upon the quickening of Visigothic power that followed Aëtius' victory over Attila, Aëtius' murder, the death of Valentinian III, and the general debilitation of imperial power caused by the loss of Africa to the Vandals, that a more realistic order began to emerge. That order, which arose out of successive emperors' failure to establish a firm control over the west, still less any coherent policy for securing Gaul against growing barbarian power and ambition (cf. King, for the possible renewal of Visigothic minting in gold after 454), was based on a progressive abandonment of co-operation with Rome. Self-help now came to the fore; the restorative work of Fl. Constantius and Aëtius was undone; and, at least in respect of its political loyalties, if not its culture, Gaul ceased to be 'Roman'. On this basis, *Fanning*, firmly dating the beginning of the breakdown of imperial authority to the mid 450s, and (like Elton) locating its climax in the period following the death of Majorian, examines the cases of Aegidius and Syagrius. His findings suggest that both men set themselves up as rulers of a northern Gallic state which was self-consciously independent of the western empire. Though our meagre sources refer to them both as 'king', this title does not indicate the rejection of the Gallo-Roman system, and Fanning demonstrates that it may be taken to mean 'emperor'. Composed of a plurality of peoples, Roman and barbarian, the 'empire' of Aegidius and Syagrius should be regarded as the local counterpart of Euric's Visigothic *imperium*.

That this could be so shows that the real power in the land was now that of the barbarian kings who, as Wes has reminded us, increasingly had to be confronted by Christian bishops rather than imperial officials. *Harries* shows how Sidonius Apollinaris, that most Roman of late antique Gauls, who none the less had to exchange the insignia of imperial office for an episcopal mitre, was gradually compelled to to come to terms with the situation. Although steadfastly loyal to the culture of Rome, and always ready to respect the status of the reigning emperor, during the second half of the fifth century he displayed a remarkable ambivalence in his attitude to the barbarians, whether Visigothic or Burgundian. In Harries' view, such ambivalence ought not to lay Sidonius open to the charge of shameless expediency: what appear as arbitrary changes of mind are explicable according to whether or not formal treaties of alliance – in Sidonius' eyes the only means of controlling and exploiting barbarian power – existed between the Empire and the people involved on the occasions in question. However, she also argues that underlying Sidonius' responses was an awareness of the political realities of his day. On the one hand, the western emperor was distant, and, as a result of the tension between Gaul and Italy that went back at least to the opening years of the century, imperial motives were suspect. On the other, Visigoths and Burgundians were close and redoubtable neighbours, who needed to be dealt with as either dangerous enemies or indispensable allies, as the moment demanded. The situation was bound to arise, as it did once for Sidonius in 474, when imperial and local loyalties were directly opposed; and, as they must, the former took second place. Thus, unconsciously and impelled by circumstance, Sidonius Apollinaris approached close to high treason; and it may be argued that in doing so he was belatedly setting out along a dangerous, unmarked path towards co-operation with the barbarians as sovereign peoples that had already been trodden by others of his background – most famously his friend Arvandus who, in 469, was found guilty of treacherous dealings with Euric.

Harries concludes that this ill-defined 'climate of treason' resulted from a practical, *ad hoc* and hence ideologically confused local movement towards acceptance of the barbarians with a view to securing the safety of the inhabitants of the Empire in Gaul. Though not intended to betray the western empire as a whole, it will have served to undermine imperial political power in the country. The same climate of treason is investigated by *Teitler*, in a study of the cases of the two Gauls who incurred punishment and ill-fame for entering into suspicious dealings with the Visigoths in the late 460s and early 470s, Arvandus and Seronatus. While harder than Harries in his judgement of the former, and indeed considering both men guilty of culpable treason rather than pragmatic co-operation, Teitler reaches conclusions very similar to hers: Arvandus and Seronatus were fundamentally correct in their assessment of the realities of Gallic power-politics; we can see Gallic circumstances causing Sidonius, even as prefect of the City of Rome, to compromise his loyalty to the Empire (in his dealings with Arvandus following the latter's arrest); and Sidonius would soon have to follow their lead and those of others of his class who, from an even earlier date, had begun to work within the barbarian, rather than the Roman, system.

CHAPTER 25

Emperors and empires in fifth-century Gaul

S. Fanning

As the fifth century opened, Constantine, a general from Britain, was put forward as emperor by his troops, having been chosen to replace the less suitable candidates, Marcus and Gratian. Constantine's subsequent career and sphere of operations is reminiscent of Postumus and the Empire of the Gauls in the mid third century, for he was active in the prefecture of the Gauls from 407 until his death in 411. Certainly claimants to the imperial throne coming from Britain and moving into Gaul were nothing new, for following Postumus there were Carausius and Magnus Maximus, and especially the most successful aspirant of all, Constantine the Great (Bury, 1923: I, 187ff.; Stevens, 1957; Jones, 1964: 185ff.).

The fall and deaths of the usurper Constantine and his sons, Constans and Julian, were followed in 411 by the rise of other would-be emperors in Gaul, Jovinus and his son and co-emperor, Sebastian. Although Jovinus was supported by the Burgundians, the opposition of the Visigoths and the few Gallic officials who had remained loyal to Honorius quickly put an end to him and Sebastian (Bury, 1923: I, 194f.; Jones, 1964: 187; Perrin, 1968: 335ff.; Matthews, 1975: 308f.; Wolfram, 1988: 161). Thereafter Gaul appears essentially to have been under the control of the official Roman government in Italy as first Constantius, the general of Honorius and later husband of Galla Placidia and briefly co-emperor with Honorius, and then Aëtius struggled to keep the Germanic tribes in Gaul loyal to their federate status.

Nevertheless, after the deaths of Aëtius and Valentinian III in 454 and 455 respectively, imperial authority in Gaul was in disorder. Avitus was put forward as a Gallic claimant for the emperorship, and, after the end of his brief rule in Italy, Majorian for a while seemed to be able to exercise some kind of authority in Gaul. But the death of Majorian effectively ended the links between Gaul and the shadowy puppets of Ricimer and Orestes, as well as the illicit rule of Odovacar (Bury, 1923: I, 200ff.; Jones, 1964: 240ff., 324, 327; Wolfram, 1988: 161, 176, 178, 232).

In Gaul, the Visigoths, Burgundians and Franks expanded almost without hindrance against the remnants of imperial authority in Gaul. The poorly known count Paul attempted to hold the Loire against the Visigoths, while Aegidius, *magister militum* under Majorian, established an independent rule centered on Soissons. One tradition had him being accepted as king over the Franks, while another named him 'king of the Romans'. Aegidius was succeeded in this 'little kingdom' by his son Syagrius, who is not known by any traditional Roman title, but is called 'king of the Romans' by our best source for Gaul in this period, Gregory of Tours. At last Syagrius was defeated by Clovis and the Franks in 486, and all of Gaul was then in the hands of one or another of the Germanic rulers (Bury, 1923: I, 341ff.; Dill, 1926: 4f., 10ff., 78f.; Jones, 1964: 246; Perrin, 1968: 340ff.; Musset, 1969: 66, 70, 124; Demandt, 1970: 688ff.; Wood, 1977: 24; Thompson, 1982: 38ff.; Wolfram, 1988: 172ff.).

Aegidius and Syagrius seem to have been acting only on a local basis in a barbarian world. As we have seen, Aegidius may have exercised some sort of authority over the Franks, and both he and his son Syagrius are said to have been *reges Romanorum* (GT *HF* 2.27; *Liber Historiae Francorum* 8), although *PLRE* (II, 11ff., 1041f.) refuses to accord this title to Aegidius, and prefers to identify Syagrius simply as a 'Roman ruler (in North Gaul)'. The inelegant and obviously un-Roman title of *rex Romanorum* has indeed excited considerable scholarly interest and derision. It has been called inadmissible and unacceptable by Georges Tessier (1964: 149), while Godefroid Kurth dismissed it as a gross error (1893: 213). Kurth said that at the most Syagrius held the title of count or duke, but that the barbarians gave him the same title of king that their own leaders carried. It was simply nonsense for the Romans actually to have called Syagrius king of the Romans, but that rather offensive title did correspond to the barbarian view of his actual position (1893: 213f.; Frouin, 1929: 140ff.). It is also suggested that Syagrius exercised a kind of Germanic army command over his barbarian troops, which made him a kind of barbarized Roman *rex* (Schmidt, 1928: 614; Wallace-Hadrill, 1962: 160; Geary, 1988: 81ff.). Or, it is thought that he was simply Master of the Soldiers (Thorpe, 1974: 139). Or again, it was as *rex Romanorum* that he wished to be known to the

Germanic chieftains in power around him (Wallace-Hadrill, 1962: 160), or perhaps he was *comes civitatum* (Kaiser, 1973: 140 and n377).

Whichever theory is put forward, it is clear that no one takes seriously the only title by which Syagrius is known in the few sources that mention him, or one of the titles attributed to his father Aegidius. Of course, the reason that this title seems so objectionable is that one of the best-known truisms of Roman history is that of the Roman hatred of kingship. After the expulsion of Tarquin the Proud, the Roman *plebs* would not allow the kingship to continue at Rome, according to Livy (*Ab Urbe Condita*, 2.1.9, 2.2.5, 2.2.7). And when the Spanish chieftains offered the title of king to Scipio Africanus during the Second Punic War, Scipio refused it, saying, again according to Livy, that elsewhere the name of king was great, but at Rome it was intolerable (27.9.4). As Rome expanded into the Hellenistic east, it gained the reputation of being inimical to monarchy and the rule of kings (Gruen, 1984: 339).

The turmoil provoked by the fears that Julius Caesar aspired to kingship in Rome is, of course, legendary, and, from Octavian on, Roman emperors sedulously avoided the title *rex*. This Roman antipathy towards kingship was an attitude that persisted even after Diocletian established the Dominate and the Roman emperors ruled as virtual absolute monarchs. Dio Cassius (*Roman History* 53.17.1–5, 18.2–5) and Synesius (*De Regno* 13; Dvornik, 1966: 703) in the east, and Augustine (*De Civitate Dei* 3.16) and Orosius (2.4.13) in the west repeated the familiar tradition of Rome's abolition of kingship, which by their time was close to nine centuries old. The Roman and early Medieval worlds were certainly aware that Romans would not tolerate the 'name and office' of king (Orosius 2.4.13).

We in our time are so sure of this Roman detestation of the title of king that when it is applied to a Roman emperor it is dismissed and explained away as having been due to barbarian influence, as in the case of Syagrius. When a gold medallion of Visigothic provenance was found featuring the emperors Valens and Valentinian I with the inscription *REGIS ROMANORUM*, it was regarded as inconceivable that an authentic original coin could have read *REGES ROMANORUM*, and the title was described as the invention of a German copyist (Wolfram, 1967: 37; 1988: 110, 145, 416 n396). It has been explained that the Visigoths thought of the Roman emperors as kings (Myers, 1982: 369).

As sure as we are that the Romans would not use the offensive title of king, there has been little consideration of how Gregory of Tours came to use it for Syagrius. While it may well have been true that it was among the oral traditions received by Gregory, its un-Roman nature would have been as obvious to him as it has been to modern historians, for he was reasonably well educated for his time (Riché, 1976: 191, 271). Moreover, in his discussion of the early history of the Franks, he showed critical abilities when assessing the accounts of his sources concerning early Frankish kings, *regales*, and *duces* (*HF* 2.9). Thus it is even more mysterious that Gregory could mention a *rex Romanorum* without a word of explanation or an inquiry into the actual position held by Syagrius.

But what is never taken into account in any discussion of this troublesome phrase is the fact that this is not the only instance of Gregory's using 'inappropriate' royal language. In his version of the story of the Seven Sleepers of Ephesus, Gregory has one of the seven address the great persecutor Decius, 'O *rex*, the precept of your *imperium* runs to the boundaries of the whole earth' (*Passio Sanctorum Martyrum Septem Dormientum apud Ephesum* 2). Obviously none of the suggestions put forward for the actual position and authority of Syagrius can be valid for Decius in the mid third century. While it may be true that in this case Gregory was intending for the word *rex* to be sarcastic or insulting when applied to a persecuting emperor, as a form of *Kaiserkritik*, it is significant that he could use such a clearly inappropriate title for an emperor, whom he called *imperator* in the *History of the Franks* (1.30): Gregory was clearly not consistently critical of Decius.

However, it must be noted that Gregory twice referred to Helena, the wife of one emperor and mother of another, as *regina* (*Liber in Gloria Martyrum Beatorum* 5). Surely Gregory could not have been intending to insult that great Christian heroine, and the Romans were as unlikely to have had *reginae* as they were *reges*. Moreover, the regal references to Decius and Helena cannot be ascribed to oral traditions, whether Frankish or Germanic. The arguable title given to Syagrius by Gregory can no longer be considered in isolation, and in fact the problem has deepened.

If one turns to a careful reading of the contemporaries and sources of Gregory of Tours, similar instances of 'inadmissible' usage can be found. In the *Life of St Martin* by Venantius Fortunatus, Maximus is referred to as *rex* at least eight times (2.1.59, 64, 99, 330, 464, 490;

3.1.522, 523), that emperor's wife is called *regina* (3.1.262) and Maximus has a *regnum* (3.1.517). One of Gregory's favorite sources, Sulpicius Severus, shows similar usage. He applies the word *rex* to the emperors Constantine, Julian, Maximus (eight times), Valentinian II, Constantius II (six times), and generally to emperors (*V. Martini* 2.2, 6.7, 20.4–7; *Dial.* 2.5.8, 2.12.1, 2.12.4, 2.38–9, 2.42, 2.45). Helena again is a *regina*, as is the wife of Maximus (*Chron.* 2.34; *Dial.* 2.6.1, 2.6.3, 2.6.5, 2.7.1–2, 2.7.5). Maximus has a *regnum* (*Dial.* 2.6.4, 2.11.11), and the Roman empire is referred to as the *regnum Romanorum* (*Chron.* 2.3).

In the *City of God* of St Augustine, which surely must be one of the basic books of the Middle Ages, this usage is also to be found. Emperor Hadrian is called *rex hominum* (4.29) and *regnum* is used regularly, along with *imperium,* for the Roman empire. One can read of the *regnum Romanum*, and the Roman state is described in general as a western *regnum* (4.1, 4.6, 4.7, 5.21, 18.2, 18.27, 20.23; 5.25). In Book Seven of Orosius' *Seven Books of Histories against the Pagans*, many emperors are called *rex* – Tiberius (who is called *rex Caesar* [4.10]) (4.7), Commodus, Constantine and Honorius (16.3, 27.10, 37.10) – and the word is used in a general sense to mean emperors (28.27). Moreover, Orosius even used the suspect phrase that Gregory applied to Syagrius when he wrote that Constantine was the first or the only one of the *Romanorum reges* to found a city in his own name (35.6). *Regnum* is used repeatedly for the Roman empire (6.1, 10.1, 11.1, 15.1, 15.11, 16.1, 17.8, 20.1, 21.4, 24.1, 24.2, 35.15), and the phrase *regnum Romanorum* is used at least three times (2.4, 22.3, 27.10).

In expanding the investigation, similar instances of this usage can be repeated. In the third century, Tertullian equated *imperium* with *regnum* (*Apologeticum* 25.12), and it is clear that it is the Roman empire that was a *regnum*. In the fourth century, Ammianus Marcellinus referred to the emperor Julian as a *rex* (23.5.8) In the fourth-century *Scriptores Historiae Augustae*, *rex* and *reges* refer to Hadrian (who is *rex Romanus*), Severus Alexander, Regalianus, Claudius II and his children, and Carinus (Had. 2.8; Sev. Alex. 38.4.6; Thirty Pretenders 10.6; Deif. Claudius 10.3; Carus, Carinus, Numerian 17.1). The wife of Severus Alexander was a *regina* (Sev. Alex. 51.3) and three emperors have *regna* (Opel. Macr. 6.6; Thirty Pretenders 10.3, 9.1).

In the fourth century, Hilary of Poitiers employs a similar vocabulary. Valentinian I is styled *sanctus rex* as well as simply *rex* four other times (*Contra Arianos vel Auxentium Mediolanensem* 7) and Hilary twice uses *regnum* for the Empire (*Liber I ad Constantium* 2; *Liber II ad Constantium* 10). Lucifer of Cagliari made repeated references to Constantius II as *rex*. On some of these occasions he was obviously applying the term unflatteringly to that Arian emperor (*stultissimus, insulsissimus*) but others are quite the opposite (*prudentissimus, aequissimus, piissimus, sanctissimus*) (Setton, 1941: 96).

Fifth-century sources follow this same pattern. Prosper of Aquitaine refers to the wife of Valentinian III as *regina*, and a *regnum* is held by eight emperors and empresses (Prosper, 1167, 1170, 1238, 1243, 1245, 1246, 1251, 1288, 1375). The *Chronica Gallica* style Galla Placidia as *regina* and six emperors have *regna* (*Chron. Gall. 452*, 1, 18, 19, 31, 89, 103, 109; *Chron. Gall. 511*, 613, 614).

In the sixth century, nothing has changed. Ennodius refers to Julius Nepos as *rex* and to the *regnum* of both Glycerius and Nepos; and he mentions the *Romana regna* (*V. Epiphanii* 79–81; *Panegyric. Regi Theoderico* 69). Jordanes uses *rex* for three emperors (*Romana* 357; *Getica* 104), and *regnum* is used for nineteen emperors, from Augustus to Augustulus (*Romana* 84, 263, 266, 280, 283, 296, 307, 321–2; *Getica* 87–9, 104, 165, 239–40, 242–3). He also refers to the *regnum Romanum, regnum occidentale, orientale regnum*, and the *regnum Italiae* (which was occupied by Odovacar) (*Romana* 327, 348, 386; *Getica* 148, 172, 244, 264, 290, 303, 309). Avitus of Vienne uses the term *rex Orientis* for the eastern Roman emperor, who also has a *regnum* (Ep. 2.3, 94). In Britain, Gildas says that *reges Romanorum* won *imperium orbis*, and he makes reference to the *Romanum regnum* (5.1, 6.1, 13.2).

From the seventh to the early eighth century, these same terms are employed for Roman emperors and the Roman empire. Pope Gregory I mentions the *regnum* of emperors Maurice and Phocas (*Ep.* 1.16a, 13.34). Isidore of Seville refers to Julius Caesar as *rex,* mentions Caesar's *monarchia*, and says that the Romans used the title *Augusti* for their *reges* (*Etym.* 5.39.25, 7.6.43; Reydellet, 1981: 559f.). Paul the Deacon writes that Tiberius II was the fiftieth of the *Romanorum reges*, and freely uses the term *regnum* and *Romanorum regnum* for the Empire (*Historia Langobardorum* 3.12, 6.36, 6.13, 4.36, 49, 4.11–12). Bede discusses the *Romanum regnum* of Nero and

Phocas, the *Hesperium regnum* that came to an end with the death of Valentinian III, and refers to the *regnum* of five emperors (*Eccl. Hist.* 1.3–5, 1.8, 1.13, 1.15, 1.21, 1.34). 'Nennius' refers to Gratian as the *rex Romanorum* and discusses the *regnum Romanorum*, the Roman *monarchia* and the *regnum* and *monarchia* of Augustus (15, 20, 27, 28).

While one might argue that this long history of royal language attached to Roman emperors and the Roman empire reflects only a popular or vulgar usage, panegyrics form a different category of source, since they were intended to flatter their subjects and to be delivered at the imperial courts. The panegyrics of Claudius Claudianus, written for Honorius and other members of the Theodosian family, indicate that emperors could indeed be called kings to their faces. Honorius is called *rex* and his brother Arcadius is called King of the East, *rex Eous* (*De IV Cons. Hon.* 262; *De III Cons. Hon.* 17). There is mention of the *reges* of the Theodosian house (*De Cons. Stil.* 2.53). Maria, daughter of the great Theodosius, is called the offspring of *reges* who is about to give birth to *reges* (*Epithalamium de Nuptiis Honorii Augusti* 252–3). Rome is the *patria regum* (De Cons. Stil. 3.175). *Rex* is used generally for an emperor (*De Cons. Stil.* 3.115), and there are the *reginae* of the Theodosian family (*De IV Cons. Hon.* 166; *De Cons. Stil.* 2.361). One can read of the *Romanum regnum*, the *regna Hesperiae*, and the *regnum Eio* (*De Bell. Get.* 457, 517; *In Rufinum* 2.1–2). In fact, one can find the appearance of *rex* in imperial panegyrics as early as the first century AD, when Statius refers to Domitian as *rex magne* in his Silvae (4.1.46).

It can now be seen that the phrase *Romanorum rex* is not peculiar to Gregory of Tours or to Frankish sources. The *Scriptores Historiae Augustae*, Orosius, Gildas, Paul the Deacon and Nennius all refer to Roman emperors as *rex Romanorum*, *rex Romanus* or *reges Romanorum*. Ammianus Marcellinus, Hilary of Poitiers, Lucifer of Cagliari, Augustine, Orosius, Venantius Fortunatus, Sulpicius Severus, Ennodius, Jordanes, Avitus of Vienne and Isidore of Seville style emperors as *rex*. Sulpicius Severus, Augustine, Orosius, Claudian, Ennodius, Jordanes, Gildas, Paul the Deacon and Nennius refer to the Roman empire as *regnum Romanum*, *regnum Romanorum* or *regna Romana*. Thus, in this larger context of Latin usage, it seems clear that, when Gregory of Tours and the *Liber Historiae Francorum* identify Syagrius or Aegidius as *rex Romanorum*, it is meant that they were, or were seen to be, claiming to be Roman emperors. Gregory could let that suspect phrase pass by without explanation because it was well grounded in the usage of his day and needed no elaboration, for its meaning was clear.

Likewise, the use of imperial vocabulary to refer to Germanic states and their rulers ought not to be seen as some sort of barbarian conceit, a claim of equality to the dying western empire, or as an appropriation of its vocabulary. It was common to see the Persian ruler as an *imperator* and his state as an *imperium*. This can be seen in Ammianus Marcellinus (17.5.5), Gregory of Tours (*HF* 4.40), John of Biclarum (3.62, 3.64), pope Gregory I (*Ep.* 5.21, 20.23) and Fredegar (*Chron.* 6.9). It was a commonplace that there were four great *imperia*, those of the Assyrians, the Persians, the Macedonians, and, of course, the Romans (Swain, 1940). This is found in Augustine (*De Civitate Dei* 4.4, 5.21, 20.23), Orosius (2.1.5, 7.2.2), and Sulpicius Severus (*Chron.* 2.3, 2.5, 2.7). Jordanes also refers to the *imperium* of Artaxerxes (*Romana* 69).

Beyond references to these great world empires, it is relatively unusual to find non-Roman states styled *imperia*, but examples are indeed to be found. The *Scriptores Historiae Augustae* mention the *imperium* of Odenathus, king of Palmyra, and of his wife Zenobia (Two Gallieni 10.1, 13.2–3). Cassiodorus, in the *Variae*, constantly refers to the *imperium* of Ostrogothic kings (1.42) and he repeatedly uses the phrase *imperium Italiae* (1.18.2, 12.22.5; Reydellet, 1981: 196). On occasion Jordanes uses imperial vocabulary for Gothic rulers (*Getica* 98, 119), but otherwise he limits such language concerning non-Romans to a Vandal king (*Getica* 170) and most frequently for the Huns (*Getica* 248, 253, 259, 272). The only non-Roman *imperium* referred to by Paul the Deacon was that of the Huns (*Historia Langobardorum* 1.27). The Visigoths were also the subjects of imperial vocabulary in the writings of Isidore of Seville (*De Laude Spaniae* 267; *Historia Gothorum* 52).

When these writers reflect on the essential meaning of *imperium*, they present a consistent theme of a state composed of a plurality of peoples, nations and *gentes*. In the third century, Origen wrote that God had prepared the nations for Christ by putting them under one ruler, the Roman *basileus*, and Augustus fused the many people of the earth into one *basileia* (*Contra Celsum* 2.30). Tertullian referred to the Roman empire as a conflation of *regna* (*Apologeticum* 25.17; see 32.2, 34.1). Jerome wrote that, before the coming of Christ, each *gens* was under its own *rex*, and no one could go from one *natio* to another, but in the Roman *imperium* all men were made into one (*Comment. in Esaiam* 5.19.23). Augustine also stressed the plurality of nations in the Empire (*De Civitate Dei* 4.4, 4.9, 5.12, 18.22, 18.27). The early fifth-century panegyrist Rutilius Namatianus described the Roman empire as one *patria* made from *diversae gentes* (*De Reditu Suo* 1.63). His fellow panegyrist Claudian stressed the plurality of peoples and languages under the emperor (*De IV Cons. Hon.* 355; *De Cons. Stil.* 1.152–4; *De Cons. Stil.* 3.159), and the same point is made by Jordanes (*Getica* 68).

When *imperium* is applied to non-Roman states, the same concept of plurality is prominent. This is found in Augustine (*De Civitate Dei* 4.6) and Sulpicius Severus (*Chron.* 2.15) concerning the Persians and Assyrians. The *imperium* of Odenathus consisted of *totus Oriens* (*Script. Hist. Aug.* Two Gallieni 10.1). When Jordanes applied imperial language to the Goths and Huns, again it was with reference to the various peoples under their power (*Getica* 73, 98, 120, 248, 253, 259, 272), and the Huns were generally well known for the many peoples they had conquered (Maenchen-Helfen, 1973: 18ff.). When Isidore of Seville attributed *imperium* to the Visigoths, again plurality, conquest and expansion are stressed (*De Laude Spaniae* 267; *Historia Gothorum* 42, 52).

This conception of *imperium* as a large state consisting of a plurality of peoples is not a product of the Middle Ages or even of the later Roman period (but see Wolfram, 1970: 16). It can be seen in the first century BC, in Sallust's *Jugurthine War* (18.12, 31.20, 79.2), and it is equally present in the writings of Tacitus a century later (*Historiae* 4.58, 4.63; *Annales* 2.2, 2.61, 6.34, 11.24, 11.9, 12.34, 11.37). Thus from Sallust and Tacitus to Jordanes and Paul the Deacon, the essence of an *imperium* and its *imperator* is the ruler over more than one people, land, or kingdom. When Ennodius makes reference to the *imperium* of Euric (*V. Epiphanii* 86), or when other writers use imperial language for Germanic or other non-Roman leaders and peoples, it is not a sign of conceit or of the appropriation of a uniquely Roman language. Instead, it accurately reflects Latin usage and conceptions stretching back for centuries.

Thus, in this survey of regal and imperial terminology as applied to holders of imperial power in fifth-century Gaul, the element of discontinuity between the earlier part of the century and the latter is much less acute than is usually supposed. It would be extremely rash to suggest that Aegidius and Syagrius were in fact Roman emperors, but it is clear that Gregory of Tours and the *Liber Historiae Francorum* were using language that meant just that. Equally it would be going too far to deny that Euric may have seen himself as the equal of the weak and ineffective emperors that he confronted as he expanded his territories in Gaul and Spain, but the use of imperial language to refer to him or to any of the other Germanic leaders of the fifth or sixth centuries is not an expression of hubris, but rather simply indicates that he or the others ruled over domains composed of a plurality of peoples. While there was a considerable decline of Roman imperial authority in Gaul in the fifth century, the indications of that decomposition are not to be found in the Latin language surrounding Roman emperors, would-be emperors, wielders of ostensibly imperial powers, or the Germanic kings that would soon hold all real power in that diocese of the Roman empire.

CHAPTER 26

Sidonius Apollinaris, Rome and the barbarians: a climate of treason?

J. D. Harries

In 475, Clermont of the Arverni was surrendered to Euric and the Goths under a treaty negotiated by four Provençal bishops. The settlement evoked from the city's leading defender and bishop, Sidonius Apollinaris, a spirited defence of the rule and values of Rome. For this purpose, history was rewritten; the Arverni were not the people of Vercingetorix but 'brothers to Latium' and 'sprung from the blood of Troy' (*Ep.* 7.7.2); the betrayal of the Arverni was thus one of true Romans by Romans. The reward for the loyalty and suffering of the Arverni, as demonstrated in their endurance of the Gothic sieges over four years and the conviction of the corrupt Seronatus, was to be abandoned and face slavery, thanks to the decisions of a clique more concerned with private gain than the public good (*Ep.* 7.7.4).

Such was Sidonius' 'epitaph for the Western Empire' (Stevens, 1933: 160), the indignant outpouring of a totally loyal Roman – or so it would seem. But the stark contrasts of freedom and slavery, of Roman and barbarian, expressed in Sidonius' rhetoric do not stand up to close scrutiny in the light of their literary context, of Sidonius' own actions at other points in his career and of the opinions advanced by him elsewhere. The importance of Sidonius' writings is not simply that, used with care, they chronicle the career and thoughts of an individual, but that they are symptomatic of assumptions held by many among the Gallo-Roman aristocracy about how to deal with the barbarians. These assumptions were not formally treasonable and there is no question of Sidonius' own loyalty to the Roman state; but, with only a little adaptation, the compromises advocated by Sidonius could lead, as in Arvandus' case, to outright treason.

Sidonius' letters as we have them are not the spontaneous outpourings of a private man writing informally to friends and colleagues. As his books of letters emerged in instalments after 476 (although part of Book I may have been circulating in 469), Sidonius himself selected what was to be made public, while allowing (so he said) some 'polishing' by others (*Ep.* 1.1.3). Both the fact of preselection and the possibility of revision suggest that Sidonius aimed not simply to inform but also to explain and justify his actions to his many aristocratic friends (cf. Wood, above p. 12). This impression is supported by the artful arrangement of letters in Book I, which points to a deliberate attempt by Sidonius to paint in favourable colours his association with the Gothic king, Theoderic II, and his friendship with the traitor Arvandus (Sivan, 1989b). The letters, therefore, like the earlier *Carmina* (published in one book in 469), have something of the character of a modern politician's memoirs or diaries: they present the writer in the most favourable light, while appearing franker than they really are. And the picture is, of course, further complicated by the conventions of rhetoric, which sacrificed accurate description to literary effect (Loyen, 1943).

If Sidonius' aim was to justify his past, it must be admitted that he was only partially successful. Viewed superficially, Sidonius' relationship with the Goths emerges as a model of inconsistency. As Avitus' son-in-law, he was associated with the pact with the Goths which put the western empire briefly in Avitus' hands; and in 463 he is found blandly accepting the Goths' and Theoderic's occupation of Narbonne, describing that king as 'the support and preserver of the Roman people' (*Carm.* 23.72). Yet in 471–5 he did everything possible to defend Clermont against those same Goths, now described as a 'race of treaty-breakers' (*Ep.* 6.6.1); finally, a further change of position, when in 477 the Gothic king is reinstated as the object of petitions from all over the world and the rescuer of the 'shrunken Tiber' (*Ep.* 8.9; *Carm.* 42; cf. Teitler, below p. 316). On religion, Sidonius is equally adaptable. In his portrait of Theoderic, the king's Arian practices are discreetly veiled (*Ep.* 1.2.4); in contrast, Euric in 474 is represented as a religious fanatic and a persecutor of bishops and churches (*Ep.* 7.6); but finally Sidonius was prepared to accept this persecutor as overlord, when restored to his see under the supervision of a Catholic *comes*, Victorius. Still less creditable may have been the secrets which may lurk behind silences not covered by the conventions of literary *politesse*. We have the minimum on the reign of Avitus (Mathisen, 1979c; cf. Chianéa, 1969: 354); nothing dating from 461–2 on the transfer of Narbonne to the Goths, only the later acceptance of the *fait accompli*, and no mention either of Aegidius or his son Syagrius, although Sidonius did have a correspondent at Soissons; nothing on the object of Sidonius' journey to Rome in 467, which resulted in his elevation to the city prefecture in 468; and nothing on that momentous event familiar to all Sidonius' readership, his consecration as bishop in about 470. While allowance must be made for the omission of material familiar to his correspondents – both his link with Avitus and the events surrounding his consecration would have been well known – cynics might still agree that what we have in Sidonius is a 'trimmer', the archetypal survivor. A man who had offered a panegyric to, and served under, the emperor (Majorian) responsible for the death of his wife's father must surely have been capable of any sacrifice of principle to expediency.

But, if Sidonius is to be 'decoded', it must be accepted that the truth is more subtle. With Sidonius we are dealing with constantly changing situations and different perspectives. The letters were written 'as reasons, people, or situations prompted' (*Ep.* 1.1.1) and, whatever polishing may have taken place, it did not extend to ironing out inconsistencies between one letter and another. Some letters were clearly tailored to the beliefs of the recipient: for example, the attack on Euric as an Arian fanatic is addressed to a bishop noted for his debating victories over the heretics; and the grovelling humility deemed appropriate by the new bishop Sidonius to the aged and formidably saintly Lupus of Troyes (*Ep.* 6.1) receives a healthy corrective in Sidonius' confession to the more approachable Fonteius of Vaison that 'I find it easier to submit in humility to such characters than to associate with them as friends' (*Ep.* 7.4.3).

Fortunately, however, Sidonius was not merely a mirror-image of his correspondents. Behind the shifting façade and the distortions of rhetoric was a set of coherent beliefs, which motivated his actions and which render them consistent when viewed in their own terms. One constant feature is Sidonius' ideal of Rome, the city that symbolized his aristocratic values and, through its rule, gave him and his peers the right, and indeed the obligation, to hold high office. Letters on this subject tended to be to people whose careers reflected this ideal. Eutropius, to whom Sidonius described Rome as 'the home of laws, the training ground of letters, the senate house of offices' (*Ep.* 1.6.2), was to be Gallic praetorian prefect in about 470; and a letter to a man who had made it as *vicarius*, Gaudentius, poured scorn on 'the arrogant sloth of your detractors and the contempt for public life typical of lazy people, when in despair of rising themselves they philosophize over the wine and extol the holiday existence of those who hold no office' (*Ep*. 1.4.2; cf. Wes, above p. 254). Through Roman office, aristocrats gained status, and the literary culture which marked out the superior person was guaranteed under the same system. With the loss of office, wrote Sidonius in about 476, only literature was left as a means of separating the best from their inferiors (*Ep*. 8.2.2); the Latin language could reach safe harbour despite the 'shipwreck' of 'Latin' military might. But, if Rome as the capital of letters was something of an abstraction, Sidonius' own career confirms his belief in the Empire as the source of offices: under Avitus, abortively, as *tribunus et notarius*, under Majorian as *comes* and finally under Anthemius, as city prefect 'by a chance stroke of the pen' (*Ep*. 1.9.8), Sidonius was consistent in his pursuit of a Rome-based career, long after contemporaries like Leo of Narbonne had thrown in their lot with the Gothic or Burgundian courts. His renunciation of that career may have been due to implication with Arvandus, despair of the Empire (suggested by his urging of Ecdicius to return and defend 'the last hope of freedom' in *Ep*. 2.1.4), fear of Euric acting on strong local patriotism, or the initiative of the Arverni themselves, but it would certainly have been no casual decision.

A second assumption which consistently underlay Sidonius' actions was the belief that Roman rule in Gaul was best protected by the existence of treaties (*foedera*); the existence or otherwise of these was the crucial test of the acceptability of Roman dealings with barbarian peoples. One of Eparchius Avitus' many qualifications for the imperial office in the eyes of his panegyrist in 456 was his ability to deliver treaties with the Goths. The pact which set him on the throne in 455 had been foreshadowed by his achievement in controlling the victorious Goths after Litorius' defeat in 439 and in renewing their treaty: 'it is enough that you ordered what the world requested' (*Carm*. 7.308–9). It was Avitus who brought the Goths out against the Huns, as Sidonius recalled (*Carm*. 7.341–2), and Avitus' assumption of the purple is encouraged by the Goths with the promise that they will be 'soldiers of Rome' (*Carm*. 7.510–11). Both Gallic people (*cives*) and senators assembled at Beaucaire are heartened by the knowledge that he has brought with him a promise of Gothic support and a treaty (*Carm.* 7.520–1), and the senatorial assembly duly proclaims him Augustus. Despite the fall of Avitus, there is no hint that Sidonius broke with the Goths in the late 450s or 460s. The first of his published letters, aside from the dedicatory epistle, is his laudation of Theoderic, who is praised for his *civilitas*, the ability to behave like a Roman, not a barbarian (*Ep.* 1.2.1), and the king's relationship with Narbonne in 463, a year after its surrender, is described as one of affection, increased by memories of its former resistance, which (we are told) will guarantee its present loyalty (*Carm.* 23.72–3). Perhaps Sidonius was to view the resistance of Clermont in similar terms.

By the time Sidonius left Clermont for Rome in 467, the parties to the arrangement of 461, Libius Severus and Theoderic II, were both dead, and the intentions of Euric uncertain. When Arvandus as praetorian prefect urged the Gothic king 'not to make peace with the Greek emperor' (*Ep.* 1.7.5), he was in effect arguing against the formal renewal of the *foedus* by the king with the new emperor. However, the status of the Goths as federates probably continued to be assumed for as long as Euric refrained from an act of war.

Even after hostilities had broken out, Sidonius retained a sense that the treaty ought to exist. To Eucherius, a vigorous opponent of the Goths, Sidonius complained of 'the tribe of federates who not only control Roman resources in violation of law (*inciviliter*) but are also undermining them at the roots' (*Ep.* 3.8.2); Euric's conduct was the opposite of Theoderic's *civilitas*. And in 471 Sidonius was still in hopes that the younger Avitus could use his authority with the Goths to urge restraint and bring about a settlement (*Ep.* 3.1.5). This was obviously self-interested, as Sidonius wished to negotiate the independence of Clermont, such as it was. But it was also consistent with the belief expressed apropos of Narbonne, that a treaty could be made and be the stronger after a period of hostilities.

Despite his hopes for peace, Sidonius was uncompromising during the sieges of Clermont. While some friends – notably his brother-in-law Ecdicius, whose military flair brought much-needed relief, and Constantius of Lyon – stood by him, others found themselves on the opposing side. The friendship with Leo of Narbonne, much valued by Sidonius in the 460s, is not acknowledged in a single letter between 470 and 475, although Sidonius picked up and vigorously exploited the relationship in 476. More significant are the hints about the reasons for his silence as a correspondent in a letter to one Calminius.

Calminius was being forced by the Goths to fight against his fellow citizens, and fear, which Sidonius will not explain further (*Ep.* 5.12.1), compels silence. In other words, Sidonius cannot correspond with one with whom he is at war. However, at the time of writing, there prevailed an illusion of truce, which enabled Sidonius to urge Calminius to write him a brief letter, as his fellow citizens were still fond of him (*Ep.* 5.12.2). It is clear here that the hope of a truce, if not a formal treaty, immediately transformed the basis of Sidonius' conduct.

Although the treaty finally negotiated in 475 was utterly unacceptable to Sidonius, who, as we have seen, protested vigorously, it nevertheless had the effect of reinstating the Goths as allies. As part of his campaign to obtain his recall from exile, Sidonius appealed to Euric through a friend at court, Lampridius of Bordeaux, enclosing a panegyric upon the king (*Ep.* 8.9). In the course of this, Sidonius interpreted the new situation in terms of a fresh pact between Euric and the rest of the world, which is represented as supplicating the king for aid. Among the suppliants are the Romans, 'so that the Garonne, strong in its warrior settlers, may defend the Tiber's shrunken stream' (*Ep.* 8.9.41–2). Over the twenty years since the panegyric of Avitus, Sidonius' belief that Roman and barbarian should live together under treaty had not changed.

Such were the principles of Sidonius, but were they adequate to guarantee his loyalty in the confused situation in Gaul in the 460s and 470s? It has already been observed that Sidonius' devotion to Rome was to an abstract, a source of offices and culture. Loyalty to Rome did not automatically mean loyalty to any given Roman emperor, and Sidonius on several occasions seems to have had difficulty in equating Rome with her rulers. Gallic alienation from Italian-based emperors did not begin with the rising in support of Avitus; in Sidonius' family the phenomenon had been present two generations earlier and went deep. On this, Sidonius was naturally discreet. When he restored his grandfather Apollinaris' tomb at Lyon, his new verse inscription commemorated Apollinaris simply as a praetorian prefect who 'after governing Gaul with integrity, was received into the embrace of his mourning fatherland' (*Ep.* 3.12; *Carm.* 6–8). There is no hint that the deceased had been prefect to the usurper Constantine III in 408–9 and that he had probably fallen victim to the purge of Gallo-Roman senators of the Auvergne carried out by Honorius' generals and his praetorian prefect, Cl. Postumus Dardanus (cf. Heinzelmann, above p.

243). Suppression of the past was also the rule when Sidonius urged Aquilinus, the grandson of Apollinaris' associate, Decimius Rusticus, to continue into the next generation the friendship of their fathers and grandfathers (*Ep.* 5.9). Although subsequently the fathers of Sidonius and Aquilinus had reconciled themselves with the Roman governments of Honorius and Valentinian III and held high office under them, the era of Constantine III was not forgotten. Friendships from that time were to be renewed (Sidonius hoped) in the third generation; his silence on the period of usurpation is more eloquent than his words.

Unlike Constantine III, Eparchius Avitus did succeed in installing himself as emperor at Rome and when, in 456, the young Sidonius delivered, before a Roman audience, a panegyric of his father-in-law, part of the poem was couched in such language as to leave no doubt that the long-standing disaffection among Gallo-Roman aristocrats was such as to threaten the basis of consent on which Roman rule was founded and without which the Empire itself could not function. The recently assassinated Valentinian III was made the object of personal abuse as a 'mad eunuch' (*Carm.* 7. 359), abuse the more telling for its public context. Loyalty based on tradition, claimed the orator, had enforced obedience to ineffectual laws; duty to the ancient order had motivated the Gauls in their toleration of the dynasty, and the 'shadow of an empire' more from habit (*mos*) than because it was right (*ius*). His language – which was to find echo in his panegyric upon Majorian in 458, referring to the downtrodden state of the Gallic nobility 'despised for so many years' (*Carm.* 5. 361) – conveyed a stern warning. Nobles in Gaul loyal to the idea of Rome were far from feeling the same towards Rome's emperors: the convention of obedience was being questioned, as was the right of Rome's emperors to rule (Teillet, 1984: 194f.).

After Avitus' fall and his reconciliation with Majorian, Sidonius' horizons were confined to Gaul, with the one conspicuous exception of his embassy to Rome in 467 and urban prefecture in 468. Contacts with the Goths at Toulouse and the Burgundians at Lyon and in the Rhône corridor had more immediate reality than the activities of distant emperors. When the crisis came in 469 and Sidonius found himself in 470 obliged to defend Clermont, he did so in the name of Rome and was supported by, among others, his brother-in-law Ecdicius, whose services were rewarded by Julius Nepos in 474 with his appointment as master of the soldiers. But neither Sidonius nor

Ecdicius had in fact any independent military power of their own and both would have been aware that they were under the protection, and therefore the power, of the Burgundians. Sidonius acknowledged as much when he wrote to Magnus Felix describing Clermont as a frontier city between two peoples; 'suspected by the Burgundians, bordering on the Goths, we confront both the rage of our attackers and the hostility of our defenders' (*Ep.* 3.4.1). As the Burgundians were technically federate, whereas the Goths in the early 470s were not, their protection of Clermont was compatible with the assertion that Clermont was being defended for Rome: the reality was that the Burgundians at Lyon had their own reasons to resist Gothic expansion into Clermont.

By 474, relations with the Burgundians were also more sensitive and Sidonius found himself faced, as he had been in the Arvandus case, with a choice between loyalty to friends and to Rome's emperor. The Burgundian prince, Gundobad, master of the soldiers in the early 470s, had been involved in the killing of Anthemius at Rome in July 472; the death of Ricimer in August 472 allowed him briefly to be the most powerful man in the west; he was elevated to the patriciate by Olybrius; and, on 3 March 473, he created a puppet emperor of his own, Glycerius. But in 474 Gundobad was obliged to return to Gaul, probably to ensure his own succession to the Burgundian throne on the death of his father, Gundioc. In his absence, Glycerius was in turn expelled by the new emperor from the east, Julius Nepos, who sent his predecessor off to safe keeping as bishop at Salonae – and appointed Ecdicius as master of the soldiers in place of Gundobad. The result of all this was that Nepos had a master of the soldiers without an army: the Burgundians continued to support Glycerius and refused recognition of, or co-operation with, Nepos, and it therefore became unacceptable in Burgundian eyes for Romans resident in the Rhône corridor to have dealings with the emperor in post.

Sidonius, for his part, accepted Nepos as emperor, penning congratulations to a new city prefect, Castalius Innocentius Audax, for living 'under a just emperor' (*Ep.* 8.7). To Papianilla, his wife, Sidonius was eloquent on the award to Ecdicius of the patriciate by Nepos, 'an Augustus supreme in war and in character' (*Ep.* 5.16.2). But when his kinsmen Apollinaris and Thaumastus, both resident at Burgundian Vaison, were accused by anonymous informers of plotting to hand the city over 'to the party of the new emperor' (*Ep.* 5.6.2, see also *Ep.* 5.7), Sidonius' tone was very different. Now it is the Burgundian, Chilperic, master of the soldiers, who is 'most victorious of men', while the informers are 'secret whisperers of poisonous fabrications', on whose iniquities Sidonius allows himself a rhetorical excursus once all is well and Chilperic's queen has interceded with their 'common patron', the king (*Ep.* 5.7.7). These references to the king as 'victorious' and a 'patron' turn him virtually into a substitute emperor. Clearly Sidonius did not equate Nepos, the Roman emperor, with Rome (not, at least, when his kinsmen's lives were at stake) and believed that the retention of Vaison by the federate Burgundians was acceptable. It is significant for the climate of confusion over loyalties now prevalent in Gaul that it seems not to have occurred to Sidonius (or, presumably, anyone else) that obstruction of the return of a city to a Roman emperor's control could be construed as treason.

This blurring of the distinctions between what was treasonable and what was not may help to explain the behaviour of Arvandus in 469 (though cf. Teitler, below). From a Roman standpoint it seemed obvious that Arvandus' letter to Euric was treasonable because it advocated the partition of Roman territory between the Goths and the Burgundians. This view was shared by the three representatives appointed by the Gallic provincial council to lodge complaints against him before the Roman senate. Yet they intended to trick him by pretending the letter was of no importance, a point which suggests that its treasonable implications may not have been so immediately apparent to a prefect used to functioning in a Gallic context. Moreover, Arvandus seemed genuinely taken aback by the outcry which greeted his admission of authorship. Sidonius, who was not present at the trial, ascribed Arvandus' reaction to his sudden realization that 'a man could be declared guilty of treason, even though he had not aspired to wear the purple' (*Ep.* 1.7.11). In other words, Arvandus, who as a two-term praetorian prefect had extensive experience of administering the law, had forgotten that treason consisted of 'an action carried out to the detriment of the Roman people or which damages its security' (Ulpian, in *Digest* 48.4.1). Such ignorance has seemed so unlikely to scholars that it has been suggested that Arvandus was relying on a secret deal with Ricimer (Stevens, 1933: 107). However, another explanation is possible. Arvandus may have seen himself as making a proposal consistent with what he saw as the political and military state of affairs in Gaul early in 469, which could be acceptable as the Goths had not yet crossed the Loire and the Burgundians were still technically federate; the arrangement could thus be made *iure gentium*, 'by the law of nations' (*Ep.* 1.7.5). He had lived with the realities of the situation in Gaul and was not to know that the Roman perception would be different: Sidonius, as Roman city prefect, had been in the capital long enough to know better.

The conviction of Arvandus shows how the habit of negotiation with Goths, Burgundians and other non-Roman peoples in Gaul, which had occasionally resulted in agreed surrender of territory, could shade into treason against the Roman state. Men of Sidonius' generation, born in the 430s, had grown up accepting the fact that no Gallo-Roman leader could defend 'Roman Gaul' without the help of barbarian federate allies. There was nothing formally treasonable, or even blameworthy, in Sidonius' contacts with the Gothic and Burgundian courts, his flattery of their kings (and queens), or even in his acquiescence in the expansion of barbarians' territory, when it could not be prevented.

Yet, paradoxically, Sidonius' acceptance of co-operation and compromise with the barbarians may have been more damaging to the survival of the Roman political order than the outright treason of his friend, Arvandus. True, when Goths became 'public enemies' in the 470s (*Ep.* 7.7.2), he defended Clermont resolutely and finally tried to negotiate the best terms possible, safeguards for catholic bishops in Gothic territory, the ransoming of prisoners and the care of refugees (*Ep.* 7.7.6). But, as we have seen, the 'freedom' he defended was an empty one. Clermont itself in the 470s hung suspended between Gothic domination and Burgundian protection, Roman only in name. Sidonius, along with some members of his family (and, for different reasons, Aegidius after 461) asserted loyalty to Rome, but not invariably to Roman emperors. People like Leo of Narbonne, who were ultra-Roman in a cultural sense, pursued political careers at the barbarian courts, as Romans. Roman Christianity, too, with its deep roots in the life of the cities, could survive the fall of imperial Rome. The fact that Rome in a political sense was now a form without substance and that there were other acceptable ways of being 'Roman' eased the transition to barbarian rule. Compromises tended to work in the barbarians' favour; they were the powers on the spot; and the existence of factions too could be exploited in their interests. We may suspect (though we cannot prove) that more cities passed silently under barbarian control through discreet intervention and negotiation in peace than in war – and that Goths and Burgundians were more dangerous ultimately to Rome as federates than as foes.

CHAPTER 27

Un-Roman activities in late antique Gaul: the cases of Arvandus and Seronatus

H. C. Teitler

'I am distressed by the fall of Arvandus and I do not conceal my distress.' With these words, Sidonius Apollinaris opens a famous letter, probably written early in the year 469, addressed to a certain Vincentius (*Ep.* 1.7).[1] The accusations against Arvandus, praetorian prefect of Gaul, his trial before the senate in Rome and the fact that he was found guilty of high treason must have come as a shock to Sidonius, whose letter testifies among other things to his *amicitia* for the man. It is precisely this aspect of *amicitia* which makes the letter especially interesting. The downfall of a senior Gallo-Roman administrator, accused of treacherous collaboration with the Visigothic king Euric, would no doubt have shocked Sidonius anyway, but what made matters worse was the fact that the condemned man had been his friend. 'Amicus homini fui', Sidonius writes, adding that on account of this friendship he himself had met with some difficulties: 'propter ipsum nuper mihi invidia conflata' (*Ep.* 1.7.1). He therefore eagerly complies with the request of Vincentius, who had asked him to tell the story of Arvandus' condemnation, and he grasps the opportunity to rectify misunderstandings, should there be any left: 'I will give you the facts shortly whilst paying all respect to the loyalty which is due even to a fallen friend' (*Ep.* 1.7.3).

Between Sidonius and Seronatus, another official suspected of treasonable relations with the Visigoths, no such bonds of *amicitia* existed. On the contrary, as far as we can judge, Sidonius had always heartily disliked Seronatus. In a letter to Pannychius he not only calls him a robber, a plague and a beast, but even exclaims that 'neither

---

[1]   I quote Sidonius from Anderson's Loeb edition.

Marcus of Arpinum, prince of orators, nor Publius of Mantua, prince of poets, would be equal to the task of describing such a monster' (*Ep.* 5.13.3).

It is obvious that the cases of Arvandus and Seronatus have similarities. Both men were high officers: Arvandus praetorian prefect; Seronatus either governor of Aquitanica Prima or *vicarius* of the Seven Provinces (*PLRE* II, 157f., 995f.). Both men were said to be in league with the Visigothic king and to have developed plans to deliver Roman territory into the hands of barbarians. Both were deemed guilty; and for both Sidonius is almost the only source. From what is said about Sidonius' attitude towards them, however, it is also clear that their cases, though comparable, are not identical. In this chapter I propose to make a few remarks on the evidence we have concerning Arvandus and Seronatus. I shall try to relate their cases to the historical background both in Gaul and in Rome. I would also like to examine very briefly the question as to whether their cases were unique or symptomatic of a much wider movement.

I start with Arvandus. Apart from the letter of Sidonius already quoted, our information about him is restricted to a word or two in Cassiodorus' *Chronica* and in the *Historia Romana* of Paul the Deacon. (I follow the authors of *PLRE* II and many others in assuming that our man may be identified with the 'Arabundus' and 'Servandus' of these authors.) According to Cassiodorus, Arvandus was exiled on orders from Anthemius 'after an attempt to usurp the throne', if indeed that is the correct translation of 'Arabundus imperium temptans iussu Anthemii exilio deportatus' (Cassiodorus, *Chron.* 1287). The relevant passage in Paul the Deacon is virtually identical: 'Sequenti anno Servandus Galliarum praefectus imperium temptans invadere iussu Anthemii principis in exilium trusus est' (Paul the Deacon, *Historia Romana* 15.2).

Two things attract attention in these statements. First, Arvandus is said to have been sent into exile, while the wording of Sidonius' letter to Vincentius implies that he was condemned to death. In the opening section of Sidonius' letter the emperor Anthemius is warmly commended because of the possibility that 'affection may be openly shown even for men condemned to death'; and in section 12 we are told that Arvandus was sentenced to death and flung into prison to await execution. The apparent contradiction between our contemporary source and the later authors disappears, however, on further consideration.

Sidonius, it is true, was in Rome when Arvandus arrived there, and he witnessed the preparations for the lawsuit against his Gallic compatriot; but he had left Rome before the actual trial took place and, consequently, before the verdict was pronounced. He heard about it only afterwards. At the time of his writing to Vincentius, he knew the general outcome of the process, but still not the whole of it. He had heard that Arvandus had been condemned to death, but that the sentence had not yet been carried out. Arvandus, he writes, had been flung into prison on the Tiber island, there to serve out the period of thirty days during which the punishment of persons sentenced to death was suspended in accordance with an old decree of the senate, dating from the time of Tiberius. I ardently hope, Sidonius continues, that the emperor may 'even at the cost of the confiscation of his property or exile, show favour to this half-dead man by holding back the stroke of the sword which threatens every moment to be loosed upon him' (*Ep*. 1.7.13). Apparently Anthemius did show favour to Arvandus. As to Arvandus' punishment, Cassiodorus and Paul the Deacon do not contradict, but complete, the story as told by Sidonius.

A little more ought to be said about Sidonius' report of the stay of execution of Arvandus' sentence. Sidonius speaks of a period of *thirty* days. Suetonius (*Tiberius* 75.2) and Cassius Dio (57.20.4), on the other hand, mention *ten* days. Tacitus also has ten days, but the text (*Annales* 3.51.2) is, unfortunately, suspect: the crucial word, *decimum*, is conjecturally inserted by the editors by analogy with Suetonius and Dio (I have consulted Koestermann's Teubner and Fisher's Oxford text; they follow Lipsius). Still, Suetonius and Dio are unequivocal, and it seems justified to assume that originally a reprieve of ten days was allowed. Sidonius may have got his thirty days from a law of Theodosius I (*CTh* 9.40.13, issued probably in 390), which stipulates that 'it is Our will that the criminal shall neither undergo punishment nor receive sentence immediately, but his fate and fortune with reference to his status shall be held in suspense for thirty days' (tr. Pharr, 1952; so Sidonius, ed. Anderson, 1936: 378, ed. Loyen, 1970: II, 26). This may be right, but one has to assume that Theodosius' law, which, strictly speaking, was meant for imperial sentences, also applied to verdicts of senatorial courts. Alternatively, the extension from ten to thirty days may have been much older. In one of the minor declamations ascribed to Quintilian we read: 'Damnatorum supplicia in diem tricesimum differantur' (Decl. 313);

and a phrase of the same kind is found in the twenty-fifth declamation of Calpurnius Flaccus (Duval-Arnould, 1888: 51ff.; Talbert, 1984: 440, 511f.).

The second apparent contradiction between Cassiodorus and Paul the Deacon, and Sidonius, in their reports of the prosecution of Arvandus is far less susceptible of easy reconciliation. Cassiodorus and Paul propose as the reason for Arvandus' exile his 'attempt to usurp the throne'. Sidonius, on the other hand, denies that Arvandus had nourished such thoughts. According to him, Arvandus discovered 'too late that a man could be declared guilty of high treason ('posse reum maiestatis pronuntiari') even though he had not aspired to the purple' (*Ep.* 1.7.11).

Sidonius' account of Arvandus' apparent naivety is, it has been remarked, not very convincing. Sidonius is right, of course, in alleging that offences other than usurpation could be prosecuted under the laws of *maiestas*: he knew his Tacitus (cf. *Ep.* 4.14, 4.22; *Carm.* 2.192, 23.154), if not the jurists (cf. *Digest* 48.4.1–11) and the Theodosian Code (9.14.3). On the other hand, the very obviousness of his observation has caused surprise. One can hardly believe, it has been argued (Stevens, 1933: 106), that Arvandus, a former praetorian prefect and in that capacity entrusted with the administration of the law, could have been as ignorant as Sidonius depicts him. I suggest that one might go even further, and see in Sidonius' very denial that Arvandus had aspired to the purple a hint that in fact he had toyed with that idea. This is, at any rate, what Cassiodorus and Paul the Deacon apparently want us to believe. Their words, though diametrically opposed to those of Sidonius and therefore at first sight less deserving of credit, should not perhaps be rejected out of hand. I am aware, of course, that it is hazardous to attach too much importance to some two or three words in late and jejune chronicles which by their nature often condense and distort complicated issues. I am aware too that, given the paucity of our evidence – and it should be noted that Sidonius' letter leaves many questions unanswered – we can only speculate about what really happened and what Arvandus' intentions may have been. But the possibility that Arvandus entertained such far-reaching plans as to think himself fit for the throne, like Avitus in former days, should not be deemed totally inconceivable. If accepted, it could give us one more clue as to Arvandus' motive for entering into relations with the Visigoths.

Against this background, let us consider more closely the prosecution of Arvandus. Collaboration with the Visigoths was not, of course, the initial charge against him. Sidonius begins by telling us that during the second term of office his friend, oppressed by the burden of debt, had abused his power; I cannot resist quoting Sidonius' own words, which contain one of those puns he is so fond of: 'Arvandus conducted his first term as prefect with great approbation ('cum magna popularitate'), his second with great depredation ('cum maxima populatione')' (*Ep.* 1.7.3). As a result, Arvandus had aroused general hatred. Before his term of office expired he was arrested and sent to Rome, where he had to defend himself against the charge of extortion (Coster, 1968: 26f.). In Rome he was kept under guard by the *comes sacrarum largitionum* Flavius Asellus, who treated him with conspicuous respect, for example, allowing him local freedom of movement. Meanwhile a delegation from Gaul had arrived, led by a former praetorian prefect, Tonantius Ferreolus, and further consisting of Thaumastus and Petronius. They were to accuse Arvandus by order of their *provinciales* on the charge of extortion, but not merely of extortion, for it was at this point that the second, and far more serious charge, began to surface. Tonantius Ferreolus and his colleagues intended to bring forward in court a letter they had intercepted, allegedly dictated by Arvandus and addressed to Euric which, in the opinion of experts, was red-hot treason ('hanc epistulam laesae maiestatis crimine ardere iurisconsulti interpretabantur', *Ep.* 1.7.5).

Before we take a closer look at the content of this letter, the *pièce de résistance* of the Arvandus affair, I would like to draw attention to the position of Sidonius Apollinaris in all this. After all, Sidonius is not only our principal witness, he was to a certain extent also involved in the case directly. Not only was Arvandus his *amicus*, as we have seen, but Arvandus' accusers also belonged to his acquaintanceship. All three of them were recipients of some of his letters (*Ep.* 2.5, 5.1, 5.7, 7.12, 8.1), and Tonantius Ferreolus and Thaumastus were even related to him (*PLRE* II, 465f., 1062; cf. Mommaerts and Kelley, above pp. 111ff.). Besides, Sidonius was prefect of the city of Rome at the time. This meant, among other things, that he had to preside over the *iudicium quinquevirale*, a panel of five senatorial judges, chosen by lot, which made preliminary investigation (the final decision was up to the emperor) of serious criminal charges against senators (Coster, 1935, 1968; Chastagnol, 1960: 99ff.). Sidonius, knowing that Arvandus' case might well be brought before him in this court, must have felt sorely embarrassed.

His embarrassment is in fact reflected in his immediately subsequent actions, which were most improper. Although he knew that the Gallic ambassadors planned to keep secret till the day of the trial their interception of the incriminating letter, Sidonius nevertheless, in co-operation with a certain Auxanius, reported to Arvandus what his enemies were up to and gave him the advice not to confess anything, no matter how trivial (*Ep.* 1.7.6). Sidonius does not claim that Arvandus was innocent; indeed, he apparently accepted that the letter, which Arvandus' secretary admitted to have been written at his master's dictation, was authentic and proved Arvandus guilty of treason. And yet the prefect of the city of Rome alerted the traitor to what was lying ahead of him and advised him not to confess anything. *Amicitia* appears to have prevailed over patriotism.

The content of Arvandus' letter to Euric is summarized by Sidonius as follows. First, Arvandus dissuaded the king from peace with the 'Greek emperor'; secondly, he insisted that the Britanni settled to the north of the Loire should be attacked; thirdly, he declared that the Gallic provinces ought to be divided with the Burgundians according to the law of nations; and there was more 'mad stuff in the same vein' that Sidonius chose not to elaborate upon (*Ep.* 1.7.5). If Arvandus really recommended such measures – and I see no reason to doubt that he did: Sidonius tells us that Arvandus recognized the letter as genuine (*Ep.* 1.7.10) – we can understand why Arvandus' accusers and judges deemed him guilty of high treason and proposed the death penalty.

Yet, as we have seen, in the event Arvandus was not put to death. He was sent into exile. Did Anthemius, the *Graecus imperator* of Arvandus' letter, still cling to the lofty ideal of imperial clemency? Or was Arvandus lucky enough to have influential friends in Rome (e.g. Ricimer; cf. O'Flynn, 1983: 118)? We do not know. But what we do know is that even after his trial Arvandus could still count on the friendship of Sidonius Apollinaris. Sidonius had in fact not been called upon to preside over the *iudicium quinquevirale* which, as Coster (1935: 35) has shown, had investigated the case. Perhaps his term of office as *praefectus urbi* had expired before Arvandus was finally summoned before this court. Another possibility is that Sidonius had deliberately absented himself from Rome for a while, leaving the case to a deputy, in order to avoid the direct confrontation of Arvandus and the Gallic delegation, with himself in between (Coster, 1935: 35). Be that as it may, Sidonius was not in Rome at the time of Arvandus' trial. However, he had not forgotten his friend and he felt sorry for him. After he had heard of the proposed death penalty he wrote: 'As for us, whether at Rome or away from it, we offer vows and reiterate prayers and supplications to the extent of our powers, entreating that the imperial generosity may, even at the cost of the confiscation of his property or exile, show favour to this half-dead man' (*Ep.* 1.7.13).

In marked contrast, as we have seen, Sidonius felt no similar compassion for Seronatus, when convicted. On the contrary, the mere thought that this man had nearly escaped the penalty he deserved upset him. 'The state scarcely had the courage to put him to death after his conviction', he writes indignantly in a letter to bishop Graecus of Marseilles (*Ep.* 7.7.2), after saying that the Arvernians had handed over Seronatus to the law (that is, presumably, to the *iudicium quinquevirale* in Rome), 'when he was lavishing whole provinces on the barbarians'. By doing so, Seronatus confirmed the apprehension Sidonius had felt before. In earlier letters he already had implored God to prevent the treasonous actions of this man (*Ep.* 5.13.4), who frequently visited the Visigothic court (*Ep.* 5.13.1, 2.1.1), who crowded the villas with barbarian *hospites* and who tried to replace Roman laws with those of the Visigoths (*Ep.* 2.1.3).

The fact that Seronatus actually carried out what he intended, while Arvandus' schemes had been nipped in the bud, may account for Sidonius' different attitude *vis-à-vis* the two men, apart from his personal feelings towards them. But those personal feelings were important enough. I have emphasized Sidonius' *amicitia* with Arvandus (*amicitia* in its good old political sense), for I venture to think that this tallies with Wolfram's observation 'that much of what strikes us as high-level politics and Romano-Gothic animosity was in reality a function of intergroup rivalries within Gaul's leading stratum' (1988: 187). It should also be noted that some time had passed between the trials of Arvandus and Seronatus. Seronatus is first mentioned in letters dating from the end of 469 and the beginning of 470 (*Ep.* 5.13 and 2.1; Sidonius, ed. Loyen, 1970: II, 246, 256), but the letter to bishop Graecus of Marseilles (*Ep.* 7.7), containing the passage on Seronatus' conviction and death, was written in 475 (ed. Loyen, 1970: II, xx). That letter, it is true, furnishes only a *terminus ante quem* for Seronatus' trial, which may have taken place at any time between 470 and 475. I think a date near 475 more probable (Heinzelmann, 1982: 692). For the moment, however, I am more concerned with Sidonius than with Seronatus.

If Sidonius had ever thought that a *modus vivendi* could be established with the Visigothic king Euric, by 475 he must certainly have lost all his illusions. Clermont Ferrand had been besieged several times and Euric was on the verge of taking possession of the Auvergne. Small wonder that in such circumstances Sidonius harboured a bitter grudge against anyone who had collaborated with the barbarian enemy. But the same Sidonius who, understandably, did not forgive Seronatus for his dealings with Euric, wrote, within a year of the aforementioned letter to bishop Graecus, a very friendly letter to the orator and poet Lampridius, who was in favour with that same Euric and lived as a citizen in his kingdom. The letter includes a poem in which the Visigothic king is addressed thus: 'it is your bands, Euric, that are called for, so that the Garonne, strong in its warlike settlers, may defend the dwindled Tiber' (*Ep.* 8.9.5, 42–4; cf. Harries, above p. 299). *Tempora mutantur.*

Times indeed had changed for Sidonius Apollinaris. In 468, when he was confronted with the Arvandus affair, he proudly held the office of prefect of the city of Rome, an office which he had obtained as a reward for a panegyric on the emperor Anthemius. As holder of one of the most distinguished offices a Roman noble could obtain, and on friendly terms with the emperor, Sidonius, we can imagine, looked forward confidently to the future. This may have influenced his view in the case of Arvandus and may have mollified his attitude towards his *amicus*. Perhaps, if the Arvandus affair had taken place later, Sidonius would have been harsher. In 475, when Sidonius, then a bishop, mentioned the conviction of Seronatus, he had personally experienced the disasters which had recently befallen Gaul as a result of Euric's aggression, and he anxiously foresaw what was still to come. After another year, which brought exile and imprisonment, he felt compelled to humiliate himself and write a flattering poem in honour of the very barbarian who was the root of all evil (Rouche, 1977: I, 19ff.; Wolfram, 1980: 219ff.; Teillet, 1984: 185ff.). Euric had won the day. Arvandus and Seronatus, although their choice for Euric had brought disaster to themselves, had chosen the winning side when they decided to enter into relations with the Visigoths.

I do not find it hard to call the relations which Arvandus and Seronatus maintained with the Visigoths 'treasonable' or, to follow

Loyen (1963: 437), to categorize the pair as 'quislings'. Not every attempt to deal with an enemy should be called treason; and there are various ways of coming to terms with former foes, depending on time and circumstances. It would be absurd, for instance, to rank the poems of Lampridius or Sidonius for Euric on a par with the activities of Arvandus and Seronatus, or to condemn every effort to find a *modus vivendi* with the Visigoths (who, after all, had lived in Gaul since the early fifth century). As regards Arvandus and Seronatus, however, in my view such a designation is justified. I assume that Sidonius' information, though biased and not in all respects clear, is basically trustworthy; and for what Arvandus and Seronatus intended and partly put into practice I can find no words other than treason and collaboration.

As far as we can judge, the motives of the two men were purely selfish. Unfortunately Sidonius is not very explicit on this, but he suggests that they both were driven by greed and financial problems (*Ep.* 1.7.3, 2.1.2–3, 5.13.2–4). Arvandus, perhaps, nourished higher aspirations. Further information is lacking, unless we should take into consideration the fact that Seronatus is called 'the Catiline of our age' (*Ep.* 2.1.1) and that Arvandus belonged to what Sidonius calls a plebeian family (*Ep.* 1.7.11). But I would prefer to refrain from speculation concerning their possible leadership of a pro-Visigoth party representing a movement of malcontents, including the lower classes, against the aristocracy (Yver, 1896: 21ff.): the evidence for it is too scanty (Stevens, 1933: 106). A more important question is whether the activities of Arvandus and Seronatus were unique.

In an interesting section devoted to, *inter alia*, defection to the barbarians, de Ste Croix remarks, citing the cases of Arvandus and Seronatus as the only examples he knows, that 'at the very highest level of society, needless to say, any outright treasonable conduct, betraying the empire to a "barbarian" ruler, was almost unknown' (1981: 486). Broadly speaking, I find this unexceptionable. However, when one comes to consider the behaviour of men like Vincentius (*PLRE* II, Vincentius 3), *magister militum* in the service of Euric, or Victorius (*PLRE* II, Victorius 4), another high army officer who served the Visigoths and for a time governed the Auvergne for Euric (cf. Heather, above pp. 91f.), one cannot help thinking that defection to the barbarians was not restricted to Arvandus and Seronatus alone, and that there was perhaps a 'climate of treason' in late fifth-century Gaul.

VIII

Conclusion

Most of the historical strands identified and investigated in preceding papers are drawn together by *Van Dam*, using fifth-century Gaul as a case-study in an assessment of contemporary thinking with regard to the Pirenne Thesis. Eschewing the modern tendency to discuss the Pirenne Thesis within the constraints of reconstruction of patterns of trade, Van Dam pays close attention to the personal experiences of four of the best-known Gauls of the age – Paulinus of Pella, Germanus of Auxerre, Salvian, and Sidonius Apollinaris. He points up, in the context of individual careers, issues and processes now familiar to us: authorial concerns; the neglect of Gaul in, and her eventual dismissal from, imperial political and military thinking; the deleterious effects of the invasions of 406–7 and their repercussions; the arrival of the Visigoths; the development of internal frontiers; the growth of private estates; continuing social disharmony; flight both away from and towards the troubled periphery; aristocratic retreat into religious devotion; restrictions imposed upon still lively aristocratic imperial ambitions that led to usurpation, treason and the setting up of personal realms; the compensation that was to be found in episcopal office; continuing ecclesiastical contact with Italy, to be set against the rise of the local bishop-protector; and, finally, accommodation with, and even the beginnings of appreciation of, the ever more successful barbarian kings. The general impression here, as throughout the volume, is one of a complex and multi-faceted society subject to chronic disruption and under great strain.

In part this strain may be interpreted as an aberration in the so far relatively harmonious relationship between the Roman empire and its Gallic provinces, explicable in terms of the specific political, military and social circumstances of the late fourth and fifth centuries. However, this should not be taken to signify that the country was lost piecemeal: that it slipped away from Roman control as a result of a series of relatively small mistakes and misfortunes, which with more application and more luck might have been overcome. Gaul should not be regarded as belonging automatically to the Roman world. The keystone of the Roman imperial structure was Roman military power; once this was damaged or removed the whole building was doomed to fall. Elton and Drinkwater have already drawn attention to the long-term significance of the Rhine frontier, arguing that it was the presence of a strong Roman garrison on this river that both ensured the safety of Gaul and gave the very concept of 'Roman' Gaul – a country united under imperial rule from the Rhine to the Pyrenees and from the Atlantic to the Alps – form and existence. Once the Rhine was lost to Rome – whether early in the fifth century or after the death of Aëtius – the rest was bound to follow: 'One either held all of Gaul, or none of it.'

Van Dam, by considering events in the perspective of the current debate concerning the exact date and circumstances of the transformation of the ancient into the Medieval world, and so appreciably extending his historical field of vision, is able to take a wider view, and to propose a much deeper cause for the growing instability in Gallo-imperial relations in the fifth century. He argues that the north and north-east of the country was its natural centre of gravity from pre-Roman into Roman times. At their height, Roman arms were able both to subdue Gaul and to counteract her tendency to fall away from the Mediterranean-based empire; but, as this power failed, the land settled once again into its proper position, facing north – to the North Sea and the Baltic – and slipped into its old, fragmented, pattern of government.

One might add that the loss of Africa, the catastrophic effects of which on the political, military and fiscal strength of the western empire are a thread running through this volume, could perhaps be seen as yet another stage in the ancient world's reversion to, borrowing Van Dam's words, its natural 'astounding diversity', and a further reflection of the way in which 'the Roman empire had imposed an artificial political unity' upon it.

CHAPTER 28

The Pirenne thesis and fifth-century Gaul

R. Van Dam

Henri Pirenne's ideas about the transition from the ancient to the Medieval world remain important still fifty years after their publication in his *Mohammed and Charlemagne*. In this book Pirenne identified two fundamental processes. One was the fragmentation of the Mediterranean world following the break-up of the Roman empire; the other was the rise of northern Europe. Pirenne's genius was to link the two. According to him, the expansion of Islam after the mid seventh century and not the Germanic invasions of the fifth and sixth centuries had led to the disintegration of the old Roman world; and once western Europe lost its Mediterranean contacts a Carolingian kingdom centered in northern France and Germany became dominant: 'without Mohammed Charlemagne would have been inconceivable' (1939: 234; epigram first published in 1922: 86).

Two obvious consequences of Pirenne's ideas were to prolong the survival of Roman culture and institutions through the Merovingian period and to postpone the appearance of a distinctly Medieval society until the rise of the Carolingians. Pirenne argued for the survival of what he called 'Romania' in different ways. He claimed that the early barbarian kingdoms were absolutist and secular, and thus similar to the Roman empire; he insisted upon the persistence of international commerce in the Mediterranean by arguing that the west continued to acquire distinctively eastern commodities (among which he slyly included the epidemics of the sixth century); and he argued that the Germans contributed nothing to Gallic intellectual life. Although he conceded that a distinctively Germanic civilization had immediately appeared in Anglo-Saxon England, in Gaul 'The new world had not lost the Mediterranean character of the ancient world.' 'There was nothing to take its place.' (1939: 14, 45).

Even though many scholars have found what is now called the Pirenne Thesis very suggestive, most have disagreed with it (and with

321

each other). Critics have argued that Merovingian society had already adopted specifically German characteristics, that the Merovingians already had strong interests in the North Sea, that the Muslims were incapable of blockading the Mediterranean, that Gallic ports continued to participate in Mediterranean trade after the eighth century, and that Pirenne overlooked regional variations (Hübinger, 1968; Barnish, 1989). The sincerest form of disagreement is imitation: some critics retain the connection between the closing of the Mediterranean and the rise of northern Europe but locate it in another century. Baynes (1929: 230ff.), for instance, argued that the writings of Gregory of Tours indicated that sixth-century Gaul was isolated from the Byzantine east because king Gaiseric and his Vandals had broken the unity of the Mediterranean already during the fifth century. With his appropriation of Roman imperial ceremonies and his interests in northern Gaul, Clovis then assumed the roles that Pirenne had assigned to Charlemagne: without Gaiseric Clovis would have been inconceivable.

Other critics have analyzed specific aspects of Pirenne's thesis. In particular, Lopez discussed the four 'disappearances' of papyrus, luxury cloths, spices, and gold currency that Pirenne had used to postpone the closing of the Mediterranean. Lopez concluded that the disappearance of these commodities in the west 'were not contemporary either with the Arab advance or with each other; indeed, it is not exact to speak of disappearances' (1943: 15). Although his important article has itself come in for criticism, one aspect of its subsequent influence is particularly noteworthy. Because Lopez emphasized primarily the circulation of specific commodities, much subsequent argument about the Pirenne Thesis has rather narrowed the discussion by stressing simply objects of trade.

This narrow focus became dominant particularly among numismatists and archaeologists. Bolin (1953), for instance, redirected attention away from the Mediterranean toward the Baltic Sea and Russia by claiming that the rising influence of northern France presupposed not commercial isolation but rather expansion. By then trying to demonstrate a correlation between Carolingian and Muslim coinage, he proposed that the Carolingians were in commercial contact with the caliphate by way of this 'backdoor' route through Russia. The Muslim conquests had therefore not isolated the Carolingians by blockading the Mediterranean; instead, they had made possible the expansion of the Carolingian economy through mutual (even if indirect) commerce. Although critics responded that internal politics and the financial needs of the Carolingians could alone account for fluctuations in the weight of coins and that their trade was in fact highly localized in northern Europe (Himly, 1955; Morrison, 1963), archaeologists continue to revive the notion that Carolingian trade was international. Hodges and Whitehouse (1983) have again stressed the importance of commerce in the North Sea during the Merovingian and Carolingian periods, and they specifically connect both the prosperity of northern France from the later eighth century and its financial decline from the mid ninth century to political developments in the Abbasid caliphate. Although their deductions are based on evidence from only a few archaeological sites that are then linked together in a chain of chronological coincidences that stretches from Frisia to the Persian Gulf and beyond, their conclusions again contradict Pirenne: Franks and Muslims were in contact, not isolated.

The lasting positive impact of both numismatic and archaeological arguments has been to emphasize the role of what Braudel (1972: 188) once called those 'other, northern Mediterraneans', the North and Baltic Seas, in the shaping of early Medieval Europe. But another legacy is more unsettling, and that is the continued emphasis on economic, and specifically commercial, history. For these critiques also presuppose two theoretical assumptions that link up with current debates over the nature of the ancient economy. As in the Roman empire, so still during the early Medieval period, kings, great aristocrats and bishops apparently derived most of their revenues and wealth from the land; except perhaps locally, trade was not influential enough to modify this resolutely agrarian economy (Duby, 1974: 106). Recently some Roman historians have dissented by proposing that taxation had in fact stimulated trade between frontier and interior provinces (Drinkwater, 1983: 128f.), and that archaeological evidence demonstrates a much higher volume and therefore a greater impact of trade on Roman society in general (Greene, 1986: 170). So in explanations of the transformation of the ancient world some current discussions likewise stress the significance of markets and trade networks as somehow generating a 'sudden and massive economic expansion'. 'The importance of trade to the Carolingian Renaissance seems to be beyond doubt' (Hodges and Whitehouse, 1983: 108, 171).

A second related assumption concerns the motivations behind what archaeologists in particular call 'trade'. The 'minimalist' perspective on the ancient economy should be so dubbed not because it necessarily minimizes the scale of the exchange of goods, but because it minimizes the existence of genuinely economizing motivations and instead includes ostensibly autonomous economic behavior in 'situations that were not in themselves of an economic nature' (Polanyi, Arensberg and Pearson, 1957: 242), and then explains that behavior instead by means of a 'common cultural-psychological framework' (Finley, 1973: 34). In the Roman empire, for instance, political necessity compelled the government to provide for the feeding of certain large cities and the provisioning of its frontier troops by means of a tied trade that operated largely outside the constraints of market demands (Jones, 1964: 827ff.). Even if some entrepreneurial trade did 'piggy-back' on this immense state-administered trade (Wickham, 1988), after the decline in the population of Rome and the eventual departure of the large garrisons from the Rhine frontier the only comparable political imperative to stimulate market-oriented trade in fifth-century Gaul would have been the local obligations to provide for the occupying armies of federate Visigoths and Burgundians. As already under the Roman empire, the social and cultural priorities of kings, large landowners and ecclesiastics still minimized strictly entrepreneurial transactions: 'Traders ... were fundamentally agents, dependents or clients of the rich, whose requirements, not abstract economic forces, dictated their activities' (Whittaker, 1983: 173). In another critique of the Pirenne thesis Grierson (1959) argued that the circulation of commodities in the early Medieval world was not necessarily an indication of a market economy, because cultural obligations and social relationships defined the dominant transactional modes. Not trade driven by supply and demand or the pursuit of markets but rather diplomatic subsidies, annual tributes, war indemnities, plunder, ransom, charity, entertainment, and the simple exchange of gifts could account for the circulation of most goods. The difference is one of attitudes and values, about which numismatics and archaeology have really little to contribute. If the circulation of commodities should therefore be interpreted as evidence for society and culture in general and not for an autonomous economy, then the transformation of the ancient world is also more of a cultural, social, and political problem than a strictly economic and commercial one; and if that conclusion is accepted, then, like Pirenne himself, we should again turn to the literary sources.

On any account, whether of continuity and survival or of discontinuity and interruption, an evaluation of the fifth century is crucial: the original *Cambridge Medieval History* began at 324, the new *Cambridge Medieval History* will begin at 500. Whatever we may think about Pirenne's conclusions, he at least posed some of the right questions about late antique Gaul. Pirenne claimed that the connection between Gaul and the eastern Mediterranean survived, and used it as proof of the continuity of Roman culture and society under the Merovingians; and he delayed the shift in priority from southern to northern Europe and therefore also the rise of the Middle Ages until the Carolingians. In order to evaluate these orientations, let us consider the perspectives of four fifth-century Gauls, Paulinus of Pella, Germanus of Auxerre, Salvian and Sidonius.

Although born overseas in Macedonia in 376, Paulinus grew up in Bordeaux as the favored son of an aristocratic family, with every expectation of repeating his ancestors' successes at acquiring offices in the imperial administration. But because of the barbarian invasions during the winter of 406–7 his life changed dramatically. He briefly served a usurping emperor supported by the Visigoths, before being forced to flee; after losing most of his family he then moved to Marseille; at the end of his life during the 450s he claimed to be virtually destitute. By then his only consolation was his conversion to Christianity.

Several aspects of his life are relevant to the debate over the Pirenne Thesis. Paulinus had contacts with the eastern empire, owing to his father's service as vicar in Macedonia, and even claimed that the east was his 'second homeland' (*Eucharisticus* 271–2). Eventually he inherited estates in Epirus and Greece, to which he considered returning after losing his ancestral lands in western Gaul (*Eucharisticus* 273, 413–21). But upon second thought he decided not to move, because his wife was afraid of the sea voyage. In this case east and west seem to have been split, not because of any blockade in the Mediterranean, but because of a man's concern for his family.

Paulinus' intention of moving to the east was hence only a passing fancy; instead, his life and thinking became resolutely more parochial and more Christian. Although his sons may have returned to Bordeaux to make careers in the ecclesiastical hierarchy and at the Visigothic court, the wider horizons available to some Gallic aristocrats during the fourth century had now disappeared (Matthews,

1975: 348ff.). By the end of his life Paulinus was concerned simply with hiding the embarrassment of his present poverty and reminiscing about his past lifestyle. During his early years he had lived out a 'Roman tradition' (*Eucharisticus* 70) that included an education in classical literature, a distinguished marriage, and even the use of Arabian perfumes (*Eucharisticus* 148). But after losing his Gallic estates Paulinus turned to Christianity, in part because in it he had rediscovered that 'ancient tradition' (*Eucharisticus* 465).

The rise of a Christianity that incorporated aspects of traditional aristocratic lifestyle and classical culture does not fit neatly into discussions of either continuity or change. Although by the end of his life Paulinus may have thought that Christianity provided him with his best link to his earlier life and its values, other Gauls, such as Rutilius Namatianus, were dreaming of a revival of the old order that did not include Christianity. Pirenne likewise largely ignored Christianity when discussing the survival of Roman culture and institutions; he thought instead that the Church became a vital influence only later because of the connection established between the papacy and the Carolingians during the eighth century, and that this later reorientation of the papacy was a clear demonstration of the rise of northern Gaul. Yet this northern focus for Christianity was not such a late development, as the career of Germanus of Auxerre indicates.

Germanus was Paulinus' contemporary. After service as a general, he suddenly in the early fifth century became bishop at his home town of Auxerre and adopted a harshly ascetic lifestyle. The episcopal career of Germanus seems to bear out both Paulinus' satisfaction upon finding ancient traditions being preserved in the Church and Pirenne's insistence that Roman culture survived the coming of the barbarians; for, although Pirenne never mentioned Germanus, he would certainly have been pleased that even after his consecration Germanus continued to wear his old general's cloak (*V. Germani* 4, 43). And despite his ascetic life Germanus continued to use his earlier 'Roman' skills: his legal training helped him make episcopal decisions, his skill at rhetoric enhanced his preaching, and even his military experience came in handy during a battle in Britain.

But in contrast to Paulinus' limited perspectives, Germanus' extensive journeys linked Auxerre with both north and south. Once, perhaps twice, he traveled to assist Christians in Britain; he also traveled to Arles in order to visit the prefect of Gaul, and finally to Ravenna to solicit the imperial court. Germanus' willingness to travel both to Britain and to Ravenna is hence a preview of the later connections between Italy and England that would eventually influence the Carolingians.

Paulinus and Germanus may have been contemporaries, but their attitudes obviously differed. Paulinus worried about barbarians such as the Visigoths, while Germanus was more concerned about invasions by demons; strongly nostalgic about his once wealthy lifestyle, Paulinus seems always to have been looking backwards, while Germanus was so deeply involved in the welfare of his and other communities that his life became a model for future bishops. Yet both men seem already to have shared an awareness of a shattering discontinuity in their lives. Paulinus singled out the invasions of 406–7 as decisive, and a few years later Germanus emphasized the importance of his consecration as bishop by publicly adopting an ascetic lifestyle. The obvious question for modern historians, of course, is whether we are therefore allowed to deduce a more general cultural and social discontinuity in fifth-century Gaul from these acknowledgements of personal discontinuity.

Other fifth-century Gauls stressed also the interruptions in their lives. Salvian, who belonged to the next generation after Paulinus and Germanus, was from northern Gaul and had once witnessed the destruction of Trier. But at some point he had followed the lead of the prefect and his court (as well as of other refugees) and moved to Provence; everywhere else, he claimed, the Roman state was barely breathing (*De Gubernatione Dei* 4.30). In southern Gaul he eventually served as a priest at Marseille, where about the middle of the century he composed a long-winded treatise offering his interpretation of the barbarian invasions.

Salvian's primary concern was with the consequences of the invasions in northern and western Gaul (7.50). A limited political perspective matched this non-Mediterranean geographical perspective; despite living close to Italy, he mentioned 'emperors' only once, and despite his proximity to Arles, he (perhaps) referred to prefects only once (4.21, 6.85). Instead, he stressed the roles of provincial governors, municipal magistrates and, especially, local aristocrats. These 'very powerful men' (4.20) were taking advantage of circumstances first to confiscate land and build up estates so huge that they no longer knew their dimensions (*Ad Ecclesiam* 1.18), and second to acquire control over men in dire straits, to whom they could now 'sell' their patronage (*De Gubernatione Dei* 5.39). Salvian had firsthand experience of this rapacity: one powerful man whom he petitioned had instead laughed at him (4.74–5). In a Gaul where decurions were noted for their plundering, soldiers for their pillaging, and the wealthy for colluding with imperial magistrates over the allotment, collection and remission of taxes, only these powerful local aristocrats benefited.

The Gaul that Salvian described was therefore a preview of Medieval France; but it is also possible to think of it as a reversion to a pre-Roman state of affairs, as if the barbarian invasions had essentially erased the effects of both the conquests of Julius Caesar and the consequent Romanization in Gaul. Regional fragmentation had reappeared, imperial authority and public services had lapsed, and private initiative had become dominant. Salvian seems not to have been particularly sorry at the disappearance of the Roman empire. His severe criticism of the lingering obsession with circus games, for instance, was not due simply to his moral strictures (6.38); for, because circus games were also closely associated with the presence and generosity of emperors, his reprimand can also be taken as oblique criticism of any revival of imperial authority. In fact, Salvian even claimed that many Gauls were now so disheartened by events that they simply rejected their Roman citizenship as 'cheap and repulsive' (5.22). Five centuries earlier Gauls had claimed that the campaigns of Julius Caesar heralded the end of their ancestral liberty and the imposition of Roman slavery (Julius Caesar, *BG* 3.8). Under the Empire, Roman citizenship had proved to be a form of liberty after all (*De Gubernatione Dei* 5.44). But by the middle of the fifth century, in a pointed reversal, Salvian claimed that in Gaul 'Romans' now actually preferred to live among other barbarians (5.37).

Salvian's comments are often difficult to evaluate, primarily because he indulged in so much moralizing overstatement. He seems to have distinguished, not southern Gaul from northern Gaul or even a Roman Gaul from a barbarian Gaul, as rather a moral Gaul from an immoral Gaul. According to him, cities in his native north-eastern Gaul deserved their misfortunes because of their vices (6.39), and cities in south-western Gaul, that 'image of Paradise' for which Paulinus of Pella still pined, were now openly 'brothels' (7.8, 16). Pirenne thought that 'Romania' survived the barbarian invasions. Salvian would have agreed with the notion of survival, since he conceded that these 'Roman' immoralities were certainly not new (4.54). But Pirenne also argued that the Germans wanted to preserve

Roman civilization. Salvian would have shuddered at that claim, since he thought that the barbarians could improve Gallic society by raising the level of justice and chastity (5.36, 7.107).

Salvian was not alone in trying to come to grips with the meaning and the consequences of the barbarian invasions. In fact, he wrote his treatise as a response to people who were concerned that God too might have followed the lead of the emperor in withdrawing his presence (1.1, 2.1). But if Salvian had attempted to answer people's anxieties about the presence of God, then other Gauls would make one last attempt to do something about the presence of an emperor. A few years after Salvian composed his treatise, the Visigoths and some Romans from central Gaul combined to support Avitus, a Gallic aristocrat, as emperor. When Avitus marched to Italy in 455, his son-in-law Sidonius accompanied him. Sidonius' father and grandfather had already served in the Roman imperial administration as prefects of Gaul; now he had the opportunity to deliver an oration at Rome in honor of the new emperor. Nor was this his only encounter with emperors or visit to Rome. He dined with the emperor Majorian at Arles in 461; he represented Clermont before the emperor Anthemius at Rome; and in 468 he served as prefect of Rome. Yet Avitus was to be the last Gallic emperor before Charlemagne, and even Sidonius could not ignore the ominous presence of barbarians. Upon his return to Gaul he became bishop of Clermont, whose 'Roman walls' (*Ep.* 7.6.6) were soon under siege. Although the Visigoths had been settled in south-western Gaul for decades, previously they had generally supported the imperial administration. But their new king Euric had expansionist ambitions, and in 475 the imperial court in Italy finally ceded Clermont to him in exchange for Provence.

Sidonius was most dismayed. Living near the barbarians was distressing enough; as a classical gentleman accustomed to a Mediterranean diet he was bemused to find Burgundians using rancid butter – as a hairdressing! (*Carm.* 12.7). But outright abandonment by an imperial court now concerned only about its 'Italian empire' was shattering (*V. Epiphanii* 80). Pirenne minimized the impact of the Visigoths by claiming that they, like other barbarians settled in Gaul, simply lost their 'heroic characteristics' (1939: 43); and many Roman aristocrats, including some of Sidonius' friends, did in fact preserve their prerogatives within the Visigothic kingdom. But Pirenne also ignored the devastating psychological impact of this betrayal on aristocrats like Sidonius, who had genuinely wanted to participate in a

Roman empire. As one argument for the survival of a Roman society, Pirenne (1939: 73) claimed that the eastern empire continued to dominate the policies of the western barbarian kingdoms. When in Rome Sidonius had certainly acknowledged the influence of Constantinople, the 'Rome of the east' that had ended the division of the Empire by sending the emperor Anthemius to Italy in 467 (*Carm.* 2.30–1, 65). But in Gaul the eastern empire had virtually no impact; an imperial constitution issued at Constantinople was finally introduced in Gaul only twenty-five years later (*Ep.* 8.6.7), and some Gallic aristocrats never conceded the hegemony of the eastern court. Instead, they had simply dismissed Anthemius as a 'Greek emperor' and preferred an alliance with the Visigoths (*Ep.* 1.7.5). By 476 even Sidonius looked for assistance not to the east, not even to Italy, but to western Gaul and king Euric, who was now to help to defend both Rome and even Constantinople (*Ep.* 8.9.5).

For Sidonius had always been mistaken about the possibility of resurrecting Roman control. Not only were imperial resources quite restricted, but many Gallic aristocrats had already begun to ensure their local positions without relying on connections with a Roman empire. Sidonius himself now stressed the precise use of 'old fashioned' Latin (*Ep.* 3.14.2, 8.16.2) as a distinguishing characteristic of a civilized aristocracy, and he had become a bishop. Other aristocrats served at the royal courts of barbarian kingdoms; patronized Christian relic cults; acquired huge estates and elegant villas; indulged in conspicuous consumption through feasts, gifts, and the acquisition of luxury goods; developed extensive networks of personal alliances, as documented through the exchange of letters; and even kept bands of armed retainers as virtual private armies (*Ep.* 3.3.7). Pirenne considered Sidonius another example of the survival of intellectual life within the barbarian kingdoms (1939: 122). Although Sidonius certainly tried to live up to that reputation, he may also have been the last Roman in Gaul, because many of the tactics that fifth-century aristocrats now used to promote themselves looked back to a pre-Roman Gaul that had featured great men and their dependents and forward to a Medieval France with similar characteristics.

Northern and southern Gaul, eastern and western Mediterranean, Romanness, Germanness, Christianity: too many divergent viewpoints emerge, sometimes from the same author, to support any particular grand Thesis. But precisely those divergences are worth brief consideration before returning to some sweeping conclusions. Too often discussion of the Pirenne Thesis has been reduced to consideration of coins or artifacts or finds; the people involved have been forgotten. Paulinus was unable to leave his wife and his family in order to reclaim his estates in the east; but he still ended up destitute and alone. As a bishop Germanus effectively abandoned his wife (*V. Germani* 2); he was therefore free to travel both to Britain and to Italy. Salvian and his wife did not communicate with her pagan parents for seven years (*Ep.* 4); he was likewise alienated from current events, a refugee dissatisfied with both imperial authority and the local patronage of great men but almost impressed by the barbarians. A statue at Rome commemorated Sidonius' oratorical skills (*Ep.* 9.16.3); but at the end of his life he was so astounded to discover that a Gallic friend had learned to speak German that he had to advise him to keep practising his Latin (*Ep.* 5.5). Love, dedication, estrangement, surprise: such ordinary emotions were the great catalysts in these men's lives, and neither Pirenne nor any of his critics has yet been able to account for these intimate habits of the heart in explanations of the shift from the ancient Gaul to Medieval France.

Was fifth-century Gaul ancient or Medieval? Even before beginning to write his great history (Ghosh, 1983: 18), Edward Gibbon had hinted that the notion of decline and fall might be a misconception, because the fragmentation of great empires and the ineffectiveness of imperial administrations were endemic features of the ancient world: 'instead of inquiring why the Roman empire was destroyed, we should rather be surprised that it had subsisted so long' (1912: IV, 161). This preoccupation seems to re-emerge in his later uncertainty over whether he had chosen an early enough starting point for his history. Beginning in the 'most happy and prosperous' period of the second century had perhaps been misleading: 'Should I not have deduced the decline of the Empire from the civil Wars that ensued after the fall of Nero or even from the tyranny which succeeded the reign of Augustus? Alas! I should: but of what avail is this tardy knowledge?' (Craddock, 1972: 338). Perhaps we ought to approach some of the problems posed by the Pirenne Thesis with as much concern over antecedents as consequences, since Pirenne's ideas are as consequential for ancient historians as for Medieval historians.

First, for too long the notion that the Mediterranean imposed a geographical unity has hypnotized ancient historians. Strabo's emphasis on the political and cultural unity of 'our interior sea' has blinkered modern historians as effectively as ancient Romans (Rubin, 1986: 15ff.), since the imposition of a Roman empire, the domination of a single emperor, and the spread of classical culture seem to have reinforced that geographic unity. Yet Strabo's account was equally a demonstration of the astounding diversity ringing the Mediterranean, and in many respects the Roman empire had imposed an artifical political unity on the Mediterranean world, in particular by linking with the Latin west a Greek east whose historical and cultural roots were firmly in the Near East. The regionalism characteristic of the Medieval Mediterranean was hence perhaps more normal than the apparent unity of the Roman Mediterranean. Once modern ancient historians begin to downplay the superficial political unity of the Mediterranean under the Roman empire, then the 'break-up' of the Mediterranean during late antiquity becomes less of a problem.

Second, for too long modern historians have adopted the same perspective as the writers of our literary sources, that is, a view from the political center that is uncomprehending or dismissive of events on the periphery. Pacification, Romanization, the spread of classical culture and a Mediterranean lifestyle: we modern historians blandly use these benign concepts to conceal the disruption required to transform Gaul into an apparent hinterland of the Mediterranean world that 'flooded' the empire with its revenues (cf. Josephus, *BJ* 2.371–3). In this Mediterranean perspective under-civilized northern Gaul remained marginal to the Roman empire; hence its later predominance seems to demand an explanation. In fact, Julius Caesar had noted immediately that the Three Gauls were orientated towards the north (*BG* 1.1, 4.20). Already, before his conquests, central and northern Gaul had extensive contacts with their own 'peripheral' regions such as Britain and Germany; from a northern perspective, as the German king Ariovistus disdainfully informed Caesar, Gaul was a province of Germany (*BG* 1.44), and formal incorporation into the Roman empire merely expanded its contacts with another, larger periphery consisting of southern Gaul and the Mediterranean (Haselgrove, 1987). Roman Gaul always retained this focus on its central and northern regions, ensured at the very least by the presence of legions on the Rhine frontier. When men worried about the appearance of a 'Gallic empire' in the first century, they thought of northern Gaul; because of barbarian pressure on the Rhine frontier during the later third century, their exact worries came true. Thereafter northern and central Gaul remained politically significant too. Throughout most of the fourth century a legitimate imperial court resided at Trier; during the later fifth century some maverick Roman aristocrats had established themselves as 'kings' in northern Gaul (James, 1988a: 67ff.), until eventually the Merovingian Franks came to dominate. During the subsequent decline of the Merovingians and the rise of the Carolingians the 'central' perspective had clearly moved to northern Gaul, since then the 'peripheral' regions that were thought to be in revolt were Aquitaine and Provence. For modern medievalists it is therefore the earlier orientation toward the Mediterranean south that should require explanation, not the reorientation toward the north as Pirenne suggested.

Ancient historians should likewise not take for granted the Mediterranean orientation of Gaul, even of southern Gaul, under the Roman empire. One response to the Pirenne Thesis therefore lies in considering the incorporation of western, central, and northern Gaul into the Roman empire as the 'distortion'; in this grand perspective of long-term rhythms, fifth-century Gaul was simply reverting to a 'normal' orientation away from the Mediterranean world. Some Gallo-Roman aristocrats nevertheless regretted the loss of that Mediterranean connection. Sidonius in fact hoped for another Julius Caesar who would reconquer Gaul for the Roman empire (Van Dam, 1985: 174). Five centuries earlier everyone had known when Caesar had arrived because of the brilliance of his general's cloak (*BG* 7.88). But after the middle of the fifth century the only men in Gaul wearing the scarlet cloak of a Roman general were local aristocrats (Sidonius, *Ep.* 4.9.3), Christian bishops such as Germanus, and a barbarian king such as Clovis (GT *HF* 2.38). Aristocrats, bishops, kings: the paradox of fifth-century Gaul is that these distinctively Medieval men were still wearing distinctively Roman attire.

References

PRIMARY SOURCES

Note: all references to Eunapius, Olympiodorus and Priscus in the text are derived from BLOCKLEY, 1983. Texts are listed under authors' names, except for Saints' Lives or Anonymi, when the title is used.

AMMIANUS MARCELLINUS, *Res Gestae*, ed. W. Seyfarth (2 vols.), Leipzig, 1978.

ANDERSON, 1936, 1965. See Sidonius.

AUGUSTINE, *De Civitate Dei*, ed B. Dombart and A. Kalb, *Corpus Christianorum*, Series Latina 47–8, Darmstadt, 1981.

AUSONIUS, ed. and tr. H. G. Evelyn-White (2 vols.) (Loeb edition), London and Cambridge, MA, 1919–21.

AVITUS OF VIENNE, *Opera*, ed. R. Peiper, *MGH*, *AA* 6.2, Berlin, 1883.

BORIUS, 1965. See *V.Germani*.

BURGESS, forthcoming. See Hydatius.

CAESARIUS OF ARLES, *Opera Omnia* I–II, ed. G. Morin, Maredsous, 1937–42.

Sermons, vol. I (1–80), tr. M. M. Mueller, New York, 1956.

Sermons au peuple, ed. and tr. M.-J. Delage, Sources Chrétiennes 175, Paris, 1971.

CARMEN DE PROVIDENTIA DEI, ed. M. P. McHugh, Catholic University of America Patristic Studies, Washington, 1964.

CASSIODORUS, *Chronicle*, ed. T. Mommsen, *MGH*, *AA* 11, 109–61, Berlin, 1894 (reprinted Munich, 1981).

Variae, ed. T. Mommsen, *MGH*, *AA* 12, Berlin, 1894.

CAVALLIN, 1952. See *V. Hilarii* and *V. Honorati*.

CHRON. GALL. A. CCCCLII, ed. T. Mommsen, *MGH*, *AA* 9, Berlin, 1892 (reprinted Munich, 1981).

CHRON. GALL. A. DXI, ed. T. Mommsen, *MGH*, *AA* 9, Berlin, 1892 (reprinted Munich, 1981).

CLAUDIUS CLAUDIANUS, *Carmina*, ed. T. Birt, *MGH*, *AA* 10, Berlin, 1892.

CLAUDIUS MAMERTUS, *De Statu Animae*, ed. A. Engelbrecht, *CSEL* 11, Vienna, 1885.

CLOVER, 1971. See Merobaudes.

CODEX JUSTINIANUS, ed. P. Krüger, *Corpus Iuris Civilis*, Berlin, 1954.

References

CODEX THEODOSIANUS, ed. P. Krüger, Berlin, 1923–6.
The Theodosian Code and Novels and the Sirmondian Constitutions, ed. and tr. C. Pharr *et al.*, Princeton, 1952.
CODICO DE EURICO, ed. E. Alvaro d'Ors, Madrid, 1960.
CONCILIA GALLIAE A.314–A.506 [*Conc. Gall.* I], ed. C. Munier, *Corpus Christianorum*, Series Latina 148, Turnhout, 1963.
CONCILIA GALLIAE A.511–A.695 [*Conc. Gall.* II], ed. C. de Clercq, *Corpus Christianorum*, Series Latina 148A, Turnhout, 1963.
CONST. EXTR., ed. R. L. de Salis, *MGH, Legum* sectio 3.2, Hanover, 1892.
COUNCIL OF LYONS, YENNE, *Galliae Concilia, Concilia Hispaniae, PL* 84, 1862.
DELAGE, 1971. See Caesarius.
DIGESTUS, ed. T. Mommsen and P. Krüger, *Corpus Iuris Civilis* 1, Berlin, 1954.
DOTATIO SANCTAE ET INSIGNIS ECCLESIAE VIVARIENSIS [*Dotatio*], ed. C. Devic and J. Vaissette, *Histoire générale de Languedoc*, vol. II, 14–21, 1875.
ENNODIUS OF PAVIA, ed. F. Vogel, *MGH, AA* 7, Berlin, 1885.
EUCHERIUS OF LYON, *De Contemptu Mundi et Saecularis Philosophiae, PL* 50, 1846, 711–26.
De Laude Eremi, ed. C. Wotke, *CSEL* 31, 177–94, Vienna, 1894.
Instructiones, ed. C. Wotke, *CSEL* 31, 63–161, Vienna, 1894.
EUNAPIUS, in Blockley, 1983.
EXPOSITIO TOTIUS MUNDI ET GENTIUM, ed. and tr. J. Rougé, Sources Chrétiennes 124, Paris, 1966.
FAUSTUS OF RIEZ, *Epistulae ad Ruricium*, ed. G. Luetjohann, *MGH, AA* 8, Berlin, 1887.
FORMULARY OF ANGERS, ed. K. Zeumer, *MGH, Legum* sectio 5, Formulae Merov. et Karol. aevi, Berlin, 1886.
FREDEGAR, *Chronicae*, ed. B. Krusch, *MGM, SRM* 2, 1–193, Hanover, 1888.
The Fourth Book of the Chronicle of Fredegar with its Continuations, tr. J. M. Wallace-Hadrill, London, Edinburgh and New York, 1960.
GENNADIUS, *Hieronymi de Viris Inlustribus Liber. Accedit Genadii Catalogus Virorum Inlustrium*, ed. G. Herding, Leipzig, 1924.
GILDAS, *The Ruin of Britain and Other Works*, ed. and tr. M. Winterbottom, London, Chichester and Totowa, NJ, 1978.
GREGORY, POPE, *Gregorii I Papae Registrum Epistolarum*, ed. P. Ewald and L. M. Hartmann, *MGH, Ep.* 1, Berlin, 1887–99.
GREGORY OF TOURS, *Historiae Francorum*, ed. and tr. R. Buchner, *Gregor von Tours. Zehn Bücher Geschichten* (2nd edn), Berlin, 1967.
History of the Franks, tr. L. Thorpe, Harmondsworth and Baltimore, 1974.
History of the Franks, ed. and tr. B. Radice, New York, 1983.
Opera, ed. B. Krusch, G. Waitz and M. Bonnet, *MGH, SRM* 1, Hanover, 1885.

Libri Historiarum, ed. B. Krusch and W. Levison, *MGH, SRM* 1 (1), Hanover, 1951.

HERIGER, *Gesta Pontificum Tungrensium*, ed. R. Koepke, *MGH Scriptores* (fol.) 7, 161–89, Leipzig, 1925.

HILARY OF POITIERS, *Opera Omnia, PL* 10, 1845.

Opera, ed. E. Feder, *CSEL* 65, Vienna and Leipzig, 1916.

HYDATIUS, *Chronicle*, ed. T. Mommsen, *MGH, AA* 11, Berlin, 1894.

Hydace, Chronique, ed. and tr. A. Tranoy (2 vols.), Sources Chrétiennes 218–19, Paris, 1974.

Hydatii Limici Subdita et Anonymorum Complurium Consularia Constantinopolitana, ed. R. W. Burgess, forthcoming.

IBN KHALDUN, *The Muquaddimah, an Introduction to History*, tr. F. Rosenthal (3 vols.), London, 1958.

ISIDORE OF SEVILLE, *De Laude Spaniae et Historia vel Origo Gothorum*, ed. T. Mommsen, *MGH, AA* 11, Berlin, 1894 (reprinted Munich, 1981).

Etymologiarum sive Originum Libri xx, ed. W. M. Lindsay, (2 vols.), Oxford, 1911.

History of the Goths, Vandals and Suevi, tr. G. Donini and G. B. Ford, Leiden, 1970.

ITINERARIUM BURDIGALENSE, ed. P. Geyer and O. Conte, *Corpus Christianorum*, Series Latina 175, Turnhout, 1965.

ITINERARIUM EGERIAE, *Egérie, Journal de Voyage*, ed. and tr. P. Moravil, Sources Chrétiennes 296, Paris, 1982; *Egeria's Travels*, ed. and tr. J. Wilkinson, Warminster, 1981 (2nd edn.).

JEROME, *Commentariorum in Esaiam Libri* 10–11, *Corpus Christianorum*, Series Latina 73, Turnhout, 1963.

Epistolae, ed. I. Hilberg, *CSEL* 54–6, Vienna, 1910–18.

JOHN OF ANTIOCH, ed. C. Müller, *Fragmenta Historicorum Graecorum* 4, 535–622, Paris, 1851.

JOHN OF BICLARUM, *Chronica*, ed. T. Mommsen, *MGH, AA* 11, Berlin, 1894 (reprinted Munich, 1981).

JORDANES, *Gothic History in English Version*, tr. C. C. Mierow, 1915 (reprinted New York, 1960).

Opera, ed. T. Mommsen, *MGH, AA* 5, Berlin, 1882.

KRUSCH, 1896. See *V. Amatori*

LAGARRIGUE, 1975. See Salvian.

LEGES BURGUNDIONUM, ed. L. R. de Salis, *MGH, Legum* sectio 1.2.1, Hanover, 1892.

LEGES NOVELLAE AD THEODOSIANUM PERTINENTES, ed. P. M. Meyer, Berlin, 1905.

LEGES VISIGOTHORUM, ed. K. Zeumer, *MGH, Legum* sectio 1.1, Hanover, 1902.

ed. S. P. Scott, *The Visigothic Code*, Boston, 1910.

LEO I, POPE, *Epistolae, PL* 54, 1846, 593–1218.

LEX SALICA, ed. K. A. Eckhardt, *MGH, Legum* sectio 1.4, Hanover, 1962.

LIBER HISTORIAE FRANCORUM, ed. B. Krusch, *MGH, SRM* 2, 215–328, Hanover, 1888.

LOWE, E. A., *Codices Latini Antiquiores*, Oxford, 1934–71.

LOYEN, 1970. See Sidonius.

McHUGH, 1964. See *Carmen de Providentia Dei*.

MARIUS OF AVENCHES, *Chronica*, ed. T. Mommsen, *MGH, AA* 11, Berlin, 1894 (reprinted Munich, 1981).

MARTINE, 1968. See *V. Romani*.

MARTYROLOGIUM HIERONYMIANUM [Mart. Hieronym.], in H. Delehaye and H. Quentin (eds.), *Acta Sanctorum* nov. II, 2, 1931.

MEROBAUDES, ed. and tr. F. M. Clover, Transactions of the American Philosophical Society 61.1, Philadelphia, 1971.

MÜLLER, 1956. See Caesarius.

NARRATIO DE IMPERATORIBUS DOMUS VALENTINIANAE ET THEODOSIANAE, ed. T. Mommsen, *MGH, AA* 9, 615–66, Berlin, 1892 (reprinted Munich, 1981).

NENNIUS, *British History and the Welsh Annals*, ed. and tr. J. Morris, London, Chichester and Totowa, NJ, 1980.

NOTITIA DIGNITATUM, ed. O. Seeck, Frankfurt on Main, 1876 (reprinted 1962).

NOTITIA GALLIARUM [*Not. Gall.*], ed. T. Mommsen, *MGH, AA* 9, 552–612, Berlin, 1892.

OLYMPIODORUS, in Blockley, 1983.

ORIENTIUS, *Commonitorium*, *PL* 61, 1861.
  Commonitorium et Carmina Orientio Tributa, ed. C. A. Rapisarda, Catania, 1958.

ORIGEN, *Contra Celsum*, ed. and tr. M. Borret, Sources Chrétiennes 132, Paris, 1882.

OROSIUS, PAULUS, *Historiarum Adversum Paganos Libri* VII, ed. K. Zangemeister, *CSEL* 5, Vienna, 1882.

PANEGYRICI LATINI, ed. and tr. E. Galletier (3 vols.) (Budé edition), Paris, 1949–55.

PASSIO MEMORII, ed. B. Krusch, *MGH, SRM* 3, 101–4, Hanover, 1896.

PAUL THE DEACON, *Gesta Episcoporum Mettensium*, ed. G. H. Pertz, *MGH Scriptores* (fol.) 2, 262–8, Hanover, 1829.
  Historia Langobardorum, ed. L. Bethmann and G. Waitz, *MGH, SRL*, Hanover, 1878
  Historia Romana, ed. A. Crivellucci, Rome, 1914.

PAULINUS OF NOLA, *Epigramma*, ed. C. Schenkl, *CSEL* 16, 499–510, Vienna, 1888.
  Letters of St Paulinus of Nola, tr. P. G. Walsh (2 vols.), Ancient Christian Writers 35, London and Westminster, MD, 1966–7.

PAULINUS OF PELLA, *Eucharisticus*, ed. and tr. H. White, Ausonius, vol. II (Loeb edition), London and Cambridge, MA, 1931.

References

PHILOSTORGIUS, *Historia Ecclesiastica*, in J. Bidez, *Die griechischen christlichen Schriftsteller der ersten Jahrhunderte*, Leipzig, 1913 (revised edn, F. Winkelmann, Berlin, 1972).

POSSIDIUS, *Sancti Augustini Vita Scripta a Possidio Episcopo*, ed. and tr. H. T. Weiskotten, Princeton, 1919.

PRISCUS, in Blockley, 1983.

PROCOPIUS, *Opera*, ed. J. Haury (4 vols.), Leipzig, 1962–4.

PROSPER OF AQUITAINE, *De Vocatione Omnium Gentium*, *PL* 51, 1861.
  Epitoma Chronicon, ed. T. Mommsen, *MGH*, *AA* 9, 341–499, Berlin, 1892 (reprinted Munich, 1981).
  Poema Coniugis ad Uxorem, ed. W. von Hartel, *CSEL* 30, 344–8, Vienna, 1894.

QUEROLUS, *Querolus Sive Aulularia*, ed. G. Ranstrand (Acta Universitatis Gotobergenisis 57), Göteberg, 1951.

RURICIUS OF LIMOGES, ed. G. Luetjohann, *MGH*, *AA* 8, Berlin, 1887.

RUTILIUS NAMATIANUS, *Sur son retour (De Reditu Suo)*, ed. and tr. J. Vessereau and F. Préchac, Paris, 1961.

SALVIAN OF MARSEILLE, *De Gubernatione Dei*, ed. C. Halm, *MGH*, *AA* 1, Berlin, 1877.
  On the Government of God, tr. E. M. Sanford, New York, 1966 (repr.).
  Oeuvres, vol. I. Les livres de Timothée à l'église, ed. and tr. G. Lagarrigue, Sources Chrétiennes 176, Paris, 1971.
  Oeuvres, vol. II. Du gouvernement de Dieu, ed. and tr. G. Lagarrigue, Sources Chrétiennes 220, Paris, 1975.
  Epistulae, Timothei ad Ecclesiam Libri IV, tr. J. F. O'Sullivan, FC 3, 1947.

SCRIPTORES HISTORIAE AUGUSTAE, ed. H. Hohl, C. Samberger and W. Seyfarth, Leipzig, 1971.

SIDONIUS APOLLINARIS, *Poèmes, Lettres*, ed. and tr. A. Loyen (3 vols.) (Budé edn), Paris, 1960, 1970.
  Poems (Carmina) and Letters (Epistulae), ed. and tr. W. B. Anderson (2 vols.) (Loeb edn.), London and Cambridge, MA, 1936, 1965.

SOCRATES, *Historia Ecclesiastica*, ed. R. Hussey, Oxford, 1953.

SOZOMEN, ed. J. Bidez and G. C. Hanson, *Griechische Christlichen Schriftsteller* 50, 1960.

STATUTA ECCLESIAE ANTIQUA, ed. C. Munier, Paris, 1960.

SUDA, ed. A. Adler (5 vols.), Leipzig, 1935.

SULPICIUS SEVERUS, *Libri Qui Supersunt*, ed. C. Halm, *CSEL* 1, Vienna, 1866.

SYMMACHUS, *Opera*, ed. O. Seeck, *MGH*, *AA* 6, Berlin, 1883.

SYNESIUS OF CYRENE, *De Regno. The Essays and Hymns of Synesius of Cyrene*, vol. I, tr. A. Fitzgerald, Oxford and London, 1930.

TERTULLIAN, *Apologeticum*, in *Opera*, pars I, *Corpus Christianorum*, Series Latina 1, Turnhout, 1954.

THEMISTIUS, *Orations*, ed. H. Schenkl, G. Downey and A. F. Norman (3 vols.) Leipzig, 1965–74.

References

THEOPHANES, ed. C. de Boor, Hildesheim, 1883.

THORPE, 1974. See Gregory of Tours.

VENANTIUS FORTUNATUS, *Opera Poetica*, ed. F. Leo, *MGH, AA* 4.1, Berlin, 1881.

VICTOR OF VITA, *Historia Persecutionis Africanae Provinciae*, ed. M. Petschenig, *CSEL* 7, Bonn, 1881.

VITA AMATORI, *Acta Sanctorum*, maius I, 50–60, 1866.

VITA ANNIANI, ed. B. Krusch, *MGH, SRM* 3, 104–17, Hanover, 1896.

VITA AUGUSTINI (POSSIDIUS), ed. and tr. H. T. Weiskotten, *Sancti Augustini Vita Scripta a Possidio Episcopo*, Princeton, 1919.

VITA CAESARII, ed. B. Krusch, *MGH, SRM* 3, 433–501, Hanover, 1896.

VITA DAN. STYLIT., ed. H. Delehaye, *Analecta Bollandiana* 32, 1913; tr. E. Dawes and N. H. Baynes, *Three Byzantine Saints*, London, 1948.

VITA DESIDERII, ed. B. Krusch, *MGH, SRM* 4, 547–602, Hanover and Leipzig, 1902.

VITA EPIPHANII (ENNODIUS), ed. F. Vogel, *MGH, AA* 7, 84–109, Berlin, 1885.

VITA GENOVEFAE, ed. B. Krusch, *MGH, SRM* 3, 204–38, Hanover, 1896.

VITA GERMANI (CONSTANTIUS), ed. and tr. R. Borius, *Constance de Lyon. Vie de St Germain d'Auxerre*, Sources Chrétiennes 112, Paris, 1965.

VITA HILARII, *PL* 50, 1846, 1219–46; ed. S. Cavallin, *Vitae Sanctorum Honorati et Hilarii Episcoporum Arelatensium*, Lund, 1952.

VITA HONORATI (HILARIUS), ed. S. Cavallin, *Vitae Sanctorum Honorati et Hilarii Episcoporum Arelatensium*, Lund, 1952; ed. and tr. M. D. Valentin, *Sermo de Vita Sancti Honorati*, Sources Chrétiennes 235, Paris, 1977; *Sermo de Vita Sancti Honorati*, tr. R. J. Deferrari, *FC* 15, 1361–94, 1952.

VITA LUPI, ed. B. Krusch, *MGH, SRM* 3, 117–24, Hanover, 1896; *SRM* 7, 295–302, Hanover, 1920.

VITA LUPICINI, ed. and tr. F. Martine, *Vie des pères de Jura*, Sources Chrétiennes 142, Paris, 1968.

VITA MARTINI (SULPICIUS), ed. and tr. J. Fontaine, *Vie de St Martine*, Sources Chrétiennes 133–5, Paris, 1967–9.

VITA MARTINI (VENANTIUS), ed. F. Leo, *MGH, AA* 4, Berlin, 1881.

VITA ORIENTII, *Acta Sanctorum*, maius I, 62–3, 1866.

VITA ROMANI, ed. and tr. F. Martine, *Vie des pères de Jura*, Sources Chrétiennes 142, Paris, 1968.

VITA SERVATII, ed. B. Krusch, *MGH, SRM* 3, 83–91, Hanover, 1896.

VITA VEDASTIS, ed. B. Krusch, *MGH, SRM* 3, 394–413, Hanover, 1896.

VITA VIVIANI, ed. B. Krusch, *MGH, SRM* 3, 92–100, Hanover, 1896.

WALSH, 1966–7. See Paulinus of Nola.

WILKINSON, 1981. See *Itinerarium Egeriae*

ZOSIMUS, *Historia Nova*, ed. L. Mendelssohn (Teubner edn), Leipzig, 1887.

    New History, tr. J. Buchanan and H. Davis, San Antonio, TX, 1967.

References

New History, tr. and comment. R. T. Ridley, Byzantina Australiensia 2, Sydney, 1982.

SECONDARY WORKS

AGACHE, R. 1973 'La villa gallo-romaine dans les grandes plaines du nord de la France', *Archeologia* 55, 37–52.

1978 *La Somme pré-romaine et romaine*, Amiens.

ALBERT, G. 1984 *Goten in Konstantinopel. Untersuchungen zur oströmischen Geschichte um das Jahr 400 n. Chr.*, Paderborn.

ALFÖLDY, G. 1985 *The Social History of Rome*, London.

ALLARD, P. 1908 'Sidoine Apollinaire sous les règnes d'Avitus et de Majorien', *Revue des questions historiques* 83, 426–52.

ALTHEIM, F. 1962 *Geschichte der Hunnen*, vol. IV, Berlin.

ANDERSON, J. G. (ed.) 1938 *Tacitus, De Origine et Situ Germanorum*, Oxford.

ARNHEIM, M. T. W. 1972 *The Senatorial Aristocracy in the Later Roman Empire*, Oxford.

ARTHUR, P. 1985 'Naples. Notes on the economy of a Dark Age city', in G. Barker and R. Hodges (eds.), *Papers in Italian Archaeology IV, Part IV: Classical and Medieval Archaeology*, Oxford, 247–59.

ASBACH, J. 1870 *Die Anicier und die römische Dichterin Proba*, Vienna.

ATSMA, H. 1976 'Die christlichen Inschriften Galliens als Quelle für Klöster und Klosterbewohner bis zum Ende des 6. Jahrhunderts', *Francia* 4, 1–57.

BABAULT B., and LUTZ, M. 1973 'La nécropole gallo-romaine de St Guillaume (St Quirin)', *ASHAL* 73.

BACHRACH, B. S. 1969 'Another look at the barbarian settlement in southern Gaul', *Traditio* 25, 354–8.

BALDWIN, B. 1980 'Priscus of Panium', *Byzantion* 50, 18–61.

1981 'Sources for the Getica of Jordanes', *Revue Belge de Philologie et d'Histoire* 59, 141–5.

BALIL, A. 1970 'La defensa de Hispania en el Bajo Imperio', in *Legio VII Gemina*, Leon, 603–20.

BALMELLE, C. 1980 *Recueil général des mosaïques de la Gaule*, vol. IV. *Aquitaine 1*, Paris.

1983 'A propos d'une mosaïque tardive de Bordeaux', in *Mosaïque. Recueil d'Hommages à H. Stern*, 21–32, Paris.

1987 *Recueil général des mosaïques de la Gaule*, vol. IV. *Aquitaine 2*, Paris.

In prep. *Recueil général des mosaïques de la Gaule*, vol. IV. *Aquitaine 3*, Paris.

References

BALMELLE, C., GAUTHIER, M., and MONTURET, H. 1980 'Mosaïques de la villa du Palat à Saint Emilion (Gironde)', *Gallia* 38, 59–96.

BALON, J. 1963 *Etudes franques 1. Aux origines de la noblesse*, Namur.

BARDY, G. 1936 'Prosper d'Aquitaine (Saint)', *Dictionnaire de Théologie Catholique* 13.1, cols. 846–50.

BARNES, T. D. 1975 'Patricii under Valentinian III', *Phoenix* 29, 155–70.

BARNISH, S. J. B. 1986 'Taxation, land and barbarian settlement in the western empire', *Papers of the British School at Rome* 54, 170–95.

1987 'Pigs, plebeians and potentes. Rome's economic hinterland, c. 350–600 AD', *Papers of the British School at Rome* 55, 157–83.

1989 'The transformation of classical cities and the Pirenne debate', *Journal of Roman Archaeology* 2, 385–400.

BARTHOLOMEW, P. 1982 'Fifth-century facts', *Britannia* 13, 261–70.

BASTIEN, P. 1972–6 'Le médaillon de plomb', *Bulletin des Musées et Monuments Lyonnais* 5, 157–76.

BAYNES, N. H. 1929 Review of H. Pirenne, *Medieval Cities. Their Origins and the Revival of Trade*, 1925, and other books, *Journal of Roman Studies* 19, 224–35.

BEAUJARD, B., et al. 1986 *Topographie chrétienne des cités de la Gaule des origines au milieu du VIIIe siècle, vol. IV. Province ecclésiastique de Lyon*, Paris.

BELLEN, H. 1971 *Studien zur Sklavenflucht im römischen Kaiserreich*, Wiesbaden.

BENOIT, F. 1951 'Le premier baptistère d'Arles et l'abbaye Saint-Césaire', *Cahiers Archéologiques* 5, 54–5.

1954 'Recherches archéologiques dans la région d'Aix-en-Provence', *Gallia* 12, 285–300.

1977 *Cimiez, la ville antique. Fouilles de Cemenelum I*, Paris.

BERATO, J., et al. 1986 'Fouilles récentes à Toulon', *Documents d'Archéologie Méridionale* 9, 135–66.

BERGENGRUEN, A. 1958 *Adel und Grundherrschaft in Merowingerreich*, Wiesbaden.

BERNOULLI, C. A. 1981 *Die Heiligen der Merowinger*, New York.

BIANCHINI, M. 1988 'Ancora in tema di unione fra barbari e romani', *Atti dell'Accademia Romanistica Constantiniana. VII Convegno Internazionale. 16–19 Ottobre, 1985, Perugia*, 225–49.

BIARNE, J., et al. 1986 *Topographie chrétienne des cités de la Gaule des origines au milieu du VIIIe siècle, vol. III. Provinces ecclésiastiques de Vienne et d'Arles*, Paris.

BILLORET, R. 1968 'Informations archéologiques circonscription de Metz', *Gallia* 26, 373–407.

BLANCHARD-LEMÉE, M. 1981 'La villa à mosaiques de Mienne-Marboué', *Gallia* 39, 63–83.

BLOCH, M. 1947 'Comment et pourquoi finit l'esclavage antique', *Annales, Economies, Sociétés, Civilisations* 2, 30–44, 161–70.

References

BLOCKLEY, R. C. 1981, 1983 *The Fragmentary Classicising Historians of the Later Roman Empire*, vols. I, II, Liverpool.

BÖHME, H. W. 1974 *Germanische Grabfünde des vierten bis fünften Jahrhunderts zwischen unteren Elbe und Loire*, Munich.

— 1976 'Das Land zwischen Elb- und Wesermündung vom 4. bis 6. Jh. — Die Sachsen und ihre Beziehung zum römischen Westen', *Führer zu vor- und frühgeschichtlichen Denkmälern* 29, 205–25, Mainz.

— 1985 'Les découvertes du Bas-Empire de Vireux-Molhain', in J.-P. Lemant (ed.), *Le cimetière et la fortification du Bas-Empire de Vireux-Molhain, dep. Ardennes*, 76–88, 131–3, Mainz.

— 1986 'Das Ende der Römerherrschaft in Britannien und die angelsächsische Besiedlung Englands im 5. Jahrhundert', *Jahrbuch des Römisch-Germanischen Zentralmuseums Mainz* 33.2, 469–574.

— 1988 'Zur Bedeutung des spätrömischen Militärdienstes für die Stammesbildung der Bajuwaren', in *Die Bajuwaren von Severin bis Tassilo 488–788*, 23–47, Munich.

BOIXANDERA, M., *et al.* 1987 'L'habitat de hauteur de Sainte-Propice', *Documents d'Archéologie Méridionale* 10, 91–113.

BOLIN, S. 1953 'Mohammed, Charlemagne and Ruric', *Scandinavian Economic History Review* 1, 5–39 (reprinted in Hübinger, 1968: 58–64).

BONIFAY, M. 1983 'Eléments d'évolution des céramiques de l'antiquité tardive à Marseille d'après les fouilles de la Bourse (1980–1981)', *Revue Archéologique de Narbonnaise* 16, 285–346.

— 1986 'Observations sur les amphores tardives à Marseille d'après les fouilles de la Bourse (1980–1984)', *Revue Archéologique de Narbonnaise* 19, 285–346.

BONIFAY, M., and VILLEDIEU, F. 1988 'Importations d'amphores orientales en Gaule', unpublished paper presented to the Association CATHMA (Céramiques de l'Antiquité Tardive et du Haut Moyen Age).

BONNASSIE, P. 1985 'Survie et extinction du régime esclavagiste dans l'Occident du haut moyen age (IVe – XIe s.)', *Cahiers de Civilisation Mediévale* 28, 307–43.

BONNET, C. 1987 'The archaeological site of the church of Saint Peter (Saint-Pierre), Geneva', *World Archaeology* 18.3, 330–40.

BORDEAUX, 1973 *Bordeaux 2000 ans d'histoire*, Catalogue of an exhibition at the Musée d'Aquitaine, (2nd edn), Bordeaux.

BORDEAUX, SAINT CHRISTOLY REPORTS Unpublished reports of excavations by the Direction des antiquités historiques, Bordeaux .

BORDEAUX, ST CHRISTOLY 1982 *Bordeaux, Saint Christoly. Sauvetage archéologique et histoire urbaine*, Catalogue of an exhibition at the Musée d'Aquitaine, Dec. 1982–Jan. 1983, Bordeaux.

BOST, J.-P., *et al.* 1987 'La villa gallo-romaine de Plassac', *Les cahiers du Vitrezais* 60, 3ff.

343

BOUBE, J. 1984 'Contribution à l'étude des sarcophages paléochrétiens Sud Ouest de la Gaule', *Aquitania* 2, 175–238.

BRADLEY, K. R. 1984 *Slaves and Masters in the Roman Empire*, Collection Latomus 185, Brussels.

BRANIGAN, K., and MILES, D. (eds.) 1988 *Villa Economies*, Sheffield.

BRAUDEL, F. 1972 *The Mediterranean and the Mediterranean World in the Age of Philip II* (tr. S. Reynolds), London.

BRENOT, C. 1980 'Monnaies de cuivre du VIe siècle frappées à Marseille', in P. Bastien, *et al.* (eds.), *Mélanges de Numismatique, d'Archéologie et d'Histoire Offerts à Jean Lafaurie*, 181–8, Paris.

BRIESENICK, B. 1962 'Typologie und Chronologie der sudwest Gallischen Sarkophages', *Jahrbuch des Römisch-Germanischen Zentralmuseums Mainz* 9, 79–128.

BROWN, P. 1981 *The Cult of the Saints*, London.

1982 *Society and the Holy in Late Antiquity*, Berkeley.

BROWN, P. D. C. 1975 'A fifth-century burial at Kingsholm', in H. Hurst *et al.*, 'Excavations at Gloucester, third interim report. Kingsholm 1966–75', *Antiquaries' Journal* 55, 290–4.

BRÜHL, C. R. 1988 'Problems of the continuity of Roman civitates in Gaul, as illustrated by the interrelation of cathedral and palatium', in R. Hodges and B. Hobley (eds.), *The Rebirth of Towns in the West*, Council for British Archaeology Research Report 68, 43–6.

BRUN, J.-P. 1987 *L'oleiculture antique en Provence. Les huileries du département du Var*, Paris.

1988 'Les amphores romaines, guide typologique I–III', *Annales de la Société des Sciences Naturelles et d'Archéologie de Toulon et du Var* 40, 1.1, 23–40; 1.3, 143–59.

BRUN, J.-P., *et al.* 1985 'L'habitat rural dans le Var à l'époque romaine. Données archéologiques récentes', *Provence Historique* 35, 233–51.

BULLETIN DE LIAISON, 1982+ Bulletin de liaison et d'information, Association des archéologues d'Aquitaine, Direction des antiquités historiques d'Aquitaine, Bordeaux.

BULLOUGH, D. 1986 'Ethnic History and the Carolingians', in C. Holdsworth and T. P. Wiseman (eds.), *The Inheritance of Historiography 350–900*, 85–106, Exeter.

BURNS, T. S. 1984 *A History of the Ostrogoths*, Bloomington.

BURY, J. B. 1923 (reprinted 1958) *History of the Later Roman Empire*, (2 vols.), London.

CALLU, J.-P., and BARRANDON, J.-N. 1987 'Note sur les sous Gaulois au Ve s. de notre ère', *Studi per Laura Breglia*, Supplemento al n. 4/1987 [Parte II] del *Bollettino di Numismatica*, 197–204, Rome.

CAMERON, A., LONG, J., and SHERRY, L. 1990 *Barbarians and Politics at the Court of Arcadius*, Berkeley.

CAPPUYNS, M. 1929 'Le premier représentant de l'augustinisme médiéval, Prosper d' Aquitaine', *Recherches de Théologie Ancienne et Médiévale* 1929, 309–37.

References

CASEY, P. J. 1987 'A fifth century Gallo-Roman gold coin from Piercebridge, Co. Durham', *Durham Archaeological Journal* 3, 5–7.

CAVALLERA, F. 1922 *Saint Jérôme, sa vie et son oeuvre*, Louvain.

CHALON, M. 1973 'A propos des inscriptions dédicatoires d'évêque Rusticus', *Narbonne. Archéologie et Histoire* 1, 223–32.

CHASTAGNOL, A. 1960 *La préfecture urbaine à Rome sous le Bas-Empire*, Paris.

1973 'Le repli sur Arles des services administratifs gaulois en 407 de notre ère', *Revue Historique* 249, 23–40.

CHIANEA, G. 1969 'Les idées politiques de Sidoine Apollinaire', *Revue Historique du Droit Français et Etranger* 47, 353–89.

CHRONIQUE D'ARCHEOLOGIE BORDELAIS annually, in *Bulletin et Mémoires de la Société Archéologique de Bordeaux*, Bordeaux.

CLARKE, G. N. 1979 *Pre-Roman and Roman Winchester*, Oxford.

CLAUDE, D. 1971 *Adel, Kirche und Königtum im Westgotenreich*, Sigmaringen.

CLELAND, D. J. 1970 'Salvian and the Vandals', *Studia Patristica* 10, 270–4, Berlin.

COLLINS, R. 1983 *Early Medieval Spain. Unity in Diversity, 400–1000*, London.

CONGES, G. 1980 'L'histoire d'Arles romaine précisée par les fouilles archéologiques', *Archeologia* 142, 10–23.

COSTER, C. H. 1935 *The Iudicium Quinquevirale*, Cambridge, MA.

1968 'The iudicium quinquevirale reconsidered', in C. H. Coster, *Late Roman Studies*, 22–45, Cambridge, MA.

COTHENET, A., and LAFAURIE, J. 1969 'Trésor de monnaies d'or de Valentinien III trouvé à Arçay', *BSFN* 24, 443–4.

COULON, G., GIRAULT, J.-L., BOURIN, J.-Y, and MARINVAL, P. 1985 'Les bains et l'environment de la villa gallo-romaine de la Pétonnière à Paulnay (Indre)', *Revue Archéologique du Centre de la France* 24, 191–214.

COURCELLE, P. 1964 *Histoire littéraire des grandes invasions germaniques* (3rd edn), Paris.

COURTOIS, P. 1955 *Les Vandales et l'Afrique*, Paris.

CRADDOCK, P. B. (ed.) 1972 *The English Essays of Edward Gibbon*, Oxford.

CROKE, B. 1987 'Cassiodorus and the Getica of Jordanes', *Classical Philology* 82, 117–34.

CROUZEL, H. 1972 'Saint Jérôme et ses amis toulousains', *Bulletin de Littérature Ecclésiastique* 73, 126–46.

CZUTH, B. 1965 *Die Quellen der Geschichte der Bagauden*, Acta Universitatis de Attila Joszef nominatae, minora opera ad philologiam classicam et archaeologiam pertinentia, vol. IX, Szeged.

DALY, W. M. 1970 'Caesarius of Arles, precursor of medieval Christendom', *Traditio* 26, 1–28.

DAUGE, Y. A. 1981 *Le Barbare. Recherches sur la conception romaine de la barbarie et de la civilisation*, Collection Latomus 176, Brussels.

DE CHAUME, M. 1971 *Les origines du Duché de Bourgogne*, Aalen.

DEBORD, P., and DOREAU, J. 1975 'Le port antique de Bordeaux', *Revue Historique de Bordeaux et du Département de la Gironde* 24, 5–18.

DELEHAYE, H. 1908 Review of A. Dufourcq, *Etudes sur les Gesta Martyrum romains, Analecta Bollandiana* 27, 215–18.

DELMAIRE, R. 1984 'Les monnaies d'or de Montay (Nord). Une réédition', *BSFN* 39, 482–3.

DEMANDT, A. 1970 'Magister militum', *RE* Supp. XII, 553–790.

DEMIRO, E. 1980–1 'Ricerche archeologiche nella Sicilia centro meridionale', *Kokalos* 26–7, II, 578–9.

DEMOUGEOT, E. 1951 *De l'unité à la division de l'empire romain, 395–410*, Paris.

    1965 'Y eut-il une forme arienne de l'art paléochrétienne?', *Atti del VI Cong. Int. di Archeologia Cristiana, Ravenna, 1962*, 491–519, Rome.

    1979 *La formation de l'Europe et les invasions barbares*, vol. II, Paris.

    1980 'Les sacs de Trèves au début du Ve siècle', in P. Bastien, *et al.* (eds.), *Mélanges de numismatique d'archéologie et d'histoire offerts à Jean Lafaurie*, 93–7, Paris.

    1983 'A propos des solidi gallici du Ve siècle apr. J.-C.', *Revue Historique* 270, 3–30.

DENEAUVE, J. 1972 'Céramique et lampes africaines sur la côte de Provence', *Antiquités Africaines* 6, 219–40.

DEPEYROT, G. 1986a 'Les émissions wisigothiques de Toulouse (Ve siècle)', *Acta Numismatica* 16, 79–104.

    1986b 'Les solidi gaulois de Valentinien III', *Schweizerische Numismatische Rundschau* 65, 111–31.

DIACONU, G. 1975 'On the socio-economic relations between natives and Goths in Dacia', in M. Constantinescu (ed.), *Relations between the Autochthonous Population and the Migratory Populations in the Territory of Romania*, Bibliotheca Historica Romaniae 16, 67–75.

DILL, S. 1905, 1921 *Roman Society in the Last Century of the Western Empire*, London.

    1926 (reprinted 1966) *Roman Society in Gaul in the Merovingian Age*, London and New York.

DOCKES, P. 1980 'Révoltes bagaudes et ensauvagement', in P. Dockès and J. M. Servet (eds.), *Sauvages et ensauvagés*, 143–262, Lyon.

    1982 *Medieval Slavery and Liberation*, Chicago.

DREW, K. F. 1987 'Another look at the origins of the Middle Ages. A reassessment of the role of the Germanic kingdoms', *Speculum* 62, 803–12.

DRINKWATER, J. F. 1983 *Roman Gaul. The Three Provinces 58 BC – AD 260*, London, Canberra and Ithaca.

    1984 'Peasants and Bagaudae in Roman Gaul', *Classical Views* NS 3, 349–71.

1987 *The Gallic Empire. Separatism and Continuity in the North-Western Provinces of the Roman Empire*, Historia Einzelschriften 52, Stuttgart.

1989a 'Patronage in Roman Gaul and the problem of the Bagaudae', in A. Wallace-Hadrill (ed.), *Patronage in Ancient Society*, 189–203, London.

1989b 'Gallic attitudes to the Roman empire in the fourth century. Continuity or change?', in H. E. Herzig and R. Frei-Stolba (eds.), *Labor omnibus unus. Gerold Walser zum 70. Geburtstag*, Historia Einzelschriften 60, 136–53, Stuttgart.

DUBY, G. 1974 *The Early Growth of the European Economy. Warriors and Peasants from the Seventh to the Twelfth Century* (tr. H. B. Clarke), Ithaca.

DUBY, G. (ed.) 1980 *Histoire de la France urbaine, vol. I. La ville romaine*, Paris.

DUCHESNE, L. 1894 *Fastes épiscopaux de l'ancienne Gaule, vol. I Provinces du sud-est*, Paris.

1907, 1910, 1915 *Fastes épiscopaux de l'ancienne Gaule* (3 vols.; vols. I, II: 2nd edn), Paris.

DUFOURCQ, A. 1900–7 *Etudes sur les Gesta Martyrum romains* (4 vols.), Paris.

DUNNING, G. C. 1968 'The trade in medieval pottery around the North Sea', in J. G. N. Renaud (ed.), *Rotterdam Papers. A Contribution to Medieval Archaeology*, 35–58, Rotterdam.

DUPARC, P. 1958 'La Sapaudia', *Comptes Rendus de l'Académie des Inscriptions et Belles-Lettres*, 371–83.

DURU, R. 1982 'La crypte de l'église Saint Seurin de Bordeaux', *La Sauvegarde de l'Art Français* 2, 57–88.

DUVAL, Y., FEVRIER, P.-A., and GUYON, G. 1986 *Topographie chrétienne des cités de la Gaule des origines au milieu du VIIIe siècle, vol. II. Provinces ecclésiastiques d'Aix et d'Embrun*, Paris.

DUVAL-ARNOULD, L. 1888 *Etudes d'histoire du droit romain au Ve siècle d'après les lettres et les poèmes de Sidoine Apollinaire*, Paris.

DVORNIK, F. 1966 *Early Christian and Byzantine Political Philosophy*, (2 vols.), Washington.

ENSSLIN, W. 1937 'Valentinians III. Novellen XVII und XVIII von 445', *Zeitschrift der Savigny-Stiftung für Rechtsgeschichte Rom. Abt.* 57, 367–78.

ESQUIEU, Y., and LAUXEROIS, R. 1975 'La nécropole de Saint-Pierre à Alba (Ardèche)', *Archéologie médiévale* 5, 5–44.

ESQUIEU, Y., et al. 1988 *Viviers, cité episcopale: Etudes archéologiques*, Documents d'Archéologie en Rhône-Alpes I, Lyon.

EWIG, E. 1973 'Observations sur la grandeur et la décadence de Trèves la Romaine', in *Economies et Sociétés au Moyen Age, Mélanges Edouard Perroy*, Publications de la Sorbonne, série Etudes 5, 28–39, Paris.

1978 'Bemerkungen zur Vita des Bischofs Lupus von Troyes', in K. Hauck and H. Modek (eds.), *Geschichtsschreibung und geistiges Leben im Mittelalter, Festschrift für H. Löwe*, 14–26, Cologne and Vienna.

FABRE, P. 1949 *Saint Paulin de Nole et l'amitié chrétienne,* Bibliothèque des Ecoles Françaises d'Athènes et de Rome 161, Paris.

FAVEZ, C. 1957 'La Gaule et les Gallo-Romains lors des invasions du Ve siècle d'après Salvien', *Latomus* 16, 77–83.

FENTRESS, E., and PERKINS, P. 1988 'Counting African Red Slip', in A. Mastino (ed.), *L'Africa-Romana. Atti del V Convegno di Studio Sassari, 11–13 dicembre 1987,* 205–14, Sassari.

FEVRIER, P.-A. 1964 *Le développement urbain en Provence de l'époque romaine à la fin du XIVe siècle,* Bibliothèque des Ecoles Francaises d'Athènes et de Rome 202, Paris.

 1974 'Permanence et héritages de l'Antiquité dans la topographie des villes de l'Occident durant le haut moyen âge', *Settimane di Studio del Centro Italiano di Studi sull'Alto Medioevo* 21, 41–138.

 1978 'Problèmes de l'habitat du Midi mediterranéen à la fin de l'Antiquité et dans le Moyen Age', *Jahrbuch des Römisch-Germanischen Zentralmuseums Mainz* 25, 208–47.

 1980 'Vetera et nova', in P.-A. Février, *et al.* (eds.), *Histoire de la France urbaine,* vol. I, 393–494, Paris.

FEVRIER, P.-A. (ed.) 1988 *Premiers temps chrétiens en Gaule méridionale. Antiquité tardive et haut moyen age, IIIe – VIIIe siècles,* Lyon.

FINLEY, M. I. 1973 *The Ancient Economy,* Berkeley.

 1985 (revised edn) *The Ancient Economy,* Berkeley.

FISCHER, H. 1976 *Die Schrift des Salvian von Marseille 'An die Kirche'. Eine historisch-theologische Untersuchung,* Bern, Frankfurt on Main.

FISCHER, J. 1948 *Die Völkerwanderunq im Urteil der zeitgenössischen kirklichen Schriftsteller Galliens unter Einbeziehung des heiligen Augustinus,* Heidelberg.

FLACH, J. 1893 *Les origines de l'ancienne France,* Paris.

FOLZ, R. 1969 *The Concept of Empire in Western Europe from the Fifth to the Fourteenth Century* (tr. S. A. Ogilvie), Westport, CT.

FONTAINE, J. 1981 *Naissance de la poésie latine chrétienne du IIIe au VIe siècle,* Etudes Augustiniennes, Paris.

FORRER, R. 1927 *Strasbourg-Argentorate,* Strasbourg.

FORTIN, E. L. 1959 *Christianisme et culture philosophique au cinquième siècle,* Paris.

FOSSARD, D. 1957 'La chronologie des sarcophages d'Aquitaine', *Actes du V. Cong. Int. d'Archéologie Chrétienne, Aix, 1954,* 321–33, Paris.

FOUET, G. 1972 'Le sanctuaire des eaux de La Hillère à Montmaurin', *Gallia* 30, 83–124.

 1975 'Exemples d'exploitation des eaux par de grands propriétaires terriens dans le sud ouest au IVe siècle', *Caesarodunum* 10, 128–34.

FOURNIER, P.-F. 1970 'Clermont-Ferrand au VIe siècle. Recherches sur la topographie de la ville', *Bibliothèque de l'Ecole des Chartes* 128, 273–344.

FOXHALL, L., and FORBES, H. A. 1982 'Sitometria. The role of grain as a staple food in classical antiquity', *Chiron* 12, 41–90.

FROUIN, R. 1929 'Du titre roi porté par quelques participants à l'imperium romanum', *Tijdschrift voor Rechtsgeschiedenis* 9, 140–9.

FUHRMANN, H. 1953 'Studien zur Geschichte mittelalterlicher Patriarchate (1. Teil)', *Zeitschrift der Savignystiftung für Rechtsgeschichte* Kan. Abt. 39, 112–76.

FULFORD, M. G. 1980 'Carthage, overseas trade, and the political economy', *Reading Medieval Studies*, 68–80.

1983 'Pottery and the economy of Carthage and its hinterland', *Opus* 2, 5–14.

1987 'Economic interdependence among urban communities of the Roman Mediterranean', *World Archaeology* 19, 58–74.

FULFORD, M. G., and PEACOCK, D. P. S. 1984 *Excavations at Carthage. The British Mission*, I. 2, Sheffield.

FUSTEL DE COULANGES, N. D. 1885 *Le colonat romain*, Paris.

GABBA, E., and TIBILETTI, G. 1960 'Una signora di Treviri sepolta a Pavia', *Athenaeum* 38, 253–62.

GAGE, J. 1971 *Les classes sociales dans l'empire romain* (2nd edn), Paris.

GARNSEY, P. 1983 'Grain for Rome', in P. Garnsey, K. Hopkins and C. R. Whittaker (eds.), *Trade in the Ancient Economy*, 118–30, London.

1988 *Famine and Food Supply in the Graeco-Roman World. Responses to Risk and Crisis*, Cambridge.

GAUTHIER, M. 1975 'La céramique estampée tardive d'Aquitaine. Un siècle de trouvailles bordelaises', *Revue Historique de Bordeaux* 24, 19–45.

GAUTHIER, N., and PICARD, J.-C. (eds.) 1986 *Topographie chrétienne des cités de la Gaule des origines au milieu du VIIIe siècle, vol. I. Province ecclésiastique de Trèves*, Paris.

GEARY, P. J. 1988 *Before France and Germany. The Creation and Transformation of the Merovingian World*, Oxford.

GERBERDING, R. 1987 *The Rise of the Carolingians and the Liber Historiae Francorum*, Oxford.

GHOSH, P. R. 1983 'Gibbon's Dark Ages. Some remarks on the genesis of the Decline and Fall of the Roman Empire', *Journal of Roman Studies* 73, 1–23.

GIARDINA, A. (ed.) 1986 *Società romana e impero tardoantico III. Gli merci gli insediamenti*, Rome.

GIBBON, E. 1912 *The History of the Decline and Fall of the Roman Empire*, (ed. J. B. Bury, 5th edn), London.

GIRAULT, M.-A. 1878 'Fouilles archéologiques de la rue Gouvion à Bordeaux. Mosaïque et constructions antiques', *Bulletin de la Société Archéologique de Bordeaux* 5, 131–50.

GOFFART, W. 1980 *Barbarians and Romans, AD 418–584. The Techniques of Accommodation*, Princeton.

1986 'Paul the Deacon's Gesta episcoporum Mettensium and the early design of Charlemagne's succession', *Traditio* 42, 59–93.

1988 *The Narrators of Barbarian History (AD 500–800)*, Princeton.

References

GOLVERS, N. 1984 'Le Querolus et le parler de Marseille', *Latomus* 43, 432–7.

GREENE, K. 1986 *The Archaeology of the Roman Economy*, London.

GRENIER, A. 1934 *Manuel d'archéologie gallo-romain, vol. II. L'archéologie du sol*, Paris.

GRIERSON, P. 1959 'Commerce in the Dark Ages. A critique of the evidence', *Transactions of the Royal Historical Society*, 5th series, 9, 123–40.

GRIFFE, E. 1956 'L'Epigramma Paulini. Poème Gallo-romain du Ve siècle', *Revue des Etudes Augustiniennes* 2, 187–94.

1964–6 *La Gaule chrétienne à l'époque romaine* (3 vols., 2nd edn), Paris.

GRUEN, E. S. 1984 *The Hellenistic World and the Coming of Rome*, Berkeley, Los Angeles and London.

GUILD, R., GUYON, J., and RIVET, A. L. F. 1980 'Recherches archéologiques dans le cloître de Saint-Sauveur d'Aix-en-Provence – bilan de quatre campagnes de fouilles (1976–1979)', *Revue Archéologique de Narbonnaise* 13, 115–64.

1983 'Les origines du baptistère de la cathédrale Saint-Sauveur – étude de topographie aixoise', *Revue Archéologique de Narbonnaise* 16, 171–232.

GUILD, R., *et al.* 1988 'Saint-Sauveur d'Aix-en-Provence, la cathédrale et le baptistère', in *Le Pays d'Aix, Congrès Archéologique de France, 143e session*, 7–64, Paris.

GUILLAUME, J. 1974–5 'Les nécropoles de Dieue/Meuse (France)', *Acta Praehistorica et Archaeologica* 5/6, 211–439.

HALSALL, G. 1988 'La 'Civitas' Mérovingienne de Metz', *BLAFAM* 12, 5–52.

HALSALL, G. forthcoming 'Civitas Mediomatricorum. Settlement and social organization in the Merovingian region of Metz', University of York D.Phil. diss.

HARRIES, J. D. 1978 'Church and state in the Notitia Galliarum', *Journal of Roman Studies* 68, 26–43.

HARRIES, J. D. 1981 'Bishops, senators and their cities in southern and central Gaul, AD 407–476', unpublished University of Oxford D.Phil. diss.

HASELGROVE, C. 1987 'Culture process on the periphery. Belgic Gaul during the late Republic and early empire', in M. Rowlands, M. Larsen and K. Kristiansen (eds.), *Centre and Periphery in the Ancient World*, 104–24, Cambridge.

HASELOFF, G. 1981 *Die Germanische Tierornamentik der Volkwänderungszeit*, Berlin.

HEATHER, P. 1986a 'The crossing of the Danube and the Gothic conversion', *Greek, Roman and Byzantine Studies* 27, 289–318.

1986b 'The Goths and the Balkans AD 350–500', unpublished University of Oxford D.Phil. diss.

HEFELE, D., and LECLERCQ, H. 1908 *Histoire des conciles*, vol. II, Paris.

HEINZELMANN, M. 1976 *Bischofsherrschaft in Gallien*, Francia Beihefte 5, Munich.

1982 'Gallische Prosopographie 260–527', *Francia* 10, 531–718.

1988 'Bischof und Herrschaft vom spätantiken Gallien bis zu den karolingischen Hausmeiern. Die institutionellen Grundlagen', in F. Prinz (ed.), *Herrschaft und Kirche, Monographien zur Geschichte des Mittelalters* 33, 23–82, Stuttgart.

HERRIN, J. 1987 *The Formation of Christendom*, London.

HERRING, G. 1987 'The society and economy of Poitou-Charentes in the Roman period', unpublished University of Oxford D.Phil. diss.

HIMLY, F.-J. 1955 'Y a-t-il emprise Musulmane sur l'économie des états européens du VIIIe au Xe siècle? Une discussion des témoignages', *Schweizerische Zeitschrift für Geschichte* 5, 31–81 (reprinted in Hübinger, 1968: 276–329).

HITCHNER, R. B. 1988 'The Kasserine archaeological survey, 1982–86', *Antiquités Africaines* 24, 7–41.

HODGES, R., and WHITEHOUSE, D. 1983 *Mohammed, Charlemagne and the Origins of Europe. Archaeology and the Pirenne Thesis*, London and Ithaca.

HODGKIN, T. 1889 *The Dynasty of Theodosius*, Oxford.

HOPKINS, K. 1978 *Conquerors and Slaves*, Cambridge.

HUBERT, J. 1958 'Evolution de la topographie et de l'aspect des villes de Gaule du Ve au Xe siècle', *Settimane di Studio del Centro Italiano di Studi sull'Alto Medioevo* 6, 529–58.

HÜBINGER, P. E. (ed.) 1968 *Bedeutung und Rolle des Islams beim Übergang vom Altertum zum Mittelalter*, Wege der Forschung 202, Darmstadt.

HUNT, E. D. 1982a *Holy Land Pilgrimage in the Later Roman Empire, AD 312–460*, Oxford.

1982b 'St Stephen in Minorca', *Journal of Theological Studies* 33, 106–7.

IONITA, I. 1975 'The social-economic structure of society during the Goths' migration in the Carpatho-Danubian area', in M. Constantinescu (ed.), *Relations between the Autochthonous Population and the Migratory Populations in the Territory of Romania*, Bibliotheca Historica Romaniae 16, 77–89.

JALLAND, T. G. 1941 *The Life and Times of St Leo the Great*, London and New York.

JAMES, E. 1977 *The Merovingian Archaeology of South-West Gaul* (2 vols.), BAR(S) 25, Oxford.

1979 'Cemeteries and the problem of Frankish settlement', in P. H. Sawyer (ed.), *Names, Words, and Graves*, 55–89, Leeds.

1988a *The Franks*, London.

1988b 'Childéric, Syagrius et la disparition du royaume de Soissons', *Revue Archéologique de Picardie* 3–4, 9–12.

JOHNE, K.-P., KÖHN, J., and WEBER, V. 1983 *Die Kolonen in Italien und den westlichen Provinzen des römischen Reiches*, Berlin.

JOHNSON, S. 1983 'Late Roman urban defences in Europe', in J. Maloney and B. Hobley (eds.), *Roman Urban Defences in the West*, Council for British Archaeology Research Report 51, 69–76.

JONES, A. H. M. 1958 'The Roman colonate', *Past & Present* 13, 1–13 (reprinted in P. A. Brunt (ed.), *The Roman Economy*, 1974, 293–307, Oxford).

1964 *The Later Roman Empire, 284–602. A Social, Economic,and Administrative Survey*, Oxford and Norman, OK.

1966 *The Decline of the Ancient World*, London.

JONES, A. H. M., MARTINDALE, J. R., and MORRIS, J. 1971 *The Prosopography of the Later Roman Empire, vol. I. AD 260–395*, Cambridge.

JONES, M. E., and CASEY, P. J. 1988 'The Gallic Chronicle restored. A chronology for the Anglo-Saxon invasions and the end of Roman Britain', *Britannia* 19, 367–98.

JULLIAN, C. 1887–90 *Inscriptions romaines de Bordeaux* (2 vols.), Bordeaux.

KAISER, R. 1973 *Untersuchungen zur Geschichte des Civitas und Diözese Soissons in römerischer und merowingerischer Zeit*, Rheinisches Archiv, Bonn.

KAUFMANN, G. 1866 'Über das Foederatverhaltniss des tolosanischen Reichs zu Rom', *Forschungen zur deutschen Geschichte* 6, 433–76.

KEAY, S. J. 1984 *Late Roman Amphorae in the Western Mediterranean*, Oxford.

KELLEY, D. H. 1947 'New consideration of the Carolingians', *New England Historical Genealogical Register* 101, facing 109–facing 112.

KELLY, J. N. D. 1975 *Jerome. His Life, Writings, and Controversies*, London.

KENT, J. P. C. 1956 'Gold coinage in the Later Roman Empire', in R. A. G. Carson and C. H. V. Sutherland (eds.), *Essays in Roman Coinage Presented to Harold Mattingly*, 190–204, London.

1974 'Un monnayage irregulier du début du Ve siècle de notre ère', *Cercle d'Etudes Numismatiques Bulletin* 11, 23–9.

KING, C. E. 1987 'Fifth century silver coinage in the western Roman Empire. The usurpations in Spain and Gaul', in H. Huvelin, M. Christol and G. Gautier (eds.), *Mélanges de Numismatique offerts à Pierre Bastien à l'occasion de son 75e anniversaire*, 285–95, Wetteren.

1988 'Fifth century silver issues in Gaul', in P. Kos and Z. Demo (eds.), *Studia Numismatica Labacensia, Alexandro Jelocnik Oblata*, 197–210, Ljubljana.

KING, P. D. 1972 *Law and Society in the Visigothic Kingdom*, Cambridge.

1988 'The barbarian kingdoms', in J. H. Burns (ed.), *The Cambridge History of Political Thought, c. 350–c.1450*, ch. 7, Cambridge and New York.

KRAFT, K. 1978 'Die Taten der Kaiser Constans und Constantius II', in K. Kraft, *Kleine Schriften*, vol. II, 87–132.

KURTH, G. 1893 *Histoire poétique des Mérovingiens*, Paris, Brussels and Leipzig.

LABROUSSE, M. 1968 *Toulouse antique des origines à l'établissement des Wisigoths*, Paris.

LADNER, G. 1976 'On Roman Attitudes toward barbarians in late antiquity', *Viator* 7, 1–26.

LAFAURIE, J. 1964a 'Monnaie en argent trouvée à Fleury-sur-Orne. Essai sur le monnayage d'argent franc des Ve et VIe siècles', *Annales de Normandie* 14, 173–96.

1964b 'Essai de répertoire des trésors et trouvailles de monnaies frappées en Gaule et en Italie pendant la deuxième moitié du Ve siècle et au cours du VIe siècle', *Annales de Normandie* 14, 197–222.

1980 'Deux trouvailles de monnaies du Ve siècle à Châtelaillon', *BSFN* 35, 715–16.

1982 'A propos de deux monnaies d'or de Sévère III trouvées en Anjou', *BSFN* 37, 194–6.

1983 'Monnaies d'or frappées en Gaule dans la seconde moitié du Ve siècle', *BSFN* 38, 270–1.

1984 'Trésor de monnaies d'or du Ve siècle trouvé en 1803 à Combertault (Côte d'Or)', *Revue Numismatique* 26, 145–60.

1987 'Les dernières émissions impériales de Trèves au Ve siècle', in H. Huvelin, *et al.* (eds.), *Mélanges de numismatique offerts à Pierre Bastien*, 297–323, Wetteren.

1988 'Monnaies trouvées dans la tombe de la nécropole de Mailly-le-Camp (Aube) (résumé)', *BSFN* 43, 379–84.

LAGARRIGUE, G. 1964 'L'opinion de Salvien sur les barbares. Interpretations actuelles', *Revue d'Etudes Latines* 42, 70–1.

1983 'Le Carmen de Providentia Dei. Optimisme religieux et espoir patriotique', in H. Zehnacker and G. Hentz (eds.), *Hommages à Robert Schilling*, 137–45, Paris.

LALLEMAND, J. 1965 'Vedrin. Sous d'or de Magnus Maximus à Anastase', *Etudes Numismatiques* 3 (Bibliothèque Royale de Belgique, Cabinet des Médailles), Brussels, 109–44.

LANGGÄRTNER, G. 1964 *Die Gallienpolitik der Päpste im 5. und 6. Jahrhundert. Eine Studie über den apostolischen Vikariat von Arles*, Theophaneia 16, Bonn.

LAUB, F. 1982 *Die Begegnung des frühen Christentums mit der antiken Sklaverei*, Stuttgart.

LAUFFRAY, J., SCHREYECK, J., and DUPRE, N. 1973 'Les établissements et les villas gallo-romains de Lalonquette (Pyrénées-Atlantiques)', *Gallia* 31, 123–56.

LAUXEROIS, R. 1983 ›Le Bas Vivarais à l'époque romaine. Recherches sur la cité d'Alba‹, *Revue Archéologique de Narbonnaise supplément* 9.

LEGENTILHOMME, P. 1943 'Le monnayage et la circulation monétaire dans les royaumes barbares en occident (V^e › VIIIe siècle)', *Revue Numismatique* 7, 45–112.

LEONARDI, C. 1977 'Alle origini della cristianità medievale', *Studi Medievali* 3a, serie 18.2, 491–608.

LEPELLEY, C. 1979–81 *Les cités de l'Afrique romains au Bas-Empire* (2 vols.), Paris.

LE ROY LADURIE, E. 1987 *The French Peasantry* (tr. A. Sheridan), London.

LIEBESCHUETZ, W. 1990 *Bishops and Barbarians*, Oxford.

LINDNER, R. P. 1983 *Nomads and Ottomans in Medieval Anatolia*, Bloomington.

LINTZ, G., and VUAILLAT, D. 1987–8 'Les poignards et les coutelas dans les sépultures gallo-romaines du Limousin', *Gallia* 45, 165–88.

LLEWELLYN, P. 1970 *Rome in the Dark Ages*, London.

1986 'The popes and the constitution in the eighth century', *English Historical Review* 101, 42–67.

LOPEZ, R. S. 1943 'Mohammed and Charlemagne. A revision', *Speculum* 18, 14– 38 (reprinted in Hübinger, 1968: 65–104).

LOT, F. 1928 'Du régime de l'hospitalité', *Revue Belge de Philologie et d'Histoire* 7, 975–1011.

1966 *The End of the Ancient World and the Beginnings of the Middle Ages*, New York.

LOUD, G. A. 1982 'The gens Normanorum – myth or reality', in R. A. Brown (ed.), *Proceedings of the Battle Conference on Anglo-Norman Studies IV*, 10–46, Bury St Edmunds.

LOYEN, A. 1934 'Les débuts du royaume wisigoth de Toulouse', *Revue des Etudes Latines* 12, 406–15.

1943 *Sidoine Apollinaire et l'esprit précieux en Gaule aux derniers jours de l'empire*, Paris.

1963 'Résistants et collaborateurs en Gaule à l'époque des grandes invasions', *Bulletin de l'Association Guillaume Budé* 22, 437–50.

1969 'Le rôle de Saint Aignan dans le défense d'Orléans', *Comptes Rendus de l'Académie des Inscriptions et Belles Lettres*, 64–74.

LUKMAN, N. 1948 'The Catalaunian battle in medieval epics', *Classica et Mediaevalia* 10, 60–130.

LUTZ, M. 1964 'Considérations sur la civilisation dite "des Sommets Vosgiens" à la lumière de découvertes récentes', *ASHAL* 63, 25–40.

1978 'Archéologie des rives de la Sarre', *ASHAL* 78, 11–39.

MAAS, H. 1985 'Bemerkungen zur Rolle der Volksmassen in der Zerfalls- und Untergangsphase des Weströmischen Reiches', *Klio* 67, 536–61.

MCKITTERICK, R. 1983 *The Frankish Kingdoms under the Carolingians, 751–987*, Harlow and New York.

MacMULLEN, R. 1966 *Enemies of the Roman Order*, Harvard.

1987 'Late Roman slavery', *Historia* 36, 359–82.

MAENCHEN-HELFEN, O. J. 1973 *The World of the Huns*, Berkeley, Los Angeles and London.

MAILLE, M. de 1959 *Recherche sur les origines chrétiennes de Bordeaux*, Paris.

References

MANSI, G. D. 1901–27 *Sacrorum Conciliorum Nova et Amplissima Collectio*, Paris, Leipzig and Arnhem.

MARCUS, G. E., and FISCHER, M. J. 1986 *Anthropology as Cultural Critique. An Experimental Moment in the Human Sciences*, Chicago.

MARKUS, R. A. 1986 'Chronicle and theology. Prosper of Aquitaine', in C. Holdsworth and T. P. Wiseman (eds.), *The Inheritance of Historiography 350–900*, Exeter Studies in History 12, 31–43, Exeter.

MARMION, C. 1984–5 'La sigillée tardive d'Aquitaine', unpublished TER, Université de Bordeaux III.

MARROU, H. I. 1952 'L'épitaphe vaticane du consulaire de Vienne Eventius', *Revue des Etudes Anciennes* 54, 326–31.

1954 'Un lieu dit "Cité de Dieu"', *Augustinus Magister* 1, 101–10.

1970 'Le dossier épigraphique de l'évêque Rusticus de Narbonne', *Rivista di Archeologia Cristiana* 46, 331–49.

MARTINDALE, J. R. 1980 *The Prosopography of the Later Roman Empire, vol. II. AD 395–527*, Cambridge.

MATHISEN, R. W. 1979a 'Hilarius, Germanus and Lupus. The aristocratic background of the Chelidonius affair', *Phoenix* 33, 160–9.

1979b 'Resistance and reconciliation. Majorian and the Gallic aristocracy after the fall of Avitus', *Francia* 7, 597–627.

1979c 'Sidonius on the reign of Avitus. A study in political prudence', *Transactions of the American Philological Association* 109, 165–71.

1979d 'The ecclesiastical aristocracy of fifth century Gaul', unpublished University of Wisconsin-Madison Ph.D. diss. (now available as *Ecclesiastical Factionalism and Religious Controversy in Fifth-Century Gaul*, Washington, DC, 1989).

1981a 'Avitus, Italy and the east in AD 455–456', *Byzantion* 51, 232–47.

1981b 'The last year of Saint Germanus of Auxerre', *Analecta Bollandiana* 99, 151–9.

1981c 'Petronius, Hilarius and Valerianus. Prosopographical notes on the conversion of the Roman aristocracy', *Historia* 30, 106–12.

1981d 'Epistolography, literary circles and family ties in late Roman Gaul', *Transactions of the American Philological Association* 111, 95–109.

1982 'PLRE II. Suggested addenda and corrigenda', *Historia* 31, 364–85.

1984 'Emigrants, exiles and survivors. Aristocratic options in Visigothic Aquitania', *Phoenix* 38, 159–70.

1985 'The third regnal year of Eparchius Avitus', *Classical Philology* 80, 192–6.

1986 'Patricians as diplomats in late antiquity', *Byzantinische Zeitschrift* 79, 35–49.

1988 'The theme of literary decline in late Roman Gaul', *Classical Philology* 83, 45–52.

MATTHEWS, J. F. 1967 'A pious supporter of Theodosius I. Maternus Cynegius and his family', *Journal of Theological Studies* NS 18, 438–46.

355

References

1970 'Olympiodorus of Thebes and the history of the west (AD 407–425)', *Journal of Roman Studies* 60, 79–97.

1971 'Gallic supporters of Theodosius', *Latomus* 30, 1073–99 (reprinted in J. F. Matthews, *Political Life and Culture in Late Roman Society*, London, 1985).

1974 'The letters of Symmachus', in J. W. Binns (ed.), *Latin Literature of the Fourth Century*, 58–99, London.

1975 *Western Aristocracies and Imperial Court AD 364–425*, Oxford.

MATTINGLY, D. J. 1988 'Oil for export? A comparison of Libyan, Spanish and Tunisian olive oil production in the Roman empire', *Journal of Roman Archaeology* 1, 33–56.

MAZZARINO, S. 1959 *La fine del mondo antico*, Milan.

MILLAR, F. 1983 'Empire and City, Augustus to Julian. Obligations, excuses and status', *Journal of Roman Studies* 73, 76–96.

MOMIGLIANO, A. 1956 'Gli Anicii e la storiografia latina del VI secolo', *Rendiconti dell'Accademia dei Licei* ser. 8, vol. II, 11–12, Geneva.

MONTURET, R., and RIVIERE, H. 1986 *Les thermes sud de la villa gallo-romaine de Séviac*, Aquitania suppl. 2, Bordeaux and Paris.

MOORHEAD, J. 1983 'The West and the Roman past from Theoderic to Charlemagne', in B. Croke and A. M. Emmett (eds.), *History and Historians in Late Antiquity*, 155–68, Sydney.

MORGAN, G. 1969 'Hagen and Aetius', *Classica et Mediaevalia* 30, 440–50.

MORIARTY, G. A. 1985 *Plantagenet Ancestry*, Baltimore.

MORRISSON, C. 1983 'The re-use of obsolete coins. The case of Roman imperial bronzes revived in the late fifth century', in C. N. L. Brooke, *et al.* (eds.), *Studies in Numismatic Method Presented to Philip Grierson*, 95–111, Cambridge.

MORRISON, K. F. 1963 'Numismatics and Carolingian trade. A critique of the evidence', *Speculum* 38, 403–32.

MOSS, J. R. 1973 'The effects of the policies of Aetius on the history of the western empire', *Historia* 22, 711–31.

MUHLBERGER, S. 1983 'The Gallic Chronicle of 452 and its authority for British events', *Britannia* 14, 23–33.

1984 'Heroic kings and unruly generals. The "Copenhagen" continuation of Prosper reconsidered', *Florilegium* 6, 50–70.

1990 *The Fifth Century Chroniclers. Prosper, Hydatius and the Gallic Chronicler of 452*, Leeds.

MÜLLER-MERTENS, E. 1985 'Servus/Sklave – Klasse oder Stand? Reflexion auf terminologische Probleme der Feudalismusanalyse', in E. Müller-Mertens (ed.), *Feudalismus. Entstehung und Wesen*, 309–25, Berlin.

MUSSET, L. 1969 *Les invasions. Les vagues germaniques*, Nouvelle Clio 12, Paris.

MYERS, H. A. 1982 *Medieval Kingship*, Chicago.

NEHLSEN, H. 1984 'Codex Euricianus', *Reallexikon der germanischen Altertumskunde* (2nd edn), V, 42–7.

NELSON, J. L. 1977 'Inauguration rituals', in P. H. Sawyer and I. N. Wood (eds.), *Early Medieval Kingship*, 50–71, Leeds.

NÜRNBERG, R. 1988 *Askese als sozialer Impuls. Monastisch-asketische Spiritualität als Wurzel und Triebfeder sozialer Ideen und Aktivitäten der Kirche in Südgallien*, Bonn.

O'FLYNN, J. M. 1983 *Generalissimos of the Western Roman Empire*, Edmonton.

OOST, S. I. 1968 *Galla Placidia Augusta. A Biographical Essay*, Chicago.

PADER, E. J. 1980 'Material symbolism and social relations in mortuary behaviour', in P. A. Rahtz, T. M. Dickinson and L. Wats (eds.), *Anglo-Saxon Cemeteries*, BAR(B) 82, 143–59, Oxford.

  1982 *Symbolism, Social Relations and the Interpretation of Mortuary Remains*, BAR(S) 130, Oxford.

PANELLA, C. 1983 'Le anfore di Carthagine. Nuovi elementi per la ricostruzione dei flussi commerciali del mediterraneo in età imperiale romana', *Opus* 2, 53–74.

  1986 'Le merci. Produzioni, itinerari e destini', in Giardina, 1986: 421–59.

PARSONS, J. forthcoming 'Victor of Vita's *Historia Persecutionis Africanae Provinciae*'.

PASCHOUD, F. 1967 *Roma Aeterna. Etudes sur le patriotisme romain dans l'Occident latin à l'époque des grandes invasions*, Bibliotheca Helvetica Romana 7, Neuchâtel.

  1975 *Cinq études sur Zosime*, Paris.

PATLAGEAN, E. 1977 *Pauvreté économique et pauvreté social à Byzance*, Paris.

PELLEGRINO, M. 1940 *Salviano di Marsiglia, studio critico*, Lateranum NS 6.1, Rome.

PERCIVAL, J. 1976 *The Roman Villa*, London.

PERIN, P., and FEFFER, L.-C. 1987 *Les Francs* (2 vols.), Paris.

PERRIN, O. 1968 *Les Burgondes*, Neuchâtel.

PIETRI, C. 1980 'L'espace chrétien dans la cité. Le vicus christianorum et l'espace chrétien dans la cité arverne (Clermont)', *Revue d'Histoire de l'Eglise de France* 66, 177–209.

PILET, C. 1980 *La Nécropole de Frénouville (Calvados)*, BAR(S) 83, Oxford.

PIRENNE, H. 1922 'Mahomet et Charlemagne', *Revue Belge de Philologie et d'Histoire* 1, 77–86 (reprinted in Hübinger, 1968: 1–9).

  1939 *Mohammed and Charlemagne*, (tr. B. Miall), New York.

POLANYI, K., ARENSBERG, C. M., and PEARSON, H. W. (eds.) 1957 *Trade and the Market in the Early Empire*, Glencoe, IL.

PORTE, P. 1980 *L'habitat mérovingien de Larina*, Grenoble.

  1984 'Le camp de Larina, forteresse mérovingienne', *Dossiers de l'Archéologie* 78, 79–82.

References

PREMIERS, 1986 *Premiers temps chrétiens en Gaule méridionale*, exhibition catalogue (Sept. 1986–Jan. 1987), Lyon.

PREVOT, F., BARRAL, I., and ALTET, X. 1989 *Topographie chrétienne des cités de la Gaule des origines au milieu du VIIIe siècle, vol. VI. Province ecclésiastique de Bourges*, Paris.

PRINZ, F. 1965 *Frühes Mönchtum im Frankenreich. Kultur und Gesellschaft in Gallien am Beispiel der monastische Entwicklung (4.–8. Jahrhundert)* (reprinted 1988), Munich and Paris.

RAGUY, D. 1978–9 'Les villes romaines dans l'Aquitaine augustéenne', Unpublished TER, Université de Bordeaux III.

RANDERS-PEHRSON, J. D. 1960 *Barbarians and Romans. The Birth Struggle of Europe, AD 400–700*, Norman, OK.

RAYNAUD, C. forthcoming *Les fouilles du Clos de la Lombarde à Narbonne*.

REINHART, W. 1938 'Die Münzen des Tolosanischen Reiches der Westgoten', *Deutsches Jahrbuch für Numismatik* 1, 107–35.

REYDELLET, M. 1981 *La Royauté dans la littérature latine de Sidoine Apollinaire à Isidore de Seville*, Bibliothèque des Ecoles françaises d'Athènes et de Rome 243, Rome.

RICH, J. W. 1988 'A bibliography of E. A. Thompson', *Nottingham Medieval Studies* 32, 11–18.

RICHE, P. 1957 'La survivance des écoles publiques en Gaule au Ve siècle', *Le Moyen Age* 63, 421–36.

1962 *Education et culture dans l'Occident barbare*, Paris.

1976 *Education and Culture in the Barbarian West*, Columbia.

RIGOIR, J., RIGOIR, Y., and MEFFRE, J.-F. 1973 'Les derivées des sigillées paléochrétiennes du Groupe atlantique', *Gallia* 31, 207–63.

RILEY, J. A. 1982 'New light on relations between the eastern Mediterranean and Carthage in the Vandal and Byzantine periods', *Actes du Colloque sur la Céramique Antique*, Centre d'Etudes et de Documentation Archéologique de la Conservation de Carthage, *Bulletin* 1, 111–21.

RIVET, A. L. F. 1976 'The Notitia Galliarum, some questions', in R. Goodburn and P. Bartholomew (eds.), *Aspects of the Notitia Dignitatum*, BAR(S) 15, 119–41, Oxford.

1988 *Gallia Narbonensis*, London.

ROUCHE, M. 1977 *L'Aquitaine des Wisigoths aux Arabes (418–781)* (2 vols.), Lille.

1979 *L'Aquitaine des Wisigoths aux Arabes 418–781. Naissance d'une région*, Paris.

ROUGE, J. 1966 *Recherches sur l'organisation du commerce maritime en Mediterranée*, Paris.

ROUSSEAU, P. 1976 'In search of Sidonius the bishop', *Historia* 25, 356–77.

1978 *Ascetics, Authority and the Church in the Age of Jerome and Cassian*, Oxford.

References

RUBIN, Z. 1986 'The Mediterranean and the dilemma of the Roman empire in late antiquity', *Mediterranean Historical Review* 1, 13–62.
STE CROIX, G. E. M. de 1981 *The Class Struggle in the Ancient Greek World*, London and Ithaca.
SALIN, E. 1939 *Rhin et Orient 1. Le haut Moyen Age en Lorraine d'après le mobilier funéraire*, Paris.
SAMSON, R. 1987 'The Merovingian nobleman's house. Castle or villa?', *Journal of Medieval Archaeology* 13, 287–315.
1989 'Rural slavery, inscriptions, archaeology and Marx. A response to Ramsay MacMullen's "Late Roman slavery"', *Historia* 38, 99–110.
SAMSON, R. forthcoming 'Knowledge, constraint and power in inaction. The defenceless medieval wall', in P. Shackle and B. Little (eds.), *Meanings and Uses of Material Culture. Studies in Historical Archaeology*, Oxford.
SAVANT, M.-O. 1985 'Les peintures murales romaines de Plassac', in A. Barbet (ed.), *Peinture murale en Gaule*, BAR(S) 240, 113–35, Oxford.
SCARDIGLI, B. 1973 *Die Goten. Sprache und Kultur*, Munich.
1976 'Die gotisch-römischen Beziehungen im 3. und 4. Jahrhundert n. Chr., ein Forschungsbericht', in H. Temporini (ed.), *Aufstieg und Niedergang der Römischen Welt* II.5.1, 200–85, Berlin and New York.
SCHÄFERDIECK, K. 1970 'Der germanische Arianismus', *Miscellanea Historiae Ecclesiasticae* 3, Bibliothèque de la Revue d'Histoire Ecclésiastique 50, 71ff., Louvain.
1976 *Die Kirchen in den Reichen der Westgoten und Suewen bis zur Errichtung der Westgotischen Katholischen Staatskirche*, Arbeiten zur Kirchengeschichte 39, Berlin.
SCHARF, W. 1991 'Germanus von Auxerre – Chronologie seiner Vita', *Francia* 18, 1–17.
SCHMIDT, L. 1928 'Das Ende der Römerherrschaft in Gallien. (Chlodowech und Syagrius),' *Historisches Jahrbuch* 48, 611–18.
SEILLIER, C. 1986 'La présence germanique en Picardie à l'époque romaine. Les textes et l'archéologie', in D. Bayard, *et al.* (eds.), *Picardie. Berceau de la France*, 55–8, Amiens.
SETTON, K. M. 1941 *Christian Attitudes Towards the Emperor in the Fourth Century*, New York.
SHAW, B. D. 1984 'Bandits in the Roman Empire', *Past & Present* 105, 3–52.
SIVAN, H. 1983 'Romans and barbarians in fifth century Aquitaine. the Visigothic kingdom of Toulouse (418–507)', unpublished Ph.D. dissertation, Columbia University, New York.
1985 'An unedited letter of the emperor Honorius to the Spanish soldiers', *Zeitschrift für Papyrologie und Epigraphik* 61, 273–87.
1986 'Funerary monuments and funerary rites in late antique Aquitaine', *Oxford Journal of Archaeology* 5, 339–53.
1987 'On foederati, hospitalitas, and the settlement of the Goths in AD 418', *American Journal of Philology* 108, 759–72.

1988a 'Who was Egeria? Pilgrimage and piety in the age of Gratian', *Harvard Theological Review* 81, 59–72.

1988b 'Holy Land pilgrimage and western audiences. Some reflections on Egeria and her circle', *Classical Quarterly* 38, 528–35.

1989a 'Town and country in late antique Gaul. The example of CIL XIII 128', *Zeitschrift für Papyrologie und Epigraphik* 79, 103–13.

1989b 'Sidonius Apollinaris, Theoderic II and Gothic-Roman politics from Avitus to Anthemius', *Hermes* 117, 85–94.

SMITH, J. T. 1978 'Villas as a key to social structure', in M. Todd (ed.), *Studies in the Romano-British Villa*, 149–85, Leicester.

1982 'Villa plans and social structure in Britain and Gaul', *Caesarodunum* 17, *Actes du colloque sur la villa romaine dans les provinces du Nord-Ouest*, 321–36.

STANCLIFFE, C. 1983 *St Martin and his Hagiographer. History and Miracle in Sulpicius Severus*, Oxford.

STEIN, E. 1959 *Histoire du Bas-Empire* (2 vols.), Paris.

STEVENS, C. E. 1933 *Sidonius Apollinaris and his Age*, Oxford.

1957 'Marcus, Gratian, and Constantine', *Athenaeum* NS 35, 316–47.

STROHEKER, K. F. 1937 *Eurich, König der Westgoten*, Stuttgart.

1948 *Der senatorische Adel im spätantiken Gallien*, Tübingen (reprinted Darmstadt, 1970).

SUNDWALL, J. 1915 *Weströmische Studien*, Berlin.

1975 (reprint) *Abhandlungen zur Geschichte des ausgehenden Römertums*, New York.

SWAIN, J. W. 1940 'The theory of the four monarchies. Opposition history under the Roman Empire', *Classical Philology* 35, 1–21.

TÄCKHOLM, U. 1969 'Aetius and the battle on the Catalaunian Fields', *Opuscula Romana* 7.15, 259–75.

TALBERT, R. J. A. 1984 *The Senate of Imperial Rome*, Princeton.

TEILLET, S. 1984 *Des Goths à la nation gothique. Les origines de l'idée de nation en Occident du Ve au VIIe siècle*, Paris.

TESSIER, G. 1964 *Le baptême de Clovis*, Paris.

THOMAS, C. 1981 *Christianity in Roman Britain*, London.

THOMPSON, E. A. 1952 'Peasant revolts in late Roman Gaul and Spain', *Past & Present* 2, 11–23 (reprinted in M. I. Finley (ed.), *Studies in Ancient Society*, 1974, 304–20, London).

1966 *The Visigoths in the Time of Ulfila*, Oxford.

1982 *Romans and Barbarians. The Decline of the Western Empire*, Madison.

1984 *Saint Germanus of Auxerre and the End of Roman Britain*, Studies in Celtic History 6, Woodbridge.

TODOROV, T. 1984 *The Conquest of America. The Question of the Other*, New York.

TOMLIN, R. S. O. 1976 'Notitia dignitatum tam civilium quam militarum', in R. Goodburn and P. Bartholomew (eds.), *Aspects of the Notitia Dignitatum*, BAR(S) 15, 189–209. Oxford.

TWYMAN, B. L. 1970 'Aetius and the Aristocracy', *Historia* 19, 480–503.
URLANIS, B. 1971 *War and Population* (tr. L. Lempert), Moscow.
VALENTIN, L. 1900 *Saint Prosper d'Aquitaine*, Toulouse.
VAN DAM, R. 1985 *Leadership and Community in Late Antique Gaul*, London, Berkeley and Los Angeles.
VANDER ESSEN, L. 1907 *Etude critique et littéraire sur les vitae de saints mérovingiens*, Paris.
VERLINDEN, C. 1955 *L'esclavage dans l'Europe medievale, vol. i. Péninsule Ibérique, France*, Bruges.
VILLEDIEU, F. 1986 'Relations commerciales établies entre l'Afrique et la Sardaigne du IIe au VIe siècle', *L'Africa Romana*, 321–32.
VIVES, J. (ed.) 1969 *Inscripciones cristianas de la España Romana y Visigoda*, Barcelona.
VOGT, J. 1967 'Kulturwelt und Barbaren – zum Menscheitsbild der spätantiken Gesellschaft', *Akademie der Wissenschaften und der Literatur Mainz*, Abhandlungen der Geistes- und Sozialwissenschaftlichen Klasse Jahrgang 1967.1, 1–68.
WAAS, M. 1965 *Germanen im römischen Dienst in 4. Jahrhundert*, Bonn.
WAGNER, A. R. 1975 *Pedigree and Progress. Essays in the Genealogical Interpretation of History*, London.
WALLACE-HADRILL, J. M. 1962 *The Long-Haired Kings*, Oxford.
   1971 *Early Germanic Kingship in England and on the Continent*, Oxford.
   1983 *The Frankish Church*, Oxford.
WARD-PERKINS, B. 1984 *From Classical Antiquity to the Middle Ages. Urban Public Building in Northern and Central Italy, AD 300–850*, London.
WARD-PERKINS, J. B. 1938 'The sculpture of Visigothic France', *Archaeologia* 87, 79–128.
WATSON, A. 1987 *Roman Slave Law*, Baltimore.
WATTENBACH, W., and LEVISON, W. (eds.) 1957 *Deutschlands Geschichtsquellen im Mittelalter III*, ed. H. Löwe, Weimar.
WELTER, T. 1906 'Die Besiedlung der Vorstufen der Vogesen unter besonderer Berücksichtigung des gebirgigen Teils des Kreises Saarburg in Lothringen. Ein Gesamtbericht über mehrjährige Ausgrabungen der Reste aus Gallo-römischerzeit', *ASHAL* 18, 371ff.
WENSKUS, R. 1961 *Stammesbildung und Verfassung. Das Werden der frühmittelalterlichen Gentes*, Cologne.
WERNER, J. 1950 'Zur Entstehung der Reihengräberzivilisation', *Archaeologia Geographica* 1, 23–32.
WES, M. A. 1987 'Gesellschaft und Literatur in der Spätantike', *Ancient Society* 18, 173–202.
WHITEHOUSE, D., *et al.* 1985 'The Schola Praeconum II', *Papers of the British School at Rome* 53, 162–210.
WHITTAKER, C. R. 1983 'Late Roman trade and traders', in P. Garnsey, K. Hopkins and C. R. Whittaker (eds.), *Trade in the Ancient Economy*, London and Berkeley, 163–80, 208–11.

1987 'Circe's pigs. From slavery to serfdom in the late Roman world', in M. I. Finley (ed.), *Classical Slavery = Slavery and Abolition* 8:1, May 1987, 88–122.

WICKHAM, C. 1984 'The other transition. From the ancient world to feudalism', *Past & Present* 103, 3–36.

1988 'Marx, Sherlock Holmes, and late Roman commerce', *Journal of Roman Studies* 78, 183–93.

WIEACKER, F. 1963 *Allgemeine Zustände und Rechtszustände gegen Ende des Weströmischen Reichs*, Institutum Romanum Medii Aevi 1.2a, Milan.

1964 *Recht und Gesellschaft in der Spätantike*, Stuttgart.

WIGHTMAN, E. M. 1970 *Roman Trier and the Treveri*, London.

1978 'Peasants and potentates. An investigation of social structure and land tenure in Roman Gaul', *American Journal of Ancient History* 3, 97–128.

1985 *Gallia Belgica*, London.

WOLFRAM, H. 1967 *Intitulatio. I. Lateinische Königs- und Fürstentitel bis zum Ende des 8. Jahrhunderts*, Graz, Vienna and Cologne.

1970 'The shaping of the early medieval kingdom', *Viator* 1.1, 1–20.

1980 *Geschichte der Goten. Von den Anfängen bis zur Mitte des sechsten Jahrhunderts. Entwurf einer historischen Ethnographie* (2nd edn), Munich.

1988 *History of the Goths* (tr. T. J. Dunlap), Berkeley.

WOLFRAM, H., and SCHWARTZ, A. (eds.) 1988 *Anerkennung und Integration. Zu den wirtschaftlichen Grundlagen der Völkerwanderungszeit 400–600*, Vienna.

WOOD, I. N. 1977 'Kings, kingdoms and consent', in P. H. Sawyer and I. N. Wood (eds.), *Early Medieval Kingship*, 6–29 (reprinted 1979), Leeds.

1980 'Avitus of Vienne. Religion and culture in the Auvergne and the Rhône valley, 470–530', unpublished University of Oxford D.Phil. diss.

1984 'The end of Roman Britain. Continental evidence and parallels', in M. Lapidge and D. N. Dumville (eds.), *Gildas. New Approaches*, 1–25, Woodbridge.

1985 'Gregory of Tours and Clovis', *Revue Belge de Philologie et d'Histoire* 63, 249–72.

1986 'The audience of architecture in post-Roman Gaul', in L. A. S. Butler and R. Morris (eds.), *The Anglo-Saxon Church*, Council for British Archaeology Research Report 60, 74–9, London.

1987 'The fall of the western Empire and the end of Roman Britain', *Britannia* 18, 251–62.

1988 'Clermont and Burgundy, 511–534', *Nottingham Medieval Studies* 32, 119–25.

1990 'Administration, law and culture in Merovingian Gaul', in R. McKitterick (ed.), *The Uses of Literacy in Early Medieval Europe*, 63–81, Cambridge.

forthcoming 'Ethnicity and the ethnogenesis of the Burgundians'.

WORMALD, P. 1976 'The decline of the western Empire and the survival of its aristocracy', *Journal of Roman Studies* 66, 217–26.

YOUNG, B. K. 1980 'Le problème franc et l'apport des pratiques funéraires (III – Ve siècles)', *Bulletin de Liaison de l'Association Française d'Archéologie Mérovingienne* 3, 4–18.

YVER, G. 1896 'Euric, roi des Wisigoths (466–485)', in *Etudes d'Histoire du Moyen Age Dédiées à Gabriel Monod*, 11–46, Paris.

ZABEHLICKY, H. 1980 'Zwiebelknopffiblen als Kennzeichen von Soldaten auf spätrömischen Denkmälern', in W. S. Hanson and L. F. J. Keppie (eds.), *Roman Frontier Studies, 1979*, BAR(S) 71, 1099–111, Oxford.

ZECCHINI, G. 1983 *Aezio: l'ultima difesa dell'Occidente romano*, Rome.

Index

Personal names are listed in accordance with the order and spelling conventions of *PLRE*. Thus, for example, Sidonius Apollinaris is to be found under 'Apollinaris'. The status of persons other than emperors, usurpers, barbarian kings, bishops and popes is given only when necessary to avoid confusion. Titles of major works are listed independently of their authors. Those who followed Alaric and his successors are referred to as 'Goths' down to their settlement in Aquitania in 418 and as 'Visigoths' thereafter. Place names are given in their modern form.

Index

Index